HITLER'S ROCKET
SOLDIERS

TATTERED
FLAG

Tattered Flag Press West Sussex

HITLER'S ROCKET
SOLDIERS

THE MEN WHO FIRED THE V2s AGAINST ENGLAND

Murray R. Barber and Michael Keuer

Published in Great Britain in 2011 by
Tattered Flag Press
PO Box 2240
Pulborough
West Sussex RH20 9AL
England

office@thetatteredflag.com
www.thetatteredflag.com

Tattered Flag Press is an imprint of Chevron
Publishing Ltd.

Jacket Design: Mark Nelson
Cartography © Tim Brown, 2010
V2 Graphic © Janusz Swiatlon

The Publisher would like to acknowledge the
kind assistance of Eddie J. Creek in the supply
and preparation of photographs for this book.

Cataloguing-in-Publication Data for this book
is available from the British Library

ISBN 978-0-9555977-5-6

Typeset and design by Mark Nelson,
Sydney, Australia

Printed and bound in Croatia

For more information on books published by
Tattered Flag visit: www.thetatteredflag.com

This book is produced using paper that is
made from wood grown in managed,
sustainable forests. It is natural, renewable and
recyclable. The logging and manufacturing
processes conform to the environmental
regulations of the country of origin.

CONTENTS

INTRODUCTION

IN the year 2000 whilst researching the script for a planetarium presentation, I discovered that the German V2 Rocket was the first man-made object to enter space. I had been aware since my youth of the V1 and V2 and that both had been used by Hitler as 'vengeance weapons'. They had been launched against London and other targets in a last-ditch attempt by the Nazis to change the outcome of World War Two. I was also aware that a military and scientific research facility at Peenemünde, on the Baltic coast of Germany, was the development centre of the Rocket.

During my initial research, I also learned that Peenemünde became the first centre of truly integrated scientific research and that its only parallel was Los Alamos in the United States where the Manhattan Project scientists would develop the first atomic bomb. Interestingly, whilst the service roads for Peenemünde were being constructed, the development of the American atomic bomb lay some seven years into the future. I also read of the political intrigues of the Rocket's development and how the most feared organization in Nazi Germany, the SS, attempted, and ultimately wrested, control of the Rocket from its creators. Following the end of the war, the Americans and Soviets acquired those creators, who willingly, or otherwise, furthered 'Cold War' military and scientific technology. Both sides had been quick to exploit not only the knowledge accrued by the Peenemünde team, but also the captured hardware. This was to bring to the Americans the greatest technological victory of the Cold War: the first man on the Moon.

As part of my occupation at that time was (and continues to be) to give lectures on scientific and historical topics, I decided it would be very useful to have a part of a V2. I was sure that if the audiences had just a modicum of my tactile nature, they would not fail to be impressed, especially if I could say that the artefact had been into space!

I have always held a great interest not only in astronomy, but also in rocketry and military history. My developing interest in the V2 Rocket combined these passions. I had owned my first astronomical telescope before my teens and later ground and polished optical mirrors for a Newtonian reflector. Rocketry however has always been the most exciting and potentially more dangerous of the interests. Inspired by the Apollo missions of the late 1960s and early 1970s, I recall that, with my fellow classmates, we drafted plans for liquid-powered rockets at school. In the light of a ban by the headmaster, we continued to pursue our interests in our own time and built increasingly larger solid fuel rockets. The experience of seeing our rockets soaring into the sky was wonderful. Unfortunately, following a dramatic explosion, confiscation of equipment, and a stern 'ticking off' from the local constabulary, the great adventure ended.

To return to more recent times: in order to acquire my 'piece of a V2', I contacted Tracy Dungan in the United States, a leading authority on the

V2 Rocket and founding member of the International V2 Research Group, to ask him his advice. Dungan assisted with the restoration of the USAAF Museum's V2 and continues to be responsible for an excellent Internet website detailing not only the technical information, but also details of the offensive use, of the weapon. He told me that every now and then V2 items appear on Internet auction websites. I decided that perhaps the most interesting and economically viable way to acquire a part of a V2 was to try to find it for myself. I remembered being told during my teens that V2 impact craters were still to be seen scattered across rural locations in southern England. Eventually, after contacting a local history society and landowner, I was given permission to begin a search of an impact crater in woodland near East Grinstead in West Sussex, some 30 miles south of London. During the course of several visits, I found many kilograms of V2 shrapnel in an area covering just under 8000 square metres (26,246 square feet). Some of the items were recognizable parts of plumbing from the V2 and have proved to be very useful props with the lectures I perform.

During this time, I was invited by Dungan to join the International V2 Research Group (IV2RG). The IV2RG is a diverse, worldwide group of historians, researchers and interested lay-people such as myself. At its inception, there were approximately a dozen or so members, one of whom was Michael Keuer of Hannover in Germany. We quickly realized that we had common interests. Michael's interest in the V2 is more personal than mine, as his late maternal grandfather, Hermann Engelmann, had worked at Peenemünde as a metalwork craftsman. During what was to become a regular feature of Sunday afternoon conversations over the Internet, Michael invited my wife and I to Germany to visit Peenemünde, the birthplace of the V2 Rocket. During the course of our developing friendship, we decided to research aspects of the V2 using the National Archives (formerly the Public Records Office) at Kew in London as well as other sources. In a relatively short time, we built up a collection of archive material covering the development and deployment of the Rocket. However, the one area of research that intrigued us was the experience of the men who actually operated the weapon. These soldiers, known as the *Fernraketen Truppen* (abbreviated to 'FR' – long-range rocket troops) had the responsibility for carrying the German war effort far beyond the front line, yet they operated in battlefield conditions. With the exception of the atomic bomb, they had handled the most technologically advanced weapon that had ever been produced. The documents we had collected from our archival research gave a dry and impersonal account of these men as their testimony had frequently been taken immediately after hostilities when they were prisoners of the Allies. Therefore, the idea for this book was born – a book that would describe the experiences of ordinary German soldiers operating a most extraordinary weapon.

The problem we then faced was how to trace these men whose numbers were, by the day, gradually diminishing. It soon became apparent that unlike the situation in the United Kingdom, no ex-servicemen organizations exist for the V2 veterans, and thus a potentially valuable line of enquiry was unavailable. We had only one other option. We placed advertisements in the German press appealing to the veterans to come forward so that we would be able to interview them. At that point we encountered a problem, which I as an Englishman had not anticipated, but it was one that caused Michael no surprise: some of the regional newspapers refused to publish our appeals! The publishers knew that the excesses of the Nazi State are fully revealed in the manufacture of the V2 and they were concerned about our political reasons for seeking such men. Modern day Germany takes no pride in its wartime technological innovations; behind the manufacture of every single component of the Rocket and other weapons, slave workers strove under appalling conditions to fulfil the vision of the Nazi leadership. Simultaneously, for many Germans, the death and destruction caused by the Rocket is tempered by the knowledge of what happened to almost every German city and major town during the Allied strategic bombing campaign between 1942-1945. Fortunately for our research, more liberally minded publishers did allow the placement of our advertisements and so we waited with much anticipation for the first veteran to contact us.

We realized beforehand that the possibility of speaking to former members of the SS Rocket Battalion (SS *Werfer Batterie/Abteilung* 500) was very poor. Our main hope lay with veterans from the German Army – the *Heer*. Eventually the first of eleven veterans contacted us and the interviews, which would take place over a period of seven years, began.

It is difficult to describe collectively the men who so graciously gave their time to us, since each one of them was very much an individual. Some of the veterans contacted us simply to satisfy their curiosity and, having done so, would refuse to be interviewed; this was a great disappointment. On two occasions, we failed completely to gain the confidence of the veterans who subsequently, following the interview, either asked never to be troubled again or made it impossible for us to contact them. One veteran was torn between desperately wanting to tell of his experiences, but being equally concerned that we might, in some way, hold extreme political views. He took the advice of friends and met with us for the first time in a public place for his safety so that he could assess our intentions. In time, we would share beers together and grow to know each other on first name terms. Two of the veterans had personal reasons for wanting to tell their stories. One wanted to tell of his former comrades and explain that they and himself had dutifully carried out their orders to defend their country. Another veteran, proud of his work on the Rocket, was delighted that in his twilight years, his memories might find a wider audience than his less-than-interested family. He was, however, quick to tell of his vanity and the personal 'millstone' carried since 1944. Another veteran, having met us, then encouraged a former comrade to contact us to tell us of his experiences.

As a consequence of the book project, two comrades were to become reacquainted, having lost contact in the final hectic days of the war over sixty years previously. Generally, the veterans were impressed that men, approximately 34 years younger than themselves, were prepared to travel great distances and at some cost simply to hear their tales of military life.

More often than not, we were invited into the veterans' homes with great hospitality and warmth, and in many cases trust slowly developed. The interviews of perhaps two to three hours duration would be recorded and the questions asked taken from a prepared list. At times, of course, the veteran would discuss related issues that varied from our prepared list, or fresh questions came about from the answers given. We never deterred deviation as we always hoped to gain information from under the surface. Later, the recordings were transcribed and painstakingly translated by Michael Keuer. In total, nearly 80 hours of recordings were made and the transcribing and translation took an estimated 240 hours to accomplish. The text would then be studied and the veterans would be asked any further questions arising by mail. Unfortunately our questions asked by letter would occasionally be answered by a simple 'yes' or 'no' and we realized that the best way to gain further information or clarification was either by telephone or by meeting the veterans 'face to face' once again. In some instances, we would meet with them on three or four occasions. Sometimes a veteran would accidentally let slip information that he would later regret and then refuse to comment further: this was unfortunate. That stated, when they did discuss potentially controversial topics, we felt obliged to further raise the issue and to research the topic to the best of our ability. It should be mentioned that neither of the interviewers has had experience in the field of journalism and therefore we apologize unreservedly for any shortcomings that may appear. However, we attempted always to interview, research and write the veterans' accounts in a balanced, non-political manner. In some instances, inevitably, duplication of events will be read in the text: this is because the experience was common to more than one veteran – for example, enduring the RAF attack upon Peenemünde or participating as extras in the Nazi propaganda film production of *Kolberg*. In most cases, the veterans allowed us to see photographs of their days of military service and these we copied to the best of our ability in their homes.

One common aspect of the stories told to us by the veterans was that each one believes that his life had been spared by service to the V2. Each man knew of friends or relatives who did not return at the end of the war, most having lost their lives on the Eastern Front. Some of the veterans had been taken directly from the front line to become 'Rocket soldiers'. Others of proven combat service, recovering from wounds suffered in battle, had received fresh orders and were dispatched to Peenemünde or to obscure distant rural locations in Poland. Others, who had demonstrated expertise in the field of science or engineering,

x

found themselves, on entering military service, ordered to Peenemünde or to the Rocket experimental firing sites of Heidelager, Poland. For the veterans of the Russian campaign, this was a blessed relief from the 'meat grinder' in the East. Battle-hardened combat veterans mixed with others fresh from initial training. Although many could not understand the reasons why they had been picked for special duties, or indeed, what those duties might be, in all cases the veterans of the Rocket Battalions have the V2 to thank for their survival whilst so many others died. Apart from the risks of operating the Rocket and possible attacks from the Resistance or Allied fighter-bombers, they were relatively safe. They were only exposed to great peril when the Rocket offensive ended and in 1945 many were forced to join infantry units in the defence of Berlin. I should mention that all of the veterans we spoke to knew that the V2 was killing defenceless civilians and that no defence was possible. Many expressed their regret.

We learned more from the veterans than simply their experiences with the Rocket. Many told of personal family disasters and those of others brought about by the war. War, no matter where or when fought and no matter the weapons used, is about people, individuals and consequences. Therefore, what follows is not purely a tale of cold machinery and 'rockets' red glare', but of men of flesh and blood.

Murray R. Barber
North Devon, January 2011

ACKNOWLEDGEMENTS

OVER the eight years this book has taken to research and write, Michael Keuer and I have been very fortunate not only to have met the veterans whose stories are told herein but also to have benefited from the wisdom of a number of technical experts and historians, many of whom are members of the International V2 Research Group (IV2RG). Formed in 2000, the membership share a common interest in the history and technical aspects of the V2 whilst remaining completely non-political. It is a pleasure to now record their names:

Sergey V. Andreev, Terry Barker, François Bayeux, Andre Bobet, Bernard Cocriamont, Robert J. Collis, the late Arnold (Arnie) L. Crouch, Raymond Delcommune, Stan Druzynski, Jan Harm ter Brugge, David Howard, Michael F. Imhoff, Mario Isack, Benno Janssen, John Kiever, Thomas Kliebenschedel, Frank Leuband, Gino Van Lommel, Charles Ostyn, Alan Scheckenbach, Manuel Thomas and Marcel Verhaaf.

We would like to make special mention of the following members of the IV2RG who kindly corresponded with us on specific areas of research and supplied us with information that would have otherwise eluded us: Laurent Bailleul, Michel van Best, Wolfgang Gückelhorn, Gerhard Helm, Jiří (Jirzy) Komprda, Bart Koopman, Henk Koopman, Gerard Laib, Cor Lulof, Detlev Paul, Volker Pelz, Reiner Sigmund, Ed Straten, and Rudi Velthuis. Special mention must also be made of Tracy Dungan, author and specialist in the V2 Rocket and John Pridge who at the eleventh hour both kindly read the manuscript and made many helpful comments.

We have also been fortunate to make contact with another extremely knowledgeable group of individuals, whose local information was a great asset – the Foundation V2Platform based in The Hague. We would like, specifically, to express our gratitude to Mart Keuning and Jos Borsboom.

Any detailed study invariably has 'crossover' into other fields of interest and we would like to thank Arthur O. Bauer of the Foundation Centre for German Communications and Related Technology; Michel Baert and Gilles Bouillon of the National Museum of Military History (Belgium) and the *Association (Belgo-Luxembourgeoise) des Musées de la Bataille des Ardennes*; Flt/Lt. Gerry Traynor of the 602 Squadron Museum; the Reverend Douglas McRoberts (regarding the history of 602 (City of Glasgow) Squadron, RAF); Craig Cabell (regarding the late Thomas L. Love); Cornelie Jochems (behaviour and history of the Duindigt llamas); Eddie J. Creek; Heiko Petermann (Hans Kammler photograph); Nicolette Faber-Wittenberg of the *Haags Gemeentearchief* (regarding photographs of The Hague); Paul Waayers (regarding Mr. Idzerda); Rob de Bie (Messerschmitt Me 163 historian); Heino Hünken (regarding the history of Welmbüttel); Jean Claude Augst of the *Association Française Buchenwald Dora et Kommandos*; Pierre Morel (regarding Maurice Moreau research).

In some instances, veterans both in Germany and the United Kingdom died before the publishing of this book and it was necessary to interview and, in some cases correspond, with relatives to learn the non-military history of the deceased. We would like to thank *Frau* Priebe (widow of the late Wilhelm Priebe, Waltraud Lorenz née Jericha (daughter of Eduard Jericha), Roland Schaepe (nephew of Eduard Jericha) and Jack Love (son of Thomas L. Love).

The staff of the following archival resources who so frequently retrieve documents, often without a word of thanks, require a special note of gratitude: the National Archives, Kew, London; Stephen Walton, Jane Fish and the staff of the Imperial War Museum in London; the staff of the *Bundesarchiv-Militärchiv* in Freiburg; and Elfi Rudolph of the International Tracing Service, Bad Arolsen, Germany.

We are extremely grateful to the frankness and generosity of the following veterans: Dr. Helmut Fredenhagen, Eduard Jericha, Heinz Junker, Walter Klein, Fritz Meibert, Wilhelm Priebe, Oswald Schneider, Franz Stolle and Heinz Wunderlich who all freely gave their time to us.

We have been fortunate that an engineer and scientists involved in the development of the Rocket have also come forward. They have given us fascinating insights into aspects of research previously unknown to us. Additionally, they recount the personalities involved in support of the Rocket from a slave worker to the overall head of development programme. We extend our thanks to Stefan Blomberg and Dr. Helmuth Frenk.

Sadly, it was not possible for us to meet in person, but we would also like to acknowledge the very interesting correspondence we enjoyed with the late Konrad Dannenberg who was able to confirm the reminiscences of others and gave us an insight into his early introduction into rocketry. *Herr* Dannenberg kindly allowed us to use his article, '*Present at the Creation*' which first appeared in *Aviation Week & Space Technology* of 24 March 2003.

Michael and I wish to thank our editor and publisher, Robert Forsyth: without his encouragement and enthusiasm, this book would never have seen the light of day. We also wish to thank Rob Cray who introduced us to Robert all those years ago.

I would also like to give personal thanks to the late David Thompson, a friend and former colleague, who always urged me to question everything. Geoffrey Rathbone who helped to open doors so that I could meet the eminent television presenter and writer, Raymond Baxter. Additionally, I would like to thank Rudolf and Andrew Kittler of Norwich who helped to re-establish contact with Konrad Dannenberg; Christopher Rostant for helpful comments; my brother-in-law, John Arnold, who offered advice; my daughter, Helen, for her enthusiasm; and my son, Phillip, who, at short notice, would visit the National Archives to research on my behalf.

Finally, I would like to thank my dear wife, Valerie who has supported and encouraged this project from the very beginning. She has read text, offered advice and spent many days alone, whilst Michael Keuer and I travelled the length and breadth of Germany pursuing our research.

Murray R. Barber
January 2011

GLOSSARY OF TERMS

Abhebekontakt	sprung loaded switch (lit. 'lift off')
Abschussplattform	firing table
'Aggregat'	machine unit
Antriebsblock	propulsion block
Bodenplatte	concrete platform
Brennschluss	close burning
Fernmeldeeinheit	Signals unit
Fernmelder	Signaller
Feuerleitpanzer	Fire Control Vehicle
Flak (Fliegerabwehrkanone)	Anti-Aircraft Gun (or AA fire)
Flugkapitän	Flight Captain (civilian title)
Fernraketen (FR)	Long-Range Rocket (as in 'troops')
Funkkommandogerät	radio equipment
Geräteraum	control departments
Gesellschaft für Raketenforschung	GEFRA – Organization for Rocket Research
HARKO (e.g.: *Höh.Art.Kdr.* 191)	High Artillery Command
'Hauptstufe'	Main stage
Heck	tail
Heer	Army
Heereswaffenamt	Army Weapons Office
Hitler Jugend	Hitler Youth
Ingenieur	Engineer
Kampfgruppe	Battle Group
Jabo (Jagd-bomber)	Fighter-Bomber
Konzentrationslager	Concentration Camp
Leitstrahl	Guidance beam
Meillerwagen	Meiller Vehicle, V2 Rocket transporter
Mittelteil	centre fuselage/section
Mischgerät	steering control
Oberkommando der Wehrmacht (OKW)	Wehrmacht High Command
Offizierskasino	officers' mess
Panzerfaust	Portable anti-tank rocket
Raketenflugplatz	Rocket launch airfield
Reichsarbeitsdienst	Reich Labour Service
Reichswehr	Defence Force
Schießzug	Firing platoon
Sicherungstruppe	Security Troop

Spitze	warhead
Stab	Staff
Staffelkapitän	Squadron commander
Stotz Stecker	umbilical plug socket
Staudruckrohr	pitot tube
V-Leute	Agents or informers
Versuchsstelle	Test Centre
VfR	*Verein für Raumschiffahrt* (Society for Spaceship Travel)
Volkssturm	People's Militia (Home Defence Force)
'*Vorstufe*'	preliminary stage
Zeitschaltwerk	time switch
Zug	Platoon

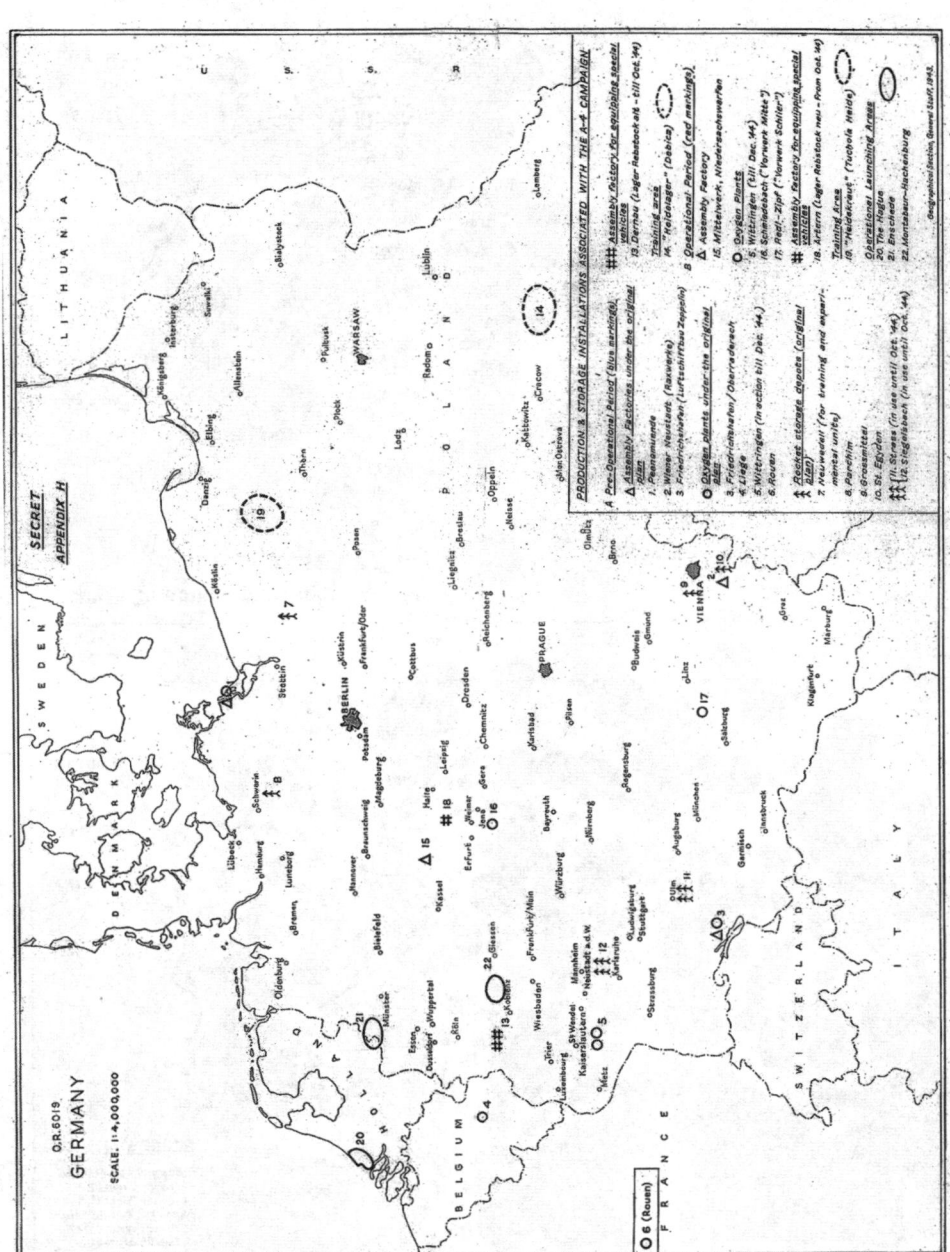

Production and Storage Installations associated with the A4 campaign.

These four maps have been redrawn directly from Allied originals (IWM)

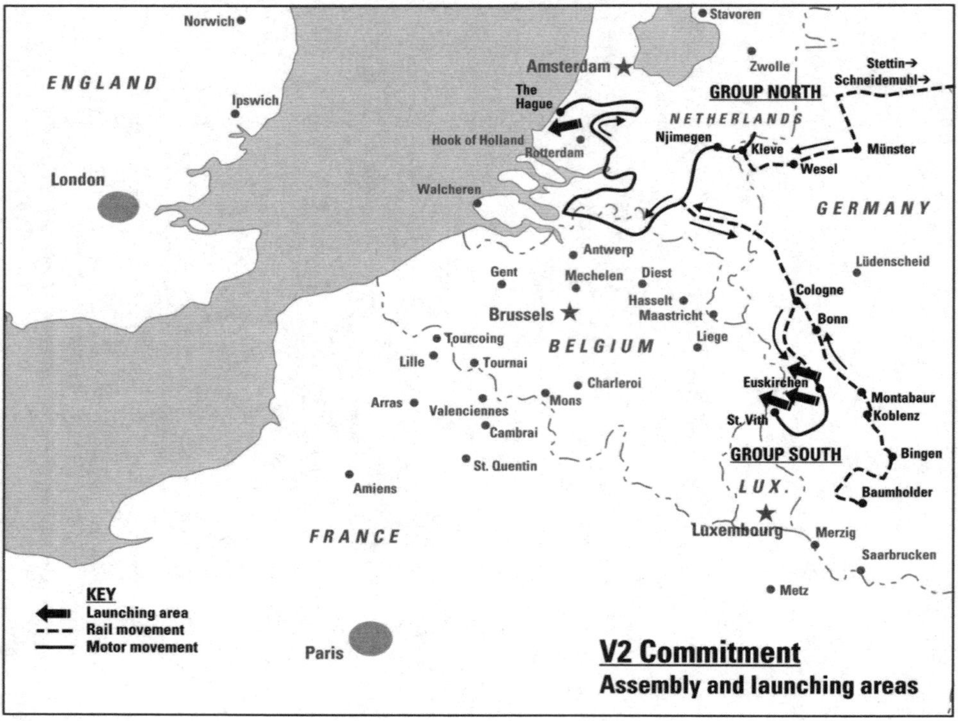

V2 Commitment
Assembly and launching areas

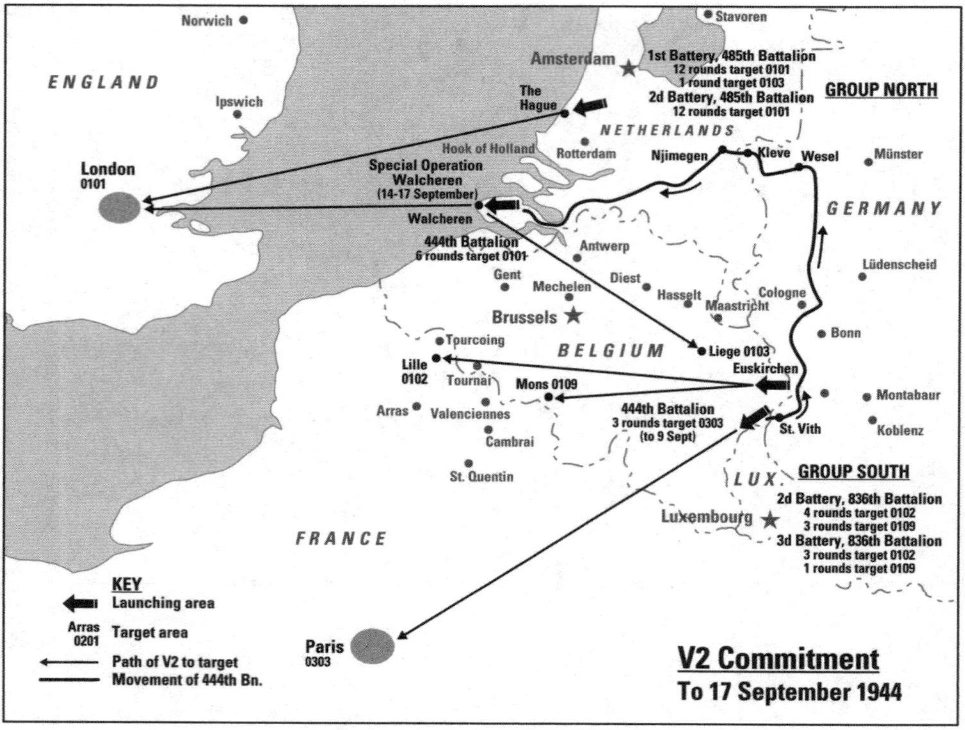

KEY
Launching area
Rail movement
Motor movement

V2 Commitment
To 17 September 1944

KEY
Launching area
Arras 0201 Target area
Path of V2 to target
Movement of 444th Bn.

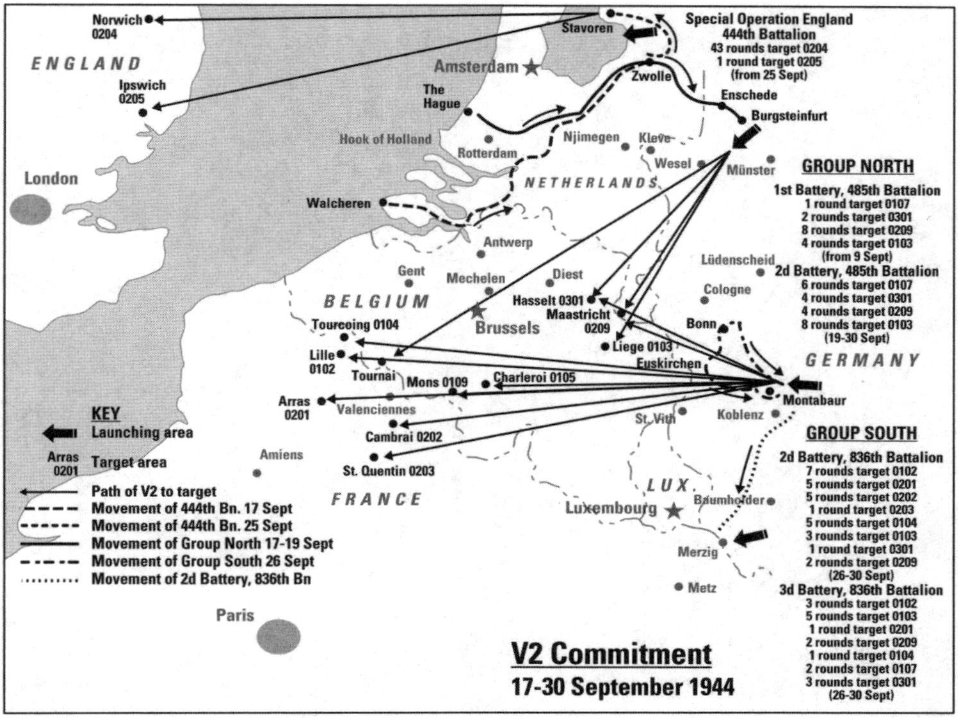

Norwich 0204
ENGLAND
Ipswich 0205
London
Stavoren
Amsterdam
The Hague
Zwolle
Special Operation England
444th Battalion
43 rounds target 0204
1 round target 0205
(from 25 Sept)
Enschede
Burgsteinfurt
Hook of Holland
Rotterdam
Njimegen
Kleve
Wesel
Münster
NETHERLANDS
Walcheren
GROUP NORTH
1st Battery, 485th Battalion
1 round target 0107
2 rounds target 0301
8 rounds target 0209
4 rounds target 0103
(from 9 Sept)
2d Battery, 485th Battalion
6 rounds target 0107
4 rounds target 0301
4 rounds target 0209
8 rounds target 0103
(19-30 Sept)
Antwerp
Lüdenscheid
Gent
Mechelen
Diest
Cologne
BELGIUM
Hasselt 0301
Maastricht 0209
Brussels
Tourcoing 0104
Bonn
Lille 0102
Liege 0103
Tournai
Euskirchen
GERMANY
Mons 0109
Charleroi 0105
Montabaur
Arras 0201
Valenciennes
Koblenz
St. Vith
KEY
Launching area
Arras 0201 Target area
Cambrai 0202
GROUP SOUTH
Amiens
St. Quentin 0203
2d Battery, 836th Battalion
7 rounds target 0102
5 rounds target 0201
5 rounds target 0202
1 round target 0203
5 rounds target 0104
3 rounds target 0103
1 round target 0301
2 rounds target 0209
(26-30 Sept)
Path of V2 to target
Movement of 444th Bn. 17 Sept
Movement of 444th Bn. 25 Sept
Movement of Group North 17-19 Sept
Movement of Group South 26 Sept
Movement of 2d Battery, 836th Bn
FRANCE
LUX.
Luxembourg
Baumholder
Merzig
Metz
3d Battery, 836th Battalion
3 rounds target 0102
5 rounds target 0103
1 round target 0201
2 rounds target 0209
1 round target 0104
2 rounds target 0107
3 rounds target 0301
(26-30 Sept)
Paris
V2 Commitment
17-30 September 1944

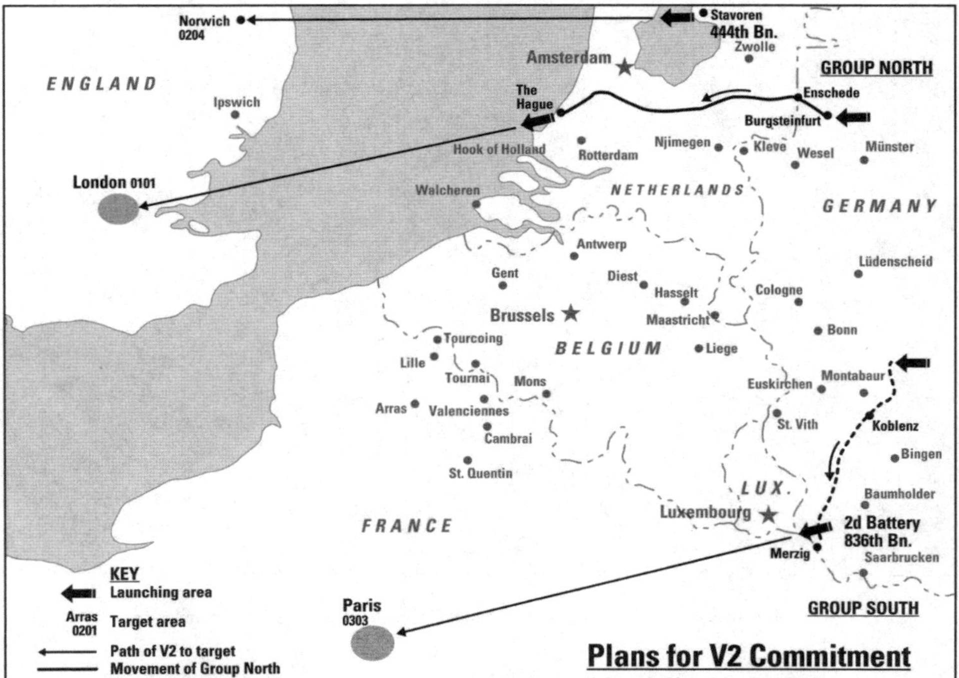

Norwich 0204
Stavoren
444th Bn.
Zwolle
ENGLAND
Amsterdam
GROUP NORTH
Ipswich
The Hague
Enschede
Burgsteinfurt
Hook of Holland
Rotterdam
Njimegen
Kleve
Wesel
Münster
London 0101
Walcheren
NETHERLANDS
GERMANY
Antwerp
Lüdenscheid
Gent
Diest
Hasselt
Cologne
Brussels
Maastricht
Bonn
Tourcoing
BELGIUM
Liege
Lille
Tournai
Mons
Euskirchen
Montabaur
Arras
Valenciennes
St. Vith
Koblenz
Cambrai
Bingen
St. Quentin
LUX.
Baumholder
Luxembourg
2d Battery
836th Bn.
FRANCE
Merzig
Saarbrucken
KEY
Launching area
Arras 0201 Target area
Paris 0303
GROUP SOUTH
Path of V2 to target
Movement of Group North
Movement of Group South
Plans for V2 Commitment
After 1 October 1944

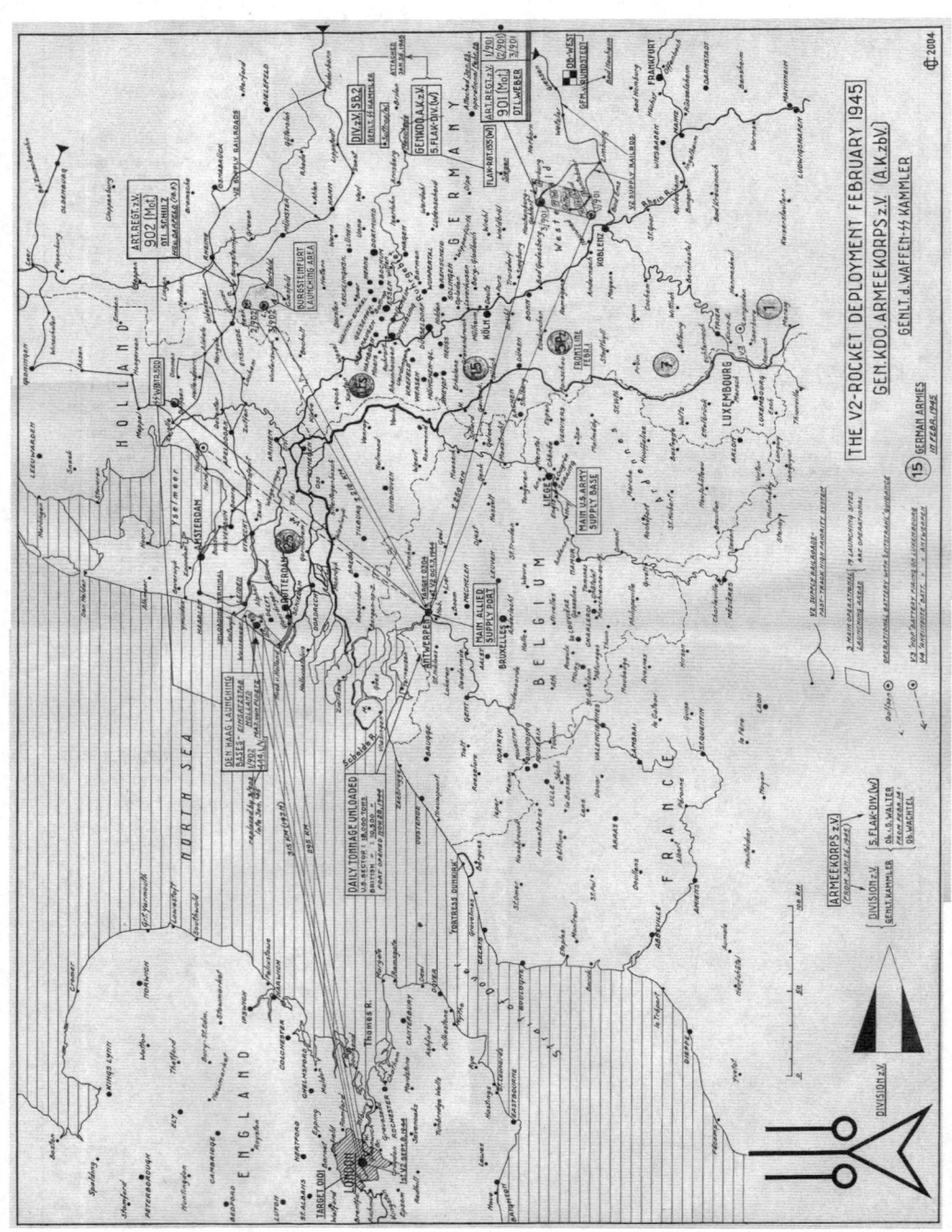

This map is provided courtesy of Mr Charles Ostyn and reproduced with permission.

FOREWORD

'*One of the most heated arguments with respect to the A-4 [V2] concerned its operation in the field. We dyed-in-the-wool rocketeers felt that it could not be fired successfully in combat unless from elaborate concrete installations containing many repair and testing facilities. This view was energetically opposed by General Dornberger [formerly Commanding Officer, Peenemünde] on the grounds that such installations would be bombed out of existence before they could go into operation. Dornberger felt that it was wiser to set up A-4 operations in the form of mobile batteries worked by trained military personnel.*

'*Against the almost unanimous objections of we technicians, he persisted in this course and was surprisingly successful.*'[1]

WERNHER VON BRAUN, 1956: FORMERLY TECHNICAL DIRECTOR,
PEENEMÜNDE

———

THE writing of any history is fraught with pitfalls. One of the most contentious subjects has to be Germany during the Second World War. The highly complex and secretive nature of the Third Reich provides problems enough, but if added to these the author has to deal with a highly classified project, the task of elucidating 'the truth' becomes exceptionally difficult. Only authors who are prepared to give their total commitment over an extended period of time can hope to faithfully piece together such topics. Therefore it is not surprising that little has been written about the structure and activities of the secret military units whose role was to protect and fire, under field conditions, possibly the most sophisticated device built during the Second World War, the A4 (V2) rocket. The present authors have achieved this objective to an impressive degree.

This book recounts in considerable detail the personal day-to-day stories of eleven of these former rocket troops including their combat experiences, attitudes, humour and interpersonal relations. Illuminating contacts between some of these veterans and notables at the Peenemünde rocket test centre such as *Dr.* Wernher von Braun, *Professor* Hermann Oberth, von Braun's mentor, *Generalmajor Dr.* Walter Dornberger and SS–*Obergruppenführer Dr. Ingenieur* Hans Kammler are documented. It is to be expected that some memories of events stretching back more than half a century may be clouded. Consequently the

———

[1.] Wernher von Braun, 'Reminiscences of German rocketry' *Journal of the British Interplanetary Society* 15 (May-June 1956): 125-145.

authors have sought to substantiate the accounts of these veterans through independent sources wherever possible.

The A4 was the world's first long-range rocket. The training of rocket troops, transport of rockets, preparation of field launch sites, erection, fuelling and firing of the rocket required the development of special equipment and protocols. All this had to be done from scratch. There were no guidelines. The principles that were evolved for the A4 field deployment would become the guiding pattern for the rapid post-war build-up of mobile rocket forces in both the West and the East.

To their credit the authors did not shy away from the more sensitive questions. Did the rocket soldiers think about the strategic and moral aspects of the rocket? Did they know about von Braun's dreams for future spaceflight and if so did they have any empathy for such ideas? The answers to these and many other intriguing questions make fascinating reading.

The authors are to be congratulated on their perseverance in finding these veterans, as no doubt very few survive. The importance of this historical research becomes patently clear when we note that several of the veterans interviewed have subsequently passed away. This important work has gone a long way to filling the void about Hitler's rocket soldiers.

Brett A. Gooden, MD, PhD, FBIS

Part One

VORSTUFE

'The air was filled with the rumbling of thunder.
We felt the vibrations through our entire bodies as well as through
the ground… I watched through my binoculars as the black and white
rocket rose faster and faster. The exhaust gases from the rocket motor
generated a flame about as long as the rocket itself.
This unforgettable sight is still the highlight of my career…'

KONRAD DANNENBERG, 2003

CHAPTER ONE

'TAIL OF FIRE'

The development of German rocketry from the
Great War to Peenemünde

IN terms of its application in the First World War, rocketry can be thought of as being benignly useful rather than aggressively significant. Rockets were used in the trenches and at sea for signalling purposes. Lines of communication were often broken on the Western Front by heavy shelling and it was normal practice for army brigades on both sides to use rockets for emergencies, indicating forward positions to troops behind the front line and for confirmation of received messages. The few exceptions to these non-aggressive applications were in aerial warfare. Over the trenches of the Western Front, rockets were used, with rare success, to shoot down German hydrogen gas-filled observation balloons. The French Navy Lieutenant, Yves Le Prieur (1885-1963), devised solid-fuel, stick-guided rockets that were fired from the wing struts of Allied biplanes such as the Nieuport fighter. Highly inaccurate and disliked by pilots, not only because of the risk of setting alight their aircraft, but also because of the short range of less than 120 metres, they necessitated steep manoeuvres to avoid collision with the target. Although observation balloons were occasional victims, not one Zeppelin was to fall to the French rockets.

Infinitely more important than rocketry during the Great War was artillery. The perception of generals on both sides was that the stalemate of heavily defended and fortified front lines could only be smashed by using artillery. On land the most powerful guns were those operated by railway artillery units, the most infamous of the rail artillery pieces being the 'Paris Gun' manufactured by Friedrich Krupp A.G. Known to the Germans as the '*Kaiser Wilhelm Geschütz*', this colossus was 34 metres long, weighed 125 tonnes and fired a 120 kg (61 lb) shell to a range of 131 kilometres. It was used against the French capital between March and August 1918. The mighty shells were airborne for just under three minutes and reached a height of 40 kilometres. This altitude would not be surpassed until the A4 Rocket launch on 3 October 1942 at Peenemünde. It could be argued that the Paris Gun was the first 'terror weapon' of the modern era although, strategically and militarily, its deployment was a wasted effort. However, the psychological effect against the Parisians and the propaganda effect for the Germans were considerable.

Following defeat in 1918, Germany faced the humiliation of the signing of the Treaty of Versailles on 28 June 1919, which demanded stringent reductions in the country's armed forces and its ability to defend itself or to rearm. It is hardly surprising that reparations were sought by the principal signatories of the Treaty. The appalling, costly war had been responsible for 8.5 million fatalities with 21 million wounded. Parts of north-western Europe had been pounded into rubble, France being the worst affected. The map of Germany was redrawn to the satisfaction of the Allied victors with Germany losing not only all of its colonies but also territories to France, Belgium, Lithuania, Czechoslovakia, Denmark and Poland. Particularly contentious was the creation of the 'Polish Corridor' through what had been German territory and the declaration that the port of Danzig on the Baltic coast was to become a 'free city'. To the east, the Saarland was to be granted special status under French control. The French were also to occupy the Rhineland as a demilitarized buffer zone for fifteen years. Further, Germany was banned from having any union with Austria and had to admit to its war criminality. The former Kaiser and other war leaders were put on trial. Reparations – mainly to France – of £6,600 million were demanded: far beyond Germany's ability to pay. It was obvious that the Allies wished to bankrupt the nation. Germany militarily was further humiliated: it was allowed no air force; the new '*Reichswehr*' (army) was to have no more than 100,000 non-conscripted men; and there were to be no tanks, heavy artillery or poison gas supplies. At sea, the *Kriegsmarine* was restricted to no more than six capital ships and no submarines. The country's once huge armaments industry was stripped of the potential to wage war.

In spite of the stranglehold of constraints created by regulations that existed in the fine text of the Treaty of Versailles, odd loopholes could be found by the German military command. The most intriguing was rocketry. This technology was not considered sufficiently important to be included in the list of prohibited military pursuits and Germany was free, under international law, to develop rockets. The significance of this was not at first appreciated – after all rockets were nothing more than a footnote in military history.

Although few practical applications for the rocket could be seen, science popularists, fiction writers and imaginative theorists had already explored the use of rocketry for space travel. The British author, H.G. Wells (1866-1946), had fired the public imagination with his novel *War of the Worlds* (1898) which featured the invasion of Earth by Martians. He also put forward the idea that space travel from the Earth might itself be possible in *The First Man on the Moon* (1901).

In the inter-war period, one man in particular, Konstantin Tsiolkovsky, developed these ideas further. The Russian-born Tsiolkovsky (1857–1935), although not widely known, was a space travel visionary and writer. Mostly self-taught, he established a theoretical basis for space travel in his book/paper, *The Exploration of the World's Space with Jet-Propulsion Instruments* (1903). He realized that liquid-fuel rocket engines had greater efficiency than those powered by solid fuel; furthermore, with the former, the thrust could be controlled.

If Tsiolkovsky was the unsung mentor of astronautics theory, then Robert Goddard (1882-1945), was to be posthumously praised as the father of modern rocketry. This American's achievements in rocketry were extraordinary. Born and raised in Worcester, Massachusetts, the scientifically precocious Goddard explored mathematically the practical means to reach high-altitude with sufficient speed to break away from the Earth's gravity. Additionally, he bench-tested various rocket engines using a combination of solid and liquid fuels. Independently of Tsiolkovsky's work of nine years earlier, Goddard came to the same conclusions on the benefits of liquid-fuelled engines. By July 1914, he obtained his first two rocket patents and in the last year of the First World War, he developed for the U.S. Army the basis for the rocket weapon, later to be known as the 'bazooka'. During his long career, Goddard was to be granted 214 patents in rocketry!

In 1919, Goddard published a pamphlet, *A Method of Reaching Extreme Altitudes*, which discussed the mathematical theories of rocket propulsion and rocket flight. He published the results of his experimentation and wrote that travel to the Moon might be a possibility. The New York Times picked up on these comments and published a sensationalist and inaccurate report under the banner heading of *A Severe Strain on Credulity!* Goddard was deeply wounded by the ensuing public ridicule. He had never courted fame and afterwards deliberately strove to avoid the 'limelight'. It is then no great surprise to discover that on the very day that the first liquid-powered rocket flight took place on 16 March 1926, very few witnesses observed the launch and the press was very definitely not invited! The Goddard rocket was a strange, spindly contraption; the fuel tanks were located below the engine and held together by thin rods. This arrangement meant that the 3.4 metre (11 ft)-long rocket was aerodynamically very unstable and, having flown into a cold but bright Massachusetts sky, it crashed ignobly into a snow-covered cabbage patch 56 metres (184 ft) away from the launch platform.

Goddard's insular manner meant the developing interest in rocketry in Europe was handicapped, as only an incomplete picture of his pioneering work was known. It was, in particular, a loss to Germany where there was a growing interest in rocketry.

Twelve years after the end of the First World War, Germany and its military services were still complying with the restrictions and constraints of the Versailles Treaty. The loophole relating to rocketry was spotted by *Oberstleutnant* Karl Heinrich Emil Becker (1879-1940) the chief of the *Ballistische und Munitionsabteilung* (Ballistic and Munitions Department) in the *Reichswehr's Heereswaffenamt* (Army Ordnance Office). These organizations were actively exploring alternative weapon technologies as a replacement to artillery.

In the spring of 1930, Becker appointed the career soldier and artilleryman, Walter Dornberger, specifically to explore the potential of the rocket. *Hauptmann Dr.-Ing.* Walter Dornberger (1895-1980) was born in Giessen in central western Germany and was to become a leading figure in the research and development of the V2 Rocket and in the recruitment of personnel for the project. He had joined an artillery regiment in the *Kaiserreichsheer* (Imperial German Army) in early August 1914 just before the outbreak of the First World War. He was later to serve in a heavy artillery unit and was doubtless familiar with the 'Paris Gun'. Following the war's end, he was repatriated from internment in France and two years later he returned to the army, renamed as the *Reichswehr*. Whilst in service he was able to continue his education which had been interrupted by the war. He studied physics at the Technical University of Charlottenburg between 1926 and 1931. Sponsorship to study rocketry was hard to come by in the early 1930s for neither German industry, nor technical colleges, had any interest. Therefore, after reviewing the work of Goddard and others, the *Ballistische und Munitionsabteilung* established a rocket test centre in late 1930 at the *Reichswehr* proving range at Kummersdorf-West, 27 kilometres (17 miles) south of Berlin, with Dornberger in overall charge.

By the time the *Reichswehr* began its rocketry assessments, an interest in rocketry among German civilians was already well established. While the military 'men in grey' destroyed rocket engines in static tests at Kummersdorf-West, men in tweed and flannels were flying rockets from the suburbs of Berlin as a weekend hobby. One outlet for the amateur interest was the *Verein für Raumschiffahrt* (Society for Spaceship Travel) which had been created in 1927 in Breslau and was known simply as the VfR. From the Berlin suburb of Reinickendorf, the VfR launched its rockets from what it optimistically called the *Raketenflugplatz* (Rocket Flight Field). The society would grow to a membership of 500 and, thanks to international cooperation, some of its members were attracted from outside Germany. Notable members included Wernher von Braun, Rolf Engel, Kurt Hainisch, Walter Hohmann, Willy Ley, Rudolf Nebel, Hermann Oberth, Klaus Riedel, Eugen Sänger, Johannes Winkler and Max Valier, to name just a few. It is, however, von Braun and Oberth whose names, historically, are so closely associated with the V2.

Hermann Oberth (1894–1989), figurehead and mentor to the VfR membership, was born in Nagyszeben in what today is known as Transylvania. He had intended to follow his father's example and become a doctor, but the First World War interrupted his medical studies. Whilst convalescing from wounds he received in action, he was able to pursue studies in a new area of research that fascinated him: astronautics. He attempted to simulate weightlessness and designed a long-range liquid-fuelled rocket. Oberth was truly a cosmopolitan man and did not hesitate to correspond with the largely unknown Tsiolkovsky and the secretive Goddard. Oberth studied for a Ph.D. at the University of Heidelberg and he produced a paper based upon his rocket designs and experiments. His ideas were rejected and the university promptly dismissed him. However, he was not easily daunted and partially out of his own pocket, he published in 1923 a book entitled *Die Rakete zu den Planetenräumen* (The Rocket into Interplanetary Space). This book, although technical in nature, was widely read and inspired writers such as Max Valier and Willy Ley to write popularized titles covering rockets and space travel. These books also fuelled the growing interest in space travel among Germans and the growth of many rocket clubs and organizations including the VfR. At a time of such austerity and political upheaval it is easy to understand how many found solace from the difficult times of the 1920s in popular science.

The VfR ran its activities on a shoestring and many members saw that only a substantial investment from an external source could lead to significant advances. A partial remedy came from the film industry. Fritz Lang (1890–1976), the famous producer of films such as *Metropolis*, commissioned Oberth in the autumn of 1928 to be a technical advisor on a new project for a film to be known as *Frau im Mond* (Girl on the Moon). Oberth was also asked to make a full-scale working rocket 'prop' for the special effects Lang was hoping to film. Although Oberth was a great theorist, he had little practical or organizational experience. These shortcomings would again be revealed many years later at Peenemünde. Some in the VfR disliked the sensationalism of Lang, but Oberth enlisted the help of several members, most notably Rudolf Nebel. However, he soon ran into difficulties. The liquid-fuelled rocket prop exploded during tests and Oberth was to lose sight in his left eye. He also had to use his own money, as the promised funds from the production company never materialized. The rocket for Lang's film was never to fly, but in July 1930 Oberth agreed to test-fire a VfR rocket engine called the '*Kegeldüse*' (conical nozzle). It was based upon his elegant designs for the *Frau im Mond* rocket. The *Kegeldüse* engine sat in a container of cooling water and was designed to fire its thrust flame towards the sky. The young engineer, Klaus Riedel, using the customary petrol-drenched burning rags on the end of a long pole, lit the engine, which started with a loud bang. The *Kegeldüse* was the first European liquid-fuelled rocket engine and performed faultlessly for a fire time of 90 seconds, consuming 6 kilograms (13 lbs) of liquid oxygen and 1 kilogram (2 lbs) of petrol, delivering a constant thrust of 7 kilograms (15 lbs).

Unbeknown to the elated members of the VfR, Goddard had already fired his rocket engine in 1926 but, typically, was not to publish his results for another 10 years. The immediate problem was that in spite of the recognition, the expected flood of backing money into the coffers of the VfR never materialized. Meanwhile the Austrian writer and adventurer, Max Valier (1895–1930), experimented with solid fuel-powered rocket engines attached to railway wagons, sledges and gliders. Again, this caused consternation within the VfR for many felt this was nothing more than a cheap publicity trick. With the cooperation of the car manufacturer Fritz von Opel (nicknamed 'Rocket Fritz'), he built the Opel RAK rocket cars. With solid fuel rockets, the Opel RAKs reached speeds of over 230 km/h (143 mph). Many hundreds watched and cheered him on as his rocket cars sped along public highways. Unfortunately Valier later died while testing a liquid oxygen and petrol-fuelled engine that exploded in his laboratory. In spite of the reservations of some VfR members, Valier's efforts gained wide publicity (albeit bad publicity) for rocket travel and were an inspiration for many young would-be scientists.

One young man who was greatly inspired by Max Valier's exploits, and whose name was forever to be linked with rocketry, was Wernher von Braun. Von Braun (1912–1977) was the second of three sons born into an aristocratic Prussian family in Wirsitz, Germany, (now Wyrzysk, Poland). His father was Magnus *Freiherr* von Braun, a politician and agriculture minister in the German government. With his privileged background, young von Braun received an extensive education, but it was his hobbies of musical composition and car-building that occupied his time. Consequently, his scholastic achievements suffered, and he was a poor student of mathematics and physics. However, his young imagination was fired by the extraordinary exploits of the rocket publicists.

As von Braun was to recall in an interview in the 1960s: 'When I was 12 years of age, I had become fascinated by the incredible speed records established by Max Valier and Fritz von Opel. So I tried my first practical rocket experiment. It resembled one tried in 1500 by a Chinese named Wan Hoo. This visionary Oriental foresaw the use of rocketry in going to the moon and he wanted to be the first to do it. Using the technology then available, Wan Hoo fastened a huge kite to a sedan chair on which he had strapped 47 solid propellant rockets. Bravely he sat in the sedan chair while coolies held torches to the rocket fuses. Wan Hoo disappeared in a burst of flame and smoke.

'Although I had not heard of Wan Hoo's fateful experiment, my approach was similar. I chose a coaster wagon instead of a sedan chair. Selecting half-a-dozen of the biggest skyrockets I could find, I strapped them to the wagon. Since there were no coolies to apply the torch, and lacking Wan Hoo's courage and determination, my wagon was unmanned, and I lit the rockets myself. It performed beyond my wildest dreams. The wagon careened crazily about, trailing a tail of fire like a comet. When the rockets burned out, ending their sparkling performance with a magnificent thunderclap, the wagon rolled majestically to a halt.

'The police, who arrived late for the beginning of my experiment but in time for the grand finale, were unappreciative. They quickly took me into custody. Fortunately, no one was injured and I was released to the Minister of Agriculture (my father).'[1]

One can only wonder what von Braun's father would have thought while reprimanding his son if he had known that in twelve years hence, young Wernher would be the director of Germany's military rocket programme! Perhaps in the hope of steering young Wernher away from dangerous rocketry pranks, his mother gave him a small astronomical telescope as a confirmation gift. The telescope brought alive views of space that he had previously seen only in school textbooks and, by the age of 14, he was well and truly besotted with astronomy and thoughts of journeys to the stars.

Von Braun read any book he could find on astronomy and space flight and it was not long before he obtained a copy of Oberth's *Die Rakete zu den Planetenräumen*. This book captivated his imagination, but not his understanding. It was far too technical to digest; Oberth's theories were in the main expressed in mathematical formulae. He complained to his schoolteacher and, to his initial dismay, was advised to study maths and physics. According to von Braun, he was determined to master these subjects and accordingly 'buried myself in their mysteries.' In 1928 he was sent to the Hermann Lietz School located on the North Sea island of Spiekeroog close to Bremerhaven. He was granted permission to study the night sky for a couple of hours before bed with the telescope his mother gave him. His interests in amateur astronomy grew and his gifts as a natural born leader and organizer first showed themselves in the building of the school's observatory at the age of 16. He led a group of volunteer student workers who, in their spare time built, from the foundations up, a complete observatory housing a 125 mm (5-inch) refracting telescope. In September 1929, an enthusiastic 19-year old von Braun made contact with the Vice President of the VfR, Willy Ley. An appointment was made for von Braun to meet at Ley's Berlin home in order to ask for his acceptance into the VfR. Ley recalled it was a wet afternoon and he arrived late for the meeting to hear the sounds of Beethoven's *Moonlight Sonata* being played on the piano as von Braun patiently entertained himself.

Von Braun's rocketry experiments with the VfR were in many ways as dangerous as his first experiments as a boy. As von Braun was to relate: 'I joined Klaus Riedel and Rudolf Nebel, two other members of the German Society for Space Travel (VfR), as Professor Oberth's assistants. Our equipment was elementary, and our ignition system was perilous. Klaus Riedel would toss a flaming gasoline-soaked rag over the gas-spitting motor, and then duck for cover before Oberth opened the fuel valves and it started with a roar.'[2] Not only did he come to terms with the 'mysteries', but graduated a year early from the Hermann Lietz School to be enrolled at the Technical University of Charlottenburg. It is quite possible that von Braun and Dornberger 'rubbed shoulders' in the corridors of the institute, for their time there overlapped. In any event, at Charlottenburg von Braun learned the mechanical practicalities of engineering that were to be so important in his later work. After two years at the Berlin Institute of Technology, he received his bachelor's degree in mechanical engineering in 1932. He was just 20 years old.

The problem of finding a safe location for the VfR to conduct potentially dangerous experiments was solved by a founding member, Klaus Riedel. From rural Bernstadt in Saxony, Riedel's family were farmers and they agreed that their land could be used as a rocket testing ground. From this pastoral setting in the summer of 1930, the VfR experimented with a series of static liquid oxygen and petrol-fuelled rockets called the '*Mirak*' (minimum rocket') series. The design was constrained by whatever materials were on hand at the time. In the case of the *Mirak* 1, the combustion chamber was 'jacketed' by the liquid oxygen fuel tank to prevent excessive heat build-up and the metre-long stabilizing tail stick was, in fact, a pressurized fuel tank of petrol. Although initially successful, the *Mirak* 1 was destroyed following a rupture of the liquid oxygen tank in September 1930. More seriously, the future use of the proving ground was jeopardized. The deafening explosion frightened the local population who knew only too well how dangerous rockets could be; after all, it had been just five months earlier that Max Valier had died in a much publicized rocket explosion.

During the experiments with the *Mirak* series, Rudolf Nebel sought an alternative proving ground to improve upon the rather public and primitive facilities of the open fields of Bernstadt. Nebel, who had a reputation as a scrounger of free materials and as an eloquent negotiator, secured a former First World War ammunition storage site for a peppercorn rent from the authorities. Although the land belonged to the city, the old blockhouses still belonged to the *Reichswehr*, hence the cheapness of the rent. Located at Reinickendorf, south of Berlin, a 300-acre site of weeds and scrub were partly cleared. Abandoned blockhouses became laboratories, test stands and bachelor quarters. A small signboard proudly proclaimed '*Raketenflugplatz Berlin*' (Berlin Rocket Field) and it was officially opened in September 1930. In its first operational year at the *Raketenflugplatz*, the VfR launched 87 rockets and performed 270 static engine tests.

From the new proving grounds the VfR developed the *Mirak* 2 which reached an altitude of 63 metres (207 ft) in July 1932. Experimentation continued and in turn led to the development of the powerful one stick 'Repulsor' rocket. This rocket shared similar features to Goddard's rocket of 1926. The water-cooled combustion chamber was carried at the front with its exhaust gases bearing down onto the guarded top of the oxygen tank, behind which lay the alcohol tank and recovery parachute. Four thin, curving fuel pipes held the engine and fuel tanks in their correct positions. The 'Repulsor' could reach altitudes of 1 km (0.62 miles). To help raise VfR funds the public paid an entry fee of one Mark to watch the demonstrations of rocket firings and the much hoped-for, and occasionally granted, explosions. The Repulsor rocket was to be indelibly etched into the minds of the VfR membership. One such flight, witnessed by a film crew, resulted in the roof of the local police station being set ablaze, threatening the banning of all further tests!

A similar organization to the VfR was the *Gesellschaft für Raketenforschung* (GEFRA – Organization for Rocket Research) based in Hannover. This group, whose membership included Konrad Dannenberg (1912-2009), was led by the unqualified, but enthusiastic, Albert Püllenberg (1913-1991). Dannenberg recalled that in the mid-1920s, he and Püllenberg attended a meeting in Hannover where Max Valier was giving a lecture. He spoke about rocketry and discussed the possibility of a manned trip to Mars. The talk convinced Dannenberg and his friends that rocket propulsion would eclipse the successes of both Charles Lindbergh's recent Atlantic crossing and those of the Zeppelins. In 1928, Dannenberg and Püllenberg – travelling by bicycle – attended Valier's rocket-propelled rail wagon tests at Burgwedel near Hannover. Valier wanted to demonstrate the capability of rocket propulsion as many at that time were not convinced that exhaust gases could generate sufficient power to accelerate a vehicle. The first and second test, although in part successful, did not achieve high speeds and Valier increased the charge considerably for the third test. Unfortunately, the huge amount of power and the tremendous acceleration derailed the vehicle and the car exploded killing its hapless test passenger – a cat.

Inspired nevertheless by the experience, Dannenberg, Püllenberg and other would-be rocketeers began a series of solid engine tests in the late 1920s. The test facility was Püllenberg's uncle's garage – until an explosion caused its complete destruction. Undaunted and encouraged by the writings of Oberth, they decided to experiment with liquid engines. Eventually, Püllenberg arranged for the GEFRA to acquire land from the *Reichswehr* to conduct further experiments in safety, north of Hannover, on the Vahrenwalder Heide. Starved of resources, a near insurmountable problem for the group was sourcing a supply of liquid oxygen, but interest from the Hannover Technical University flying club helped it to obtain liquid oxygen from a local air-separation plant. Dannenberg left the group but kept in contact with Püllenberg who continued the research.[3]

In the background to all this activity in civilian rocketry was the *Reichswehr*. Dornberger courted amateur rocketry groups for recruits as they had courted him for finance. The *Heereswaffenamt* would award research contracts to rocketry groups to build and demonstrate rockets. The *Reichswehr's* finance was very scarce and it felt it was important to meet and evaluate the rocketeers on their own home ground. The difficulty for Dornberger and his colleagues at Kummersdorf-West, however, was the internal rivalries and ridiculous claims of technological prowess of which the various groups boasted. Dornberger visited the GEFRA facility and despite the enthusiasm he witnessed, he concluded that the group was working towards a dead end. Following an interview with Püllenberg, he recommended that he should take an engineering degree and, perhaps, in the future, he might have a job for him. Püllenberg followed Dornberger's advice and was later invited to join the military Rocket development team. Püllenberg discreetly told Dannenberg of 'highly interesting activities' that he was involved with although he could never mention the word 'Rocket'. Eventually however, Püllenberg suggested that Dannenberg should make an application and join him. Dannenberg, who was drafted into the *Wehrmacht* in 1939, took part in the invasion of France in May 1940. He was able to leave the military, and as a civilian worker, began work at Peenemünde, becoming a propulsion specialist working under *Dr.-Ing.* Walter Thiel.

In 1930, the scene was set for a very famous encounter between *Hauptmann* Dornberger of the *Reichswehr's Heereswaffenamt* and the scientifically prodigious member of the VfR, Wernher von Braun. Dornberger visited the *Raketenflugplatz* to view the work of the VfR membership; the shrewd and knowledgeable student, von Braun, impressed him. Physically striking and memorable, he was to recall von Braun's height and 'broad massive chin'. The most important attribute in Dornberger's mind, however, was von Braun's ability to grasp problems and to expose difficulties. This skill was apparently missing from the other members of the VfR and from the other groups. Von Braun joined a short list of technical specialists whom Dornberger thought could further the *Heereswaffenamt* projects.

Von Braun remembered the first meeting with Dornberger thus: 'I remember that of the many visitors we had, there were three men in mufti who came in what looked like a military car, but with civilian licence plates on, and they were greatly interested in what we were doing. And I remember that after the demonstration of one of our crude little rocket motors on the captive test stand, they invited us to give them a free flight demonstration on the army proving ground of Kummersdorf.'[4]

Dornberger gave the VfR team funds to build a rocket and von Braun worked through the spring and summer of 1932 to produce the device. At that time, a VfR rocket had its size defined by whether it could be lifted by one hand or two hands. It was one of the 'two-hands' large rockets that was to be demonstrated – the 3.8 metre tall one-stick 'Repulsor'. The demonstration took place in June 1932 at the *Reichswehr's* Kummersdorf-West proofing ground with mixed results. The rocket took off perfectly, but with only four small stabilizing fins and no guidance system, a stiff wind blew it off course and it flew horizontally at a height of 250 metres. As the flight was so unexpectedly short, the timing mechanism did not eject the chute and the rocket crashed into woods some 3 kilometres (2 miles) away from the launch site. For its part, the VfR considered it to be a successful demonstration of the liquid-fuelled rocket, but the military was not so enthusiastic; after all, it had paid for a rocket that had neither reached its expected altitude of several kilometres or landed by parachute.

Dornberger, however, had been impressed by the demonstration and was keen to extend the involvement of the *Reichswehr* with the VfR. His main anxiety was security: the VfR's open nature and public operations at the *Raketenflugplatz* did not suit a military research programme. Dornberger made an offer that von Braun considered impossible to refuse; he stated that the *Reichswehr* would support the development of liquid rockets but only if they (the VfR) would accept military terms and move the whole operation behind the fence of a military facility.

Suddenly, the official recognition craved by the VfR became a 'two-edged sword' that ultimately was to prove divisive to the membership. Von Braun and Nebel argued. Surprisingly, although Nebel knew better than anyone else of the perilous financial situation, he thought that the VfR could impose conditions on the *Reichswehr*. Von Braun, however, realized that the VfR was broke and only substantial new finance could move the rocket project along. The VfR would have to accept the conditions and restrictions imposed by its new master. Von Braun accepted Dornberger's offer; initially the rest of the VfR declined. Nebel and his supporters continued to work at the *Raketenflugplatz* for another two years until, at last, fading finances and other pressures meant they had to give up in January 1934 and the site reverted to its former use as an ammunition dump. The disbandment of the VfR soon followed. The new Nazi government outlawed all amateur civilian rocket firings and international cooperation.

On 1 October 1932, von Braun began his contract work as a civilian researcher behind the barbed wire of Kummersdorf-West. He started modestly with just one mechanic/engineer at his disposal. The rockets subsequently developed over the next 12 years were named uniquely, but for the genesis of the V2 development, the nomenclature was the letter 'A' followed by an ascending number. The 'A' stood for '*Aggregat*' (machine unit).

The A1 never got off the ground – it was never supposed to. Harking back to the 19th century and experiments to improve the accuracy of torpedoes, the A1 featured a 41-kilogram (90 lb) stabilizing gyroscope located in its nose. Within the 1.4 metre (4.5 ft)-long body of the rocket, the liquid oxygen tank was located inside the ethanol alcohol tank. The A1 was expected to develop 300 kilograms (661 lb) of thrust for a burn time of 16 seconds. The first static test-firing was made in December 1932 and was a disaster; it ran for a fraction of a second before the fuel tanks exploded. The development of rockets with propellant tanks within propellant tanks was abandoned.

The next development from the Kummersdorf-West team was the A2. Two such rockets were made and were called *Max* and *Moritz* after the well-known German cartoon child characters drawn by Wilhelm Busch in 1865. The mischievous and rebellious boys also appeared in the New York Journal's *Sunday Supplement* as the *Katzenjammer Kids*. Like their predecessor, the A2s used liquid oxygen and alcohol in a 1:3 ratio. The heavy gyroscope, however, was mounted 'amidships' with the two separate fuel tanks either side. Unlike their namesakes, *Max* and *Moritz* were very well behaved. Both were successfully fired in December 1934 from the North Sea island of Borkum, reaching an altitude of 2.4 kilometres.

The next step was the A3. In the summer of 1937, an A3 was transported from Kummersdorf-West to the island of Greifswalder Oie for flight-testing, 13 kilometres away from Peenemünde. Apparently, this was the same island that Winkler had attempted to get permission to use for his independent rocket tests in the early 1930s. Permission in the past had been denied as the authorities were concerned that the lighthouse might be damaged. Such fears were dismissed, however, when the *Heer* used the site! The 7.65 metre (26 ft)-long A3 was fuelled with liquid oxygen and alcohol. The design of the A3 represented a great advance on its predecessors. Deviations in the flight path were intended to be sensed by three gyroscopes and two integrating accelerometers. Corrections were to be applied by molybdenum jet vanes positioned in the flow of the combustion chamber's exhaust. After three launches of the A3 series, test results were mixed. The 1500-kilogram (3,300 lb) thrust engine and rocket structure was deemed a complete success, but the steering mechanism proved to be a complete failure. All of the A3s tested climbed a few hundred metres before losing guidance control and falling into the Baltic.

The setbacks to the A3 were an enormous problem for the von Braun team. At the same time that the A3 was being constructed and tested, a rocket twice the size was taking shape in the drawing offices. Although the specifications had not yet been determined, it was called A4. The guidance control problems of the A3 temporarily halted development of the A4 as it was decided that the A3 must be made to work first. By this stage, the A3 had such a bad reputation that it was thought it would be a good omen to change the name to A5. The A5 was first flown without guidance in 1938 and in the spring of 1939 it flew with a perfected, fully functioning guidance system. The principle of the guidance system was essentially the same as that used in the A4. The A5, however, could not be thought of as a long-range missile for its range was only 26 kilometres with a vertical ceiling of 16 kilometres. The work on the A5 was completed by the summer of 1939 and was deemed a complete success.

A lack of official recognition of the rocket programme's potential and its low financial priority were perpetual problems for the rocket team. Irrespective of the important military personages who corralled around the Kummersdorf-West proofing stands, one man alone proved to be the greatest threat to the whole project: Adolf Hitler. On 29 March 1939, Hitler visited the facility in the company of the Deputy *Führer*, Rudolf Hess, as well as *Reichsleiter* Martin Bormann (Hess' personal secretary), and *General der Artillerie* Becker. With Dornberger as tour leader, they visited the proof stands and laboratories. They walked under grey, leaden skies from one test stand to the other as both the 295-kilogram (650 lb) and 1090-kilogram (2,400 lb) thrust engines were fired. The normal reaction to the spectacle of the vivid, dancing blue thrust flame and gut-wrenching sounds was unanimous euphoria, but Hitler reacted with apparent indifference. It seemed to Dornberger that Hitler's thoughts were elsewhere. Indeed, he may well have been distracted because on 15 March 1939 he had completed his invasion of Czechoslovakia in defiance of the Munich Agreement. Hitler knew that talk of appeasement with the British and the French was over and conflict was inevitable.

Returning indoors, the tour concluded with von Braun describing the marvels of the proposed A4 using a mock-up model appropriately coloured to show the flow of propellants. Again, Hitler feigned complete disinterest. It was customary on such occasions to lavish guests with a fine dinner, accompanied by cognac and cigars to conclude a memorable visit. However, the *Führer* neither smoked nor drank and he forbade anyone to do so in his presence. His mood began to lift, however, as he sat down to a meagre meal of vegetables with mineral water. Hitler chatted with his intimates and Becker about what he had seen during the day. Then he turned to Dornberger and enquired if it would be possible to build the fuel tanks of the proposed A4 rocket using steel rather than aluminium. Hitler was perhaps concerned about the demands of aluminium upon aircraft manufacture. Dornberger explained that although possible, it would cause delays. Hitler gazed absent-mindedly and commented: 'It certainly was terrific!' [5]

This was the only sign that Hitler had been impressed by his visit to Kummersdorf-West and it troubled Dornberger. Hitler's attitude to the A4 development programme continued to vacillate for a further four years.

The 'A' range of rockets for the *Heer* were not the only projects being handled by the von Braun team. *Major* Wolfram *Freiherr* von Richthofen of the *Luftwaffe Technisches Amt* (Technical Office), a distant cousin of the famous First World War fighter ace, showed early interest in the work at Kummersdorf-West. Von Richthofen was Dornberger's *Luftwaffe* counterpart and with remarkably imaginative flair, he foresaw a time when aircraft could be powered by rocket engines. However, it was not until 1936 that he became sufficiently interested to ask the *Heer* research team to develop a rocket engine that could be used to propel an aircraft. The Kummersdorf-West team duly developed a 300 kilogram (660 lb) thrust, liquid oxygen and alcohol rocket to the *Luftwaffe's* specification. It was fitted to the rear of the piston engined, propeller-driven Heinkel He 112 fighter. Although two He 112s were destroyed during tests, the third airframe flew with spectacular success on 1 April 1937 from Neuhardenberg, Germany with *Flugkapitän* Erich Warsitz (1906-1983) at the controls. Warsitz flew the He 112 to an altitude of 800 metres (2,635 ft) and then ignited the engine in the rear of the aircraft to become the first person to fly solely by rocket. Warsitz went on to test-fly not only the Heinkel He 176, the first aircraft ever to fly purely on rocket power, but also the famous Messerschmitt Me 163 rocket interceptor.

Because of this work and von Richthofen's enthusiasm, the von Braun team was awarded grants by the *Luftwaffe* to develop RATO's (Rocket Assisted Take-Off) units. These rockets provided heavily overloaded aircraft with additional thrust to become airborne and were used successfully on the huge Messerschmitt Me 321 *Gigant* (Giant) transporter. Weighing in at 34400 kilograms (34 tons) and with a wingspan of 55 metres (180 ft), the formidable *Gigant* normally required three towing twin-engine Messerschmitt Bf 110s to achieve take-off!

According to von Braun, the *Luftwaffe* became so excited about rocket development that it wanted to greatly expand the entire endeavour. Furthermore, it had identified that the scientists were too crowded at Kummersdorf-West. To von Braun's very great surprise the *Luftwaffe* offered him and the team 5 million Reichsmarks to move to a much larger base. (By the standards of the year 2000, 5 million Reichsmarks were equivalent to £15,593,505 or 25,573,348 Euros or US $23,626,522). Von Braun was alarmed by this talk of so much money, so he discussed the situation with his superior *General der Artillerie* Becker. Von Braun was later to recall Becker's reaction as, 'Well I'm not going to let the *Luftwaffe* run the wheel of this business. I'm going to be the majority stock holder in this enterprise.'[6]

Becker then offered von Braun an additional 6 million Marks. With promised funds of 11 million Reichsmarks (2000 value £34,305,711 or Euros 56,261,365 or US $51,978,348) the world's first fully integrated centre for scientific research was to be born in which both the *Heer* and *Luftwaffe* were to have control.[7]

But where should it be sited? A position close to the sea would be ideal for security, secrecy and also for safety. Germany is landlocked in all directions bar the north. To the north lies Denmark. The 75-kilometre wide Danish frontier is flanked by the North Sea to the west, and the Baltic to the east.

On 2 April 1936, Becker, Dornberger, von Braun and the *Luftwaffe* men, von Richthofen and newly-promoted *Generalleutnant* Albert Kesselring, head of the *Luftwaffe's* Administration Office, met to discuss the situation. Initially the beautiful, white chalk cliff island of Rügen in the Baltic was considered, but this was already spoken for by the *Deutsche Arbeitsfront* (German Labour Front) organization. Following a suggestion made by von Braun, with Kesselring's agreement for the *Luftwaffe* to pay half the costs, Peenemünde on the Baltic coast was chosen. The Baltic coastline had always been popular as a holiday destination for Germany's city dwellers. One place in particular, the island of Usedom, became so popular with the citizens of the capital city that it became known as 'Berlin's bath tub'.

The shape of the wooded and sand duned island of Usedom can best be described as an irregular triangle with its longest side of 50 kilometres (31 miles) running from north-west to south-east facing the Baltic. On this side of the island, there are picturesque fishing hamlets set upon a shoreline of dense pine forests. The other two sides of the island are bounded by the River Peene. Von Braun's memory of his maternal grandfather's hunting expeditions on Usedom had prompted his initial suggestion. Wild boar, deer and countless wildfowl populated the tranquil and unspoilt interior. Ten kilometres (6 miles) due north of the cathedral town of Wolgast lay the village of Peenemünde, which is so named as its position is at the 'mouth of the Peene'. To the east lie the popular holiday destinations of Zinnowitz and Zempin. The great geographical attraction of this location was that rocket tests could be performed over the sea with the trajectory running parallel to the coast. The east–northeast track of this trajectory was 500 kilometres (311 miles) in length before reaching the coast of Lithuania.

The *Heeresversuchsstelle* Peenemünde (*Heer* Research Centre at Peenemünde) was to become a reality with remarkable speed; the move into the new facility from Kummersdorf-West was made in the spring of 1937. Trees were felled to make tracks through the forest upon which cobbled stone service roads were laid. The site as dictated by the financial situation was divided rather unequally between the *Heer* and the *Luftwaffe*, the latter occupying the western side known as Peenemünde West and the *Heer* area known as Peenemünde East (Peenemünde *Ost*). The *Luftwaffe* was to construct an airfield and support buildings, whilst the *Heer* built accommodation quarters for both scientists and technicians within the security zone. Further to the south and outside the security boundary, was constructed the Karlshagen *Siedlung* (Housing Estate): it was the most modern estate in Germany, being home to 3,000 people.

Planned as a model village for the families of scientists, technicians and administrators, schools, shops, sports facilities and leisure clubs were all provided. Further to the south of Karlshagen was Trassenheide, the hutted camp for foreign prisoner workers encircled by chain-linked fencing (anecdotal information suggests the fence may have been electrified). At its height the *Heeresversuchsstelle* Peenemünde was to employ 20,000 people. A railway line fed scientist, technicians and workers from the settlements and nearby villages to the enormous 'Development' and 'Pre-Production' factory halls and numerous other smaller buildings. One such smaller building housed a revolutionary supersonic wind tunnel. Three kilometres to the west of the factory halls, at the village of Peenemünde, the tranquil harbour and docks were enlarged to accommodate the increased flow of construction materials, a new 30,000-kilowatt coal-fired power station and liquid oxygen plant forever disfiguring the village skyline.

More than thirteen *Prüfstände* ('Proof Stands' – test platforms) were constructed. Strung out at the end of a line of six test stands were the most famous of all: *Prüfständ* VII and *Prüfständ* X. These platforms were launch pads for the later A4 Rocket. *Prüfständ* VII was set within a raised embankment forming a round-ended amphitheatre that was approximately 200 metres (656 ft) long by 150 metres (492 ft) wide overall. The embankment, intended to reduce the risk of crosswinds from the Baltic was approximately 38 metres (125 ft) thick. The distinctive earthworks and launch area were commonly known as the 'Arena'. At the northern end of the Arena, beside the launch platform, stood a moveable 30-metre (98 ft) tall preparation tower. Underground tunnels ran from a bomb-proof control bunker to the launch pad and from the top of the embankment, photographers operating cine cameras captured the disasters and triumphs of the Rocket tests. More or less centred in the Arena was the firing position and the '*Schurre*', a concrete ditch system that directed the engine blast and carried the pipelines of water needed to cool the test stand.

Great thought was given as to how the facility could best be disguised from the air and to this end, the felling of trees was kept to an absolute minimum. Peenemünde kept its natural charm and for many that lived and worked there it was called the 'Sleeping Beauty'.

Rocket development was not the only work that took place at Peenemünde and mention should be made of the V2's stablemate, the V1. In the early 1930s, the *Luftwaffe* became interested in the concept of cheap, pilotless aircraft. At first, the V1 was a joint project between the *Luftwaffe* and von Braun's own department in the *Heeresversuchsstelle*. By 1940, it was realized that the ramjet (stovepipe engine) originally designed for manned flight was the logical engine for the V1; an air-breathing, winged missile. Additionally, it was decided that the *Luftwaffe* would   separately develop airborne missiles and the *Heer* would concentrate on ballistic, wingless missiles that would travel through airless altitudes. Developments and project responsibilities swapped, and the von Braun team played no further part in the V1 development. The *Luftwaffe* accordingly brought in the manufacturer Fieseler to develop its airframe.

On 1 September 1939, Hitler invaded Poland and war broke out. This changed the situation at Peenemünde dramatically. As von Braun was to recall: 'The Army told us in very clear terms that either we had to produce something of promise as a weapon in the very near future or we must go out of business.'[8]

Fresh appraisals were made of the existing plans and it was decided to continue the aerodynamic configuration of the A5 in order to save wind tunnel studies. The A4 was twice the size of the A5 and similar in proportion, except that the A4 had larger stabilizing fins and rudders. The ultimate factor in deciding the length and breadth of the A4, however, was the ease of transportation through railway tunnels. The development team was then asked what specification a larger version of A5 in payload and range might have. The reply was one metric ton of explosives with a range of over 275 kilometres. On this basis the *Heer* endorsed the plans and the development of the A4 began.

Throughout 1940-1941 the components of the A4 were developed and static engine tests were performed. The A4 combustion chamber was mounted on gimbal rings on the test stand to evaluate the guidance systems. The first A4 test launch in June 1942 was a failure. The second test, on 16 August 1942, was a partial failure as the sand-filled warhead broke off and the rocket disintegrated as it reached record-breaking supersonic speeds. With pressure building for a successful launching, Konrad Dannenberg, a rocket propulsion specialist, recalled the tension, excitement and ultimate success: 'It was of extreme importance that we succeed this time, because we had been told the Army's effort would be cancelled if we failed, and all personnel would be sent to the Russian Front. The date was 3 October 1942, a beautiful and sunny day. Preparations for the launch had proceeded without any major problem. The missile had been erected on its launch table in the centre of *Prüfständ* VII. It was there, about a month before, that a few static firings with the same missile had been successfully conducted in a mobile test tower positioned over the flame deflector that we could see just behind the vehicle. As one of the last operations before launch, the rocket's tanks had been filled with liquid oxygen, indicated by the frost which formed on the outer skin. The frost would drop away at lift-off and would not be a weight penalty. The rocket's fins and boat tail were made of steel, and so would not be damaged by the impact of these icy flakes.

'The launch area had been cleared of all personnel. Thiel and the operating crew were in the control bunker. Wernher von Braun and General Walter Dornberger were on the roof of the Measurement House about a kilometre away. A television set had been installed there, and a Doppler receiver would indicate the speed of the vehicle during its entire flight. Some observers, a photo-crew and I had climbed on the roof of the assembly building, about 100 yards away from the launch pad. On previous attempts, I had seen the launch from inside the control bunker, but from there the view was severely limited to just the first few seconds of lift-off. I wanted to see more of the later trajectory of the forthcoming flight. Loudspeakers announced the countdown progress to all observers.

'From our position on the roof, we could clearly see the A4 sitting on its launching table. It was still connected by an umbilical cord to the instruments in the control bunker and to an electric power supply to save the flight batteries' power. It was just before 4 o'clock when the loudspeakers finally announced: "X minus three." Oxygen vapour was still coming out of the vent line, but this stopped suddenly when an operator in the control bunker remotely closed the vent valve. The oxygen tank was now being pressurized. The fuel tank had been pressurized earlier. The missile was now ready to go.

'When the loudspeaker announced "X minus one", a small solid propellant rocket was fired nearby to ascertain if wind conditions were acceptable. A few seconds later, the final countdown was announced: "X minus 10-9-8-7-6-5-4 (I knew the high-speed recorders and the oscillographs would be turned on now) 3-2-1... (Ignition)." A bright yellow-orange pre-stage flame was leaping out from the rocket chamber. The turbo-pump was not yet running, so the generated thrust was low. The rocket was operating in "*Vorstufe* (Pre-stage)" mode. When the test conductor saw the exhaust flame burning properly, he pulled a switch and announced: "*Hauptstufe* (Main-stage)". The umbilical cable fell off, and the turbo-pump was turned on. This increased the flow of propellants into the rocket engine and the thrust level. In about a second, the thrust was equal to the weight of the rocket. It left the launching table, very slowly at first but then faster and faster until the thrust reached about twice the weight of the rocket. The A4 was now accelerating with 1g, equal to Earth's gravity. The air was filled with the rumbling of thunder. We felt the vibrations in our entire bodies as well as through the ground. After all, we were much closer than you can get today to any rocket launch.

'I watched through my binoculars as the black and white rocket rose faster and faster. The exhaust gases from the rocket motor generated a flame about as long as the rocket itself. This unforgettable sight is still the highlight of my career, watching it rise vertically off the launching table for the first 5 seconds and then gradually tilting in the desired flight direction steered by graphite control vanes in the jet exhaust. This flight showed that the A4 could be controlled. It did not start to rotate, as in previous launches. The rocket went through the "sound barrier" and stayed under control.

'A few seconds later, a white vapour trail formed, which led some people to announce an explosion. We later found out that this vapour formed at great altitudes because the exhaust gases condensed due to the low pressure and the low temperatures. I observed this event without my binoculars.

'The loudspeaker finally announced "*Brennschluss* (cut-off)," the end of the propulsive phase of the trajectory. "*Brennschluss*" happens in two phases: first the steam flow into the turbine is decreased by closing the main hydrogen peroxide valve, but leaving an 8-ton valve open. Thus, the 25-ton thrust level decreases to about 8 tons. This permits a more exact termination of thrusting to obtain a more accurate cut-off velocity, which determines the length of the trajectory. You could see the effect because the formation of the condensation cloud became smaller. I seem to recall that I could still see the glowing jet vanes for several additional seconds after *Brennschluss*.

'Dornberger and von Braun had left their observation post to come to Proof Stand VII to inspect the launch site and to congratulate the operating engineers and especially Thiel, who was still sucking on his cold pipe, which he hardly ever lit. This launch experience gave him many ideas how to improve future operations. The launch crew was delirious with joy. There was great emotion all around. People embraced, shook hands and congratulated each other. The evening featured a terrific party with plenty of beer and hard liquor.

'Dornberger gave a congratulatory talk in which he expressed his hope that the Peenemünde team could continue further development of the A4. He stressed that this would be the No. 1 task in the immediate future. But he also told us that we had put a human-built article in outer space for the first time and had used this novel medium to travel from one point on Earth to another one. We had just started the Space Age.'[9]

Remarkably, the Peenemünde team had to wait a further nine months after the successful firing before Hitler at last gave the development top priority in July 1943. Dornberger was to write with much understatement: 'The great struggle for recognition appeared to be over.'

The reality was that the great struggle had only just begun.

CHAPTER TWO

VERGELTUNGSWAFFE 2 (V2)

Anatomy of the Rocket

THE principles of a rocket engine can be understood by a simple analogy: stand at the stern of a rowing boat and throw a heavy weight! This action produces a movement in the opposite direction of the thrown weight. Rocket engines work in accordance to Isaac Newton's third law of motion, '*every action has an equal and opposite reaction*' and consequently, are known as reaction engines. A rocket engine is actually throwing weight (more correctly 'mass') in the form of a high-pressure gas created by the burning of fuels. The ignition of the gases accelerates the mass of the converted fuel, at high speeds, out of an opening in the combustion chamber called the venturi. If the combustion chamber was a perfect sphere, the explosive force would be the same in all directions, but the venturi and the divergent nozzle directs it. The outward force pushing on the sides of the sphere is equal, but the force upwards on the top of the combustion chamber, and opposite towards the venturi, is not. The downward force of the exhaust escaping through the nozzle pushes the combustion chamber and rocket, upwards.

Although rocket fuel can be either solid or liquid, its mass does not change even though it has been turned into a gas, but its expulsion from the engine accelerates the mass and produces thrust. The fuel known as a propellant is often in two parts, fuel and an oxidizer. Although many fuels cannot 'burn', a special oxidizer mixed with the fuel can produce a rapid chemical reaction – effectively 'burning'.

The V2 Rocket was the first long-range ballistic weapon to enter space and to be deployed in modern warfare. Standing 14.03 metres high (46 ft), it was approximately as tall as a five-storey building. Powered by alcohol as a fuel and liquid oxygen as an oxidizer, it had a cylindrical body that tapered to a sharp point whilst the tail section held the combustion chamber and four stabilizing fins set at right angles, each equipped with air rudders. Gyroscopes controlled flight stability by adjusting the air rudders and four vanes placed in the exhaust. The external sheeting of the Rocket was of steel, welded, riveted and braced by an internal structure of steel stringers and formers. Further materials used for internal items such as fuel tanks, pipes and other plumbing were made from aluminium. Cheaper materials, such as wood, were also used whilst the tip and combined fuse of the nose cone was made of glass. Internal insulating material between fuel tanks and the internal bodywork were made of glass wool. Special paint for the Rocket's external surfaces was introduced to reduce premature mid-air explosions due to 'burn through'. Moulded plastic was used for the antennae in the tails.

For the purposes of describing the V2 Rocket, it can be conveniently divided into five parts: *Spitze* (warhead); *Geräteraum* (control departments); *Mittelteil* (Middle Fuselage); *Antriebsblock* (propulsion block), and the *Heck* (tail).

Spitze (Warhead)

The 6 mm-thick (¼ inch) mild steel of the warhead contained 994 kilograms (2,187 lb) of explosive – 60% Amatol and 40% ammonia nitrate. The odourless explosive has been variously described as being grey or yellow in colour.[1] Apparently, at Peenemünde and elsewhere, during training sessions with *Fernraketen* (abbreviated to 'FR' – long-range rocket) troops, an instructor would pound the explosive with a hammer and even throw it into an open fire, but it would not detonate! Its true explosive effect was demonstrated, however, with the use of an appropriate priming charge.[2]

The electrical detonating system of the Rocket was called the Sterg unit. The warhead was detonated on impact by a combination of five separate fusing systems; a simple crush type contact device encapsulated in glass, a pair of 'trembler' inertia switches in the nose and a pair of similar switches mounted in the base of the warhead.[3] The combination of the fuses constituted a safety device.

The glass tip of the Rocket contained a simple electrical contact switch. On impact with the ground, contact between the metal surfaces completed the circuit and electricity would pass to the fuse thus detonating the warhead. The inertia trembler switches, constructed of ceramic and Bakelite would close when subjected to a *g*-force of 130 times normal gravity during the sudden deceleration as the Rocket impacted. The inertia switches were electrically connected to an igniter in an exploder tube of pink penthrite wax in the warhead. Regardless of the angle of impact, inertia switches were positioned so that the fuse would always detonate. The design was a compromise as it had been impossible to manufacture a detonating system that would explode the warhead at an altitude of 18 metres (60 ft), to cause maximum effect. The Sterg device contained a safety feature that was controlled by ground radio and could be used to detonate the warhead if the Rocket went off course or was likely to fall on friendly territory.[4]

The warhead was attached to a flange on the Rocket by twenty screws inserted through countersunk holes drilled around the circumference of the warhead base. To aid fitment of the warhead in the normal horizontal position, two sling points were provided at either side of the casing in addition to two at the rear mounting plate. The junction of the warhead to the body of the Rocket formed one of two mounting joints for use when the Rocket was transported on the purpose-built transporter known as the *Meillerwagen*. Close to the tip of the Rocket's warhead, an open aperture called the *Staudruckrohr* was located. The purpose of the *Staudruckrohr* was to replace pressure loss during the consumption of propellant during flight. From the open hole in the warhead casing, a flexible metal pipe was connected to the upper propellant tank containing alcohol. Although the propellant tank was pressurized before flight with nitrogen, the 'ram air' effect created as the Rocket sped into the sky maintained pressure at the correct working limits.

The *Geräteraum* (Control Departments)

The Control Departments were located below the warhead and above the propellant tanks. This section was divided by means of plywood into four equal compartments, centrally braced with four steel brackets set at right angles to each other. Each compartment was equipped with an external detachable panel to allow easy access. As seen in plan-form, the partitions bisect the angles between the fins by 45 degrees. The compartments were identified with reference to the fins below. Hence, the *Geräteraum* 1 was directly above fin 1. Two of the compartment panels were bolted into position whilst the other two formed hinged doors.

The disposition of the various instruments was as follows:
Geräteraum **I** (Compartment 1) contained a pair of 16-volt batteries for the operation of avionics; for example: radio equipment, gyroscopes, control amplifiers and solenoid valves. The compartment also carried the *Verdoppler* radio receiver but only when the *Brennschluss* (BS) system was in use. Additionally, within the compartment was the *Funkkommandogerät* (radio equipment) that allowed emergency fuel 'cut-off' up to the moment of launching. This cut-off is not to be confused with '*Brennschluss*'. In rocket terminology, *Brennschluss* (close burning) is the moment the engine stops (either intentionally or due to exhausting its propellants) and the rocket continues under its own momentum until it falls to the ground. Control of *Brennschluss* in the V2 was important because it determined the range and therefore the accuracy of the weapon. Several *Brennschluss* systems were developed for use with the V2. They were either carried internally, or operated in conjunction with ground radio equipment.

Geräteraum **II** (Compartment 2) contained the main electrical distribution box, a fuse circuit box and the *Stotz Stecker* (umbilical plug socket) for ground power supply and control with the manned *Feuerleitpanzer* (fire control vehicle). When the Rocket was launched, the *Stotz Stecker* was released by a solenoid and the plug was thrown away from the Rocket's side by a spring-loaded mechanism. Additionally, Compartment 2 contained the Sterg unit and the *Zeitschaltwerk* (time switch) which governed the sequence of events after take-off.

Geräteraum **III** (Compartment 3) contained gyroscopes and their alternators with regulators that supplied alternating current (36 volts, three phased at 500 cycles per second).[5] The gyroscopes known as '*Horizont*' (pitch) and '*Vertikant*' (yaw/roll) required a minute to reach the maximum 30,000-rpm.[6]

Compartment 3 also contained the *I-Gerät*, which measured acceleration and integrated acceleration over time to obtain a velocity value.[7] When a predetermined value of velocity on the optimum trajectory was reached, a contact closed and the supply of propellant was either shut down or reduced to 1/3rd of normal thrust for a short period of adjustment. The *I-Gerät* was entirely self-contained and resistant to intentional jamming or interference. A great advantage of the system was that the FR troops were able to dispatch a Rocket without the necessary support of a cumbersome radio organization.[8]

If the *I-Gerät* was not installed, the compartment held the *Brennschluss* (BS) command receiver. The BS was an alternative means of determining velocity instead of the *I-Gerät*. The BS system was able to determine the velocity of the Rocket and at the correct moment, shut the engine down. It used the principles of 'Doppler Shift', in which a change of frequency is experienced by an observer moving relative to the source. BS required an accurately positioned ground-based radio station working in conjunction with two mobile units. One of the units was a transmitter/receiver station, the other was connected by cable. The radio station transmitted a signal to the ascending Rocket and a modified signal to the mobile transmitter/receiver in addition to a signal to the second unit via a land cable. The signal that reached the Rocket was 'Doppler'-shifted due to the Rocket's motion relative to the transmitter. The *Verdoppler* in the Rocket then modified the signal by doubling the amount of shift and then transmitted an amplified signal to the transmitter/receiver mobile unit. The received signal was compared with the signal of the cable-connected unit and the frequency difference of the two signals represented the rocket's velocity. When the correct velocity had been achieved, a signal was transmitted to the Rocket to terminate the engine. Although BS was the most accurate means to determine velocity and hence engine shut-down combined with targeting accuracy, it was vulnerable to enemy radio jamming.

Nevertheless, in the early part of the V2 campaign, most launching sites had a BS radio facility.[9]

A sophisticated item of equipment carried in Compartment 3 was the *Mischgerät* (steering control) which consisted of an amplifier of five independent panels mounted on a common base plate. It took signals from the gyroscopes and then translated the information into a signal which directed the servo steering mechanism and steering vanes to correct attitude deviations in powered flight. Passing through Compartment 3 was the *Staudruckrohr* from the warhead.

Geräteraum IV (Compartment 4) contained three compressed air bottles and a high-pressure safety valve for pressurizing the alcohol fuel tank after fuel cut-off. When fitted, the compartment also carried the *Leitstrahl* (guidance beam) radio receiver equipment.[10] *Leitstrahl*, based on the Lorenz blind-landing system used by aircraft before the war, was an attempt to improve the bearing accuracy of the Rocket. It worked in conjunction with radio signals transmitted by two carefully positioned ground stations. Detected variations in the received signals were interpreted and corrections were accordingly applied via the *Mischgerät*. Apparently, when the *Leitstrahl* equipment was not used, the void was filled with additional explosives. Realistically, however, the increase in the weapon's destructive force would have been minimal.[11]

Mittelteil / Middle Fuselage

The main body of the Rocket housed the propellant tanks and was constructed in a manner that was similar to aircraft manufacture at that time. It was made up of two half-shells of circular formers and longitudinal stringers with an outer skin of sheet steel secured by spot-welding and riveting. The thin steel sheeting of the Rocket, although heavier than aluminium, was able to withstand the 649 degrees C (1200 F) temperature of the re-entry phase of the Rocket as it passed through the Earth's atmosphere. The specification of the steel used in the external surfaces was improved to reduce the risk of mid-air break-up. Rocket ruptures caused by 'burn through' and buckling of the outer skin were common when an inferior grade of mild steel had been used in early test-firings.[12]

Two reinforced joint rings allowed the Rocket to be built in sections and served to carry the weight of the internal structures e.g. propellant tanks and engine. The joining rings also supported the weight of the Rocket whilst it was being transported. Ports in the middle fuselage allowed for the equilibrium of changing pressures during the flight. The propellant tanks had a capacity of 4546 litres (1,000 gallons) each and were positioned, one on top of the other. Both tanks were insulated on all sides by glass wool. Alcohol was supplied to the turbo-pump unit by a large diameter pipe that passed directly through the liquid oxygen fuel tank and to prevent the alcohol from freezing, the feed pipe was double walled with a layer of glass wool.

The fuel tanks were arranged such that the centre of gravity of the Rocket was hardly affected whether the tanks were full or empty. The tanks were mounted in such a way that they were relieved of structural stress and free to expand or contract with variations of temperature. The total fuel load of the liquid oxygen and alcohol tanks was 8.29 tonnes. Both tanks were of welded aluminium construction and light enough that four men could carry them with ease. The alcohol tank was cylindrical over most of its length, but tapered at one end to accommodate the streamline frontal aspect of the Rocket. The liquid oxygen tank was cylindrical over its entire length. Both tanks had domed ends. To prevent the accidental freezing of the alcohol, a servo-operated valve was located at the outlet of the alcohol tank and would open at the appropriate time before a launching operation. The Rocket could only be fuelled in the upright position. If an attempt was made to fuel the Rocket in the horizontal position, the fuel tanks would probably collapse, destroying the Rocket. Filling connections for both tanks were located in the rear sections of the tanks. The alcohol tank was vented during fuelling by a short curved standpipe located at the top of the tank and this was closed by a screw cap at the end of fuelling. The liquid oxygen tank had a relief valve connected to an internal pipe passing through the bottom of the tank and open at its upper end. This not only allowed venting but it also acted as an overflow for the liquid oxygen tank. It is believed that the liquid oxygen tank was always filled to capacity to compensate for evaporation. Expansion and contraction of the whole system was allowed for by large diameter concertinas of coppered brass flexible joints between pipe connections of the propellant tanks.[13]

The pressurization of the liquid oxygen tank was accomplished by passing some of the liquid oxygen through a heat exchanger in the combustion system, vaporizing it and leading it back to the tank.[14] Exhaust gases from the heat exchanger were fed through flexible hoses to an aerodynamically shaped fairing at the base of the Rocket's main body. For symmetry, a second fairing was located directly opposite the first to screen the vent pipe of the oxygen tank.

Originally, ethanol alcohol was used and was consumed (famously) by practically anyone who came into contact with the Rocket. Although ethanol gave the Rocket an advantage of increased range by approximately 17 kilometres (11 miles), toxic methanol alcohol was introduced. Methanol, in spite of warnings, quickly gained an appalling reputation for poisoning, blinding and even the occasional death among the FR troops.[15]

Antriebsblock / driving block or propulsion block

The combustion chamber of the Rocket required alcohol and liquid oxygen to be pumped at very high volumes and pressures. One solution to this requirement was simply to pressurize the two fuel tanks. However, this was not possible because this would require extremely heavy tanks to withstand the enormous pressure involved. The alternative used in the Rocket were two high-speed, high-volume centrifugal pumps, driven by a single steam-powered turbine. To achieve the high horsepower, the comparatively small turbine unit was driven by the violent reaction of a mixture of hydrogen peroxide and calcium permanganate. They were known by the FR troops as *T-Stoff* (hydrogen peroxide) and *Z-Stoff* (either potassium or sodium permanganate). The *T-* and *Z-Stoff* were fed separately into the turbine combustion chamber. Bottles of compressed nitrogen forced the *T-Stoff* from its elliptically shaped tank and when mixed with *Z-Stoff*, they reacted vigorously, producing energy in the form of super-heated steam of oxygen and manganese dioxide. The exhaust stream, passing through nozzles drove the turbine of 354 moving blades and 112 fixed blades at 5000 rpm, developing 675 bhp. The pumps were mounted either side of the turbine in a casing made largely from light aluminium. The alcohol pump was splined directly to the turbine rotor shaft while a flexible coupling drove the oxygen pump. The combined pumps would deliver 140 litres (31 gallons) of propellant per second and to prevent failure at high speeds, the pump bearings were lubricated by liquid oxygen. The compact turbine was held centrally within a framework with its rotor at right angles to the length of the Rocket.

The liquid oxygen, having passed through the pump and control valves, would flow through six distributors. Each of the six distributors had a triple union so that, in total, eighteen aluminium pipes fed the combustion chamber. An additional outlet pipe from the valve body of the pump supplied liquid oxygen to the heat exchanger.

The alcohol supply from the pump was first divided into two distributor branches. Each branch was connected to a triple branch union so that in total, six pipes supplied alcohol to the combustion chamber.

The turbine, pumps, tanks of chemicals, bottles of compressed nitrogen and ancillary equipment were held securely in a remarkable support structure called the Thrust Frame. The frame additionally attached the combustion chamber to the reinforced joint ring of the Rocket's lower body. Although the frame was of minimalist design for economy of weight, it was immensely strong as it was able to transmit the power of the combustion chamber to the main body of the Rocket and withstand the sudden shock when the propulsion system developed full power.

Of particular note, *T-Stoff* was used in several German weapons of World War Two including the Henschel Hs 293 glide-bomb and the famous rocket-powered interceptor, the Messerschmitt Me 163 *Komet*. Of particular note, hydrogen peroxide was used to launch the FZG 76, otherwise known as the V1 pilotless 'flying bomb' and the V3 *Hochdruckpumpe* (High Pressure Pump or HDP).

The V1 used a pulse-jet engine that could only operate when a specific airspeed had been achieved to create a ram air effect in its combustion chamber. Hydrogen peroxide was used as the means to accelerate and launch the V1 from a sloped ramp. The V3 or 'London Gun' was intended to use hydrogen peroxide to progressively accelerate a projectile along the bore of a long-barrelled gun. Although Allied bombers harassed its construction, Luxembourg was attacked by an HDP installation at Lampaden, 13 kilometres (8 miles) south-east of Trier. The site was eventually overrun by American forces in February 1945.

Combustion Chamber and Venturi

The Rocket's engine consisted of a large spherical steel welded combustion chamber that contained inlets for propellants and venturi through which exhaust gases passed via a divergent nozzle. For the most part, the combustion chamber was double walled for liquid cooling, which prevented 'burn through'. The extreme rear of the venturi was not double walled but was lagged with glass wool to reduce the risk of heat transfer to the servo control motors of the vanes.

Pipes from the turbo-pump supplied liquid oxygen to the 18 burner cups that were arranged in concentric circles of six and twelve on the top of the triple-walled constructed combustion chamber. Each burner cup sprayed fuel directly into the combustion chamber through a sprayer rose. The walls of the burner cups had three rows of liquid oxygen jets and two rows of plain openings through which the alcohol entered via the skinned wall. The presence of the alcohol openings in this part of the combustion chamber was to reduce the risk of 'burn through' using a technique called 'thin film cooling'. This process created a relatively cool insulating blanket upon the internal surfaces of the combustion chamber.

Six delivery pipes supplied alcohol to the engine via the large raised annulus at the rear of the venturi. The alcohol then flowed forward towards the burner caps through the cavity of the double wall and along four external pipes contoured to the shape of the combustion chamber. This arrangement allowed not only the passage of cooling alcohol along the length of the engine but also allowed the supply of alcohol through ringlets of holes into the combustion chamber for supplementary cooling.

The major part of the remaining alcohol reached the burner cups through the outer triple-walled head at the top of the combustion chamber. It was then injected through jets and holes into the cups. A supplementary supply of alcohol was fed through a single pipe that connected to the top of the combustion chamber, surrounded by the 18 burner cups.

A means of controlling the flow and therefore the power output of the engine was afforded by a servo-operated blanking valve plate at the centre of the walled head. This gave two alternative methods of flow. If the valve plate was closed, the alcohol was bypassed back to the alcohol pump. If, however, the plate was open, the bypass circuit would close and all the alcohol would pass through the triple wall and into the combustion chamber. The thrust developed varied between Rockets either because of difference in manufacture or the burning of the engines. However, thrust was assumed to be within working tolerances set during manufacture and no control was available operationally.

Heck / Tail

The tail unit was not intended to transmit the thrust of the engine; instead, it was a fairing for the combustion chamber and was a means of stabilizing and controlling the Rocket's flight.[16]

In powered flight, the Rocket was stabilized by four large fins on the tail and the trajectory was controlled by four vanes operating in the thrust exhaust of the combustion chamber, together with four air rudders at the extremities of the fins. The driving mechanism for the vanes was mounted upon a large aluminium casting that formed the seating for the end of the venturi. Electrical hydraulic servomotors drove short steel shafts to which the vanes were bolted. The vanes were made of graphite to withstand the high temperature of 2650 degrees C created by the combustion chamber.

The air rudders on the stabilizing fins were operated by a chain and sprocket mechanism. One pair of rudders was coupled to the servomotors and functioned in unison with the graphite vanes. The second pair operated entirely independently using separate electric motors. Fins 1 and 3 were parallel to the rotational plane of the turbine and were aligned directly towards the intended target. Fins 2 and 4 were at right angles to the plane of the trajectory of the Rocket in flight. Between the bases of all four fins, cowling vents allowed the exhaust of the steam turbine to exit the Rocket body. The base of fin 4 had a socket for an emergency fuel cut-off line and fin 1 was fitted with a sprung loaded 'take-off' switch known as an *Abhebekontakt*.

During launching, the propellants were delivered into the combustion chamber in a two-stage sequence. Stage one, known as '*Vorstufe*' (preliminary stage), was operated by ground equipment held in the *Feuerleitpanzer* and allowed atomized propellants to flow under the influence of gravity into the combustion chamber where it was ignited by a pyrotechnic device. The igniter, placed high in the combustion chamber, held four cardboard fireworks in a form resembling a Swastika. Rotating at high speed, the igniter produced a showerhead of sparks. Initially the thrust produced was only 8 tonnes and was insufficient to launch the Rocket. However, it allowed the firing crews a few seconds to observe the quality of flame pattern on the *Abschusstisch* (firing table). If the firing crew was satisfied, the main electrical umbilical *Stotz Stecker* plug was released by a solenoid initiating stage two, known as '*Hauptstufe*' (main stage). To avoid damage, the plug was captured by a net and electrical relays automatically operated solenoid fuel valves allowing the steam turbine unit to deliver fuel at full capacity. The thrust would suddenly increase to 25 tonnes and the Rocket would become airborne. Secondary umbilical plugs with rubber seals would simply shear away as the Rocket lifted off.[17]

Having left the *Abschusstisch*, the Rocket would climb vertically for the first 4 seconds thereafter and, controlled by the *Zeitschaltwerk* (time switch motor), pitch would change in accordance with a predetermined programme in the direction of the target. The Rocket was held at a constant inclination until *Brennschluss*. No attempt was made to control the programme from the ground. The pitch programme lasted for approximately 43 seconds by which time the inclination of the Rocket was 47 degrees to the vertical. Approximately 65 seconds after launching, the propellant supplied to the combustion chamber would either be terminated or moderated for a few seconds to a reduced thrust known as 8-*Tonnestuffe*. The initial acceleration was equivalent to that of gravity (1*g*), but thereafter it increased as the propellant load lessened and air resistance decreased until the acceleration at fuel cut-off was approximately 5*g*. The Rocket at this point of its flight would have reached an altitude of approximately 35 kilometres (22 miles). The trajectory up to this moment would have been in a straight line; thereafter the Rocket would follow a parabolic curve, attaining an altitude of about 88 kilometres (55 miles) under its own momentum and behave like a conventional artillery shell to impact. The maximum speed during powered flight was 5760 km/h (3,578 mph) and the impact speed was approximately 3960 km/h (2,460 mph).

Firing at a specific target meant that velocity had to be determined and the integrating accelerometer set accordingly. The FR troops used setting and range tables that had to take into account amongst other things, the effects of the rotation of the Earth. In order to further increase the range of the Rocket it was decided, in December 1944, to increase the speed of the turbine unit. This was accomplished by adjusting the settings of the turbine pressure-reducing valve. This increased the range by a further 18 kilometres (11 miles). Rockets fired from The Hague had an average range of 330 kilometres (205 miles), but it was also possible for Rockets to travel between 360 and 380 kilometres (224–236 miles) allowing for the full capacity of the fuel. Although the greatest wartime range known was 425 kilometres (264 miles), apparently this was never taken into account in deciding upon a target! The absolute minimum range the Rocket could achieve was determined by the *Zeitschaltwerk* which governed the sequence of events. Although range tables were accordingly determined to a distance of 80 kilometres (50 miles), they were never used.[18]

CHAPTER THREE

'ZUR BESONDEREN VERWENDUNG'

The development
of the V2 operational infrastructure

FOR students of military history, the study of the V2 Rocket's development and offensive infrastructure would be immeasurably easier to comprehend if just one organization had been conceived, operated and eventually ceased. However, the *Fernraketen* ('FR' – long-range rocket) organization was constantly changing both in title and personnel. Additionally it was handicapped by rivalries within the *Heer* (German army) and between the omnipresent SS who strived and ultimately succeeded in gaining overall control. Following the end of the war, Intelligence Officers in both Britain and the United States made exhaustive studies into this convoluted organization, its machinations and operations. Fortunately for the historian and researcher, those once highly classified reports are now a matter of public record. To reproduce their detail here is beyond the remit of this work. This book is concerned primarily with the reminiscences of veterans' experiences at the secret German rocket-testing and development centre at Peenemünde and during the V2 offensive against Belgium, France and Great Britain. However an overview is possible using archival information and other sources.

It seems extraordinary that in spite of the research facility at Peenemünde having been established at enormous cost in 1937, primarily to develop one weapon system, no serious consideration appears to have been given to the practical offensive utilization of the A4 Rocket – the weapon that would become known infamously during the offensive as the 'V2'. In fairness however, it should be mentioned that the Peenemünde facility was not fully operational until the spring of 1943 and the whole Rocket programme suffered from funding problems as Adolf Hitler vacillated as to its worthiness. Nevertheless, in spite of the difficulties, development of the A4 and its predecessors continued during the centre's construction, perhaps overshadowing the ultimate goal.

The first major document to address the issue of field deployment of the A4 was produced in April 1943 by *Generalmajor* Walter Dornberger, head of *Wa Prüf* 11 (the Weapons Research Section).[1] The booklet entitled '*Entwicklungskommission für Fernschiessen*' (Proposals for the Operational Employment [of the A4 Rocket]) was also a blatant piece of promotion. Dornberger optimistically proposed that 5,000 A4s would be fired per annum at a rate of up to 100 Rockets in eight hours subject to any supply problems. He also turned his attention to the requirement for propellants – typically 70,000 tonnes of oxygen per annum, although in the subsequent planning, these figures were amended downwards. He further proposed that the A4 Rocket Regiments (*Abteilungen*) would consist of three Batteries (*Batterien*) and that each *Batterie* would have three firing platoons (*Züge*). Although it was considered that the A4 might be launched from railway wagons, Dornberger envisaged that a fully motorized *Abteilung* would require a large force of 560 vehicles.[2] Dornberger was guilefully vague as to specific targets that the new weapon might be used against, thus avoiding the thorny topic of the A4's inaccuracy. However he did suggest the target area of southern England from firing sites in northern France. It is believed that *Reichsminister* Albert Speer, Hitler's armaments minister, was the first to voice the notion earlier in 1942 that fixed firing sites should be constructed.

Dornberger had high hopes that his booklet would have a wide readership in the higher echelons of the military but, ironically, the sensitive nature of the text meant that the Chief of the Armed Forces Supreme High Command, *Generalfeldmarschall* Wilhelm Keitel, ordered that all but three copies should be confiscated in order to preserve the secrets of Peenemünde. Nevertheless, the existence of the booklet did catch Hitler's attention, which, it can be presumed, was always Dornberger's intention. What Dornberger could never have predicated was that Hitler, following a prophetic experience in March 1943, would remain ambivalent. He had dreamed that the A4 would never reach England![3]

Hitler's attitude is even more difficult to understand since he was doubtless aware that work was already well in hand in northern France creating the first of the Rocket firing sites at Watten. Speer had been appointed head of the *Organisation Todt* (OT), the civil and military construction and engineering organization named after the engineer and prominent Nazi, Fritz Todt, who had died the previous year. In this capacity, Speer had earlier authorized the drafting of plans in conjunction with military personnel and Peenemünde experts. The construction of fixed firing sites for the A4, as well as Rocket storage facilities and oxygen liquefaction plants, was progressing according to plan.

The A4 site at Watten, also known as the 'Bunker of Éperlecques', was 27 kilometres south-east of Calais and 175 kilometres south-east of London. The 'bunker' was of extraordinary proportions – 28 metres high and weighing an estimated 300,000 tons.

Forgetting, briefly, the *Führer's* conscious and subconscious feelings, the A4 programme had had to jump many hurdles before the full support it needed was eventually given. One such hurdle was competition for funding from its stablemate, the Fieseler Fi 103 (or FZG [*Flakzielgerät*] 76), later to be known as the 'V1' Flying Bomb. First flown from the *Luftwaffe* airfield of Peenemünde West on 24 December 1942, the pilotless pulse jet-driven bomb could deliver 830 kg of explosive to a range of 238 kilometres at a speed of nearly 656 kilometres per hour.[4] Unlike the lengthy and ongoing development project of the A4, the V1 went from concept to test-flight in a mere 18 months. On 26 May 1943, Albert Speer arrived at Peenemünde with an evaluation team, the Long Range Weapons Development Commission, to review both the V1 and A4 and to make their findings known to Hitler.[5] A negative assessment following a poor demonstration could easily close the entire A4 programme. In the event, both A4 test Rockets (V26 and V25) performed well, impressing the evaluation team which included high-ranking dignitaries such as *Generalfeldmarschall* Erhard Milch, (as the *Generalluftzeugmeister* of the *Luftwaffe* responsible for all aviation technical development) and *Admiral* Karl Dönitz of the *Kriegsmarine* (the *Befehlshaber der Unterseeboote,* [BdU], commander of the U-boat arm). The demonstration of the V1, however, was a failure, the weapon crashing into the sea shortly after lifting off the launching ramp. Demonstrations aside, the evaluation team also had to consider the cheapness of the V1, its economy of fuel, modest size and hence the ease of transport. When compared to the relatively small footprint of the A4's *Abschusstisch* (firing table), it was realized that the V1's launching ramp would be highly visible to Allied air reconnaissance. Additionally, the airborne flying bomb would be detectable by radar and hence vulnerable to both fighter aircraft interception and ground anti-aircraft fire. The A4 however, once launched, was invulnerable. To the relief of the two development teams, both weapons received support from the commission, for it was felt that the benefits and drawbacks would, in time, equalize and that both weapons working together in a combined offensive would create a massive effect upon the enemy. Hitler, however, did not fully subscribe to the report's findings.

The first V1 was to fall on southern England in the small hours of 13 June 1944, some three months before the V2 became operational. Approximately 5,811 Flying Bombs would fall upon England before the assault ended on 29 March 1945.[6] The V1 campaign ended in the early hours of the following day with a final few shots against Antwerp.

On 7 July 1943, Dornberger and Wernher von Braun met with Hitler, Keitel, Speer and the military commanders, *Generaloberst* Alfred Jodl (Chief of the

Operations Staff of the Armed Forces High Command [*Oberkommando der Wehrmacht* – OKW]) and *General der Infanterie* Walther Buhle (Chief of the Army Staff of the OKW) at the *Wolfsschanze* (Wolf's Lair), the *Führers's* Eastern Front Headquarters close to the town of Rastenburg (now Kętrzyn in Poland). As the black-caped figure of Hitler walked into the conference room to the shouted proclamation of 'The *Führer!*', Dornberger was shocked at his appearance recalling, 'bowed, hunched shoulders … He looked a tired man … only his eyes retained their life.'

Hitler had changed greatly since their meeting at Kummersdorf-West four years earlier. Following Dornberger and von Braun's enthusiastic presentation and the dramatic screening of the A4's first successful firing ten months earlier, Hitler appeared to have had an epiphany. He shook Dornberger by the hand and whispered, 'I thank you. Why was it I could not believe in the success of your work? If we had had these rockets in 1939 we should never have had this war.'[7]

Hitler was perhaps thinking that the threat alone of such a weapon could have won appeasement at the negotiating table without a single shot being fired. By 1943 however, the war situation was dire. In the East, the failure to capture Stalingrad, in spite of heavy losses, was a very bad omen. To the south, the campaign in North Africa had ended with a withdrawal. In the West, RAF Bomber Command's nightly offensive against Germany was intensifying, particularly along the Rhine-Ruhr valley. Hitler was unable to order proportional reprisal air attacks, for the *Luftwaffe* could no longer mass fleets of bombers to '*Blitz*' British cities. Aircraft, air and ground crew now had to be divided on three fronts and, in any case, RAF night fighters using the rapidly advancing science of Airborne Interception (A.I.) radar systems, would have wreaked havoc in any protracted nocturnal heavy bombing campaign. Irrespective of this, a financial perspective showed that the cost of an A4 (excluding research and development) was one-thirtieth of the cost of manufacturing a German heavy bomber and investment in training its crew which, in all probability, would not return from its mission.[8] It must have occurred to Hitler (then, if not before) that as a new 'wonder weapon' the A4 was the perfect means for revenge and might yet be Germany's salvation. Whatever tactical thoughts were passing through Hitler's mind, he demonstrated a stunning lack of practicality when he ignored any conversation regarding mobile Rocket batteries and then asked Dornberger if the A4 could carry a ten-ton warhead. Dornberger explained that this would require a brand new rocket and commented that when work originally started on the A4 project an 'all-annihilating effect' was not thought of. Hitler in rage shouted, 'You! No, you didn't think of it, I know. But I did!' Keitel artfully defused the situation with a change of subject and, once calmed, Hitler promised full support and a status of top priority to the Peenemünde men.

The summer of 1943 proved to be tumultuous for the A4 programme as six weeks to the day after Hitler had given his tacit support, Peenemünde was seriously damaged by an RAF bombing raid on the night of 17–18 August. The RAF attack was code named 'Operation Hydra' after the Herculean multi-headed beast that grew two heads for every one lopped off. Ironically, the attack forced a wide dispersion of both manufacture and training that previously had been concentrated at Peenemünde. Factory production of the A4 moved to a facility underneath the Harz Mountains near Nordhausen and the training of the FR troops was redirected to the safety of the remote SS *Truppenübungsplatz* (Troop Training Ground) at Heidelager in Poland.

In spite of the lack of an SS presence at the important aforementioned meetings, it would be wrong to presume that it was only after the RAF attack on Peenemünde that this infamous organization became involved with the A4. *Reichsführer*-SS Heinrich Himmler first visited Peenemünde unexpectedly in early April 1943, more or less as a sightseer. No A4 firing demonstration was laid on for him, but a tour of the facilities was conducted and a static motor test. On his departure, Himmler spoke to Dornberger before clambering into his aircraft. His parting comments were, 'I am very interested in your work. I may be able to help you.'[9] This, however, was not the first high-level contact Peenemünde personnel had had with the SS. Not long after the first successful firing of the A4 in October 1942, production experts at Peenemünde petitioned the SS for prisoners to make the A4.[10] Dornberger must have known of the contact, but von Braun, so deeply committed to research, may not have.

A member of the SS who was to become very closely associated with the A4 was *Dr.-Ing.* Hans (Heinz) Friedrich Karl Franz Kammler. Kammler had joined the SS in 1934 and was a career bureaucrat. Formerly he had been a deputy to Oswald Pohl at the SS *Wirtschafts-Verwaltungshauptamt* (WVHA – the SS Economic Administration Main Office) which had overseen the building of the *Konzentrationslager* (Concentration Camps) and later the *Vernichtungslager* (Extermination Camps). Kammler, who would achieve the rank of SS *Obergruppenführer*, had overseen the installation of the infamous crematorium equipment at Auschwitz–Birkenau and initially, took a personal interest in the activity of Peenemünde.[11] A month after the air raid of August 1943 however, he was appointed by Himmler to take charge of moving vital industrial installations into secure underground sites in anticipation of mass manufacture of the A4. The most notorious of these sites was the *Mittelwerk* at Nordhausen, which was to become the sole final assembly plant for the Rocket. The workforce was to be formed predominantly of slave labour.

Upon meeting Kammler for the first time in Berlin in September 1943, Dornberger was at first impressed by the striking, athletic and handsome looks of the man. However as they talked, Dornberger noticed that it was impossible to converse with him as topics changed rapidly without pause or reflection. Kammler was quick to boast of 'what a splendid fellow he was' and of the exceptional influences he had at high levels.[12] Dornberger was to later admit that he had yet to realize that the man was dangerous.

Kammler's motivation for his commitment to the A4 programme is not fully understood. Rather than any fascination with the spectacle of 'wonder weapons' roaring across the sky, it may have occurred to him that via his association with the Rocket and Flying Bomb he could accelerate his climb further up the echelons of the Nazi regime. Possibly it might have been the huge sums of money that had been invested and would continue to be ploughed into the weapons' development that appealed to him. Alternatively, he may have perceived a weakness in the *Heer* leadership of the A4 programme and believed genuinely he could have a positive role to the benefit of the nation and state. Whatever the reason, he dedicated himself fanatically to acquiring the whole endeavour. He was gifted with a skill to use the shortcomings and disagreements of others to his own benefit. Not satisfied with the existing FR structure, he established an SS V2 firing unit, known as the SS *Werfer Batterie* 500. The meteoric climb of Kammler was much to Dornbergers' chagrin. Dornberger was to comment wryly that Kammler had a truly fantastic military career, particularly since he had never served a day as a soldier and had had no military training whatsoever.[13]

On 4 September 1943, Dornberger was appointed as *Beauftragter zur besonderen Verwendung Heer* (*B.z.b.V* – Army Commissioner for Special Tasks). The *B.z.b.V* had been created tactically by Dornberger, superseding his previous position as Chief of *Wa Prüf* 11. The new organization was essentially a 'miniature self-contained army' and, in effect, gave Dornberger control of all aspects of the A4 including organizing, equipping and training of the FR units for field deployment. This promotion was quickly followed by Hitler confirming, on 4 October 1943, Dornberger's appointment as commander of the *Höhere Artillerie Kommandeur (Motorisiert) 191*, (*HARKO* 191 – Higher Artillery Commander [Motorized] 191), which essentially extended Dornberger's responsibilities for recruitment and the training of the FR troop. Additionally, he was made responsible for establishing the logistical infrastructure for the supply of all materials needed for the A4 offensive. Most importantly *HARKO* 191 gave Dornberger operational command of the A4 as and when the campaign was ordered to commence.[14]

Following the encouraging meeting with Hitler in July 1943, Dornberger shortly afterwards appointed *Oberstleutnant* Gerhard Stegmaier to command the *Lehr- und Ersatz-Batterie (mot.).93* (Motorized Demonstration and Depot Battery 93). This was the first military unit to be exposed to the new A4 Rocket. Stegmaier had been present with Dornberger when the first successful firing of the A4 had taken place in October the previous year and had formerly been in charge of the Pre-Production Works (South) at Peenemünde. The 'Mot. 93' was soon renamed the Lehr- und Versuchsbatterie 444 (Training and Experimental Battery 444) and as it grew it took personnel from the reservoir of men already gathered at the Versuchskommando Nord (VKN – Test Command North) at Karlshagen close to Peenemünde. Because of Batterie 444's importance, Stegmaier could call upon any personnel he wished, even men directly from front line service. Eventually, under the command of Major Wolfgang Weber, Batterie 444 was to consist of one battery of three firing Züge. At first, the primary purpose of Batterie 444 was to determine operating and firing procedures for the A4 empirically and its support equipment whilst liaising closely with scientists at Peenemünde. Many helpful and practical suggestions made by the soldiers were implemented. During the process, training procedures were determined and detailed in anticipation of the A4 Rocket Abteilungen (Battalions) yet to be created.

Shortly after Batterie 444 moved to Heidelager in September 1943, it was joined by the recently formed artillery battalions, Artillerie Abteilung 485 (mot.) and Artillerie Abteilung 836 (mot.). The new units were not concerned with test and evaluation of the A4 but, rather, training. The more experienced Batterie 444 then supplied Art.Abt. 485 and 836 with the instructors to commence a field-training programme with the A4. As Batterie 444 and the other A4 battalions grew, they were supplied by men from two Pomeranian based facilities: the Kommando-Stelle S at Köslin (a V2 Training School, named after Stegmaier) and the training camp at Groß Born.

Following the basic plan laid out in Dornberger's booklet, 'Entwicklungskommission für Fernschiessen' (Proposals for the Operational Employment [of the A4 Rocket]), Art.Abt. 485 and 836 were intended to have separate headquarters and technical batteries. Each Artillerie Abteilung was to have three launching batteries with each battery having three Züge, making a grand total of 18 Züge. However, operational and supply problems meant that this could never happen. The growing Artillerie Abteilungen would require a large supply infrastructure as and when they were pressed into service. However, changes were afoot that would see a radical reappraisal in the manner in which the A4 offensive would be conducted.

In northern France, the Bunker of Éperlecques at Watten was bombed on 27 August by the US Eighth Air Force, less than two weeks after the RAF had attacked Peenemünde. The Allies' 'Operation Crossbow' (launched in response to the threat of the A4) and 'Operation Noball', (to counter the V1) were proving very successful in identifying and destroying the developing Rocket facilities and fixed V1 'Ski' launch ramps. Subsequent attacks rendered the Watten site useless for the Rocket offensive and serious work ceased. Undeterred, Organisation Todt was given instructions to commence the building of a new hardened bunker that was to be known as *La Coupole* (The Dome) 12 kilometres south-east of the Bunker of Éperlecques. Although the facility was to make use of natural geology and an existing quarry, it was correctly presumed that it was impossible to hide such a structure from the prying cameras of enemy photo-reconnaissance aircraft. Therefore, *La Coupole* was built as a massive structure intended to render Allied bombs useless. The principal feature was a 71-metre-wide reinforced concrete lid, five metres thick. Under this 55,000-ton structure, the ground was excavated and the walls of the void were then reinforced to form a polygonal shape, 21 metres deep in which Rockets could be safely fuelled and armed. When ready for firing, massive 1.5 metre thick steel doors would open and the A4 would be drawn out for immediate launching on a carriage and track system. In common with Watten, both structures swallowed up an enormous amount of money and material. The *Organisation Todt* employed local French building companies at first for Watten but later, because of security concerns, German construction companies were used on *La Coupole*. Both construction sites used prisoners from the Low Countries and Russians from the Eastern Front.[15] The work was hard: 12-hour shifts around the clock with poor food and constant armed guards. The human cost is not known with certainty.

La Coupole proved to be a very difficult target for the Allies, but it was rendered useless after it was bombed by the RAF which used 12,000 lb 'Tall Boy' bombs dropped from Avro Lancasters in June 1944. Following the landings on the coast of Normandy on 6 June, all V-weapon related facilities in northern France were destined to be made redundant. Dornberger had never liked the concept of fixed sites for the A4 because of their vulnerability (as was proven) to air attack. He had bravely attempted to sway Hitler away from the grandiose concrete monolith sites in northern France without success in July the previous year. Dornberger's insightful proposal that the A4 should be a mobile weapon, operated by motorized firing batteries would come to the fore.

Although the A4 had been successfully launched in October 1942, very significant problems began to surface during the continued field-testing and training conducted at Heidelager in Poland in late 1943. Rockets would suddenly lose power shortly after taking off or, having climbed to a range of one to two kilometres, would suddenly explode. However, the most significant problem was a catastrophic structural failure in the final moments of descent that would shower the target area with debris. Dornberger referred to this effect as 'Air Burst'. These problems required Dornberger to spend a considerable amount of time away from his other duties with the *B.z.b.V* and *HARKO* 191 while he attempted, with Peenemünde's scientists, to determine remedies from the tangled wreckage of the failed A4s.

The diverse demands upon Dornberger were too much and he relinquished his control of *HARKO* 191 and, by November 1943, Hitler appointed

Generalleutnant Erich Heinemann as the new commander of *Generalkommando* LXV. *Armeekorps zur besonderen Verwendung* (Army Corps for Special Purposes).[16] The 'special purposes' of the *Armeekorps* were the field deployment of the A4, V1 and other weapons to be used against England. Heinemann apparently had no knowledge of the existence of the V-weapons but was an experienced artillery commander, a quality that Dornberger did not have. In the final days of 1943, Heinemann appointed *Generalmajor* Richard Metz, who had commanded an artillery unit on the Eastern Front with distinction, as an A4 tactical commander. In common with Heinemann and others brought into the A4 organization, he too had no previous knowledge of the V-weapons but quickly proved to be a practical and able leader in spite of the reservations of others on Dornberger's staff. After a familiarization period of three months, Metz began a report into the readiness of both equipment and personnel in anticipation of the V2 offensive.[17] In March 1944, he visited Peenemünde, Heidelager and the A4 training schools of *Kommandostelle S*, Köslin and Groß Born. The findings of his report were, in part, lamentable. Although Metz had been impressed by the enthusiasm he had seen at the training schools, he was appalled by the quality of some of the commanders and the lack of both a tactical doctrine and coordinated training procedure. He was also critical of Dornberger's policy that one man should be trained to do one job. Metz, sensing a disaster, requested a transfer. This was denied.

In May 1944, the LXV. *Armeekorps z.b.V* determined that the V2 offensive would begin in September under the cover code of *'Operation Pinguin'* (Operation Penguin). Many difficulties remained, however, most notably in transport, delivery and supply of A4s and spare parts to the anticipated FR operational areas. From his own staff, Dornberger instructed the logistics officer, *Oberstleutnant* Wilhelm Zippelius, to investigate solutions. Zippelius was later to recall during an interview with British intelligence officers, a meeting with Heinemann. The British had asked Zippelius to sum up the 'chain of command' within the *B.z.b.V* and *HARKO*. 'Oberst Thom and I travelled to *Maisons-Lafitte* [Headquarters of the General Command, LXV, St. Germain-en-Laye, 18 kilometres north-west of Paris], to clarify important and burning issues regarding the operation. General Heinemann constantly looked out of the window into the garden. Then suddenly during this most important meeting, he stood up, went out into the garden and shot a squirrel, which he had been observing all of the time. On his return with the poor creature, he was congratulated by the chief of staff, Oberst Walter with the words "*Waidmann Heil*" (a salutation meaning Good Hunting)'! Zippelius also commented that the general command lacked selfless idealists.[18]

Shortly afterwards, on 8 July, in the presence of three Generals at Heidelager, Kammler set about a tirade of character assassination of von Braun and Dornberger. Kammler accused von Braun of being childish, supercilious and arrogant. The greatest venom, however, was reserved for Dornberger who was accused of draining Germany and weakening capacity both in armament and men in order to bring into existence a chimera. For this, Kammler said that Dornberger should be court-martialled and not another penny should be devoted to such a hopeless project. What Kammler hoped to achieve with this outburst is not known, but shortly afterwards Himmler and Kammler met with Hitler and proposed that Kammler be given full charge of all A4 operations to the exclusion of LXV. *Armeekorps z.b.V. Generaloberst* Jodl objected for he feared that new organizational changes so close to the A4 offensive would be harmful to operational efficiency.[19] Irrespective, the motion made by the SS men was carried, and Kammler secured the position and became Special Commissioner for V2 Matters.

On 31 August, Kammler summoned Dornberger, Metz, Heinemann and other senior officers to a meeting in Brussels. Kammler presented his new position as a fait accompli and immediately began to give new orders. In spite of loud protests, his detractors could give no opposition; the rubber-stamping from on high could not be questioned. Metz immediately lost his post, but was doubtless happy to depart having requested a transfer on more than one occasion. Kammler rapidly reorganized LXV. *Armeekorps z.b.V* and *HARKO* 191 into a Divisional Staff, the whole formation now known as *Division z.V.* (Reprisal Division).[20] The exalted position that Kammler now enjoyed was one that Dornberger had always sought. Kammler had authority over all aspects of the V2; not only operational deployment but also V2 production in Germany and elsewhere. Dornberger's rankled state of mind had been noticed and according to *Oberstleutnant* Zippelius, the following conversation had taken place:

Kammler: 'After all Dornberger, we could be friends.'
Dornberger: 'You can never expect that of me. I have devoted my life's work to the careful making of an instrument which you have taken out of my hands, to play on it in your own clumsy fashion. I can carry out your orders, but I can never be your friend.'[21]

At the very beginning of September, Himmler ordered Kammler that the V2 offensive code named *Operation Pinguin* was to begin on the 5th of the month. A preliminary order instigated by Kammler was issued by the *Oberkommando des Heeres* (OKH – High Command of the Army) that FR personnel were to move to pre-designated areas in anticipation of operations. The V2 campaign was to be divided between two organizations, *Gruppe Nord* (Group North) and *Gruppe Süd* (Group South). A total of 6,306 men and 1,592 vehicles were available. On 5 September 1944, the V2 Artillery Battalions were arranged as follows:

Gruppe Nord under the command of *Oberst* Hohmann consisted of *Artillerie Abteilung (Motorisiert)* 485. The first and second batteries (*Art.Abt.* 1./485 and 2./485) were to risk near capture by the Allies on 7 September in the area of Tilburg. However, the following day, from Wassenaar close to The Hague, *Art.Abt.* 2./485 fired two V2s almost simultaneously in the early evening to begin the campaign against London. *Art.Abt.* 3./485 was still in training and would not fire its first V2 until 21 October from the area of Burgsteinfurt, Germany, against Antwerp.[22]

Gruppe Süd under the command of *Major* Weber comprised elements of *Artillerie Abteilung* 836 (*mot.*) and *Lehr- und Versuchsbatterie* 444. The second and third batteries of *Artillerie Abteilung* 836 prepared to fire at targets in northern France while *Art.Abt.* 1./836 was in the east continuing experimental work. *Batterie* 444 moved into the region of the Ardennes in anticipation of firing upon Paris.[23]

The long awaited campaign, which might yet spare Germany a humiliating defeat, was about to begin.

Part Two

ROCKET SOLDIERS

'Your men must finally learn to see blood flowing...'

SS-OBERGRUPPENFÜHRER DR.-ING. HANS KAMMLER
TO OFFICERS OF *LEHR- UND VERSUCHSBATTERIE 444,*
SEPTEMBER 1944

WH-1583409

CHAPTER FOUR

'THE ROCKET LIFTED OFF AND I HELD MY BREATH'

HELMUTH FRENK
Heeresversuchsstelle Peenemünde

HELMUTH Frenk was born in 1916 in Wetzlar, in the state of Hessen, western central Germany. While he was a young boy the Frenk family moved to Ehringhausen a few kilometres west of Wetzlar where their father was a policeman. He had two younger brothers, Herbert and Eberhard. Young Helmuth showed a greater aptitude at school than his brothers and had a natural flair towards physics. Typical of a precocious scientific mind, he needed to know how machines worked and recalled that, 'A tremendous curiosity drove me on with anything technical...'

During his school holidays he enjoyed working with a local engineering company and learned not only how to operate engineering equipment, but also how to service cars. To discover the workings of an electric motor, he decided to build one for himself. Spurred on by the scientific atmosphere that prevailed in Germany in the late 1920s and early 1930s caused by films such as Fritz Lang's *Die Frau im Mond* (Woman in the Moon) and the national media preoccupation with dramatic demonstrations of science, Frenk built gun powder–fuelled rockets that would fly to an altitude of 30 metres. His attempts at rocketry, however, caused his father embarrassment when the smouldering, spent rockets would land on the roofs of local factories! The behaviour of the son of a policeman was expected to be exemplary, but his parents' chastisement was short for they always encouraged their boys in their pursuits.

Helmuth excelled in his favourite school subjects of physics and chemistry and decided that he would be an engineer at the end of his studies. However he applied firstly to the armed forces for the post of Weapons Officer as this would ensure that the state would pay for his education and would relieve the burden upon his family of three sons. He was therefore obliged to work as an industry trainee at the cement manufacturing company of Buderus in Wetzlar for a year commencing in April 1935. Frenk very much enjoyed his time in industry and on one occasion of high-spirited daring during a lunchtime, he demonstrated the adventurous and exhibitionist side of his personality by taking on the challenge of climbing the factory's 86-metre (272 ft) tall chimney to the astonishment and excitement of his work colleagues. During his free time he enjoyed the growing popular activity of glider flying. Many of the fellow glider pilots Frenk became friendly with worked for the famous optical company of Leitz in nearby Wetzlar. These contacts were later to prove very useful.

From Buderus, he joined the *Reichsarbeitsdienst* (Reich Labour Service) for six months in Frankenberg near Chemnitz, in central eastern Germany. His attitude to his service was ambivalent, and he felt that the high school graduates were unjustly stressed and pushed too hard. In October 1936 he was called up for military service as a weapons officer in a motorized artillery battery in Würzburg. He was pleased with the new posting, and considered it to be 'substantially more humane' as so many artillery units at this time used horses to draw gun carriages. Additionally, and to the relief of his parents and younger brothers, he could continue to receive an engineering education at the state's expense. Frenk was chosen to perform the mathematical calculations to aid the artillery accuracy of the 15 cm Schwere *Feldhaubitze* (Heavy Field Howitzer), nicknamed *Immergrün* (Evergreen), a gun based upon a much earlier First World War weapon. Although somewhat out of date, it was the *Immergrün* that would nevertheless see widespread use in the forthcoming conflict.

Whilst performing artillery calculations with pencil and paper to determine direction angles and distances, it occurred to Frenk that a mechanical computer could spare some of the repetitive and tiresome calculations. He reported his ideas to his battery superior, *Hauptmann* Walter Hohmann, who was sufficiently impressed to allow Frenk temporary relief from normal 'creeping in the dirt' duties so he could produce constructional drawings and an operating description for the computer. Several weeks of work brought about rewards, some instant, some much delayed. As Frenk recalled: 'The equipment was appreciated from 'above' and I was praised. I even got a patent. Thereafter, I heard nothing more. Years later, after I had given up a career as a Weapons Officer and had become a Second Lieutenant of the Reserve in my third year of voluntary service, I received a telegram from Supreme Command: *"The suggestion of Schütze (Private) Frenk is good, perhaps the computer should be used and that Frenk be promoted to non-commissioned officer."* Seldom have I laughed so.' Frenk was, of course, already a non-commissioned officer.

It was at Würzburg that he met the young and ambitious Martin Rysavy. Rysavy, although also called to the motorized artillery, desperately wanted to be re-posted to the *Luftwaffe* to train as a fighter pilot. His wish was to be granted and he and Frenk would cross paths again, albeit tragically, in northern France.

By 1938, Frenk was a Second Year NCO and was posted to join the *Eisenbahn-Artillerie Batterie* 764 at Fürth in Bavaria to train on the top secret 24 cm *'Theodor Bruno'* railway gun. The location of the gun and its operation were so secret that Frenk was ordered to travel to his new posting in civilian clothing.

During the First World War railway guns had proved useful, as they could be deployed rapidly to the front or to a coastal position. Although railway-mounted weapons were potentially vulnerable to air attack, it was a relatively straightforward task to repair bomb-damaged railway lines and to retreat the guns under the cover of darkness. Railway artillery pieces fitted perfectly into the plans of the *Blitzkrieg* war that was being drafted by military strategists in Berlin. The difference between the *Immergrün* and the *Theodor Bruno* was enormous. The *Immergrün* had a total length of approximately 4.5 metres (14.7 ft), while the barrel alone of the *Theodor Bruno* was nearly twice the length at 8.5 metres (27.8 ft).

During an idle moment one day at Fürth, Frenk was roaming around the billets and by pure chance found a wooden box with a Leitz label on it. As a 'Wetzlar' man and knowing many *'Leitzianer'* employees from his gliding days, his curiosity was aroused. Upon opening it, he discovered an artillery theodolite known as a *'Richtkreis-Kollimator'* (judging circle collimator) and an optical collimator known as a *'Bunker-Kollimator'*. The Leitz engineer, Rudolf Stützer, had developed both devices sometime after the First World War. Frenk studied the manual and with growing astonishment realized that the equipment had an application as a targeting aid for heavy artillery. The *Richtkreis-Kollimator* had the appearance of a sophisticated surveyor's theodolite. The *Bunker-Kollimator*, no longer than 30 cm, had the appearance of a small telescope with a profile similar to a binocular – narrow at one end, but gradually increasing in diameter at the opposite end, the whole having the means to be bolted securely to a surface. Attached to the narrow end was a light source and at the wider opposite end was a convex (magnifying) lens. Mounted internally in the collimator was a transparent screen upon which graduated adjusting figures could just be glimpsed with the naked eye. In use, the collimator would be attached to an artillery weapon with the lens facing outwards. The collimator would then be examined from a distance of no greater than 12 metres (40 ft) by the *Richtkreis-Kollimator*. The adjusting figures of the collimator would now appear to be highly magnified as seen with the *Richtkreis*, and correcting adjustments to bring the artillery weapon 'back on station' could then easily be undertaken in an objective manner. Frenk realized that the devices were substantially more accurate and faster in application than the usual theodolites and judging circles then being used on the railway guns. He reported his discoveries to

Hauptmann Hohmann who, again, was greatly impressed. Both men realized that they would have to proceed with considerable caution. Firstly, although destined for the artillery, the true recipient of the collimators could not be established. Why they had been left and forgotten was to remain a mystery. Secondly, the application for use with the *Theodor Bruno* gun was not 'established procedure'. Hohmann wrote out a receipt to 'officially procure' the collimators and instructed Frenk to set about determining the operating instructions and drawings in their use. Frenk's artillery unit then started to train with the innovation.

Frenk, now aged 22, remembered the famous meeting between Adolf Hitler and the British Prime Minister, Neville Chamberlain on 30 September 1938 which defused the so-called 'Munich Crisis' with the signing of the peace treaty. The breaking of the treaty with the occupation of the Sudetenland seven months later on 15 March 1939 caused Frenk much anxiety for he now found it difficult to believe that Hitler was an honourable man. He feared the worst and felt sure that a war in Europe would be a disaster. To voice such an opinion would have been very unwise and so he kept his anxieties to himself. Frenk's worst fears were to be confirmed as war lay less than six months in the future.

In April 1939, whilst on leave in his home town of Wetzlar, Frenk was introduced by his *'Leitzianer'* glider-flying friends to Rudolf Stützer who was delighted to learn that his collimators were being put to good use: previously the *Heer* had declined his innovation. Stützer arranged for Leitz to put at Frenk's immediate disposal three complete collimator systems so that each gun in his unit was equally equipped.

Training continued on the railway tracks of abandoned mines in the Saar area close to the French border until 10 May 1940, when Germany invaded France. Frenk's artillery unit was pitted against the defensive French Maginot Line. Just before going into action *Hauptmann* Hohmann had a private cautionary conversation with Frenk about the unauthorized use of the *Richtkreis-* and the *Bunker Kollimator*, warning his subordinate: 'Frenk, if this does not work, we will both face court martials.'

However it became obvious that the unit's 24 cm railway guns were firing a greater number of rounds on French positions than other less able units. This success did not go unnoticed, and Hohmann and Frenk's superiors praised them. Leitz subsequently received an urgent order from the *Heer* for the immediate delivery of several hundred examples. The collimator was then introduced officially into German artillery units. Frenk was ordered to the *Oberkommando der Wehrmacht* (OKW – *Wehrmacht* High Command) at Zossen near Berlin and not only wrote the official operating regulations and hosted instruction courses for officers, but also appeared in an educational training film. In acknowledgement of his work Frenk received the *Kriegsverdienstkreuz 1. Klasse* (War Merit Cross 1st Class).

Seconded to the *Lehr- und Ersatz-Abteilung für Eisenbahn-Artillerie (mot.)* 100, (Instructional and Supplementary Detachment for Railway Artillery [mot.] 100), Frenk undertook training exercises at several locations including Rügenwalde which was 160 kilometres away to the east from Peenemünde along the same Baltic coastline.

Promoted to the rank of *Major*, Hohmann was appointed the head of *Eisenbahn-Batterie* (Railway Battery) 702. *E-Battr.* 702 operated the most modern artillery weapon in the whole of the *Heer* arsenal, the Krupp 28 cm K5 *Eisenbahngeschütz* (railway gun). Considered to be probably the best gun ever built for the *Heer* railway artillery force, the K5 saw service on many fronts, including Italy, where the gun was nicknamed 'Anzio Annie' by the besieged Allies.

Operating from the area of Calais in north-west France, Hohmann requested that Frenk should join the battery at Wissant to plan firing operations across the English Channel against ports and other targets in southern England using the new innovation. The contrast between the 'K5' and the 24 cm *Theodor Bruno* that Frenk was familiar with was considerable. The super-long-range K5 introduced in 1936 had a barrel 21.5 metres (68 ft) in length, a staggering 13 metres longer than the *Theodor Bruno*! Crewed by 42 men, it sat upon a pair of twelve-wheel bogies and weighed 218 tonnes. The K5 fired a 256 kg (563 lb) splined shell through a deeply grooved barrel. More unconventionally, an experimental shell designed at Peenemünde, called the 'Arrow Shell', was developed, increasing range to 42 kilometres (53.7 miles) and fired from smooth bored barrel versions of the K5.[1] Although Frenk never saw this innovation, this fin-stabilized shell, when fired with a special propelling charge, increased the range of the K5 to 150 kilometres (93.5 miles).

During the summer of 1940, in the area of Calais and Cap Griz Nez, seven artillery batteries bore their guns upon not only shipping in the English Channel, but also ports and radar installations in south-east England. Three of these batteries included a rail unit each equipped with two K5 guns. Initially installed in support of the failed invasion of Britain, '*Operation Seelöwe* (Sea Lion)', these guns became part of the 'Atlantic Wall' in defence of the occupied territories, although some were later sent to other fronts. The ports of Dover, Folkestone and even the far afield seaside town of Margate were assailed. The K5s operated on purpose-built rail-switching and turntable systems. The English Channel and its shipping were completely dominated. The offensive began on 12 August 1940 when the first shell fell upon Dover. Throughout the war, 2,226 shells hit Dover and its total civilian death toll was 205, with 946 buildings destroyed.

Throughout the Battle of Britain and beyond, from his battery position close to Wissant 60 kilometres south-west of Calais, Frenk witnessed formations of *Luftwaffe* aircraft flying across the Channel to England. Many *Luftwaffe* units were stationed close to the battery's position including the famous *Jagdgeschwader* 26, whose pilots were known as the 'Abbeville Boys'. The famed, charismatic, cigar-smoking fighter ace, *Oberstleutnant* Adolf Galland, was to lead JG 26 from August 1940 to December 1941 and who, it was rumoured, instructed his ground crew to install a cigar lighter in the cockpit of his Messerschmitt Bf 109. Neighbouring personnel from both the *Luftwaffe* and artillery batteries would call upon each other out of courtesy – and curiosity. During such a sociable meeting, Frenk met again his old friend from his early days at Würzburg, Martin Rysavy, who had joined the *Luftwaffe* before the outbreak of war. Frenk was delighted to learn that Rysavy was now an *Oberleutnant* and *Staffelkapitän* of 2./JG 26 with aerial 'kills' to his name. As Frenk recalled: 'We didn't speak much about the war and our respective "jobs" – just our personal adventures.'

The billets for *E-Battr.* 702 were close to the sea and one day Frenk remembered seeing a 'local' Bf 109 flying at an altitude of only a metre above the waves to make a 'wheels–up' crash-landing on the beach. The pilot, with a bullet wound to the stomach, was pulled from his aircraft just as the machine burst into flames. Although the aerial combats were followed with keen interest with battalion binoculars, and in spite of the blazoned German black crosses or RAF 'cockades' (as the British roundel was known by the Germans), it was very easy to misidentify an aircraft during a 'dogfight' especially far out over the sea. On one occasion, Frenk and his comrades ran in the direction of a descending parachutist with side arms drawn expecting to take a prisoner, only to discover it was a German airman.

In addition to the warmly welcomed 'Abbeville Boys', the tedium of the posting was also broken by less popular visits and inspections from higher ranks, including no less than the *Führer,* Adolf Hitler, who visited the area whilst inspecting *Luftwaffe* airfields and artillery batteries in December 1940. 'He had a special interest in long-range weapons,' Frenk recalled, 'But overestimated their possibilities.'

During the first half of 1941, Frenk's battery was frequently 'shot up' by a persistent, lone RAF Spitfire. The Spitfire would dive down from the sun to shoot up the K5 emplacement and the battery anti-aircraft support. Remarkably, the pilot tended to make his attacks very consistently at noon. Although no artillery crew members were ever hit, it was decided that this had to stop. Very special attention was given to scanning the skies in anticipation of the next attack. When it came, it was to have most unexpected results. At noon on 2 July 1941, the battery's Flak unit waited patiently for the expected nuisance attack by the rogue Spitfire. It was not to be disappointed. An aircraft was sighted from out of the sun, flying towards the unit's position. The Flak guns opened up at once and struck their target. With a heavy heart, it was realized almost immediately that it was a Bf 109 which, having been hit, had crashed close to the position. Tragically, the smashed airframe contained the body of Martin Rysavy. This shook the unit and affected the personnel deeply. Rysavy, a *Staffelkapitän* for less than seven weeks was shot down returning from convoy escort duty. His final tally was eight kills in 177 combat sorties. His replacement, *Leutnant* Horst Uhlenberg, was killed in action just ten days later. The story of the Battle of Britain is well known, but what is often forgotten is that the attrition in the air continued over southern England, the Channel and north-eastern France well beyond October 1940. [2]

The changing strategic situation with regard to the air war was never known to Frenk and his comrades, but given that they continued to be stationed in the same location into 1942, there were no doubts as to the overall progress of the war. However, to voice any concerns was extremely dangerous as so many comrades were also ardent Nazis. Both Eberhard and Herbert had joined the military services and Frenk recalled a rare moment during which he was able to speak openly when a spell of home leave coincided with that of his brother, Eberhard. Eberhard was seven years younger and Frenk recalled that 'Eberhard, was an easy-going type, well liked by his friends, but not that successful at school. He read a great deal, especially detective stories. Since our father was a policeman and esteemed in the local population for his good nature, Eberhard decided that his profession would be as a police detective. Therefore, he applied to the police. My parents·supported this application, hoping that in the police he could be exempted from the dangers of the front, for Herbert and I were already soldiers. Just about this time, Himmler acquired command of the whole of the police force. One of his first orders was that every police applicant had first to apply to the *Waffen*-SS. Eberhard, aged 17, joined the *Waffen*-SS in 1941 and after a year of very tough recruit training in Ellwangen, he was immediately sent to the Russian Front to fight with the 3. SS-*Panzergrenadier-Division "Totenkopf"*.' In fact, earlier than Frenk remembered, on 17 June 1936 *Reichsführer*-SS Heinrich Himmler became *Chef der Deutschen Polizei im Reichsministerium des Innern* (Chief of German Police in the Interior Ministry) following a Hitler decree to '… unify the control of the Police duties in the Reich.'

Frenk and his brother's respective 'fronts' were separated by an extraordinary distance of approximately 2300 kilometres (1,440 miles). The Western Front had remained relatively unchanged, but in the East the resolve of the Red Army was strengthening. As they exchanged news, Eberhard spoke of a recent recruit into his '*Totenkopf*' ('Death's Head') division who had previously worked as a concentration camp guard. This man bragged that he had personally murdered one hundred Jews. Apparently, no one in the division spoke to this man or sought his company thereafter! Frenk recalled: 'They [the *Waffen*-SS] were taught to kill and die without twitching an eye. The '*Totenkopf*' Division was used pitilessly. My brother earned an Iron Cross, which, for a simple soldier, was something special. For his memory I see my task as emphasizing that one cannot describe every member of the *Waffen*-SS as necessarily being a criminal. I fully consent to declare all misdeeds against Jews and other civilians, especially in the concentration camps, as exceptional crimes. But there were also decent individuals and these men paid with their lives for joining the wrong organization.'

During their shared home leave, Eberhard saw their mother listening in to a broadcast from the BBC on the wireless. Horrified, Eberhard announced that he would report her to the authorities. Understandably, it devastated Frenk's mother to think that she would be denounced by her own 'flesh and blood' and she was deeply concerned about the possible consequences that would follow as a result of such a move on the part of her son. In any event, she was not reported for she had 'learned her lesson'. Listening to foreign radio stations was a highly dangerous activity.

By the summer of 1942, both of Frenk's brothers had been killed in action on the Eastern Front. Eberhard had fallen in July somewhere between Leningrad and Moscow. Herbert, a forward artillery observer in the *Heer*, died on the same sector but further to the south. Due to a decree of Hitler, to 'spare the tears of mothers', Frenk was now no longer eligible for front line service and returned to Germany from France to work in the armaments industry. It was then, following a recommendation by *Major* Hohmann, that he was ordered to Peenemünde in early April 1943 to work on the adjusting procedures of the A4 Rocket. Although it would have been dangerous to openly express relief over such a non-combatant role, he was overjoyed with the new posting for his education, scientific interest and inventive mind could now come to the fore.

The rocket facility of Peenemünde was then known under the cover name of *Heimatartilleriepark* 11 (Home Artillery Park 11) – or 'HAP 11' as stated in Frenk's documents and travel permits. Frenk was billeted in a private room in House 30 within the *Entwicklungswerk* (Development Works) at Peenemünde, 2.5 kilometres south-southeast from the main Rocket test platform. His immediate neighbour was the famous *Professor* Hermann Oberth with whom he became very friendly. Also sharing the accommodation of House 30 were members of the *Luftwaffen-Versuchsstelle* team at Peenemünde West including several test pilots working on the Messerschmitt Me 163 rocket-powered interceptor. The swept-wing Me 163, later known as the *'Komet'*, was yet another extraordinary piece of technology that came from the stable of German 'wonder weapons'. Designed as a high-speed, high-altitude interceptor, this remarkable and diminutive aircraft was powered by hypergolic fuels. The fuel, a mix of hydrazine hydrate and methanol, would combine with the oxidizer, hydrogen peroxide (also used in the A4/V2) and spontaneously ignite producing high levels of thrust. The Me 163 was capable of speeds in excess of 950 km/h (590 mph) and altitudes of over 12 kilometres (7.45 miles). Frenk recalled one of the pilots who lived in House 30; Max Mayer complained that the ink in his fountain pen would boil at high altitudes, ruining his shirts! In spite of its innovation, in 1944 the Me 163 failed to thwart the armadas of American heavy bombers which pounded the Reich's cities almost daily. Its highly volatile propellants meant that more pilots were lost in accidents, especially in landings, than in combat.

Unlike others who had been posted to Peenemünde directly from the front, Frenk realized that the contrast of the Rocket centre to what would have been employment in more conventional military industry was extraordinary: 'Life in Peenemünde was like it was in peacetime; an oasis in the middle of the war. Although we were fed quite well in the *Offizierskasino* (officers' mess) and met others there in the evening, one could go for a meal, using food cards, in Greifswald. I and others were glad that we were allowed to work in our native country legally without having to go to the front. Of course one would never have been allowed to say that out loud! Instead one said, "I would prefer to be at the front, so that I could earn the Iron Cross."'

However, the high security at Peenemünde was very unlike anything experienced in peacetime. Security badges had to be worn at all times, although apparently Frenk was required only to show a single pass.

Throughout his nine years of military service he built up a collection of personal photographs, but not one exists from his time at Peenemünde since photography was strictly forbidden. Frenk had only been at Peenemünde a relatively short time when he heard that a woman telephonist, while on her night shift, had mentioned 'V2' during a conversation with a person resident in a distant town. The conversation was overheard during a spot-check of telephone 'traffic' by the Gestapo. The woman was sentenced to death and executed.

Frenk observed that most of the men seconded to Peenemünde were described officially as having the status of 'UK', meaning *unabkömmlich* (indispensable), exempting them from front line military service. It was a great stroke of luck for these men, for a thousand Germans a day were perishing on the Eastern Front. Frenk was assigned to the military staff of *Leutnant* Gerhard Stegmaier who was in charge of the Pre-Production Works. Frenk's first duty was to develop the artillery settings for the A4's aim. Initially however, for the first few weeks, he had to become fully acquainted with the full function of the Rocket. Armed with his security pass, which was the envy of many other engineers, he was able to visit development laboratories, construction departments and the launch platforms, known as *Prüfstände* (Proof Stands). The cooperation that he received from every person he came into contact with was excellent. A *Dr.* Strobel, who headed the Trajectory Calculation Department, was sufficiently impressed with the young *Leutnant* that he suggested that it would be possible for Frenk to pursue his doctorate at Peenemünde. Frenk was obliged to decline because of the pressure of his new duties.

During his tour of the Peenemünde facilities, Frenk quickly learned the importance of the gyroscopes that controlled the A4; as he recalled: 'The gyros, *Vertikant* and *Horizont*, controlled the position of the Rocket during the flight. Deviations from the 'normal' position were measured and computed into commands and given to rudders. The position of the Rocket fins at launching did not play a role in target accuracy. They only had to align with the gyro axles. At *Prüfstand* VII the fins were adjusted using a theodolite and the controlling gyros were installed without exact adjustment. That was not accurate enough and so the first firing I witnessed, on 14 April 1943, had a deviation of 30 kilometres to the right and impacted on the Pomeranian countryside.'

In addition to the inaccurate installation of the gyroscopes and many other issues, Frenk also noticed that mounting holes for the gyros into the control department were oversized. The gyroscope mounting bolts were 4 mm in diameter and passed though pre-drilled holes 5 mm in diameter! Frenk calculated that the error caused by the engineering mismatch would be responsible for a deviation as great as one degree. This error could cause an impact inaccuracy of 5 kilometres. For a Rocket that had a range of 330 kilometres targeted upon cities, this may not appear to be too great an error, but it was a specific and easily corrected factor that was detrimental for a weapon in which so many uncontrollable variables existed. Although his study of the installation of the A4's avionics and manufacturing errors was not part of his brief, Frenk decided to report his findings and suggestions for correction directly to von Braun via official channels.

Following his arrival at Peenemünde, Frenk quickly became familiar with the name of Wernher von Braun, the Technical Director of the Rocket facility at Peenemünde, a man he came to admire and a man he was later to describe as 'a genius'. Frenk also envied, albeit never grudgingly, the leadership of von Braun, who was only one year older than he was. During his time at Peenemünde, Frenk was to experience work of the greatest personal satisfaction, but his experiences were also to be marred by what he himself describes as a '*faux pas*' with the one man he least wished to embarrass. However, with this incident yet to unfold in the near future, Frenk's report duly arrived upon von Braun's desk. Von Braun was somewhat taken aback by the report, which had come not from his own staff, but from an outsider and newcomer who had only been at Peenemünde a few weeks. However, he called his staff together and after discussing Frenk's report, it was deemed that his comments were indeed valid. Von Braun demanded of his staff why they had not detected the mounting error for the gyroscopes themselves. The answer was simple: everybody was so busy with their own specific area and, furthermore, communication was hampered by secrecy. Changes in the A4's manufacture were implemented and von Braun made a careful note of the 'newcomer's' name for the future.

In spite of any improvements, Frenk and his colleagues would express the greatest reservations in confidence about the usefulness of the Rocket: 'We had all heard the widespread propaganda speeches of *Dr.* Goebbels about *"Vergeltung"* (retribution) on the radio, but everybody knew that the V2 was only yet another weapon that would be just a pinprick to the enemy. The V2 would never be decisive in a war. At that time, we compared it to a boxer who has the choice with the last of his strength to fend off the opponent or to miss his final punch. That was the V2. All my colleagues at Peenemünde knew that it would be impossible to reverse the fortunes of the war. Nor did we agree that the V2 was always preferable to the *Wasserfall* anti-aircraft rocket. Serious aerial attacks on German towns were taking place but the anti-aircraft rocket was always put back. We seldom saw the brown nitric acid exhaust of the *Wasserfall* in the skies of Peenemünde. We spoke to one another as far as we were confident enough to do so. However, making public these opinions could cost you your life. "Spreading defeatism" was the name of that crime.'

The *Wasserfall* rocket was one quarter the size of a V2 and similar in appearance apart from the stubby mid-body stabilizers and enlarged tail fins. Its engine, designed by *Dr.* Walther Thiel, used a hypergolic propellant system of Visol (vinyl isobutyl ether) and Salbei (90% nitric acid, 10% sulphuric acid) which instantly combusted upon mixing, creating thrust and the characteristic brown exhaust trail that was remembered by Frenk. Guided by remote control, it was intended that the 235-kg warhead would explode in a 'box' of enemy heavy bombers causing damaged aircraft to crash into one another like a tree falling in a crowded forest. Although much supported by Albert Speer, Minister for Armaments and War Production, who believed that *Wasserfall* could have stalled the Allied strategic bombing offensive against Germany's industries, Hitler considered the anti-aircraft weapon as a defensive system and as such it was anathema to him. The *Führer* looked upon the A4/V2 Rocket as an offensive weapon and eventually it would receive full priority; the defensive *Wasserfall* received consistently either low or non-existent funding. Could the *Wasserfall* have stemmed the bombing campaigns of the RAF and USAAF? Even today, this notion is still controversial.

Whenever his duties allowed, Frenk enjoyed watching the test-firing of the A4 from very close range. The elliptical raised earthworks surrounding *Prüfstand* VII that formed the Arena had parapets built into the upper ramparts which held four camera positions; another two were located further afield. The images recorded would be carefully reviewed following every launch to learn as much as possible. Hard information as to the behaviour of the V2, and its components in flight, was very difficult to obtain in the days before sophisticated telemetry systems and 'black box' flight recorders. One of the four camera positions of the Arena was an unmanned television camera that stood directly in front, some 26 metres from the firing pad. Its relayed images were examined from the BSM (*Bord-, Steuer-* und *Messgeräte* – Flight, Guidance, and Telemetering) building, 2 kilometres away in the Development Works. A second camera position was located at ground level 72 metres west from the firing platform beside the main entrance to the Arena. The remaining two camera bunker platforms were built into the top of the raised embankments of the Arena and had commanding views looking downward. The southernmost of these platforms was 96 metres away from the *Prüfstand* but the closest of the elevated camera positions was located 82 metres away to the south-east.[3] This was the position that Frenk often chose as it offered an excellent view.

He recalled: 'From the time of my arrival in 1943 to the end [of the test-firings] in 1945, I saw many test-starts of the A4 at *Prüfstand* VII. About half of them failed: some immediately after ignition; some, after a few seconds in the air, would fall down and burn out; some exploded in the air. There was an earth wall around the launch area of *Prüfstand* VII; I always positioned myself on the earth embankment above. This was actually the location for the photographers, but occasionally it was not occupied and from such a free foxhole I observed most starts. Before the launch, I could see how the Rocket was lined up. If a Rocket took off, the ground trembled as the engine developed 25 tonnes of thrust and I always felt levitated some half a centimetre above the ground. The noise was about 120 dB and because I did not clap my hands over my ears, I later became hard of hearing. When it began the tilt and went into the clouds, there was a weird droning. My feelings? *Sheer enthusiasm!* It was an ecstasy of adventure to be near the blustering power, feeling the hot air storm in one's face and the vibrating earth under one's feet – the multiple thunder striking the ears; to be in the crew who 'tamed the dragon' in a world of technical peak performance… to have entered space.'

Although Frenk believed the volume of sound made by the roaring combustion chamber to be 120 dB, the sensation of being levitated above the ground, and the air vibrations, suggests an even greater value than 120 dB. Assuming a correct value of 128 dB, it is interesting to note that the volume of the Rocket's engine heard at a distance of 1 metre would be approximately 164 dB which is hardly surprising, for it is similar to the internal sound of a large jet turbine motor![4]

When failed A4s crashed close by to the launch area, the cameramen would continue to man their cameras, desperately trying to keep the doomed device in their sights. Spectators like Frenk would hurl themselves into their foxholes clutching their steel helmets. Following the inevitable explosion caused by the liquid oxygen and the alcohol, and once the shower of shrapnel had subsided, Frenk and his fellow observers would run down the embankment and other locations around the Arena towards the ebbing flames. Armed with an assortment of pliers and other useful salvaging tools which they always carried, Frenk and his comrades would hunt through the wreckage looking out for any undamaged items. Frenk would seek out accumulators (batteries), which drove the gyroscopes. These electric cells were used to make pocket torches (flash lights). Occasionally amplifiers and undamaged pipes could be found and these would also be fashioned into useful items. This practice was not frowned upon too greatly as the destroyed Rocket was considered to be – fiscally at least – a write-off, but the practice of picking over the carcass of a failed Rocket was highly dangerous. Streams of burning alcohol not consumed in the explosion of the liquid oxygen ran across the ground and an anxious eye was always turned towards the Rocket's oddly shaped, elliptical 'T-*Stoff*' fuel tank containing 128 kg of hydrogen peroxide, a highly reactive oxidant.

Frenk recalled: 'We had a routine: one of us always looked out for the hydrogen peroxide tank. If it began to boil, the watcher would shout, *"The T-Stoff is brewing!"* We then grabbed our spoils and ran away as fast as we could from the Rocket. The T-*Stoff* would soon explode and sweep everything away that had remained. *"Alte Hasen"* ['Old Rabbits', meaning more experienced men] had told us that we could do this.'

Apparently some time before Frenk's posting to Peenemünde, an A4 failure had occurred and not only had the device rotated about its vertical axis but it had then flown off in the opposite direction to its intended trajectory. Within Stegmaier's staff, the suggestion was made that perhaps the A4 had been set upon the firing platform incorrectly by 180 degrees. Undoubtedly however, this particular misfire was caused by a failure of the gyroscopic guidance system, but nevertheless the doubt remained. Stegmaier took it upon himself always to check that Rockets had been correctly placed on the firing platform. Becoming tired of this somewhat irksome task, he decided to delegate it to the newest member of his staff. He took Frenk to one side and quietly gave him the new responsibility, stating: 'I have personally checked that Fin 1 is pointed to the target direction but this task will now be yours and you'll make a protocol for this.'

Initially Frenk felt that Stegmaier's brief was a great responsibility and demonstrated a high level of trust in him. He realized very quickly it was nonsense! It was near impossible for the firing crews to make such a mistake. Not only were the fins of the A4 clearly marked, but their position was also related to the hatches and control compartments: to make such an error the firing crew would have to be blind! Additionally, waiting for an officer to sign off the corrected orientation officially wasted a great deal of time.

However, because a procedure had already been adopted, no one in a position of seniority was prepared to take the possible risk of rescinding the task. Frenk was acquainted with *Dr. Hans Friedrich* who had overseeing responsibilities at *Prüfstand* VII. Friedrich was bemused by the protocol and, in conversation with Frenk, commented, 'This military control always costs us a lot of time. It is really superfluous.'

Frenk was not at all anxious to suggest that his new duty, which had until recently been that of Stegmaier's, was a waste of time as it might have angered his superior, but nor could he refuse the task. So Frenk suggested, to the relief of Friedrich, that he would telephone *Prüfstand* VII directly prior to a launch to confirm with him that Fin 1 had been correctly positioned. Friedrich agreed and this ad hoc procedure became the new unofficial protocol. Flawed as this arrangement was, it was to cause unforeseen and near deadly consequences on the morning of 29 June 1943.

The evening before, *Reichsführer*-SS Heinrich Himmler arrived at Peenemünde with very little fanfare, having driven himself in a *Kübelwagen*. After a modest meal and after adjourning to the Hearth Room at the *Offizierskasino*, Himmler engaged in conversation with the leading 'illuminati' of Peenemünde. The atmosphere would have been awkward, as it was well known that Himmler abhorred both smoking and drinking. Apparently the *Reichsführer* listened attentively to the tales of the early days of the rocket men and sympathetically to their concerns that Hitler remained cautious about Rocket development.[5] In reality, Himmler had been working away quietly in the background to gain control of the A4 programme. After he had outlined the 'new world order' as he perceived it, steeped in Nazi lore, the conversation drew to a close with the promise that later that very morning the *Reichsführer*-SS would see two Rocket test-firings from *Prüfstand* VII.

Just five hours later, standing on the viewing platform of the roof of the BSM building, Himmler, accompanied by SS officers and a *Wehrmacht* escort, gazed north towards the raised embankment of the *Prüfstand* Arena just over 2 kilometres away. At approximately 0915 hrs, rising above the nearby forest, the A4 Rocket, V38, began its ascent into the sky. Also watching was Frenk who was feeling particularly anxious, since not only was he aware that this had to be a successful firing for the important visitor, but also because on that particular morning he had been so busy with other duties that he had neglected to call the *Prüfstand* to speak with Friedrich. The alignment of Fin 1 had not been confirmed! He recalled: 'The Rocket lifted off and I held my breath. It flew off in the opposite direction. It looked as if it had been lined up wrongly. It impacted with a tremendous detonation and smoke cloud on the edge of the nearby airfield where the V1 was under development. My heart sank at my predicament and Stegmaiers' first thought must have been *"Has Frenk not checked the fins?"* I called Friedrich by phone and asked whether he could confirm my checks. He said, with some embarrassment, "But, *Herr* Frenk, when I am asked under oath, I cannot say that... I must tell the truth. I am sorry!"'

Meanwhile, on the roof of the BSM building, the atmosphere of shock and dismay was broken as Himmler turned to von Braun and Dornberger; commenting sarcastically 'You have a pretty effective close-range weapon here.'[6]

Frenk desperately needed to know if the impacting Rocket had injured or killed anyone over at the airfield. He promptly commandeered a *Kübelwagen* and drove as quickly as he could towards the slowly dissipating cloud of smoke 3 kilometres roughly to the south-west of *Prüfstand* VII. He arrived at the airfield to find the windows of nearby buildings blown out and, by the edge of the runway, three blast-damaged Heinkel He 111 bombers, the worst affected of which had been preparing for flight. The bomber's extensive front canopy had been blown in by the blast, and the impact crater's edge was only about 30 metres away. He peered into the front of the aircraft expecting to see a corpse, but to his relief the pilot, although somewhat pale, was not injured and remained, alive, in the interior of the wrecked cockpit. From the Heinkel, Frenk ran towards the smoking 30-metre-diameter crater. Rocket V38 had carried no warhead; it had been the kinetic energy of the falling device from its 15-second flight and the potential energy of eight tons of propellant that had wrought the destruction. As he gazed into the crater, Frenk became aware that others were approaching: 'While I stood there for a couple of minutes, another *Kübelwagen* drove up – and who was it who got out? Heinrich Himmler and an SS companion. They came towards me and stood beside the crater's edge. There was a rumour that Himmler would kill people he viewed as suspicious, those who could risk the *'Endsieg'* (final victory). We (fellow comrades) already knew that one could end up in a concentration camp or at the gallows if Himmler regarded one as not quite 'loyal' to the regime. He would simply make a dismissive hand gesture to his aide and that would be your end. Would he ask me what I was doing inside the team? Perhaps Stegmaier had already spoken about his speculation? Even at a normal court martial I would have been condemned not only for an order refused but for sabotage or similar. After a fearful minute of silence he held his hand a little in front of his body towards me. I had *"Hosen voll"* ['full trousers'] and didn't dare give him my hand. Instead I formally greeted him then quickly walked away and "disappeared".'

Frenk walked as calmly as he could back to his vehicle, leaving behind an ever-growing group of spectators congregating in, and around, the crater. He drove at speed directly back to the Rocket centre's Film Processing Department. He felt that the film footage shot by the Arena cameramen would surely exonerate him. As he made his way to the dark rooms he was told by his comrades that his name had already boomed out of the Rocket Centre's loudspeaker address system. The cine films had already been processed and dried. Frenk quickly examined a reel and soon saw that the reason for the failure had nothing whatsoever to do with the orientation of Fin 1. The A4 had indeed developed a guidance failure for he saw clearly that it rotated along its flight axis and the probable cause was due to a carden (universal joint) bearing failure causing the gyroscope to abruptly turn and guide the Rocket in the wrong direction. He recalled: 'With that result I ran to Stegmaier: "*Herr Oberst*, I have the reason for the failure!" He hadn't asked for the fin check and praised me for quickly determining the cause of the fault. I could breathe again!'

Later that afternoon, Himmler witnessed the second firing of the day. Rocket V40 was deemed a success and instead of falling 3 kilometres away, it impacted 236 kilometres down range into the Baltic Sea.

As a small footnote, unknown to Frenk, in the 1990s an excavation took place beside the old airfield runway at Peenemünde to unearth the remains of the A4 Rocket, V38. The discovered bent nose cone now resides in the entrance foyer of the Peenemünde Historical and Technical Museum at Usedom.

Shortly after Himmler's visit to Peenemünde, Frenk's work which had caused such a stir earlier with von Braun was rewarded. In acknowledgement of his 'failed A4' report he was moved from Stegmaier to von Braun's staff. Working in *Technische Direktion* 5 (TD 5 – Technological Management Department 5) Frenk was given the task of recording all faults, including misfires, in the hope of eliminating them. An example of his work is to be seen reproduced in some copies of Walter Dornberger's book '*V2*'.

Frenk realized that the principles used to align precisely the artillery guns using the *Richtkreis* and *Bunker-Kollimator* optical devices could be used to accurately position crucial parts of the A4's avionics. Many factors were responsible for the accuracy of the Rocket's 'fall of shot', one of which was the precise positioning of the *Vertikant* (vertical) gyroscope so that its axis was parallel with the stub axles of the corresponding graphite rudders positioned in the exhaust jet of the combustion chamber. This was a difficult undertaking as access to the gyroscope was awkward and it was impossible for the eye to have reference to both the top of the Rocket and its combustion chamber some 10 metres below. The answer was to manufacture into the housing of the *Vertikant* a reference area that worked in combination with the *Richtkreis* and *Bunker-Kollimator* attached to the ladder of the *Meillerwagen* which had sight of the engine's rudders. Very delicate and precise adjustment could then be made to bring the axes of the gyroscope and rudders into perfect congruence. The test-firing of 14 May 1943 proved Frenk's hypothesis as the deviation in the Rocket's flight was greatly improved. The technique became standard procedure and changes in manufacture were implemented.

Additionally, Frenk took it upon himself to produce a second, unsolicited, report for the attention of von Braun. The report detailed ideas that Frenk had on the topic of jet propulsion and related subjects. Frenk was never to hear directly what von Braun thought of his ideas. As he recalled: 'I was proud of my inventions, my military patents and the introduction of the Bunker Collimator against existing orders; I was so eager to produce new proposals but the state of A4 development I now realize made my ideas absolutely useless.'

On one occasion, Frenk called upon von Braun's anteroom and enquired of his secretary if von Braun had seen his report. She replied to his enquiry, *'Yes, but it has not been accepted.'* Instead of simply turning upon his heels and walking out, Frenk decided to embark upon a rant in the company of the girl whom he knew socially and began, foolishly, to rail against von Braun. Without any caution Frenk used the word 'dilettante' and, having uttered this and similar expressions, he became aware that von Braun's office door was ajar! With a sinking heart he felt the presence of von Braun and knew that his words had been heard — the consequences of which had an almost immediate effect and were to haunt him for the rest of his life. 'From this point of course, I fell into his disgrace. This was 100 per cent my fault. My *faux pas*, which led to a break with von Braun, caused by my own stupidity. Staying a fan of his geniality and his grand success was pretty painful for me. But I cannot find a fault in his behaviour: only disappointment in him bearing a grudge for all time.'

Shortly after the suspected debacle with von Braun, Peenemünde was attacked by the RAF. The mission, known as 'Operation Hydra' was intended to destroy both the laboratories and workshops and to kill the senior personnel at the rocket facility.[7] Frenk remembered that during the first alert on the night of 17 August 1943 he decided to remain in bed despite the opening salvos of the local anti-aircraft guns, for this he considered was the correct behaviour for a dignified man. He changed his mind, however, when the first wave of bombers flew directly over the test centre. He dressed hurriedly, grabbed a *Volksempfänger* (people's radio receiver) and ran out into the night. The air was filled with the blast waves of exploding bombs and flashing lights. In the eerie light he stumbled on something along the pathway; his skin turned to gooseflesh as he looked down and saw the bottom section of a pair of pyjamas from which protruded a dismembered foot. Frenk made his way to House 30's nearest air raid shelter and having caught his breath, attempted to tune his radio receiver so as to listen in to reports of the air raid. The *Volksempfänger,* however, was intentionally designed to have limited reception so the listener could receive only local radio transmissions (and not those from the short waveband on which the Allies transmitted to occupied Europe and Germany), but the weakened signal having passed through the thick concrete made reception impossible. Suddenly from the air raid shelter door came a heavy pounding of fists. The door was opened to reveal none other than *Generalmajor* Dornberger. Frenk was struck by his dishevelled, partly-dressed appearance as the *General* attended to the buttoning of his breeches. Dornberger later wrote: *'Inside* [the bunker], *a crowd of abruptly awakened and hurriedly dressed people were huddled in a long, brightly lit room. Here one could hear only the "plop, plop, plop" of the sticks of bombs bursting in the muffled sand. The AA fire sounded incredibly far away. Now and then the shelter shuddered and reeled like a ship in a storm. Faces grew paler and eyes grew wider with unspoken questions.'*

While waiting for the air raid to end, Frenk became aware that a woman sitting beside him was staring at him very intently and smirking. Their gaze met and Frenk recognized the woman as a member of the kitchen staff from the *Offizierskasino*. She had noticed that rivulets of perspiration were breaking out across his face. Frenk had a feeling that the woman was about to say something mocking or humiliating; as he recalled: 'This impudent woman said, "Oh *Herr. Oberleutnant*, you are afraid. Look how the sweat pearls on your forehead." This annoyed me greatly but on the other hand, I could say nothing for I really *was* sweating. I leaned close to her and hissed, *"You look after your own fear."* When, a little later, the bomb explosions grew closer I said to her: *"I wonder? Will it be this one or the next one which will hit us? Who's afraid now?"* I was angry and wanted to take revenge! The woman just screamed, *"Shut up! Shut up!"* Every close impact to the bunker felt like an earthquake. But, mercifully, the thick walls held.'

With the breaking of dawn on 18 August, Frenk could see that Peenemünde had changed forever. Gaping craters had transformed the landscape into a weird, lunar-like scene. Fires continued to burn and smoke bellowed from buildings as the fire services worked feverishly to dampen down the embers. The administrative offices had been gutted by the flames and to the south-east, the Trassenheide forced labour camp, for which no shelters had been built, had ceased to exist. The Development and Pre-Production Factory Halls, although still standing, had been damaged. The housing settlement and the hostels for the *Stabshelferinnen* (female staff assistants) close to Karlshagen had been destroyed. Frenk saw hundreds of mainly dead young women laid out awaiting collection and burial which would not take place for another three days. At the time of the authors' interviews with Frenk, although he was aware of the controversial, post-war accounts of victims of the air raid being machine-gunned by the RAF, he remained grimly confident that the victims died as a result of the bombs.

That morning Frenk heard for the first time that the eminent propulsion specialist, Dr. Thiel, his wife and two children had died when their earthwork bunker had received a direct hit. Only a few evenings before, Frenk had enjoyed Thiel's company together with Dornberger, von Braun, his secretary and a few colleagues over a glass of wine. Frenk recalled that Thiel was a '…sympathetic scientist and highly appreciated by all.' Thiel's death was not only a great loss to the development of the A4 but also dealt a mortal blow for the impoverished *Wasserfall* anti-aircraft missile programme. Later that morning, Frenk sought out von Braun. It was only then that Frenk's worst fears that his earlier, ill chosen words to von Braun's secretary had indeed been overheard: 'I said to him [von Braun] *"Please let me do something to help the clearance work – something technical perhaps…"* He replied: *"OK. There is now a great danger of epidemic following the raid. You can make sure that sufficient latrines are built!"* I had really fallen out with him – something I regret even to this day, for he was a genius. He soon transferred me out of the Technological Management Department 5.'

At that time von Braun's thoughts must have been taken up with the loss of personnel, some of whom were close friends. He was surrounded by destruction which could threaten the A4 project to which he had dedicated his life and yet, extraordinarily, he delivered his cruel *'coup de grâce'* to Frenk. The whole sorry episode affected Frenk very deeply and was to come back to haunt him many years later: 'There were of course many colleagues who watched my friendship with von Braun's secretary and some of them asked me "Isn't von Braun jealous?" I always denied it, as did the girl. Our relationship ended amicably after one and a half years. In 1945 she and her husband, also a colleague, went with von Braun to the USA and we continued to exchange yearly greetings.'

Following the air raid Frenk, and all the other staff at Peenemünde, were temporarily billeted in nearby villages and small towns. This was done not only for security but also for practical reasons as so much of the accommodation had been destroyed. Frenk was quartered temporarily in the village of Koserow, 18 kilometres (11 miles) south-east of Peenemünde along the Baltic coast. It was not long, however, before he was told that he could return to his usual accommodation at the *Entwicklungswerk* (Development Works). The building had suffered blast damage but once the broken windows and roof tiles had been replaced it had been decided that, in spite of cracked walls, it was still habitable. Frenk's transfer from von Braun's staff was swift and he was now employed in the Gyroscope Acceptance Test Department, which was overseen by *Dr*. Schneller. Schneller was a gyroscope specialist who had worked at the Darmstadt Technical University before his employment with the A4 programme. He was also a very keen pilot and would often fly the works' Siebel Si 204 twin-engine courier aircraft.

Frenk joined the Gyroscope Department at a hectic time because manufacturing changes were being hurriedly introduced in an attempt to improve the accuracy of the A4. Because of the importance of this work, Frenk was able to call to Peenemünde any person whom he considered would be useful to the department. His friend, Günther Kaiser, who had been studying to be a lawyer at Göttingen, was summoned from the Eastern Front. Kaiser was forever grateful knowing that his life had almost certainly been spared by his friend.

Frenk was sent to the *Mittelwerk*, an underground V2 and jet aircraft manufacturing plant adjacent to the *Konzentrationslager* (KZ – concentration camp) of *Mittelbau-Dora*, built deep in the Kohnstein Mountain near Nordhausen. He instructed German technicians in the new procedure of gyroscope alignment. Frenk was not oblivious to the appalling suffering and inhuman conditions that were being endured by the slave workers in the *Mittelbau*: 'Everybody knew about the existence of the KZs, everybody was conscious that it was inhuman and not right to confine people because of their race or because of a word of criticism spoken against the State. But nobody knew quite how inhuman, or how cruel the conditions in the camps were. There is a big difference between an acceptable level of hard work and scarcity of food, and torture, starvation and murder. After the liberation, 90 per cent of Germany came to know that the latter case was the reality.' Frenk believed that most of the subsequently recorded deaths that had occurred had taken place during the construction of the underground galleries and factories of the *Mittelwerk*. He was, however, aware that the standard response of the SS guards to the ever increasing acts of sabotage perpetrated by the slave workers was execution.

Frenk's superior, Schneller, had determined that the bearings that supported the gyroscope were deviating by two to three degrees during a one minute run. A mounting error of one degree was considered acceptable and this had to be achieved to reduce the failure rate. A slight misalignment of the gyroscope axis was causing an excessive amount of friction and this, in turn, caused a build-up of heat up to 200 degrees C in the bearings. As the temperature increased it exacerbated the fault. The problem was responsible for a staggering 50 per cent of the gyroscopes to be declared as unserviceable. Many experimental modifications were made by both Schneller and Frenk in an effort to reduce and eliminate the problem. A solution devised by Frenk was to replace only the upper of the two gyroscope bearings with a new design and this change ultimately reduced the failure rate to an acceptable 10 per cent.

The experimental phase of gyroscope changes necessitated visits to the Gyroscope Mounting Workshop at Buchenwald to oversee the introduction of new work practices and equipment. Schneller and Frenk flew the 400 kilometres south-west of Peenemünde to Buchenwald using the works Siebel. En route, Schneller, who had made the journey many times, invited Frenk to try his hand at the aircraft's controls. Frenk who had considerable experience flying gliders felt that the aircraft was somewhat out of trim but dismissed the thought as he returned control to Schneller for landing. He was soon to wish he had voiced his concerns.

Arriving at the Gyroscope Workshop, Frenk discovered that it was manned by slave workers from the nearby *Konzentrationslager*. The infamous concentration camp at Buchenwald had 140 sub-camps known as 'KZ-*Aussenlager*' covering a large area in central Germany. The workshop that Frenk visited was a smaller facility of which several existed just outside the fence of the main camp. These workshops were collectively known as *Kommandos*. One of these was the *'Außenkommando Optik-Fichtenhain'* and it is possibly from here that Zeiss had a manufacturing presence under the cover name of 'J.W. Optik der H. Za. Kal'.[8] The workers were of sufficient skill that they assembled cameras, binoculars and other delicate pieces of military equipment. Frenk began to instruct the men, dressed in their blue and white vertically-striped prison uniforms, in twenty different experimental patterns of the new ball bearing assembly and mounting procedures for the gyroscopes. Of his impressions of the camp and workshop, Frenk recalled: 'An SS soldier escorted me nearly all the time I was there. When he was called away briefly, I quickly took the opportunity to ask a prisoner to tell me how bad conditions were. He replied: "This is a relatively good place for us," adding "We're glad we can work with technology. They want to keep our working strength up and therefore we have better food, but sleeping is bad. We have sometimes one plank bed for three prisoners." Upon my question as to why he was there, he told me that he had offended a Party functionary. The SS man then returned and I instantly finished my questions. Anything concerning the interior conditions (of the camp) I could get no knowledge of.'

The slave worker who engaged in conversation with Frenk took an enormous risk in confiding even a single word of dissent regarding his circumstances. His negative comments could have been reported to the returning SS guard who probably, in turn, would have taken the slave worker out of the building and shot him. Frenk made no comment to the SS. At the end of the day, Frenk was escorted off the camp site and, with suitcase in hand, walked the five kilometres to the airfield at nearby Nordhausen as no vehicle was available to drive him. It had been agreed that Schneller would fly in with gyroscopes collected from Zeiss Ikon in Dresden and, having picked Frenk up, then travel on to Peenemünde before nightfall. However, having arrived at the airfield, a radio signal message was waiting for him from Schneller: *'Can only arrive tomorrow.'* Frenk was impatient to return to Peenemünde as he had arranged a 'date' with a girlfriend that very evening, so rather than spend a night at Nordhausen he arranged for a message to reach Schneller and he caught a train to Peenemünde. The following morning in the *Offizierskasino,* Frenk's coffee was interrupted by Eberhard Rees, the technical plant manager and von Braun's deputy: 'Rees, as white as chalk, came to me and gasped: *"The works aircraft has just come down!"* We then all ran to the crash site. The corpses had burned faces. Perhaps the aircraft had been overloaded or the trim was incorrect? Later, von Braun visited the crash site and wondered how I had been able to recognize the bodies? I said that I had recognized *Dr.* Schneller by his jumper. It was only by accident I was not in this aircraft.'

Eventually, Frenk became the head of the Gyroscope Quality Control Department, a position he was allowed to maintain until the war's end. His promotion was due not only to *Dr.* Schneller's death but also because of an acknowledgement that the design changes to increase gyroscope reliability had been Frenk's innovation.

In June 1944 a series of A4 launch tests were conducted from the Baltic island of Greifswalder Oie, 12 kilometres (7.5 miles) north-east of *Prüfstand*VII.The sole purpose of these firings was to discover the reason for the mid-air break-ups that were occurring, not only at Peenemünde, but also as reported by the *Fernraketen* (long-range rocket) troops training in the operational use of the Rocket at Heidelager. As mentioned in Chapter Three, test Rockets were often victim to one of three different types of mid-air disintegration. The first could occur when the device was a mere 20 metres (66 ft) above the ground when a vibration effect caused a failure. A second failure could occur at anything above 1000 metres (3,280 ft) altitude. Von Braun was later to recall the in-joke within the Rocket development team, *'I think the argument was never quite settled as to whether the V2 ever got to the point where the target was more dangerous than the launching site.'*[9] The third type, which had initiated the Greifswalder Oie tests, occurred during final stages of the Rocket's descent when, over the target zone, a sudden white cloud was seen followed by two sharp 'bangs'. The Rocket would then fall to earth as a shower of metal parts, the largest recovered components being the sand-filled warhead and the combustion chamber. Before the tests, von Braun and Dornberger had accidentally discovered that it was possible to see the approach of a descending Rocket if positioned in the target zone. This discovery, however, nearly cost them their lives when a Rocket fell just 90 metres (300 ft) away from them near the village of Sarnaki approximately 235 kilometres (150 miles) north of the Rocket training camp at Heidelager in Poland.

The difficulty of catching first sight of the approach of a A4 at the end of a semi-parabolic trajectory was challenging and potentially dangerous, so the simple answer was to fire the Rockets vertically with no tilt programme. The Rocket could then be observed all the way from take-off to impact. This formed the nature of the Greifswalder Oie tests. Frenk was instructed to attend with von Braun who led the test-firings which began on 11 June 1944. Many of the tests were conducted at dusk, under clear skies, and attempts were made to collect information via radio telemetry direct from the Rocket. The flights of the Rockets with sand-filled war-heads were closely followed using different optical aids including 10x80 *Flakfernrohr* (Flak binoculars) and *'Scherenfernrohr'* scissor telescopes which greatly increased the perspective. These telescopes were mounted on alt-azimuth mounts so that lateral deviations could be observed and quantified. Frenk also observed the trajectories with binoculars and would simply lie on his back: 'We would see the Rocket very high, more than 100 kilometres up as a white point, shining like a star. This was either because the sun was shining upon it or because of the white-hot glow of the [combustion chamber] rudders. Then the Rocket would come down entering the dense layers of the atmosphere and the light would begin to flash. The reason was that the Rocket was oscillating, but when it reached the denser air, the fins would stabilize it and then only a fixed point of light could be seen. Often we noticed that the Rocket would burst during re-entry into the atmosphere. Why? The Rockets at the peak of their curve were in airless space; they fell back with the rear end downward. As soon as the "birds" got back into denser air levels, their flights became "fidgety", because now and again the air started to "press" upon their fins. They started to swing and we on the ground saw a few seconds of blinking. The nearer to the ground, the swinging increased, until we saw only clouds of smoke. Diagnosis: the Rocket bodies were painted with a nitro paint. Due to the large surface area, however, the thin layer of paint, of course, weighed a few hundredweight and it would burn during re-entry and the thin metal skin would glow. Thereafter the Rockets couldn't stand the high physical stress due to the pendulum movement and would burst. After these findings we used a non-burning varnish and strengthened the "tin-trousers" (*Heck*, rear tail section).'

As Frenk was now outside von Braun's team he was no longer a party to all the conclusions or the additional attempts that were made to reduce mid-air bursting. Thermal insulating fibreglass was introduced around the propellant tanks in addition to steel strengthening reinforcing sleeves riveted around the tanks which also appeared to give positive results. However, no single remedy could be found to eliminate the problem altogether. Even when the V2 was introduced operationally just three months later, the problem continued without resolution.

On one occasion Frenk witnessed a potentially very hazardous test-firing from Greifswalder Oie. The observers, armed with Flak binoculars, called out that the deviation of the A4's trajectory along the lateral axis was minimal, and that the Rocket was following a fixed course almost directly along the crosshairs of their instruments. This could mean only one conclusion; four tonnes of Rocket would shortly fall at a speed of nearly 4000 km/h (2,440 mph) close to the firing platform! According to Frenk: 'The probability of being hit by the Rocket was very small, since the theoretical point of impact was about 2.5 kilometres west from the point of start because of the Earth's rotation, and the Rocket's accuracy was an area of only 5 by 5 kilometres. We were inside the 50% dispersion circle of 2 kilometres. By then anyone within Germany – soldier or civilian – was in a dangerous position and we were conscious that in the front line we would have to undergo much, much higher dangers. Having similar thoughts, nobody in the Greifswalder team fell into a panic. In fact the impact was perhaps 300 metres away from the launch pad and did no harm or damage.'

One of the more curious sights that Frenk saw during his service at
Peenemünde was when the somewhat pathetic figure of *Professor* Hermann
Oberth sat by himself on the pavement in front of House 30. As far as Frenk
could ascertain, von Braun had called his old mentor to Peenemünde in an act
of charity to protect him from some lowly engagement and perhaps enlistment
into the military services. Oberth, famed for his writings on the subject of
space travel, had been a leading figure in the pre-war days of the VfR. However,
Frenk's interpretation of the situation was that Oberth was simply not sufficiently
qualified to be in von Braun's team. Nevertheless, Frenk had strong sympathies
for Oberth and the feelings grew stronger after Frenk's own 'fall from grace'
from his mentor, von Braun. The two men became friends, the younger man
keeping a watchful eye on the famed *Professor* who was nearly twice his age:
'Oberth was a modest old man. He lived in the room beside mine. It was
impossible to integrate him into the [Rocket] development crew. He was not
consulted regarding the development work and now the Rocket was in
production, one could no longer have discussions on its principles. So he sat in
House 30 without any tasks and, of course, without contentment. Von Braun's
workload did not allow him time to find an appropriate employment for Oberth.
He [Oberth] often complained to me about it. This was tragic, but even I
couldn't see a better way. Often on a Sunday morning, Oberth would be seen
sitting beside the roadside outside House 30 pounding a piece of metal into the
form of a model. While we had the most modern equipment at our disposal,
he was making things using the most primitive means.'

Although von Braun admired Oberth and would often speak positively about
him, Frenk had the feeling that other colleagues did not afford him the same
respect, nor did they treat him as well. On one occasion in the Mess, Frenk
remembered hearing the sound of crockery and cutlery crashing to the ground.
He turned to see that the hapless individual who had just lost his entire meal
onto the floor was Oberth. To the amusement and exchange of smiles of the
younger engineers around him, Oberth, ever mindful of wartime shortages,
proceeded to squat down and to feed himself directly from the floor. It annoyed
Frenk that a man of Oberth's reputation became the centre of ridicule and
embarrassment. Oberth with his characteristic shock of hair, thick eyebrows and
pencil constantly seen above one ear, had the appearance of the stereotypical
absent-minded professor. With a complete lack of motivation or direction, fairly
small incidents would grow out of all proportion. One such memorable incident
regarded the theft of sugar from Oberth. On the notice board in House 30,
Oberth had chalked, '*A bag of my sugar has been stolen.*' Underneath the bold
banner announcing the crime, Oberth had written: '*The sugar has been laced with
a tasteless Red Indian arrow poison which will be fatal in a few days.*' Two days later
an unidentified person wrote underneath Oberth's words '*I am already*

in the hereafter!' [signed] *'The sugar thief'*. Frenk considered this to be a somewhat impertinent, but comic gesture on the part of the thief. Oberth was in the habit of hiding away small items of value in his bunker and it was from there that the theft had occurred. Following the air raid of August 1943, Oberth became extremely anxious that perhaps the Allied bombers might return. Through the crack in the wall between his apartment and that of Frenk caused by the devastating RAF air raid, Oberth would call out *'Herr Oberleutnant,* I think we're going to have an air raid warning' as well as bombarding Frenk with more mundane questions. On one occasion, Frenk answered his apartment door late one evening to find Oberth standing in front of him with his pencil yet again above his ear. Oberth wanted to know the date, but seeing that Frenk was entertaining a girlfriend, became acutely embarrassed and with many repeated apologies quickly wished Frenk a good night and returned to his adjacent apartment.

During the operational deployment of the V2, a subject of conversation that often occurred among the FR troops was the use of materials other than the usual explosive that was used in the Rocket's warhead. However, Frenk never heard of any attempt to use phosphorus as was sometimes rumoured. Similarly, the use of biological or chemical weapons, as far as he was aware, was simply not considered. To the controversial and persistent speculation of the Rocket and the nuclear bomb, Frenk clearly recollected overhearing a most illuminating conversation that took place between von Braun and a visiting dignitary: 'Once, by accident, I overheard an exchange between von Braun and a visitor, who asked: *"Why do you not use an atomic bomb in the V2?"* With a sneer, von Braun replied: *"Because we do not have one!"'*

Was von Braun's attitude to this question a reaction to being asked it once too often? Or was his cynical response simply voicing his frustration that the stalled development of German nuclear technology meant that such a weapon would never be delivered? If the latter was the case, it suggests that the offensive use of the first atomic bomb might have been London, or perhaps Antwerp, instead of Hiroshima. Ignoring such wild speculation, Frenk recalled to the authors that experiments were conducted to increase the explosive effect of the A4. At the FR troop training ground at Heidelager Frenk witnessed a test in which the normal explosive of the warhead was exchanged for nitropenta, one of the most powerful explosives available at that time. Also known as pentrite (pentaerythritol tetranitrate) it was decided not to pursue this research as the explosive was not only scarce but also expensive. In November 1943, Frenk, although not a chemist, was assigned to investigate as a low priority project, the use of a class of Sprengel explosive (named after the German chemist, Hermann Sprengel 1834-1906,) called oxyliquit. In 1895, the German Scientist, Professor Carl von Linde (1842–1934), discovered that mixing liquid oxygen with a fuel, for example carbon or some other organic material such as cork powder, could make an explosive material. The mixed organic material is able to absorb several times its own weight of liquid oxygen, producing an explosive that is between 4% to 12% more powerful than dynamite. Frenk and others realized that once 'Brennschluss' had occurred, the Rocket's propellant tank would still contain unspent liquid oxygen from the original 4900 kilograms (10,800 lbs) with which it was launched. The next step was to determine how much liquid oxygen would be available and to determine which organic materials would create the greatest possible explosive yield. The greater the Rocket's range implied of course that less liquid oxygen would be available. Extrapolating from Frenk's calculations made in 1943, it would appear that at the upper limit of the Rocket's range of 330 kilometres (205 miles), the amount of liquid oxygen left in the near empty tank would have been less than 50 kilograms (110 lbs). This paltry amount was simply not worth considering, but if the Rocket's range was between 150 kilometres to 250 kilometres (93 to 155 miles) then the quantity of unspent liquid oxygen ranged from 750 kilograms to 275 kilograms (340 to 605 lbs). Consideration was even given to the remaining liquid oxygen in the Rocket's plumbing and heat exchanger. In any event, this made the proposition of using oxyliquit worthy of investigation and, unlike pentrite, it was a cheap alternative that might increase the destructive force of the Rocket. Tests using sawdust and cork with different mixing ratios were considered and experiments using soot-laden oxyliquit were performed at Prüfstand V. A problem that had to be overcome was how the ingredients could mix efficiently in the body of the disintegrating Rocket as it impacted into the ground. It was decided to investigate the placing of prepared packets of oxyliquit in the hollow spaces between the propellant tanks of the Rocket. Perhaps the one overriding problem that led to the abandonment of the oxyliquit project was the excessive amount of time that it took for the organic material to absorb liquid oxygen. Without some very complicated technology to inject oxyliquit directly into the propellant tank during the descent stage, the idea that held such promise seemed to be doomed. Frenk was withdrawn from the oxyliquit research in February 1944 to work on other more pressing projects. The opportunity to return to oxyliquit research occurred during a relatively quiet period of inactivity in January 1945. Frenk suggested to Walther Riedel that the reactivation of the project might be worthwhile. Riedel headed the rocket engine development team following Thiel's death in August 1943 and in the following year he had become the Director of the Development facility at Karlshagen.

Riedel agreed to further research into the use of oxyliquit but the problems that previously had been identified had still to be resolved. Frenk realized that during the descent stage of the decelerating A4, the liquid oxygen would tend to pool at the top the propellant tank. Frenk's proposal was that a membrane in the top of the tank would burst shortly after *Brennschluss* allowing the liquid oxygen to flow out into the void between both the liquid oxygen and the alcohol tanks. The void was to be pre-filled with a mix of coal powder and cork dust during the Rocket's preparation for launch. The descent stage of the Rocket to impact was known to be approximately four minutes and Frenk reasoned that this would allow sufficient time for the liquid oxygen to be absorbed into the organic compounds to produce the explosive, oxyliquit. Upon impact the volatile mix would have been ignited with the explosion of the warhead and Frenk had determined that this procedure, subject to the Rocket's range and quantity of remaining liquid oxygen, would double the explosive effect. Although Frenk appeared to have resolved the earlier difficulties, one important issue however would have remained. At the instant of *Brennschluss*, it would have been essential for the Rocket to arrest any rotational movement along its major axis. Any centrifugal force would have pinned the liquid oxygen to the walls of the propellant tank thus impeding the absorption effect Frenk was trying to achieve. Although the Rocket's rudders were set to a 'zero' position, this only took place after *Brennschluss*. Thereafter, the Rocket behaved like an artillery shell and rotational movement could take place. The reality of the ever-worsening war situation meant that time was running out, and following renewed explosive tests which broke more than one window pane at Peenemünde, the project was cancelled indefinitely and to the best of Frenk's knowledge, oxyliquit was never used in a V2.

Frenk, naturally, appreciated the accolades from his superiors for his innovations that were often born from independent thought. Much of his progress from his earliest days in military service came as a result of personal recommendations. Given the nature of the Nazi military regime and the penalties for an error of judgement, these recommendations were much prized. However, one recommendation that Frenk could well have done without was made in the early days of 1945. It came from Frenk's comrade from his earlier service in the artillery, *Hauptmann* Hohmann. Promoted to the rank of *Oberst*, Hohmann now served on the staff of the ruthless, highly intelligent and ambitious bureaucrat, SS-*Obergruppenführer und General der SS Dr.-Ing*. Hans Kammler.

With a doctorate in civil engineering, Hans Kammler (1901-1945) had been ordered by Himmler to take charge of construction tasks required for the A4 development programme. This was the first move in a convoluted 'chess game'. Ultimately Kammler would replace Dornberger as 'Special SS Commissioner for V2 Operations' in January 1945 and, by April, he was further appointed 'Plenipotentiary of the *Führer* for Jet Aircraft Production and Operational Deployment'. Hohmann was aware that Kammler was constantly drawing valuable men to his ever-increasing staff and, without any hesitation, he drew attention to Frenk's name. On 15 January 1945, Frenk received a telex in which Kammler personally ordered his transfer to the *Division zur Vergeltung (Division z.V)* ('Retaliation Division'). Frenk's superior, *Generalmajor* Josef Rossmann, immediately responded and informed the SS-*Obergruppenführer* that Frenk could not be spared. Kammler would have none of this and repeated the order to Dornberger who responded in a similar fashion and again refused the transfer. Kammler, who was not used to constant refusals, would tolerate no further procrastination and a few days later sent a final telex to Rossmann that could not possibly be refused. It stated that Frenk was to be transferred to the *Division z*.V on 15 March 1945. Kammler reasoned that any further rejection of his order would now be impossible as he was giving full notice which would allow more than enough time for a replacement for Frenk to be found for Rossmann's staff. Additionally, Kammler was giving plenty of time for Frenk to complete any work in which he was currently engaged.

Frenk now faced not only the prospect of joining Kammler's staff but also of being forced to take the rank of SS-*Obersturmführer*. Frenk was keenly aware that the war would soon end and that an association with the SS could mean an extended internment by the Allied POW (Prisoner of War) system – or worse. Rossmann sent a final letter on 19 February again explaining that even beyond mid-March Frenk could not be spared from his duties at Peenemünde and that no replacement would be found for him. Shortly afterwards and with Kammler still not placated, Dornberger decided that the only way forward was to argue the case 'face-to-face' and a meeting was convened with Kammler in the Netherlands. Frenk recalled that the rendezvous occurred at the SS-*Obersturmführer's* headquarters at Apeldoorn. Kammler's main base in early 1945 was at Warstein, 22 kilometres south of Lippstadt, and it is believed that the facility in Apeldoorn may have been a temporary headquarters manned by a skeleton staff. Kammler was renowned for meetings on the move, occasionally at road junctions and it is also possible that his aides may have requisitioned a suitable property at short notice for the meeting. Travelling by air was impossible and so Dornberger, Frenk and a driver travelled the 600 kilometres (372 miles) from Peenemünde to meet with Kammler. Travelling cross-country in a *Kübelwagen* gave the two men time to talk at length: '*Generalmajor* Dornberger was the son of a chemist from Gießen near Wetzlar, my birthplace and close to my parent's home town. Normally I had no personal contact with him but our talk was friendly. He was a good-natured man with none of the attitudes of a "Prussian General".' En route, Frenk and Dornberger realized that they had been spotted by a marauding Allied fighter which dived down to attack them. Careering to a stop they dashed from the *Kübelwagen* to take shelter in a drainage ditch. They lay beside each other as machine gun fire raked the road. As the enemy aircraft disappeared, Frenk looked up to see Dornberger grinning broadly in excited relief. Having arrived safely at Apeldoorn, a meeting was hastily convened and at the appropriate time, Dornberger introduced Frenk to Kammler: 'Kammler sat opposite me. My impression of him was that he was conscious of his power and he possessed a demeanour of cool politeness. Of course, other important things were the main subjects of conversation. But Dornberger did reach settlement because after this I never heard from the SS again.'

From the beginning of 1945, Frenk's time was spent at both Peenemünde and Nordhausen where at the *Mittelwerk* he oversaw gyroscope work. He was often accommodated in the homes of German civilian workers in the surrounding countryside of the Harz Mountains. These men were later to be pressed into the service of the home guard militia of the *Volkssturm*.

By the middle of January 1945, it was becoming clear that it was only a matter of time before defenceless Peenemünde would be overrun by the Soviets and plans were made for an evacuation. The first of several trains of employees and their families departed on 17 February. Convoys of employees who had cars, military vehicles and horse-drawn carts were making their hazardous way to Bleicherode 570 kilometres (354 miles) to the south-west. The dangers of the journey came not only from the Allied fighter-bombers which strafed or bombed anything that moved but also from SS men who were seeking out deserters. Bleicherode was to become the new centre of operations just 16 kilometres (10 miles) west of Nordhausen. But to expect the infrastructure of Peenemünde to move to Bleicherode and to continue pre-evacuation activities was totally unrealistic given Germany's impending collapse. Frenk left Peenemünde for the last time in one of the officially arranged evacuations. In the days just before his departure, he heard that men had escaped from the foreign workers' camp at Trassenheide and had made their way to the *Luftwaffe* airfield on the western side of Peenemünde. This act of desperation might well have been because the workers feared what would happen to them when production ended and they were no longer required. Apparently a group of nine slave workers led by a Russian fighter pilot, Mikhail Petrovichu Devyatayev, who had been shot down seven months earlier, commandeered a He 111 and had flown off. Frenk had no idea as to their fate.

In fact, after a hair-raising take-off and avoiding German attempts to intercept, Devyatayev flew east and crossed the River Oder. Flying over Soviet-held territory, Russian AA fire damaged the aircraft, but Devyatayev successfully landed. Although he and the other escapees provided important information about the activities of Peenemünde, the NKVD (People's Commissariat for Internal Affairs) refused to believe that the 'escape' was made without the cooperation of the Germans. Consequently, he and the others were sent to a military penal unit and six of the hapless men were to die in the Battle of Berlin. Devyatayev himself was not fully 'habilitated' until 1957.

Frenk carried off in his personal luggage a few mementos of his days at Peenemünde: a 7 cm diameter gyroscope and supply transformer recovered from a crashed A4. In taking such mementos, he was taking a great risk; if his suitcase had been searched by over-zealous SS guards conducting spot road checks, he could have been shot as a spy. Frenk stayed in Bleicherode for a few weeks until his outspokenness yet again got him into trouble. A young Major of Frenk's acquaintance was profiteering on the 'Black Market'. With Germany falling apart and with seemingly the whole population in turmoil, it struck Frenk that a soldier of rank should set a better example. Frenk denounced the officer publicly but the accused man apparently was well connected and the matter continued. To shut Frenk up, he was unexpectedly ordered to join a small convoy that was about to drive to Salzburg in Austria, some 600 kilometres (372 miles) to the south-east: 'We had two lorries for the journey, one with a petrol engine and one with a wood/alcohol carburettor. Since we didn't have petrol, the wood carburettor vehicle pulled the other lorry. On the way, an American tank shot at us. We then heard that on a nearby airfield some German fighter aircraft were about to be blown up. We fetched some 100 litres of petrol from there. We abandoned the wood carburettor and drove with the other lorry to Salzburg. We saw the Armistice there on 8 May 1945 and shortly afterwards some American soldiers suddenly appeared in front of us with machine guns. We were taken to a POW camp at Lofer near Salzburg. Then we were moved to another camp at Munich. I was only a POW for a brief time and was treated well. Nobody knew about HAP 11 [the security cover name for Peenemünde] and luckily nothing of the V2 Rocket could be seen in my papers, so I was dismissed in June. I was very lucky and I then returned to Ehringshausen.'

Unknown to Frenk, on 3 April 1945 von Braun and approximately 450 Peenemünde scientists were ordered by Kammler to move from Bleicherode to the resort town of Oberammergau 400 kilometres (249 miles) south, in the district of Garmisch-Partenkirchen in Bavaria. Dornberger had suspected that the scientists would either be used as bargaining chips with the Allies or simply murdered. Oberammergau, famed for its Passion Play, was to be the scene for Kammler's final bloody act – the execution of the scientists at the behest of Hitler. Dornberger confided his worst fears to von Braun and it was decided to make contact as quickly as possible with the advancing Americans and to surrender. On 2 May 1945, von Braun's younger brother, Magnus, nervously cycled to the American line and surrendered the entire contingent of scientists.[10] Under the auspices of the Joint Intelligence Objectives Agency, the Americans, who had been actively searching Germany for the Peenemünde scientists, engineers and technicians, now had to decide who, from the many hundreds of Germans, would be sent to the United States to work on future defence projects. As the investigations and dossiers on the Germans grew, the most important candidates were paper-clipped to produce a list of men to be sent to the United States. Subsequently these most gifted Germans were to be known as the 'Paperclip Scientists'.

Dornberger's situation worsened when the Americans handed him over to the British. He was to be investigated for war crimes and the use of slave labour in the production of the V2. However, the British also needed the assistance of Dornberger in connection with 'Operation Backfire'. 'Backfire' was a British-led evaluation and documentation programme intended fully to evaluate the V2 Rocket and its support equipment. 'Backfire' culminated with three V2 launches in October 1945 from Cuxhaven in northern Germany. Although Dornberger was involved with procedures, he was not allowed to come into direct contact with the former German FR and technicians cajoled by the British into working on 'Backfire'. It was felt that his 'considerable influence might be embarrassing.'[11] He was eventually sent back to England when it was felt he could contribute nothing further. Dornberger then spent two years' confinement in Bridgend, South Wales before he was released and able to travel to the United States as a 'Paperclip Scientist'. Thereafter, he worked on American defence programmes and held positions of military consultancy before retiring to Germany. He died in Obersasbach, Baden-Württemberg in 1980.[12]

Frenk knew many of the 'Paperclip Scientists': Riedel, for example, was destined to be involved in the designing of a much larger version of the V2 engine which was used in the American Redstone short-range surface-to-surface ballistic missile. Ironically, the Redstone was first deployed in West Germany in 1958 at the height of the Cold War. Ultimately the research and development work conducted by the Germans in the employ of the Americans would lead to the mighty engines that powered the Saturn V multi-stage booster which proved crucial to the success of the Apollo lunar landing programme.

Frenk had been a soldier for nearly nine years, but during that time, with the exception of the final two years, he had been able to pursue his academic studies at the State's expense. With the war now over, Frenk was again fortunate, for not only did the Leitz company, which knew him from his military work, employ him but it also supported his continued education. Frenk returned to Göttingen University in October 1945 and in spite of the chaos following the war's end, he and 5,000 other students enrolled. Eventually he received his doctorate which had eluded him during the war. Frenk married in 1947 and thereafter enjoyed not only a happy and satisfying life, but also a rewarding career with over sixty patents to his name working for Leitz at Wetzlar.

Shortly after he was married, Frenk was approached by an old Peenemünde colleague, 'Paperclip Scientist' and friend, Dr. Eberhard Rees. Rees, who had started work at Peenemünde in 1939, had become a manager of A4 assembly and later was appointed as the Director of the NASA Marshall Space Flight Center at Huntsville, Alabama. Rees and several hundred other scientists had joined von Braun's team to further America's interest in ballistic missiles and other areas of military research. Rees and Frenk's meeting was to be the first of several that took place in the years following the war's end.

On numerous occasions Rees encouraged Frenk to emigrate to the United States to work at Huntsville. Frenk always declined in preference to his wife's wishes. On a subsequent reunion at Frenk's home, and while talking about the 'old times', Rees told Frenk that von Braun had, on more than one occasion, told the 'Frenk and latrine' story to fellow Peenemünde people. Rees asked Frenk why von Braun hated him? The answer perhaps was, in part, that von Braun expected total loyalty from his staff. Frenk had, all those years before, attempted to ingratiate himself with von Braun's very own secretary and at von Braun's expense. This was something that von Braun could not tolerate, nor could he ever forgive. It is also conceivable that a pang of jealousy in von Braun might have been aroused.

Frenk met other Peenemünde veterans in 1970 at the 21st International Astronautical Congress held at Konstanz in southern Germany, the two most notable being Dr. Krafft Arnold Ehricke and Professor Hermann Oberth. Ehricke (1917-1984), who had been employed as a propulsion engineer at Peenemünde, had become one of the 'Paperclip Scientists' at the end of the war. Having completed his American government service, Ehricke enjoyed a successful career with Bell Aircraft Corporation and Convair (Consolidated Vultee and Aircraft Corporation). Frenk remembered how he and Ehricke stood together facing an A4 that towered above them at *Prüfstand* VII back at Peenemünde. Ehricke had said, whilst pointing towards the combustion chamber, '...with four or five motors, this could make it all the way to the moon!' That conversation had taken place over a quarter of a century before, but now Frenk sensed an insular change in his old colleague who did not wish to know him any more. Worse was to follow, however, upon meeting Oberth. The visionary founding father of rocketry and astronautics was now nearly seventy-six years old and Frenk felt that perhaps the passage of the years had not been kind to his old friend. Oberth could not remember his neighbour from House 30, Peenemünde. Frenk prompted him, and Oberth replied, 'Frenk? Diploma physicist? I knew a *Leutnant* Frenk.' Frenk replied: *'But I am he!'* – but to no avail, for no flash of recognition came to Oberth's eyes.

It is perhaps surprising, given his experiences, that Frenk's attitude to the 'Paperclippers' and von Braun is so positive. It has often been commented that a feeling of resentment was levelled at the scientists who 'abandoned' their countrymen at a time when their presence could have been of great value to the rebuilding of Germany and her industries. Frenk felt that with the uncertainties of post-war Germany and the possible introduction of the so-called

'Morgenthau Plan' (the post-war American notion that Germany should revert to being an agricultural nation), it was a case of, 'Everybody had to save his own skin in those days.'

Some of the recollections of 'those days' at the start of the 21st century do not fit comfortably into the perception of what Frenk berates as 'Political Correctness', and the manipulation of thought, which he considers has unpleasant parallels with the 'old days': 'I had promised the gyroscope [taken in the final days at Peenemünde] to the museum in Nordhausen close to the *Mittelwerk*. I called a member of staff at the museum and he said: 'That is very nice – thank you, but we [the museum] are concerned that visitors will feel that it will glorify the deeds of the technicians of Hitler. We shall have to let this "disappear" into storage.' The reproaches, which get louder today, are "You were all Nazis. You wanted to help Hitler to get the rockets!" Yes, but those who didn't want to go along with that were just sent off to the front. We thought, we must win otherwise we will have very bad times later. My two brothers fell in 1942. As a result I could not be ordered to the front, but had to work in the armaments industry. The Rocket was only one part in an arsenal of weapons and it was the task of the armaments industry to destroy the enemy. The highly technical work was food for a prospective physicist. I worked positively on the V2, although I knew that it would be used as a weapon. I even collaborated in an attempt to increase the explosive effect of its impact! The V2 would never be a decisive weapon of war; everyone knew it would only give the enemy a few pinpricks. We didn't agree that the V2 was always preferable to the anti-aircraft rocket, the *Wasserfall*. Devastating attacks on German towns were taking place, but the *Wasserfall* was always put back. To win the war the Rocket was a waste. In order to advance rocket technology, however, it was *not* a waste. The first landing of a man on the moon was an event which was due to von Braun's team and comparable perhaps to the invention of the steam-driven engine or the computer. The V2 was an epoch in science.'

The physicist and inventor, Dr. Helmuth Frenk, died after a short illness in Wetzlar, in November 2005.

CHAPTER FIVE

'NOBODY CAN BEAT THIS'

STEFAN BLOMBERG
Versuchskommando Nord and *'Rebstock Lager'*

STEFAN Blomberg was born in Lippstadt, northern Westphalia, in May 1923. He was one of eight children, three of whom were brothers. His family was supported by the wages of his father who was a gardener. Having completed elementary school, Stefan became an apprentice toolmaker. He excelled in his studies and he demonstrated his competence in design and engineering in competitions organized by the overseers in the factory where he worked. Having received his indentures as a qualified journeyman, he began manufacturing control tools in a local ammunition factory which produced anti-aircraft and naval shells. Simultaneously he and his parents were asked if he wished to attend the *Adolf Hitler Schule* (Adolf Hitler School – ASH).

The *Adolf Hitler Schule* and the older more established *Nationalpolitische Erziehungsanstalt* (National Political Educational Establishment – commonly referred to as either NAPOLA or NPEA) were secondary boarding schools, primarily for boys. Entrance to these organizations was highly selective and was considered a great honour. Racial origins, physical fitness and outstanding qualities either demonstrated within the Hitler Youth or, as in the case of Blomberg, within industry, were important criteria for selection. Both the ASH and NAPOLA were operated on a military basis and were organized by the Hitler Youth and the SS respectively. The curriculum at both establishments was varied but could include sports, linguistics, science, arts, humanities and German rites. The ultimate goals of both organizations were to train young people in leadership skills and from this resource, groom future members for the Nazi managerial hierarchy. Blomberg remembered: 'I refused to join – not because I was an anti-Nazi, but because I had had enough of schools. It was war and I wanted to enjoy my life now.'

Because of his exceptional skills in engineering, he was excused from service in the *Reichsarbeitsdienst* (Reich Labour Service) and so as a young man wishing to 'enjoy his life', he entered military service! Having joined the *Heer* in 1941 and after completing basic training at Eschweiler, 15 kilometres west of Aachen in North Rhine-Westphalia, Blomberg awaited his orders for duty. During his initial training he had been assessed as a good *'Schütze'* (gunner) and his new orders were that he was to report to barracks at Cologne for further training to gain a full military driving licence so he could drive both tanks and half-track vehicles. Just before his departure to Cologne, he was ordered to report to the company commander with whom he had developed something of a rapport over the months: 'He said, " I have a letter from Berlin. They're looking for men with your profession. You're not the type of man who will become a good soldier and so I've put your name on the list." I think he liked me, it was like a father/son relationship.'

In late May 1942 Blomberg was granted a weekend's leave and he returned to his parents' home not knowing what the future held for him or where, ultimately, he would be posted. He did not have to wait long for he was soon ordered to report for very special duties at Peenemünde. He travelled by rail to Hamburg and then on to Mecklenburg where, in darkness, the train pulled into a railway siding for a stopover of an undetermined length of time. From the carriage window Blomberg could see a Red Cross station which promised the prospect of a hot meal. Blomberg enquired of a railway employee when the train would resume its journey. The response was at 0600 hrs the following morning when a new locomotive would be coupled to the carriages in order to continue the journey north. Blomberg felt hungry and impetuous. He turned to a fellow soldier traveller who evidently also shared his hunger. Blomberg recalled the unexpected consequences: 'I said to the soldier, "Come on, lets go to the station." We returned two hours later, but the train had gone! The stationmaster told us to take the next regular train, a fast train to Swinemünde and said, "If you're lucky, it will overtake your train. Leave the train at such-and-such station and ask the stationmaster to stop your train. Then you can get back onto your carriage." And it worked! Nobody had missed us. But just at the moment we climbed aboard, the *Feldwebel* [NCO] was making his rounds and saw us. He shouted at us and threatened us, "I'm going to report you! I'll have you court- martialled!" We were so worried but when we arrived at Swinemünde we were quickly separated into work groups and thus out of the control of the *Feldwebel!'*

Upon arriving at Peenemünde in June 1942, Blomberg was assigned initially to accommodation with the 7. *Kompanie* of *Versuchskommando Nord* (VKN – Test Command North) close to the centre of Karlshagen. The *Versuchskommando Nord* settlements, constructed for the thousands of staff that worked at Peenemünde, were fully equipped and enjoyed central heating and running water. Instead of having the appearance of a military camp, the environment was more like a seaside holiday village. The entire place was almost 'make believe', with an atmosphere that gave many the feeling that the war was far away and nothing could ever happen to spoil the idyll. The settlements were well cared for and neat pathways ran from tidy buildings through peaceful pine forests. Everything appeared very tranquil and beautiful. The barracks were shared with the *Heereshelferinnen* (Women's Army Helpers). These female auxiliaries wore civilian clothing and thus the general atmosphere at Peenemünde was completely different to Blomberg's previous experiences. It was not too long before he found himself a girlfriend. One of the many bonuses was the opportunity for all personnel to take evening classes and to further their education.

The central and multi-purpose building at the VKN was given the curious nickname *'Die ewige Pellkartoffel'* (literally translated, 'the eternal unskinned potato'). This was a reference not to the boring food but for the time-saving habit employed by the kitchen staff of the VKN canteen in perpetually serving boiled potatoes unpeeled!

'Die ewige Pellkartoffel' would often host special entertainment evenings with stage productions and operettas featuring well-known artists of the day from Berlin taking the leading roles. The invited 'celebrities' would never be told the true purpose of Peenemünde and how it was in the middle of nowhere that such huge audiences would gather for entertainment. Blomberg recalled that the 'silver screen' film star, Albrecht Schönhals (1888-1978), performed on the stage at the rocket base. In reality, Schönhals' film career had been in the doldrums since 1940 when he had refused to take on the lead role *Jud Süss*, the infamous anti-Semitic film produced under the control of Josef Goebbels, the 'Minister for Public Enlightenment and Propaganda'.

Initially Blomberg was set to work in the *Zusammenbauwerkstatt* (assembly shop) of the Development Works building. Travelling to work wearing his military uniform he would change into green-grey overalls for the day's labours: 'All would wear the same, whether they be an NCO or private soldier. A private could have been the director and an NCO could have cleaned the halls. Military rank and saluting didn't play a role. Smoking was only allowed in the toilet or outside.'

It was in the assembly shop that he saw, for the first time, an object that he was to discover was nicknamed the *'Ofen'* (oven). The red-painted object, which sat on the concrete floor, was in fact a Rocket combustion chamber. At first Blomberg was convinced that the entire facility was producing sea mines. Due to the extraordinary security measures in force, it took him four weeks to discover the true purpose of the object. He and his colleagues never spoke about technical or work-related matters out of work hours. Secrecy was of paramount importance and this was constantly stressed.

His first job was inserting the fuel injector jets into the steel combustion chambers of the A4. However, it was often discovered that the welding of the metal combustion chamber would damage the delicate phosphor bronze threads for the injectors and it was necessary to run a 'tap' down the threaded bore holes to clean out the threads. This was not an easy exercise as access to the threads was difficult. Blomberg created a special tool which was equipped with a hinge so that it was possible to 'run the threads through' no matter what angle was presented to the engineer. The injectors would then be screwed by hand using the same tool into the combustion chambers. The engineers would judge by hand the tightness of the fitment because, as Blomberg recalled, he and the others did not have use of a torque wrench for this procedure. Different 'forms', round and angular, were experimented with to find the best manufacturing procedure to assemble the nozzles of the combustion chamber. Once established, Blomberg had the task of building the forms that held the parts accurately for welding. Combustion chambers that had been tested on the static test platform would be returned to the assembly shop for examination and the fuel injectors would be removed and closely examined.

Blomberg was also involved in the production of the steel outer skin for the Rocket. Every single section required its own pattern and was manufactured to bespoke standards. Welded parts of either the outer skin or the *'Ofen'* would be made on jigs. Larger sections of the Rocket would necessitate proportionally larger jigs and this increased the need for the jigs to be absolutely level, otherwise the finished item would suffer from irretrievable faults. After assembly, the components would be checked for alignment. Every step of the production was controlled to the highest possible standard; the smallest of errors would render a part or assembly useless. Later he was to work on the production of the aluminium propellant tanks which held the liquid oxygen and alcohol.

Blomberg remembered his enthusiasm for the weapon even without seeing the completed Rocket. He recalled his feelings and those of his colleagues at this time: 'There was such a euphoria. We were young men and enthusiastic. I was 19-years old and one of the youngest among us. We were at war and we wanted to win. The English wanted to win and we wanted to win. We, however, had the sense that we were the more advanced. We had a better weapon. When this weapon was deployed, the war would be over!'

Whatever the task, Blomberg took great pride in his work. As far as he was concerned, work furthered his knowledge, fulfilled his great interest in technology and also his personal development. He was not in the least surprised to discover many years later that the Rocket combustion chambers would occasionally survive high-impact speeds. Even with the detonation of the warhead, the largest single relic left smouldering in an impact crater would be the combustion chamber. He recalled: 'The combustion chamber was made from thick cast steel and I'm not surprised that it would survive impact. The metal skin of the Rocket was a minimum of 8 mm thick. We discovered that, when airborne, the (external) rivets would be burnt away and this spoilt the Rocket. Later the Rockets were welded. This was one of my jobs.'

The central area of the enormous Development Works building was sufficiently high to allow completed Rockets to be assembled in the vertical position, surrounded by tall ladders and scaffolding. It was here that he saw for the very first time a completely assembled Rocket. His first thought was: 'What is that?'

He and his colleagues discovered that the closer they got to the more complete A4, the greater the level of security. Of the many thousands who worked on the component parts, only forty or fifty staff from the assembly shop would ever see a complete Rocket. Security badges worn on the left breast indicated the department in which the wearer worked and whether the person was allowed access to an engine test or launching: 'During the Rocket firings,' Blomberg recounted, 'the factory hall doors would be closed. Only few were allowed to watch the launches. I think that most of the employees at Peenemünde never saw the A4 Rocket. We followed the orders for secrecy, and the work was absolutely top secret. Every division had special identity cards. I had permission for the whole area. With a normal job you would speak about your experiences with a colleague after work. When I think back to that time, we never spoke about work in the barracks. I had no idea what the other peoples' jobs were. Not one person in my barracks worked in my division and I would not see them throughout the entire day.'

With his security pass, Blomberg was able to watch the 'fruits of his labour' being prepared for launching: 'I thought to myself, "This is impossible. Simply impossible." But when I saw the first Rocket flying, I thought, "Nobody can beat this."'

Blomberg was fortunate enough to see the successful firing that took place on 3 October 1942. Strangely, those in the workshops did not feel the excitement that was felt by Wernher von Braun, his close circle and superiors; rather, as Blomberg recalled: 'I witnessed all the trial launchings in 1942 and 1943. Many *Prüfstand* VII launches failed and crashed into the surrounding woods, cutting aisles into the forests. The crashed parts would be gathered together. Other Rockets crashed far away into the Baltic Sea. The test-shot on 3 October 1942 was confirmation that the body of the Rocket had to be welded and riveted. Just rivets alone would loosen and lead to an airburst. The success of this firing was an enormous relief. There were no further discussions.'

On returning to his billet at the end of the working day, Blomberg would change out of his military uniform into casual clothes. Depending upon the season, if the weather was good, he would wear sports clothing and perhaps enjoy the sun and sea at the beach. Only if the weather was cold would he wear his uniform for the entire day. During his time at Peenemünde neither he, nor his comrades, ever experienced military 'drill' exercises. For entertainment, Blomberg and his comrades enjoyed sporting activities such as tennis, swimming in the Baltic Sea and table tennis in the settlement sports clubs. Another activity enjoyed by the young men was flirting with the female staff and workers of Peenemünde.

The standard of pay was excellent. Blomberg recalled that during his service at Peenemünde, the pay for an enlisted man in any of the three military services was one Reichsmark per day, and for a German factory worker whose pay was salaried, the highest possible hourly rate was one Reichsmark per hour. Blomberg, however, was paid 1.6 Reichsmarks per hour which equated to not too far short of 90 Reichsmarks per week: 'Honestly, we didn't know what to do with all of the money! I had so much money I would send it home. My father was cross with me and "went up the wall" because he thought I was involved with some illegal business. My parents thought I would be arrested. But I couldn't explain to them.'

Popular places to 'dispose of earnings' were the nearby taverns of Swinemünde and the cathedral town of Wolgast, the latter of which had a dance hall close to its harbour. With their disposable income, Blomberg remembered that he and his friends were 'number one' as they rubbed shoulders with others on leave. On one occasion Blomberg recalled enjoying a quiet drink in one of the local taverns when suddenly raised voices were heard. The commotion was caused by a well-known, highly decorated, Eastern Front combat-hardened *Luftwaffe Oberfeldwebel*. The man, a test pilot who was stationed in the *Luftwaffe* area of Peenemünde, suddenly went into a vodka-induced rage and started to hurl his medals around the bar. The *Feldgendarmerie* (Military Police) had to be called and the airman was driven away. Blomberg had heard that just a few kilometres away, the *Luftwaffe* was testing the highly dangerous Messerschmitt Me 163 *Komet* rocket interceptor and also the Mistel composite aircraft in which a twin-engine Junkers Ju 88 bomber fitted with a hollow-charge warhead in place of its cockpit was delivered to its target by a detachable smaller piloted aircraft, either a Messerschmitt Bf 109 or Focke-Wulf Fw 190. Perhaps the strain of these projects had become too much for the airman. The following evening Blomberg saw the man again in the tavern in a somewhat sullen mood.

The high level of secrecy was extended to the travel permits and 'leave' documents with which Blomberg was issued. Over the years that he was involved with the V-weapons, his employment papers indicated his assignment with spurious companies and addresses in the town of Stettin – yet he had never set foot there! For official purposes, a company called the *Elektromechanische Werke* which was, apparently, based in Karlshagen 'employed' him; this was, of course, a cover for the development works.

Many components for the Rocket were outsourced and Blomberg recalled, as an example, that parts of the aluminium propellant tanks were manufactured by the Fehig company in Salzkotten while components of the electrical batteries were supplied by companies based in North Rhine-Westphalia.

Watching the preparation for either a static engine test or actual launches brought Blomberg into personal contact with Wernher von Braun. It astonished Blomberg that a man who was just eleven years older than he had such responsibility and yet it struck him that in spite of his position, von Braun came across as a 'cordial fellow' and it was easy to strike up a conversation with him. Blomberg recalled one such conversation: 'Remarkably, Wernher von Braun would announce after every firing, "The firing was 100 per cent successful" no matter what the outcome. We didn't know what purpose each test-firing was to serve. Sometimes materials were tested, while another time it could be the guidance system – which was often problematic. But the trials were always "successful".'

Blomberg was aware that von Braun had a great interest in space travel and had heard that he had commented on his ambition '... to explore the Moon and space'. He also heard a rumour that in the Peenemünde supersonic wind tunnel, a much larger Rocket was being evaluated and he presumed that von Braun was perhaps testing a variant intended for space travel. In reality however, it might have been the long-range A-9/A-10 that was being studied. This, the so-called 'America Rocket' would have been approximately twice the length and speed of an A4 with a range of 5000 kilometres (3,107 miles). If this multi-staged weapon had been built, it would still have fallen short of reaching the eastern seaboard of the United States.[1]

Blomberg also recalled that von Braun introduced work practices for German workers at Peenemünde that were very different to the accepted norm in factories elsewhere in the Reich: 'Of the personality of von Braun, I can tell you that when Goebbels declared "Total War" in his speech given at the *Sportpalast* in Berlin (18 February 1943), German industry, including the Peenemünde complex, extended its working day from 0600 hrs to 1800 hrs but when von Braun returned from a visit to Berlin, he changed our hours back to 0800 hrs to 1800 hrs. Von Braun said, "We are involved with research, not mass production." During the Christmas and New Year festivities he permitted only a skeleton staff comprising fire brigades, heating technicians and other such essentials, whilst everyone else departed from Peenemünde by special trains to all directions. Such a boss you would want even today!'

One day Blomberg observed workers digging air raid slip trenches close to his accommodation building. Up until this time he had been aware only of one air raid shelter and that was simply a shelter room at the settlement's school. He did not give this a great deal of attention until a few days later when, on the evening of 17 August 1943, the sirens wailed. It was not uncommon for the night-time siren alarms to be shrugged off and as had happened many times before, the sleep-disturbed residents of the barracks merely pulled their blankets a little higher. Peenemünde had heard the siren many times before and on all occasions it would prove to be a false alarm. But not that night. It was just 35 minutes to midnight when the alarm went off, which was followed quickly by fully dressed and helmeted officers running into barracks shouting '*Alarm!* Get up! *Alarm!*' The sleepy occupants emptied out into a misty night by their nearest exit. Lit by a near full moon shining low to the south, they sheltered in the trenches. High above Peenemünde, twelve RAF Mosquitos had begun a diversionary operation that would see them flying over Berlin 450 kilometres away to the south. But at Peenemünde, once again nothing happened and the drone of aircraft gradually faded. Although the 'all-clear' was not heard, Blomberg and the other men returned to the beds that they had left just thirty minutes before. Blomberg recalled: 'This had never happened before and it set us thinking. We had left our room hurriedly through the windows wearing our sportswear and jumped into a trench. But after a short time of inactivity we decided to return to our beds.'

However, an hour or so later the sound of approaching aircraft returned to be followed by the most intensive and concentrated attack by RAF Bomber Command since the outbreak of war. Blomberg recalled: 'There were so many aircraft! We could see their bomb doors opening and the bombs falling. I cannot remember having seen any Flak defence. It was lucky for our barracks that the *Kriegsmarine* had laid smoke about the island. Because of the westerly wind, the fog drifted eastward and the aircraft dropped their bombs directly into it. The fog soon disappeared however because of the pressure of the explosions. The bombed area stretched from the assembly shop, House 4, over to Trassenheide but missed the *Heer* barracks. Many civilians became casualties of the raid but Trassenheide camp suffered the highest death toll. I believe the electrified overhead railway cables came down on the camp perimeter fence and many people who wanted to escape died climbing over the fence. Peenemünde was a fireball!'

Blomberg had previously experienced the devastating air raid on the city of Cologne on 31 May 1942 just before his posting. On that occasion the RAF had massed its first '1,000 bomber' attack. In that raid, 13,000 homes were destroyed and 469 died, but the air raid on Peenemünde was of a completely different magnitude. He recalled: 'I think, the air raid against Peenemünde was the heaviest up until that time. We thought it was the end of the world. And yet nowhere was it mentioned on the radio or in the newspapers. Later I experienced several other air raids – Munich and Berlin – it was as if the air raids followed me. But I never saw such a heavy raid as at Peenemünde. Many people who spend their holidays on the island of Usedom say, "It is so beautiful." I say, "Yes, and if the war for me had another end, I would have never left the island"!'

The RAF had brought to bear 596 bombers to strike at Peenemünde in three waves of attack. The total tonnage of bombs dropped was 1,528 of which 267 tonnes were incendiary bombs. The first wave dropped the majority of bombs on the foreign workers' labour camp at Trassenheide in error, as the main target had been the housing estate. This attack, of fifteen minutes, was conducted without any harassment by *Luftwaffe* night fighters which had been distracted by the presence of the Mosquitos over Berlin. The second wave was intended for the V2 production area, the factory halls in which Blomberg worked. However, the majority of the bombs fell onto the beach and sea. As this 11-minute attack ebbed, the *Luftwaffe* night fighters which had been directed to Berlin started to arrive upon the scene. The third and final attack began as the second wave of Lancasters departed. The target was now the Experimental Works and this time the RAF received a considerable mauling from the night fighters. Of 560 RAF aircraft that are believed to have participated in the attack on Peenemünde, 39 failed to return, one was written off and 245 aircrew lost their lives.[2]

For Blomberg several mysteries remained from that dreadful night. Was it just a fortunate coincidence that a few days before the attack someone decided to issue orders for the hastily constructed slip trenches? Why did the officer corps appear to have been prepared for the attack when they kicked the slumbering soldiers out of their beds? Blomberg is of the opinion that no matter how bizarre it might seem, the German High Command had 'notice' of the pending attack and that the RAF had been betrayed. There had, in fact, been no betrayal – other than that caused inadvertently by an increase in enemy aircraft reconnaissance sorties in the area prior to the raid. Because of this, *Generalmajor* Dornberger had received a warning from Berlin of imminent air attack a few days before 17 August.

As the morning of 18 August dawned, Blomberg and many others gravitated towards the school at Karlshagen for news and to receive instructions in support of the search and rescue operations. Rescue parties set to work hunting through the rubble of houses and collapsed cellars searching for victims. Throughout the morning Blomberg helped friends billeted in the barracks as they sifted through the rubble for their possessions and for survivors. He visited his place of work in the Development Works assembly shop where only the day before he had been assembling combustion chambers. The building had been destroyed, but the nearby Rocket-firing position *Prüfstand* VII was hardly touched.

For the first day after the attack, Blomberg and others in his billet were housed temporarily at Hohendorf close to Wolgast and in the evening he was detailed to return to Peenemünde to guard *Prüfstand* VII for the night. For Blomberg and the other guards the anxiety was not that the RAF would return to wreak further destruction, but the possibility of an aerial invasion by British commando paratroopers. Blomberg recalled that he and the other guards felt very apprehensive that night as they patrolled around the raised earthworks of *Prüfstand* VII flanked on two sides by the dark forests. He confessed: 'Even if a fox had come out of the woods, we would have run away!'

Fortunately the bombers did not return and nor did the sky fill with British parachute silk. Later the following day Blomberg remembered: 'We helped people to move to other places on the island or the mainland, but there was little organization. Many of them were in a state of shock. A person could have swam to Sweden and nobody would have missed him. Such chaos. But two days later some form of military organization came into being again. First, a sign appeared: "Looters will be shot!" For the next two weeks we cleaned up, bringing bodies out into the street.'

Blomberg and his comrades stayed in Hohendorf for about two weeks, daily walking the 3 kilometres from the village to Wolgast railway station before catching a train, then changing at Zinnowitz for Peenemünde. Afterwards he was billeted at Swinemünde, which was considered to be a better location for security reasons.

Sometime shortly after the air raid Blomberg remembered that von Braun, who now held the title of *Professor*, called for a meeting in the huge factory hall. Von Braun intended to motivate the demoralized workforce. Standing in front of hundreds of technicians and engineers he pronounced: 'They can try to destroy us here, but production is up and running and it cannot be stopped.'

Yet an immediate problem of supply had to be resolved. The destruction wrought by the bombs had caused the loss of all factory forklift trucks and 'electro cars'. These had to be replaced immediately. In a command of nine other men Blomberg was ordered to travel to the Mirag-Werke in Oberramstadt near Darmstadt in order to secure fresh replacements and arrange their transportation back to Peenemünde so they could be put to work as quickly as possible. Blomberg had been at Oberramstadt for a few weeks when he received telegrammed orders to travel to '*Rebstock Lager*' (Vine Camp) located halfway between Remagen and Ahrweiler and about 20 kilometres south of Bonn. This camp was the billet for German military personnel who worked at '*Rebstock*' which was the codename given to the underground factory at Dernau–Marienthal west of Ahrweiler.

'*Rebstock*' was an underground fortress factory complex that Blomberg recalled was built around three disused railway tunnels under the mountain at Marienthal. It was a perfect location that was safe from Allied bombing. Blomberg discovered that the tunnels had been constructed before the

First World War to service communication between Berlin and Paris, but the tracks had never been laid. He was to work in the main tunnel that ran between Dernau and Maischoß. The cover story concocted to protect the complex's true purpose was that the site was part of the factory organization of the steel construction company of Johannes Gollnow & Sohn based in Stettin. In truth, from the summer of 1943, a 7,000-strong labour force of mostly slave workers, overseen by German technicians and guarded by SS personnel, worked in 'Rebstock's subterranean industries, producing military equipment for the V-weapons.[3] Fifty of these individuals worked in the division in which Blomberg was deployed. He recalled: 'We assembled the movable launching pads (*Meillerwagen*) and from 'Rebstock' they were taken by the *Wehrmacht* and went off to the front. We had one complete V2 with which we were able to test all electrical connections and functions to the different vehicles we manufactured.'

Not only did the A4 slave workers build the *Meillerwagen* mobile launch vehicles, but also the *Feuerleitpanzer* (see Chapter Two), the Opel Blitz mobile radio vehicle that would transmit the emergency *Brennschluss* signal, and other supply vehicles and trailers. The slave workers were mainly Russian, but after the capitulation of a former German ally on 3 September 1943, increasing numbers of Italian prisoners of war were also used. Blomberg remembered that the Italians refurbished the tunnels that had previously been used in the cultivation of mushrooms. Later technicians, engineers and mechanics were scoured from the vast concentration camp organization of the Reich and the occupied territories, many being sourced from the infamous *Mittelwerk* at Nordhausen, including nationals from Poland and France. Conditions for the slave workers were appalling as they toiled in caves that seeped with dripping water. Blomberg recalled: 'Our prisoners lived in the tunnel and never came out, but they lived in better conditions than those in the *Mittelwerk*. For every German worker there would be two or three helpers. Guarded by the SS, it was strictly forbidden to talk with them. The name of one I will never forget: Maurice Moreau, from Paris. He was about my age, and spoke a little German, and I a little French. When you work together with a man for three months, a lot of information comes across. He was such a fine fellow. One day the SS checked the lockers of the workers and found food – apparently stolen. I asked Maurice, "What will they do with you now?" He replied, "They'll give us a beating tonight". I then reported to my superior. The next morning only the prisoners of our department came to work. The others reported ill.'

Research into the wartime occupation of Maurice Moreau proved to be very representative of the experiences of many thousands who worked on the V2. The hardships endured by the foreign and slave workers should not be forgotten. From official documents it is known that Moreau was born on 19 July 1924 in Paris. During the early part of the occupation he, like many thousands of his countrymen, was employed by the Germans as a 'foreign worker' in the Reich's expanding military industries. In October 1940 he was employed as an unskilled worker at the *Russwerke*, a soot factory in Dortmund. Extraordinary though it might seem, soot, far from being a polluting waste, is in fact a valuable material that has many useful industrial applications and in this regard the account given previously by Helmuth Frenk is a perfect illustration. It is believed that at the *Russwerke*, Moreau was trained as a milling machine operator when, in February 1941, he was further employed at the BMW factory in Munich. His movements and employment are not known with certainty, but in September 1942 whilst possibly in Belgium, Moreau was treated by German doctors for a suspected stomach ulcer to which he responded well. It was further reported by the doctor who administered to him that Moreau was of 'light build' and was in less than average physical condition in spite of good lungs and heart. In January 1943, while in Berlin, Moreau signed a further one year contract of employment with the *Deutsche Vemittlungsstelle* (German Exchange Office) and was sent to work with an unidentified employer in south-west Germany. However on 15 March 1943, Moreau was admitted to a hospital in Sigmaringen, 77 kilometres south of Stuttgart, having complained yet again of stomach pains. The doctors were not convinced however, and believed that he was feigning illness to avoid work! In any event, the doctors discharged him from hospital declaring him 'unfit for work' on 1 April. It is not known why Moreau may have been feigning illness. Perhaps he was simply 'homesick'. Breaking his contract on the grounds of ill health would mean he could officially return to his home in Paris. Thereafter Moreau was presumed as unemployable but on 30 June 1944 he was arrested for 'political' reasons in Saint Denis and transferred to the prison of Fresnes. On 15 August he was deported by train and arrived five days later at the concentration camp at Buchenwald. Upon arrival he was given the prisoner identification number 77462.[4] His stay at Buchenwald was short as he was then transported to the sub-camp of *Rebstock* on 4 September 1944 where he was to meet Blomberg.

In stark contrast to the slave workers, Blomberg and his colleagues were accommodated two kilometres away in the *Neuenahrer Hof* hotel in the small town of Bad Neuenahr-Ahrweiler where, by his own admission: 'We lived like dukes.'

It is not known how many slave workers died at *Rebstock* but it is believed that at the *Mittelwerk* 20,000 workers died. The V1 and the V2 share the grisly statistic that more died in the production of these weapons than were actually killed during their deployment.

It was at *Rebstock* that Blomberg became aware of the presence of the *Fernraketen* troops. Of course they were present at Peenemünde, but Blomberg's responsibilities were such that he never had direct contact with them. In the underground tunnels he recalled seeing the FR troops receiving instruction and being trained in the use of the *Meillerwagen*. Blomberg recalled: 'The *Meillerwagen* and the moving of the Rocket upon the *Abschusstisch* (firing table) worked very well. Any soldier with a little technical understanding could do this; for example, a car mechanic. However the launching procedure, and the computing of the position and direction required specially trained, mostly university-educated men.'

During his stay at *Rebstock*, Blomberg was ordered to Peenemünde briefly and was amazed at the changes he saw. Due to the distractions of his work he had forgotten the destruction that had befallen the research centre. The natural beauty of the pine forests had been wrecked by gaping craters, the trees had either been blown down by bomb blasts or reduced to splintered stumps. The pathways, once well-tended, were now abandoned and nature was reclaiming them. Buildings remained shattered intentionally in order to give the impression to Allied reconnaissance aircraft that Peenemünde had ceased to function. He also noticed the ever-increasing number of SS uniforms. He recalled: 'Peenemünde was like a dead town with no life in it. Before the air raid we had a relatively free life, but afterwards the *Waffen*-SS took very strict control over everything.'

On one occasion, Blomberg was returning to *Rebstock* following official business away when enemy aircraft attacked the mountain: 'I and others were just walking up to the tunnel entrance. Suddenly we saw the fighter-bombers coming in and we found ourselves at the receiving end of a low-level enemy air attack. The air ventilation system for the tunnels was located in the outskirts of the town of Maischoß, which lay approximately two kilometres south-west of *Rebstock*. This installation was destroyed during the attack. We believed that one of our fellow soldiers, who lived in Aachen and who had not returned from a weekend leave at the time of the capture of Aachen by the Allies, had been caught and betrayed the works' location.'

From Blomberg's account, this incident must have taken place sometime after 21 October 1944 when Aachen became the first German city to be taken by the Allies. The area around *Rebstock* was becoming increasingly insecure due to the Allied advance. By mid-December 1944, the facility was abandoned in the face of the advance of the US First Army. Blomberg, his colleagues and the practice V2 used for testing support equipment, moved from the underground factory to a new location some 285 kilometres to the north-east at the facilities of the Kyffhäuser Maschinenfabrik Artern GmbH, a metal fabricating company 40 kilometres north of Weimar in the province of Thüringen. In peacetime Kyffhäuser Maschinenfabrik manufactured agricultural equipment but, in common with other metal fabricators in Germany, its production lines were turned over to the war effort. Approximately 50 slave workers, including Moreau from *Rebstock*, arrived at Artern on 28 December 1944. Blomberg, his colleagues and the slave workers continued to prepare launching equipment. It was at Artern that Blomberg was to see the war's end, but not so the unfortunate slave workers.

On 30 January 1945 Blomberg was officially dismissed from the *Heer* and was thereafter employed as a civilian by the Elektromechanische Werk at Karlshagen (EMW). The EMW was, again, a 'cover name' to protect the security of the Development Works at Peenemünde and, as such, Blomberg was no longer required to wear his military uniform. This would cause enormous problems when travelling and when on 'home leave'. It was the practice at the time that military men would always wear their uniforms when not on duty and especially so when enjoying furlough. As a young fit man of obvious military age, not only was he challenged at security checkpoints, but friends and relatives would also question his occupation. His official papers would, of course, satisfy the security men, but his family and friends – without an explanation of his employment – remained curious and mystified.

Work continued at Artern in spite of the nearby railway station and the slave workers' camp being attacked by Allied aircraft on 31 March 1945. Suddenly, and without warning, on 2 April the slave workers, including Moreau, disappeared from their accommodation shed, never to be seen again by Blomberg. Not knowing the fate of the Parisian, Moreau, has given Blomberg cause for much consternation throughout his life. Following the end of the war, and with the growing knowledge of the brutality meted out in the final days of the Third Reich to its slave workers, he had always feared the worst.

During the preparation of this work, the writers were able to study certain documents held in archives in France and others from sources in Germany. As a result, they were able to establish that Moreau and 250 other slave workers from Artern were transported by foot under SS guard to the crowded concentration camp of Rehmsdorf, 30 kilometres south-west of Leipzig. Due to the barbarity of the SS in the final days of the war, this journey and many others that took place, became known as 'Death Marches'. For Moreau and others from *Rebstock* and Artern, the journey to Rehmsdorf of 93 kilometres lasted three days. On 6 April the SS began to implement the closure of the camp and the transportation of the prisoners to Czechoslovakia. Later that night, Moreau and 2,500 other surviving prisoners were crammed into open-topped rail wagons – so tightly that movement was impossible. Their destination was to be Theresienstad and, ultimately, their extermination. The 250 metre-long train had to return several times to Rehmsdorf because the railway line ahead was constantly under attack from Allied fighter-bombers. During the repairs to the track, the prisoners were not allowed to disembark, nor were they fed or watered. As the weaker prisoners perished under the snow-laden skies, their deaths gradually improved the cramped conditions for the living. Having started the journey some eight days earlier, the train had only travelled a straight-line distance of 82 kilometres when it arrived at the sidings of Gelobtland, just three kilometres south of Marienberg on 15 April. With no end to the misery in sight, the guards and inmates alike heard the sounds of approaching Allied fighters. The prisoners were forced to stay in the wagons while the SS guards sought shelter, not only under the carriages, but in the woods that ran parallel to the track. As they came in to attack, the American fighter pilots observed the uniformed men running for cover and as they swooped down, they strafed the woods either side of the railway track with heavy machine gun fire. It is believed that it was at that moment of great commotion that Moreau and two other French nationals, Bernard Guerin and Rene Vanicel (who had both been members of the Resistance), took their chance. Although in a dreadfully weakened state, they fled their wagon and, risking not only the rifle fire of the SS guards, but also the machine gun fire from the American fighters, escaped to the cover of the woods. It was indeed most fortunate that Moreau seized his opportunity for freedom when he did, for what followed was a further descent into a hell of unimaginable depths. Following the air attack, the SS guards quickly regained control and the train continued its journey, the surviving number of prisoners having fallen to 2,000. The following day as the train was approaching the village of Reitzenhain, American fighters attacked again, not only destroying the tracks in front of the locomotive, but also holing the locomotive's boiler. Many prisoners were gunned down as they attempted to escape and over the next two days other escapees were rounded up and shot. Now that rail travel was impossible, the SS decided to continue the remaining journey of 80 kilometres on foot to Theresienstad. Just five kilometres from the camp, the guards separated the 1,000 Jews from the remaining prisoners who then marched into the camp where they were soon mercifully liberated by the Soviets. Nine hundred remained alive. It was decided by the SS that the other 800 non-Jewish prisoners should be sent to Dachau, but this was impossible because all of Bavaria was occupied by the Allies. Instead they were loaded back onto wagons and spent the next two weeks without food or water, being transported backwards and forwards, with stationary periods lasting as long as seven days at railway sidings before being liberated by the Czechoslovakian partisans on 8 May 1945.[5]

By means unknown, Moreau and his two fellow escapees avoided capture, then travelled the breadth of Germany, over 580 kilometres, to cross the border back into France at Sarreguemines a few kilometres south of Saarbrücken, on 1 or 2 May. He returned to his home in Paris about two days later.

With the deportation of the slave workers, V2 support vehicle and ground support equipment production at Artern ended on 15 April 1945 when the area was overrun by the Americans. Curiously, Allied soldiers passed by on their advance and took no notice of the factory in spite of the equipment that was being manufactured within its halls. It is possible that the Americans knew that two weeks earlier the management of the Kyffhäuser Maschinenfabrik had set about the systematic destruction of all electrical devices within the factory. Blomberg speculated that the Allies may have assumed that it was only a technical unit, but whatever the reason, eight uneasy days passed until eventually orders from the Americans were given that none of the 150 men who had worked at Kyffhäuser Maschinenfabrik were allowed to leave the town of Artern until further notice. Unfortunately, a former colleague – an Italian – attempted to denounce Blomberg to the Americans as a combatant and accused him of masquerading as a civilian. The Americans, having now penetrated so deeply into Germany, would have seen many such instances of men hiding their former membership of organizations such as the SS and so Blomberg was closely scrutinized. However, his paperwork was correct and indicated that he had, indeed, been dismissed from the military and was now in the employment of the Elektromechanische Werk in Karlshagen. Nevertheless, his papers did not indicate why he had left the *Heer* and the Americans pressed him for an explanation. Blomberg responded, 'lung disease'. This satisfied the inquisitors temporarily but doubtless careful notes were made about his paperwork.

Blomberg and a colleague, Günther Nöcker, who had also been in the *Heer* but was now dressed as a civilian, decided to take matters into their own hands. Blomberg recalled a conversation he had: 'I said, "Günther, I don't trust them. In the end, they will shoot us as war criminals because we worked on the secret weapons. We need to escape."'

As luck would have it, in the dusty factory hall, Blomberg and the other technicians discovered a complete railway wagon which, despite its military livery, was, in fact, fully laden with the private property of either the manager or the owner of Gollnow & Sohn. The wagon was awaiting a steam train so that it could 'disappear' to the West. They broke into the wagon and discovered a treasure trove that included food, spirits, hunting rifles, furniture and, curiously, new bicycles. The first items to be taken were bottles of cognac, food and a pair of bicycles. Following an impromptu private celebration of 'victory', Blomberg and his friend decided to escape on the bicycles and, using a military map, navigated their way along quiet lanes and forest tracks, avoiding Allied soldiers. Feeling confident, Blomberg interrupted his journey to stay a night at his girlfriend's parents' home in Nordhausen. Just 90 kilometres from home, at the entrance of a village near Kassel, Blomberg and Nöcker were challenged by a Belgian soldier who asked to see their travel permits. They presented their discharge papers which had been prepared by the secretarial staff of Kyffhäuser Maschinenfabrik. The papers had been written in both English and German, neither of which the guard could read, but nevertheless they seemed to satisfy him and they were waved on. After three days travel of approximately 175 kilometres, Blomberg finally reached his parents' home in Lippstadt on 3 May 1945. Now, at last, he could tell his mother and father of his important wartime service in the production of the V2 wonder weapon and that he was not a shadowy gangster dealing in the black market. They were both relieved and astounded to hear of his experiences dating back three years.

With what was left of German industry in turmoil, Blomberg decided to work temporarily at his brother's farm, but hoped that one day he could return to his former employment as an engineer. In October 1945, whilst working in the fields, he heard that in the town of Lippstadt, British and American officers were enquiring as to the whereabouts of a certain Stefan Blomberg! He had no idea why they were making such enquiries but presumed it must have had something to do with his work on the V2. Perhaps the interest related to his interrogation by the Americans at Artern? In any event, by keeping a low profile and with no local people informing the officers as to his location, he was able to avoid any further questioning.

The local Labour Exchange was sending unemployed men to work in the nearby potash mines, which was an occupation Blomberg wanted to avoid. The mines were hungry for workers but Blomberg was fortunate to be advised by a friend he knew at the exchange that his best option was to either continue being a farmer or alternatively to become a builder. Taking the advice, he worked for three months as a handyman and bricklayer until the demand for miners had ebbed. Then he made approaches to an engineering works and started to work for Rote Erde GmbH in Lippstadt. He disliked shift work but eventually was able to get employment at the Hella company, also in Lippstadt, where he worked in the development section until his retirement.

Blomberg considers himself to have had an extraordinarily lucky life during the war. All of his comrades from his home town of Lippstadt who joined up when he did, died very early on the Eastern Front. He considers himself very fortunate to have been chosen to work on the Rocket – work that he found extremely satisfying. The memories of working and living at Peenemünde, and how it was before the devastating RAF raid on the night of 17 August 1943 left a deep impression on him. In spite of the dangers of the 'old times', in particular the air raids at Peenemünde and elsewhere, Blomberg recalled that when the war ended, he had 'tears in the eyes'. These were not tears of relief or of regret but were brought about by the knowledge that for him, now just twenty-two years of age, a most extraordinary episode of his life had come to a close. The future was uncertain and perhaps would never quite compare to what had gone before.

CHAPTER SIX

'AN INDESCRIBABLE AND UNFORGETTABLE IMPRESSION...'

WALTER KLEIN
Lehr- und Versuchsbatterie 444

WALTER Klein was born in 1922 in Stuttgart, Germany. As a young boy, he joined the *Hitlerjugend*. Contrary to generalized post-war perceptions, he was never aware of any brutalizing indoctrination or brainwashing in the Nazi youth movement; instead his memories are of summer camps, group singing and friends who, like himself, were not in the least politically minded. The reality, of course, was that the Germany in which he grew up changed radically around his eleventh year when the Nazis came to power. One sweeping change to school education was that the teaching of foreign languages was banned as, in time, it was said all countries would ultimately speak German.

Having completed his grammar school education and final examinations, he enlisted for three months' service in the *Reichsarbeitsdienst* (Reich Labour Service). Thereafter he volunteered as an infantryman in the *Heer* in September 1940. After basic military training his first day of action as a nineteen-year old was also the first day of Operation *Barbarossa*, the German invasion of Soviet Russia on 22 June 1941. The experience of his service in Russia was so terrible that more than 60 years after the event, it was impossible for him to discuss it without emotion. As he was to remember: 'Of my life on the Eastern Front, one could write a whole book. I was almost a year in action from the beginning of the Eastern campaign, fighting in the Smolensk area until we reached about 18 kilometres (11 miles) from Moscow, and then back. From the so-called Central Sector of the Eastern Front, from 50° C in the summer, to minus 50° C in winter, to the Southern Sector in heavy defence and a fighting retreat. One always had death, injury or captivity in mind, but the view then was to do one's duty, to win the war and save the west from Bolshevism.'

Klein, amazed that he had survived so far without serious injury, volunteered to attend *Kriegs-Offiziersschule* (War Officers' Training School) back in Germany. Having completed four months of education and training, he was then thrust back into action in the southern sector of the front, north-east of Dnipropetrovsk in the Ukraine in April 1942.

The town of Dnipropetrovsk on the Dnieper River had been the scene of a desperate series of battles during which the average life span of an infantry lieutenant at the front was just six weeks. Two-thirds of his fellow comrades from the *Kriegs-Offiziersschule* were to die. Constantly changing front lines resulted in many casualties until ultimately, the Red Army forced a break in the German defensive line to establish a small bridgehead across the Dnieper on 21 September 1943. Five weeks later, the town fell to the Soviets, which in turn led to the liberation of Kiev.

Fortunately for Klein, in July 1943 he received instructions to report, with the utmost urgency, from the Eastern Front to the *Heimatartilleriepark* 11 (HAP 11 – Home Artillery Park 11) at Peenemünde. His orders were to present himself to the Chief of Development, *Oberstleutnant* Gerhard Stegmaier. Travelling by train directly from Dnipropetrovsk to Peenemünde in a goods wagon, he was in a filthy condition by the time he reached Lemberg in Poland and had to be deloused.

In early July 1943, *Lehr- und Versuchsbatterie motorisiert* 93 (Motorized Demonstration and Depot Battery 93), the first military Rocket unit for training, testing and evaluation of the A4, was formed under *Oberstleutnant* Stegmaier. The unit was known by its abbreviated nomenclature of '*Mot.* 93'. By mid July 1943, the *Mot.* 93 was renamed *Lehr- und Versuchsbatterie* 444 (Training and Experimental Battery 444) but was commonly referred to as *Batterie* 444. Later, Stegmaier founded *Kommando-Stelle* S, the long-range missile and V2 training school at Köslin.

Stegmaier was able to draw upon the readily available staff of the *Versuchskommando Nord* (VKN – Test Command North) stationed in Peenemünde and a railway artillery unit in Rügenwalde, but because of the priority of the Rocket programme, he could call for personnel from any of the armed services. As Klein remembered: 'I had known Stegmaier since 1942, for my sister, Erika, was his civilian secretary at Peenemünde. He knew me and after Erika put my name forward, he wanted me. I would not be alive today if this new posting had not happened. A prerequisite was that the selected personnel were reliable, trustworthy and dedicated. Apparently, Erika had told Stegmaier that her brother was one such man. These requirements for men went over the heads of the Supreme Command of the Armed Forces in Berlin.'

Klein decided to take advantage of the time between postings. By a happy coincidence, his sister was due to marry in his home town of Stuttgart.

The question arose of how he could justify the detour if he was pressed to explain his delay in reporting to Peenemünde. The answer was simple, for at his parents' home, stored in safe keeping in the cellar, was his spare uniform. Returning home his father greeted him and explained that the rest of the family were at the local church as the marriage was taking place that very hour. His father immediately set off for the church whilst Klein quickly changed into his spare uniform. He arrived at the church at the precise moment that the pastor announced to the congregation that it was regrettable that the bride's brother could not attend as he was serving on the Eastern Front!

Klein was now faced with a dilemma. Firstly, he had made an enormous detour to collect a uniform and he had already delayed his departure to Peenemünde because of the wedding ceremony. In spite of wishing to stay for the wedding reception, he decided that he must not delay any further reporting to Stegmaier. With a very guilty conscience and expecting a severe rebuke for his delay, Klein later entered Stegmaier's office at Peenemünde and reported for duty. Stegmaier, like Klein, was from Swabia, a rural area of Germany's south-western state of Baden-Württemberg, its capital being Stuttgart. Stegmaier was imbued with many of the qualities associated with a native of the region – slow, affable and correct. Stegmaier looked up from his desk and said: 'Ah! Klein you have arrived already. I didn't expect you so early.'

Klein now realized that he could have not only stayed for his sister's wedding reception but also delayed his departure to Peenemünde by several days. Stegmaier was a man in his forties and Klein remembered: 'He was a very good reserve officer, but at the same time a good comrade – reliable and honest. Everyone liked him. Most officers were arrogant, but not him. He was a teacher at a professional school in Göppingen. Within the officers in our group he was called "Papa" Stegmaier and that describes him very well.'

The move from active service on the Eastern Front to duties at Peenemünde convinced Klein that his life had been spared and, not only that, but he now served in a battalion that he was to describe with much understatement as *'Interesting!'*

Klein now had a Batman, or *Bursche* ('fellow'), his own chauffeur-driven car and after the appalling conditions of the Eastern Front, his own bed and private quarters. He too, like many other servicemen posted to Peenemünde from the Eastern and Southern Fronts, was struck by the casual peacefulness of the new environment. As he was to recall: 'I felt that Peenemünde was extremely peaceful – like paradise. With regard to equipment and catering, Peenemünde, and later Heidelager, enjoyed a certain priority in the armed forces. Not only more high quality food, but also petrol at a time when it was very scarce. They (the superiors) wanted to encourage us to have the V2 operational as soon as possible. We enjoyed the better food but I don't think it had any influence one way or the other on deployment.'

The two-storey barracks for the *Fernraketen* (long-range rocket) troops was sited in a conifer forest approximately 2 kilometres south-west of Karlshagen and close to the village harbour. A surprising but welcome aspect of life for the men posted to Peenemünde was the extraordinary number of young women who worked and lived at the centre. Located on the opposite side of the cobbled street to the FR troops was the accommodation for the *Stabshelferinnen* (female staff assistants) who had been called up for war service. The women worked in the numerous departments in either secretarial or in clerical roles, and one of the young residents billeted opposite Klein's quarters was his sister, Erika.

The sounds of Rocket tests and static test-firings by the scientists and the trainees of *Batterie* 444, supported by civilian engineer specialists at *Prüfstand* VII, routinely shattered the quiet idyll of Peenemünde. Eventually the specialists would be put into uniform and given the rank of *Gefreiter* (Lance Corporal) and were later appointed '*Sonderführer*' ('special leaders') at Heidelager and in the field. It was the practice that these men would be called upon in the event of the launching crews experiencing difficulties with the Rocket. Initially at Peenemünde, the Rocket was hoisted onto the *Prüfstand* by the use of motorized cranes and hydraulic lifts. By September 1943, *Batterie* 444 was able to carry out launches independently.

Among his many duties, occasionally Klein would be ordered to courier sealed secret reports and documents between Peenemünde and the offices of the *Oberkommando der Wehrmacht* (OKW – *Wehrmacht* High Command) in the Tirpitzufer in Berlin. The duty would begin with a short journey from Peenemünde using the private military railway service to the seaside village of Zinnowitz. From here he would change to the national railway for the 175 kilometres (110 miles) journey south to the capital. Travelling invariably alone by train, Klein did not particularly enjoy this duty. The standard procedure for security was that the conductor would lock the courier into his compartment, having emptied out the passengers. The displaced passengers then had to make themselves as comfortable as possible on an already crowded train, now minus one complete compartment. Additionally, to add to the woes of fellow travellers, the locked interconnecting doors of the compartment excluded access to the toilet. Women with children would snarl harsh words at him that he simply had to ignore. Upon arriving at the OKW, he would hand the sealed documents to a named officer and to no one else.

On one occasion, returning from Berlin to Peenemünde via Zinnowitz on the evening of 17 August 1943, he heard from the train's conductor the first reports of a major air raid taking place ahead of him. His immediate thoughts were for the safety of his sister and comrades. During the first wave of the RAF attack, the bombers flew parallel to the coast and attacked the Peenemünde housing complex. The prevailing winds then drove the smoke caused by the destruction towards the south-west where, approximately one kilometre (0.5 miles) away, the *Heer* barracks and billets of *Batterie* 444 were located. Klein was convinced that the dense smoke saved not only his sister, but also his unit from the following two waves of attack.

As a temporary safety measure against continued air attacks, *Batterie* 444 was billeted outside the Peenemünde area in the nearby villages of Hanshagen and Wusterhusen. Although Klein was spared the fury of the raid, he witnessed the horror of the aftermath as he and his unit assisted in cleaning up tasks and burying the remains of 600 victims. During the recovery of corpses, Klein heard that the mainly civilian workers of the housing complex had attempted to escape the exploding inferno and took to the water of the Baltic Sea to be then machine-gunned by a British aircraft. It is difficult to imagine how unescorted aircraft of RAF Bomber Command flying at a minimum altitude of 4,000 feet (1260 metres) could have picked out swimmers to machine-gun in the dark. This inexplicable event was investigated and discussed by Martin Middlebrook in his book *The Peenemünde Raid*. Having interviewed survivors of the housing complex, Middlebrook concluded: 'Something unusual must have happened... it is unlikely that the full truth will ever be known.'

Following the research conducted for this book, the authors put forward this theory: the effects of blast injury and death from shock waves are very well known, but what is perhaps less well known is that shock waves travelling through the medium of water can be far more damaging. Reconnaissance photographs taken after the raid by the RAF show that a number of bombs fell upon the beach and therefore, it is probable that many also fell and detonated in the sea. Victims fleeing the conflagration at the housing complex would have been spared only the flames. The concussive and magnified effects of the pressure waves from the exploding bombs travelling through the water of the Baltic Sea would have ruptured internal organs, causing death. It is understandable that the rescuers had drawn the wrong conclusion as to the cause of deaths as they collected the bodies floating in the water and those washed up on the long, sandy beach. The victims had died because of the air attack, but not in the way the frayed minds the recovery teams had imagined.

The atmosphere at Peenemünde changed forever following the air raid; the Allies had demonstrated that they knew the importance of the site and subsequently its personnel lived in mortal dread that the RAF would return. In the event, they never did, although American bombers were to attack in two daylight raids before Peenemünde was finally occupied by the Soviets in 1945. Many changes occurred to the Rocket's development following the devastating attack. In addition to moving the manufacture of Rockets to other sites, it was decided that the training and test-firing programme had to be moved to a new location away from the hazards and disruption of air raids. Although the first successful launching had taken place nearly a year previously, the A4 still had many faults and was far from ready for operational use. In great secrecy, in September 1943, *Batterie* 444, was loaded as a unit onto rail cars and began a ten day journey from Peenemünde direct to the SS *Truppenübungsplatz* (Troop Training Ground) at Heidelager in Poland.

The suggestion that Heidelager should be used for training of the FR troops and test-firing of the Rocket was made by Himmler who saw an opportunity to increase his influence over the entire A4 programme. Following the invasion of Poland in September 1939, the SS began the development of the *Truppenübungsplatz* close to the village of Blizna to hold some 12,000 SS personnel. The inhabitants of the village were evicted and in spite of the disappearance of the settlement, the location was still occasionally referred to as Blizna. Heidelager lay some 130 kilometres (81 miles) east of Krakow and, more importantly, over 1400 kilometres (870 miles) away from the English coast and the range of RAF Bomber Command. The extension to Heidelager was hastily prepared by the *Heer* for the new arrivals from Peenemünde and from the A4 training schools. The new facility was completely independent of the existing SS personnel already stationed at Heidelager and contact between the SS and the *Heer* was discouraged.

At this time *Batterie* 444 was commanded by the *Batteriechef, Hauptmann* Jung, his two launching officers being *Oberleutnant Dr.* Helmut Fredenhagen and *Leutnant* Klein. The *Batteriechef's* involvement was mainly concerned with tasks surrounding the Rocket and not the device itself; the launchings were always conducted by the other officers. The three *Schießzüge* (launching platoons) of *Batterie* 444 were led by a *Wachtmeister* (Regimental Sergeant), or *Oberwachtmeister* (Staff Sergeant). Each *Schießzug* consisted of thirty-two men, among them *Unteroffiziere* (NCOs) and technicians, supported by ordinary soldiers. Within the FR troop there was a wide range of ages and Klein felt uncomfortable and embarrassed giving orders to men, some of whom were twice his age and old enough to be his father.

Although ten years his senior, Klein became friendly with his much-liked fellow launching officer *Oberleutnant* Fredenhagen, a close relationship that was to last beyond the war. Fredenhagen, in addition to security duties at the firing sites, had the added responsibility of organizing the precise procedures for every man in the launch site team. Firing and safety regulations were overseen by a *Hauptmann* Kröhn. Kröhn did not play a significant technical role, having arrived late in the training programme. The A4 facility at Heidelager was under the overall command of *Major* Wolfgang Weber. Weber apparently shared many of the positive qualities of Stegmaier. Klein recalled: 'I had good fortune to have those superiors. Weber was an excellent man and very correct. Today you would call him a "mate". After the war he visited me and that was a very great pleasure.'

Klein also became acquainted with *Oberstleutnant* Paul Moser whom Stegmaier had seconded to his staff to serve as his deputy. Additionally, Moser was in charge of an evaluation office which had responsibilities to correlate all information and performance data related to the A4. Moser, a colourful character with a flirtatious reputation, was frequently the butt of many a private joke within the upper echelons of the *Batterie* 444.

The Heidelager facility was further expanded during October and November to accommodate the newly formed FR Battalions, *Artillerie Abteilung* 485 (*mot.*) and *Artillerie Abteilung* 836 (*mot.*). The new units having finished initial training conducted at the FR school at Köslin, joined *Batterie* 444 for final instruction. The 3./*Art. Abt.* 836 arrived on 27 January 1944 and were accommodated within the SS camp. Their training period was less than five weeks.

The barracks at Heidelager were comfortable with an adjoining annexe for eating meals cooked by the unit's own field kitchen. Officers were installed in simple timber barracks apart from the other men and Klein shared a telephone-equipped billet with Fredenhagen. To make the billet even more comfortable, Klein's 'boy' built up a rustic wooden veranda, complete with table and chairs made from timbers from the forest. Equipped with a wireless, Klein enjoyed socializing here with fellow off-duty officers. Visitors and guests, whether they be personnel from Peenemünde or generals, were accommodated in railway coaches seconded to *Batterie* 444 and referred to as the MCI railway train.[1] The comfortable, stationary carriages were installed on a spur of railway track so as not to impede transport to Kochanovka, the next station along the line. Each coach was able to accommodate two separate quarters.

For recreation, the troops would entertain themselves by playing musical instruments, whilst officers played billiards in the *Offizierskasino*. Klein, however, enjoyed horse riding in the woods which surrounded the camp. In addition to Rocket training, the troops had drill and rifle-firing exercises and as a result, Klein was to learn the names of most of the firing crews. The atmosphere was unusually congenial for a military camp, but nevertheless all ranks were very committed to the task in hand.

Internal security to counter spying and sabotage was monitored by just one of Kammler's men, SS-*Obersturmführer* Hans Lohse who, against expectations, was remembered as 'a pleasant fellow'.[2] Later, however, he was to die in a car accident en route to Peenemünde. His successor was SS-*Obersturmführer* Schüppenhauer who was also a similarly agreeable man. Unofficially these SS men were agents who reported to Kammler. Before his assignment at Heidelager, Schüppenhauer explained that he had had a similar duty at his previous posting in the subterranean *Mittelwerk* factory near Nordhausen in the Harz Mountains where, as described elsewhere in this book, concentration camp inmates worked under appalling conditions assembling A4s. Schüppenhauer explained that the slave workers would exploit any opportunity to sabotage a Rocket, including urinating and defecating into the aluminium propellant tanks. Schüppenhauer did not indicate what steps were taken to resolve the problem.

The Heidelager site was protected by both anti-aircraft and anti-tank gun emplacements supplemented by an infantry platoon; the SS had the responsibility of guarding the perimeter. The security was so stringent that nearby SS personnel had no access; not even the commander of the SS *Truppenübungsplatz* (Troops Practice Ground) was allowed to enter the camp. Although often flouted, the surrounding area was considered to be 'out of bounds' due to the risk of partisans.

The training that had been suspended following the attack upon Peenemünde was resumed in earnest. Launchings from Heidelager were initially prepared in open countryside but later, to imitate the situation at the front, the firing positions were prepared in the forests. Klein recalled that a large trench held three manned switchboards for the engine, radio communication and guidance sections. Additionally, a fourth man operated a field telephone. Parked beside the trench was an electric generator vehicle and air compressor for test operations. Electrical operating and power cables ran some 60 metres to the Rocket. The members of the firing team would observe the firing procedure from 'slip' trenches some 500 metres away.

Klein recalled the first such launch on the bitterly cold morning of 27 October 1943. It should be mentioned that other sources, including *Generalmajor Dr.-Ing.* Dornberger, incorrectly indicate that the incident about to be described took place on 5 November. Whatever the case, all accounts detail an inauspicious start to the Heidelager live tests. This firing coincided unhappily with a visit from *General der Artillerie z. V.* Erich Heinemann, of the *Höherer Artillerie-Kommandeur* 302 (Higher Artillery Commander – *HARKO* 302). Heinemann was to have a very close association with the A4/V2, for one month later, on 28 November 1943, he was appointed to command LXV. *Armeekorps z.b.V.* This *Armeekorps* was created as a tactical command in anticipation of the V2 campaign.

Hauptmann Jung was to command the test-firing whilst *Oberleutnant* Fredenhagen was the firing officer. The A4, serial designation V 27, was to be launched from a freshly made *Bodenplatte* (concrete pad), but it was discovered that the concrete had not fully set![3] However, under enormous pressure 'from above' due, in part, to the presence of Heinemann, it was decided the firing must go ahead. The *Abschusstisch* for the Rocket was set up upon the open ground with no other foundation than that of the natural sandy soil and the penetrating frost. To make matters worse the blast deflector plate had been incorrectly positioned.

The standard procedure, as Klein recalled, was as follows: 'The launching *Batterieoffizier* asked the *Batteriechef*, *"Feuer frei (free to fire)?"*, for launching clearance. This was done, for example, to ensure that no enemy aircraft were in the area. The *Batteriechef* answered *"Feuer ist frei!"* The *Batterieoffizier* then gave the launching orders to the crew at the switchboard, who pressed a key for *Vorstufe* ('preliminary stage') followed by *Hauptstufe* (main stage).'

However during *Vorstufe*, one of the four legs of the firing table began to slowly sink into the ground as the sand and defrosted soil was blasted away by the Rocket's jet flame. At *Vorstufe* the Rocket was leaning at a dangerous angle, but remarkably Jung gave Fredenhagen permission for *'Hauptstufe!'* Sure enough the Rocket lifted off. The Rocket's guidance system attempted to right the trajectory but quickly lost control and the device exploded into the forest some 3 kilometres (1.8 miles) away. Eventually however, the difficulties of soft ground were subsequently resolved with the use of heavy tree trunks set into the ground and covered by thick metal sheets. This proved to be perfectly satisfactory and was used operationally at rural firing locations. Following this spectacular failure, *Hauptmann* Jung was reprimanded and ordered to report with Fredenhagen to Peenemünde. Jung, who had something of a predilection to alcohol, was subsequently replaced by a new *Batteriechef, Hauptmann* Müller. Of Müller, Klein described him as: 'A very nice, highly intelligent man, but a *'spinner'* (eccentric). He knew nothing of the Rocket. He was a keen game hunter. Later, at Heidekraut, a colonel or general once said to me, "Send Müller out to hunt as often as possible, so he's not a nuisance." After the war I met him a few times although he died shortly after.'

After the first failed firing an order was received from Peenemünde that the second firing was to take place immediately. The responsibility for the next launch fell upon an extremely anxious twenty-one year old *Leutnant* Klein. On the eve of the launch, to calm his nervous and excited state of mind, he took a sleeping pill. Of the launch itself Klein remembered: 'I was not fully prepared to do it. The evening before, however, I studied the launch procedure. Luckily the launch was OK. There was a gigantic cloud of grey and yellow. The ground in the surrounding area shook and there was considerable buffeting from the air pressure. It was strange, the Rocket took off so slowly, like an elevator but then accelerated. An indescribable and unforgettable impression. I felt very happy and proud.'

To commemorate Klein's first launching of a Rocket, a comrade in the battery carved a wonderfully scaled model of the A4 from a length of wood. It stood proudly on Klein's desk in the barracks and was much admired, especially by Jung's replacement, *Hauptmann* Müller. Müller, of senior rank, was to later remind Klein that SS-*Obergruppenführer Dr.*-Ing., Kammler's 43rd birthday would fall on 26 August 1944 and that a gift would have to be found for him. Müller's eyes then alighted and lingered upon the wooden Rocket. Having taken the hint, and with a heavy heart, Klein handed over the model. A few weeks later a telegram of gratitude arrived. It thanked the FR troops for the '…ingenious wooden V2 model.' To the astonishment of Klein, the sender of the telegram was not Kammler, but the *Reichsführer*-SS Heinrich Himmler! Why Kammler had done this, Klein simply could not fathom, and the ultimate fate of the wooden Rocket was never known. The giving of presents by officers to Kammler was not restricted to just his birthday. Official records indicate that the *Division zur Vergeltung* (*Div.z.V*), the special command with overall responsibilities for V- weapons, arranged for Kammler's children to receive a pony and coach as a Christmas gift for 1944. Kammler reciprocated by sending all of the officers in the Division inscribed cigarette and cigar boxes.[4]

The training of the soldiers in the preparation and firing of the Rocket was closely monitored at Heidelager to determine best practices and the results of these observations formed the basis of the A4 *Fibel* (Primer), a technical guide for the operational use of the Rocket at the front. Strangely, very few copies, if any, of this publication were actually destined to reach the FR troops in the field. Certainly, Klein never saw a copy of it. In order to catch the attention of the reader of the A4 *Fibel*, mottos and humorous cartoons, many showing images of women with plunging necklines or wearing swimsuits, were liberally sprinkled through its pages. During the production of this book, Klein saw a copy of the A4 *Fibel*. He was not especially amused and commented: 'The funny sketches – often with women – is not at all fitting to the *Fibel*. The (modern) reader will come to the conclusion we were in some sort of "fun club". We, the V2 soldiers, fulfilled our tasks in a totally serious manner and with the knowledge that every firing meant innocent people lost their lives. Incidentally, anyone who looks at the *Fibel* will have the impression that working with the V2, and especially the launching, was a very complicated matter. This was not the case. Our method was a very simple one and there were few difficulties.'

One introductory passage beside a cartoon in the A4 *Fibel* showing a soldier with one hand held over his mouth and the other pointing skyward, is of interest because it perhaps explains why so few men saw the work. It states in somewhat unrefined and simplistic tones: '*The whole stuff about the A4 is top secret – just remember this! Whoever speaks about it, perpetrates treason, it hurts you and the State! Just remember one thing, do not take part in any debate! Make yourself no more clever than you already are, because it is not of your own knowledge. Stay away from discussions – you will only get into trouble! And if you are asked by an outsider, an informer or a smart ass, then just go into full retreat. Otherwise you could lose your head! Put on your stupidest face and say: "My name is Rabbit. I know nothing!"*'

Because the A4 *Fibel* was so detailed, it may have been decided that from a security point of view it was potentially dangerous for too many men to have such a thorough overview of the whole launching procedure. Additionally, there may have been concerns over the document falling into enemy hands. Ironically, its detail was perhaps the downfall of the A4 *Fibel*.

Visitors to Heidelager were allowed to witness test-firings but only once security clearance had been granted, and even then spectators had to introduce themselves to *Oberleutnant* Fredenhagen for final approval. On one occasion, however, Fredenhagen was unavailable and the duty temporarily fell upon Weber. During the lunch following a successful morning firing, Klein had a brief conversation with Weber's adjutant. He remarked to Klein: 'Imagine, *Oberstleutnant* Paul Moser intends to bring along his secretary [to attend a firing]. *Major* Weber of course has refused him.'

Klein commented to the adjutant that he was sorry to hear this. Shortly afterwards the telephone rang in his billet and he was ordered to report to Weber's office. Upon reporting, Weber mentioned that Moser was seeking permission for his secretary. Weber went on to say that he was aware that the young woman concerned was in fact Klein's girlfriend, Käthchen! Klein had met her through his sister Erika, at Peenemünde. Weber said: 'If you take full responsibility for her safety, I will amend my response and he [Moser] will be allowed to bring her along.'

Klein agreed and was quietly pleased that Käthchen would be able to attend. In fact her presence became something of a talisman for Klein. It soon became known by fellow officers and troops of lower rank that when she attended a launch with Klein as the firing officer, the launch would usually be a success. However whenever Fredenhagen was the firing officer, the opposite was true! It was of course nothing more than pure chance but Käthchen was proud that, whatever the reason, her presence had such a positive influence.

Oberstleutnant Moser, a veteran of the First World War, was easily twice the age of Klein and it was commonly known that he had a keen fondness for his young secretaries. The younger officers were amused that an 'old man' like Moser was constantly trying to woo the young girls, and his 'love life' was the cause of much hilarity behind his back. Bizarrely, Moser believed that bringing Käthchen to Heidelager and by ingratiating himself upon Klein by insisting that they should be on first name terms, he could somehow control relationships. Then, by some 'sleight-of-hand' simultaneously Moser would be able to draw himself closer to her. Klein refused the familiarity of calling an older man of high rank by his first name and irrespective of that, Käthchen was not in the least interested in the prospect of any advance from Moser. Moser however was not so easily put off, even when it became obvious to others that his advances were foolish.

Käthchen was granted permission to take her meals in the *Offizierskasino* and when possible and not on duty, Klein would dine with her. As Klein recalled: 'On one occasion Käthchen and I left the *Offizierskasino* after we had finished a meal while most other officers stayed to smoke and talk. Having left, my colleagues looked at their watches and noticed that after just two minutes Moser followed us. Käthchen and I walked through woods towards her accommodation beyond which was the MCI railway train. In his haste, Moser reached the train and fell between the coach buffers injuring himself. He later explained that he had simply fallen over, but I told my colleagues what had really happened. Everyone laughed at him, it was a big joke.'

On the next occasion that the three principal players of the farce found themselves in the *Offizierskasino*, the officers watched keenly as a very special entertainment had been prepared. Klein and Käthchen, having finished their meal and having exchanged parting pleasantries, exited the *Offizierskasino* as if to make the journey towards the accommodation train. Having left the building, they walked briskly around its perimeter to the opposite side, while the remaining officers glanced at their wristwatches. Sure enough, at an interval of two minutes, Moser made his excuses and left the building in pursuit. Closely following Moser's exit were all of the officers privy to the joke who dashed out of the *Offizierskasino* to watch the unfolding comedy. Moser could be seen walking towards the woods with urgency in pursuit of two disappearing figures who appeared to be in close embrace. In reality, he was pursuing two officers, one of whom was dressed as a woman wearing a similarly brightly coloured sweater to that which Käthchen had been wearing. Moser, who had appeared completely oblivious to the fact that his irrational behaviour had not gone unnoticed, now realized that he had been made a fool. Although greatly humiliated and embarrassed, he did not attempt any form of retribution on those of lower rank who had perpetrated the masquerade.

In spite of being fully conversant with the preparation to launch the Rocket and intimate with the fire control desks, the battery continued to experience failures in spite of the questionable effects of their talisman. As far as Klein was concerned: 'All faults were due to technical failures of the equipment and not human failure.'

The extremely low temperature of the liquid oxygen propellant caused frequent problems. Again and again fuelling times would extend the preparation from the normal three to thirteen hours. The intricate network of the plumbing of the fuel lines would often freeze in spite of internal heaters, and in extreme cases it was necessary to 'de-tank' the Rockets. Those working closest to the propellants and pumps would wear asbestos suits to protect them from the burning effects of the liquid oxygen's temperature of minus 183° C.

Dornberger was to concede in his book, '*V2*', that only 10 to 20 per cent of all firings were successful in the early days at Heidelager. Perhaps these figures were over-optimistic as *Major* Weber recorded a success rate of 10 per cent with only 6 per cent falling in the target area up to April 1944. Given the astonishing level of Rocket failures, it is perhaps equally astounding that only one fatal incident occurred when a Rocket failed shortly after 'lift-off' and crashed onto a slip trench in which three soldiers were sheltering. Eight tonnes of propellant ignited into a fireball. After the flames had died down and the wreckage had been cleared, no physical remains of the men were left to recover.

On the rare occasions that a Rocket was successfully launched, the Heidelager stationed Fieseler *Storch* light reconnaissance aircraft would fly out with a pilot and observer to locate the impact site. More often than not, launch failures would bring Rockets down close to the camp. The seemingly successful Rockets that did travel further afield gave the Peenemünde scientists and the firing crews an unexpected surprise. As Klein explained: 'At Peenemünde we always fired into the Baltic Sea and there were colour bags inside the Rocket that helped the aerial reconnaissance aircraft to find the impact site. From Heidelager, however, we fired into almost uninhabited countryside. We were completely shocked as the device was always bursting to pieces when dipping into the atmosphere, only debris falling to the ground. We had to solve this problem and this was very difficult. We tried applying different heat resistant paints to the outer skin because of course the heat (in descent) was enormous.'

It was believed that the heating of the Rocket's steel skin caused structural weakness during the descent stage and caused mid-air break ups and explosions. Experiments, however, with special paints intended to reduce the heating never fully answered this difficulty, as was seen when the Rocket was used operationally. Experiments were also carried out to determine the best camouflage colour schemes for the Rocket while in transport. The black and white square colour scheme synonymous with the Peenemünde tests was replaced with shades of *Heer* green.

During the first half of 1944 the frequency of visitors from Berlin and staff from Peenemünde, among them von Braun and Dornberger, increased. Klein recalled an occasion during a visit by Heinrich Himmler when von Braun was seen wearing an SS uniform in which he made a most striking impression.[5] Klein's opinion having met and spoken with von Braun several times was that: 'He was never a Nazi ... I had a good impression of him.'

Although von Braun denied membership of the SS after the end of the war, on Dornberger's advice he had enrolled as an SS-*Untersturmführer* (Second Lieutenant) in 1942. He quickly advanced to the rank of SS-*Obersturmführer* (Captain) and ended the war as an SS-*Sturmbannführer* (Major).[6]

Sometime after 5 March 1944, Klein had a conversation with a friend, Liselotte Lau, who was the principal secretary to Klaus Riedel (1907–1944), a technical director at Peenemünde and a deputy of von Braun. Lau had been present during the famous occasion when von Braun and several of his friends and colleagues were relaxing at the Schwabe Hotel at Zinnowitz near Peenemünde. During the course of the evening the subject of space travel was brought up and von Braun was to voice words of very poor judgement for such a public place. Lau recited the comments to Klein in the strictest of confidence. Klein recalled that she said of von Braun: 'He does not intend to use the A4 as an instrument of murder against women and children.'

Lau further commented that von Braun wanted to fly to the moon! These admissions unfortunately were also overheard by spies of Himmler placed amongst the population of Zinnowitz to monitor, very specifically, the scientists. Ten days later von Braun, Riedel and others who had been present at the party were arrested by the *Gestapo* and charged with sabotage. This extraordinary accusation stemmed from the notion that talk of space travel was either a deliberate or culpably negligent incitement to sabotage. Dornberger later wrote that he was able to argue the case at the SS Security Office in Prinz Albrecht Strasse, Berlin, that von Braun and the others were indispensable to the project. Following heated and protracted arguments during which the SS threatened Dornberger with a similar accusation, the men were freed and returned to work. Behind the scenes Himmler was moving closer to his ultimate goal of seizing control of the entire operation.

Later Klein heard von Braun give, fatalistically, these words of advice: 'After the war is lost, only five million Germans will remain. One should try hard to be one of those five million.'

By the summer of 1944 *Batterie* 444 and the other FR units receiving training at Heidelager were introduced to the *Feuerleitpanzer* (firing control vehicle). The armoured half-tracked vehicle was built upon the existing Büssing-NAG or Krauss-Maffei/Daimler-Benz Sd.Kfz. 7 chassis already in service with the *Heer*. These converted chassis with modified bodywork were designed specifically for field-launching of the Rocket. Derived from design studies undertaken in consultation with the FR troops, the *Feuerleitpanzer* would normally hold four men and allowed the launching officer a relatively safe view of the Rocket. As a launching officer, Klein was to become very familiar with this purpose-built machine. As he was to recall: 'The *Feuerleitpanzer* contained three control desks – one each for the engine, control system and radio. There was a radio telephone link to different stations at the firing position, which were on top of the upper platform of the *Meillerwagen*. Additionally, a connection was made to the battery commander who had to authorize the device's 'signing off' after completion of the preparations for firing. Originally the *Feuerleitpanzer* had a *Dreierschaltung* (three-way-switch) so that three firing sites could be managed by one vehicle. Later, for better mobility, every *Schießzug* got its own *Feuerleitpanzer* and the *Meillerwagen* was equipped with its own exchangeable compressed air bottles (for pressurization of propellant tanks and field-testing).'

It was the practice that the *Feuerleitpanzer* was reversed into a prepared, wide, sloping trench to protect the firing officer and his immediate team. Only the very top of the vehicle was exposed, allowing observation of the Rocket's jet flame via a narrow, closable flap in the top hatch. Once the troop commander gave the order to launch, Klein, as the firing officer, would give the final commands to the men operating the control desks, from initiating the pyrotechnic igniter to pressing the final button marked '*Hauptstufe*' which would send the Rocket aloft. Klein recalled: 'One had to wait before the main stage and this was dangerous... We always dug the *Feuerleitpanzer* in (to the ground) because of our worry about the vehicle; we were safe inside, but many Rockets exploded near the vehicle and everything would be wrecked.'

Rocket failure immediately after lift-off was particularly dangerous for the firing troops as had already been demonstrated at Heidelager. During training, Klein and his comrades had a very close brush with death while sitting in the *Feuerleitpanzer*. Klein remembered watching a Rocket lifting off from the open hatch. The engine started to lose power, but the thrust that remained nearly equalized gravity. The Rocket seemed suspended in mid-air. It then pitched over at an angle and having regained full thrust, started to move rapidly towards the *Feuerleitpanzer*. In no time at all, the Rocket travelled the 60 metres (195 ft) from the *Abschusstisch* towards Klein and his comrades. Klein quickly dropped from his position and slammed the hatch shut. The men in the *Feuerleitpanzer* waited for the worst to happen as time seemed to stand still. The Rocket roared over the top of their vehicle and exploded in a huge fireball just 100 metres (327 ft) behind the *Feuerleitpanzer* which shuddered in its trench.

Events near and far were to have an enormous impact upon the Rocket batteries. The Allied invasion of Normandy had begun with a massive sea and airborne assault upon the German defensive 'Atlantic Wall' on 6 June 1944. At a stroke, the entire infrastructure intended to supply and fire Rockets from northern France against England was lost. The giant launching bunker at Sottevast, the protected launching site at Brecourt, and the enormous prepared complex in the Forêt d'Eperlecques, near Watten in northern France, were monuments to Hitler's grandiose schemes. An enormous amount of money and man hours was written off as silo sites, storage depots and oxygen manufacturing plants were abandoned in front of the advancing Allied forces.

Of more immediate concern to the Rocket soldiers at Heidelager in the early summer of 1944, was the advance of the Soviets from the east. In spite of fierce German resistance, by May the Russians had succeeded in recapturing the Ukraine. Plans were drafted for the evacuation of Heidelager and relocation to the west. With increasingly bad news from the front and with the Soviets 256 kilometres (160 miles) away, Heidelager was finally abandoned on 24 July, its personnel making off on a 448 kilometre journey (280 miles) to the north-west by rail and to the military barracks and new test site of Heidekraut.

Set in an enclave of the spruce and pine forests of the Tucheler Heide, Heidekraut was in the middle of the so-called 'Danzig Corridor' which had featured so greatly in Nazi propaganda before the War. However, due to the speed of the Soviet advance, insufficient preparations were made for the FR troops at the Heidekraut barracks and they were temporarily billeted in the village of Suchen. Test-shots continued apace from the beginning of August, with rounds fired from north to south, just one month before the Rocket was to be pressed into service.

Klein recalled seeing Kammler perhaps just once at Heidelager, but at Heidekraut he made several appearances. On one occasion he announced that he wanted to see the crater made by a recent failed shot that had exploded a short distance away. It was decided that Klein would lead the way by horseback and that Kammler, who was well known by the FR officers as being a most unpredictable and ruthless character, would follow in his armoured open-topped Mercedes-Benz. However, as they travelled into the forest, Klein became aware that Kammler's vehicle was very close to the horse's heels. Apparently Kammler decided that progress was far too slow and he intended to quicken the pace. Klein reluctantly 'put the spurs' to the horse. By now, galloping along the forest tracks, Klein stole a quick glance behind to see Kammler waving his pistol in the air to encourage even greater speed. Eventually they arrived at the crater's rim, the horse foaming with sweat. As a lover of horses by his own admission, this distressed Klein. As he dismounted, Kammler bounded over and launched into an extraordinary tirade that Klein had tortured the 'poor animal'!

In spite of his rebuke, Klein had impressed Kammler, who was always keen to draw into his entourage exceptional officers of the *Heer*. Klein recalled: 'Kammler had always wanted me to be "promoted" into the SS as his officer aide. Fortunately, with the help of my supervisors, and with the excuse that I was busy with the launchings, I was able to turn him down. The aides of Kammler were only with him a short time and would lament his inhumanity.'

Then the fateful day arrived. Orders were received and on 2 September 1944 an advance party of *Artillerie Abteilung* 836 (*mot.*) and *Batterie* 444 under the supervision of *Oberstleutnant* Schulz from *Art. Abt.* 836 (*mot.*), including Klein as well as two NCOs and corresponding staff of the other batteries, drove west. Their instructions were to survey launch site firing positions in the region of

Maubeuge on the French–Belgian border. The third *Schießzug* (firing platoon) under *Oberstleutnant* Moser remained at Heidekraut to continue training duties with other batteries. The following day found the rest of *Batterie* 444 disembarked at Euskirchen, near Cologne, after which it drove to join the advance party in Belgium to prepare firing sites.

From a modern perspective, it will seem particularly ironic that after all the work carried out in advance of the Rocket offensive, it fell to the FR troops themselves to establish firing sites. This, however, was to prove a near impossible task because of the speed of the Allied advance into France. In spite of frequent engagements from the emboldened Resistance movement, a favourable firing site for *Batterie* 444 was found at the crossroads of Baraque de Fraiture, 46 kilometres (29 miles) south-east of Liège in Belgium. For a temporary command post, the *Batterie* 444 used the nearby inn, the 'Auberge de Carrefour'.

Under the cover of darkness on 6 September, two Rockets were prepared for a dawn launching against recently liberated Paris, some 300 kilometres (186 miles) away to the south-west. Both failed, burning out on their launching tables. *Batterie* 444 relocated to a nearby firing position at Stavelot in Belgium and from here, on 8 September, two Rockets were successfully launched at 0840 hrs and 1100 hrs. The men of *Batterie* 444 had made the very first firings in the West. Although the first Rocket exploded at high altitude, the second device, after a flight of 303 kilometres (188 miles), impacted at Maisons Alfort, a suburb of south-eastern Paris, killing six and injuring thirty-six.[7] No sooner had the Rockets been launched, than *Batterie* 444 had to evacuate because of the advancing Allied front line.

After a brief return to Germany between 9–14 September, *Batterie* 444 was billeted at Reichswald near Kleve. Hitler now forbade Paris as a target; but instead ordered that London should now be attacked. To gain range on the new target the *Schießzüge* then drove during the night of 14 September to the Dutch peninsula of Walcheren Island via Breda and Rosendaal. Klein considered the move to be a 'suicide order'. The risk of entrapment and capture was great, for although Walcheren is approximately 60 kilometres (37 miles) in length, at its narrowest it is just a few kilometres wide. Just 24 kilometres (15 miles) from this narrow position lay the strategically important Belgian port of Antwerp. The deep-water port had been liberated by British 11th Armoured Division on 4 September. With enemy aircraft roving freely over the flat landscape, a little distance to the south, Allied troops were moving forward from the strategically important city. At any time the *Batterie* 444 officers expected the worst and orders were given that all support vehicles and important equipment, including Rockets, were to be armed with demolition charges; only the most necessary of field equipment was to move forward with the *Schießzüge* to the firing positions. Every soldier was equipped with just a few days of rations as the mobile field kitchen would be left behind. In the event of being 'cut off', or if the dykes were breached, arrangements were made to transport *Batterie* 444 by boat to the safety of the Netherlands' more northerly coast.

In spite of the enormous risk of attack from marauding enemy aircraft (which was never to materialize), on 16 September *Batterie* 444 fired its first Rocket at 0732 hrs followed by a second less than an hour later. The first V2 impacted at Southgate in north London, killing sixteen people and injuring twenty-two. The second device impacted in Wembley to the west of London with one injury. Both Rockets fell approximately 15 kilometres (9 miles) from central London.[8]

London was a mere 250 kilometres (155 miles) away and because of its huge area and the lack of targeting precision of the Rocket, it made an ideal target. A heavy bombardment of Walcheren Island ensued from Allied coastal batteries, due in no small part to the presence of the FR troops, and *Batterie* 444, fearful of entrapment, was obliged to withdraw.

Klein and a handful of comrades formed the rearguard as the column drove to the comparative safety of the mainland. On one occasion, during this fraught and anxious time, scanning the skies for enemy aircraft, Klein noticed that adjacent to a bakery facing the road, stood an ice cream stand! Life in Walcheren was continuing as normal as it had done throughout the occupation and traders were open for business. Klein, who admits to a lifelong passion for ice cream, told the driver to stop so that he could satisfy his appetite. One can only imagine the bemusement of Klein's comrades as he walked back to the vehicle to continue the emergency retreat of *Batterie* 444 with an ice cream in his hand! Perhaps for Klein, having experienced a year on the Eastern Front, the military situation in the Netherlands was, by comparison, not so dire.

Shortly after *Batterie* 444's rearguard had left Walcheren, access to the mainland was cut off. What followed for the German forces left behind became known as the 'Battle of the Scheldt' (or the Battle of the Dykes). Raging from 2 October to 8 November 1944, this often forgotten and costly campaign saw the Allies fighting for control of northern Belgium and south-western Holland. Controversially, the dykes were intentionally breached causing many civilian deaths, but forcing the occupiers onto high ground. Eventually the German commander of Walcheren surrendered and 10,000 troops went into captivity. The success in securing the Scheldt gave the Allies unrestricted use of Antwerp. Supplies from the sea, essential for the advance to the Reich, could navigate the Scheldt Estuary free from German artillery batteries formerly situated along the peninsula of Beveland and Walcheren. The Allies' success meant that the target list for the V-weapons would soon be increased by one more entry – Antwerp.

For *Batterie* 444, now free from entrapment, a dangerous journey began under skies completely controlled by the Allied air forces, which ended with a rendezvous with other components of the unit on 23 September 1944 at Stavoren, Friesland, in the northern Netherlands. The reason for the hasty retreat was Operation 'Market Garden' which began on 17 September. This combined Allied air and ground assault was intended to secure crucial bridges over the main rivers of occupied Holland from which the Allies would cross the Rhine directly into Germany. The hope of the optimistic British planners was to end the war by Christmas. However, by 25 September the well-known debacle of 'Market Garden' ended in complete failure and the Rhine would not be crossed until March 1945. Nevertheless, on 25 September from two firing positions in the woodland of Rijsterbos approximately 9 kilometres (5.5 miles) east of Stavoren, *Batterie* 444 resumed its campaign, but not against London. The primary target of England's capital now lay over 420 kilometres (261 miles) away and beyond the range of the A4. Kammler, the man of action and never prepared to 'sit on his hands', decided that the targets were now to be primarily Norwich and Ipswich some 300 kilometres (186 miles) to the west. From a tactical perspective, the enterprise was a complete waste of time and precious resources. None of the 75 Rockets fired fell upon the provincial market towns.

For the first time since the Rocket became operational, Kammler made his presence known to the FR troops and visited *Batterie* 444. Now that the Allied threat from 'Market Garden' to the south had been eliminated, Kammler ordered *Batterie* 444 to travel south to new firing sites to gain range on London. Prior to its departure however, *Batterie* 444 fired the first opening round against Antwerp on 13 October. Since Kammler was concerned about the preservation of the secrecy surrounding the Rocket, he gave *Hauptmann* Müller the order that before moving off, 500 local civilians from the area of Stavoren were to be rounded up and executed. He ended this chilling command by stating: 'Your men must finally learn to see blood flowing...'

Kammler, who had no front line battle experience, was a bureaucrat with a background in civil engineering. He ignored the fact that those he was speaking to had already seen plenty of 'blood flowing'. Neither Müller, nor his officers such as Klein, who had seen action on the Eastern Front, required any such lessons. Kammler, who had overseen the systematic destruction of the Warsaw Ghetto following the Jewish uprising the previous spring, reasoned that the massacre of Dutch citizens would serve two purposes: firstly, witnesses to the dramatic firing of Rockets would be disposed of and, secondly, the action would act as a deterrent to otherwise loose tongues. *Hauptmann* Müller, at great personal risk, decided to ignore the order and the troops departed, travelling south to Wassenaar, a suburb north-east of The Hague. Travelling by night and joining other FR batteries on or around 20 October, *Batterie* 444 continued the offensive exclusively against London. The other FR batteries had been ordered one week earlier on 13 October to add the city of Antwerp to their target lists.

During the frequent journeys Klein made across the Netherlands, he had been impressed by the natural charm of the Dutch countryside, but now operating from The Hague he became acutely aware of the understandable enmity of the Dutch to the German forces of occupation. Unlike the Walcheren area, the Resistance in the central Netherlands was a constant threat and security was an increasingly important issue. At any time the RAF, acting on a 'tip off', could appear and attack the billets or firing sites of the FR troops. The greatest act of resistance was a strike by railway workers at the behest of the Dutch Government in exile in England which became effective on 17 September. Although chiefly intended to support the advance of the Allies, the strike threatened seriously to affect the Rocket offensive by disrupting supplies. For the Dutch civilians, however, the strike action was to backfire very badly when it became apparent that the 'Liberation' was stalled. The Germans introduced their own personnel from the *Deutsche Reichsbahn* (German State Railway) to operate trains and signalling equipment.[9] As a reprisal against the Dutch rebellion, the *Reichskommissar* for the Netherlands, Arthur Seyss-Inquart (1892-1946), imposed an embargo on the transport of food. In spite of a partial lifting of the embargo in early November 1944, the situation, in conjunction with the winter weather and the general chaos of the war, led to the appalling 'Hunger Winter' of 1944-45. The Netherlands was to suffer the worst famine seen in Europe in modern times, and 10,000 died.[10] None of this was to endear the occupying Germans with the Dutch. A simple, but infuriating, passive resistance which Klein experienced was that Dutch pedestrians would impede the passage of German vehicles by intentionally walking in front of the vehicles. This action prevented overtaking and occasionally stopped the vehicle altogether. Consequently, and especially on Rocket-firing operations, Klein was obliged to carry a rider's crop which he would use leaning out of the vehicle window. More seriously, he was aware that it was not uncommon for German soldiers to be found murdered in The Hague and therefore, in the final months of hostilities, off-duty soldiers would be seen walking in pairs, but never at night.

With movements of Rockets and supplies only possible under the cover of darkness, by 22 October, *Batterie* 444 fired its first Rocket towards London from The Hague. Operations settled down to what Klein described as: 'A systematic, well-coordinated and regulated firing operation.'

In The Hague many of the Rocket firings took place in restricted areas away from prying eyes that were known as the *'Sperrgebiet'* (restricted area). One such area was a strip of land 3 kilometres (1.8 miles) wide which ran parallel to the coast and had been evacuated during the building of the 'Atlantic Wall' defence network. By the time *Batterie* 444 had arrived in The Hague on 20 October 1944, the restricted areas, especially around the firing sites of Wassenaar, had grown. This had been brought about following aerial attacks by the RAF.

The increase in the restricted area not only reduced civilian casualties but it also gave the FR troops even greater choice of secure firing locations relatively close to their billets.

Dutch civilians were normally prohibited from entry to secure zones whilst members of the FR batteries carried special security passes allowing them access to the *Sperrgebiet*. The firing zones were prohibited even to Seyss-Inquart, who had no authority over the Rocket batteries. Klein remembered that a Dutchman was shot as a suspected spy, under the orders of *Hauptmann* Müller, having been found in a restricted area. Although not present at the shooting, Klein was doubtful that the Dutchman had been a spy but, rather, mentally ill. This incident would not have been an isolated event with the *Sicherungstruppen* (security troop) protecting the V2 sites during the offensive in The Hague. Nevertheless, the executed man may have been the flamboyantly named Hanso Henricus Schotanus à Steringa Idzerda. Idzerda (1885–1944) was an internationally known, pioneering radio engineer who was the first person to schedule regular radio transmitted entertainment advertised in the press. He called the programme 'Soirée-Musicale' and it ran from 1919 until 1924, broadcasted on Thursday evenings for three hours. His transmissions reached listeners far beyond the Hague including the United Kingdom, where Idzerda's programme became very popular. The success of Idzerda's broadcasts encouraged the London publishers of the *Daily Mail* newspaper to explore the possibility of establishing a broadcasting company. However, the British government of the time became anxious with the emergence of foreign and British amateur radio transmitters. The government feared that unrestricted transmissions would interfere with military radio users and consequently, via the General Post Office, a licencing system was introduced. Additionally the government worried about the possible use of radio for nefarious purposes, either within the United Kingdom or from foreign powers. Consequently, the government adopted a policy of 'if you can't beat them, join them' and in 1922 the BBC (British Broadcasting Company Ltd) was formed. Doubtless, it would only have been a matter of time before the BBC would have been brought into existence, but its creation was hastened by the pioneering work of Idzerda.[11]

The Idzerda family home in the autumn of 1944 was at Parkweg 3 in an area known as Waterpartij, between The Hague and Scheveningen. Importantly, the house was located within the *Sperrgebiet* and close to the firing sites used by the V2 batteries. On 2 November 1944, the doctors and patients of the temporary hospital located at the *Eerste Vrijzinnig-Christelijk* Lyceum school adjacent to Parkweg, heard the sounds of shouted commands and the movement of heavy vehicles. Preparations were being made for the firing of a Rocket in the nearby woods at 'Launch Site 47' as it was known to the FR troops. Two minutes before midnight the relative peace was shattered as *Batterie* 444 fired its sixth Rocket of the day.[12] The local residents, including the Idzerda family, listened nervously as the Rocket began to rise from the parkland area of Van Stolkpark at Scheveningse Bosjes. Without any warning, it suddenly exploded and the blast threw shards of glass from facing windows onto the beds and occupants in the Idzerda household. Daylight revealed more extensive damage and as replacement windows were very difficult to acquire, the Idzerdas moved to temporary accommodation closer to The Hague at Koningin Emmakade, 2 kilometres (1.25 miles) to the south.[13] Later the same morning, Idzerda returned to the scene of the Rocket misfire. Driven perhaps by his interest in technology and aviation, he was keen to collect parts in much the same way as a beachcomber would collect flotsam and jetsam. The larger remains of the Rocket would have been recovered but the remaining smaller parts appear to have been Idzerda's quarry.

A group of patrolling German soldiers who were presumably part of the security forces saw Idzerda in the vicinity of Van Stolkpark and challenged him. The Germans believed his protestations of innocence and having warned him of the dangers, ordered him away. Unfortunately Idzerda, driven by curiosity, returned within the hour to the crash site where the Germans again saw him with his sixteen-year old son, Bart. He was immediately apprehended and a search revealed that he had Rocket parts in his possession.[14] The Germans perhaps decided that his seemingly irrational behaviour of ignoring warnings could only be explained by Idzerda acting on behalf of the Resistance. Irrespective of this, his fate was sealed; this was the last time that Bart saw his father. Idzerda was taken directly to the grounds of Filmstad (Film City, the film-making area of the city) and executed. His body was discovered by accident on 28 September 1945 in Park Oosterbeek by a local unemployed fisherman who was prospecting for items that might have been left behind by the occupying forces. The fisherman correctly presumed he had discovered a shallow grave when he unearthed the remains of a peaked cap and spectacle frames. The local police were called to attend and their report detailed that the body, in a state of advanced decomposition, was wearing a long black overcoat, dark grey lounge suit with silver tiepin and brown shoes. An initial investigation showed that Idzerda had been executed standing in front of a tree some seven metres away from the grave and 100 metres from Filmstad. The report adds a bizarre and unfathomable observation regarding the bullet-riddled tree: 'In large print in brown paint and on a red cross was painted the words *Butter Dose.*' *Butter Dose* is German for butter dish.[15] It is possible that the painted marks and wording on the tree related to German surveyor marks used in the precise alignment of the Rocket, as it is known that numerous devices were fired from the area. There is, however, an additional enigma surrounding the tragic incident. If his captors felt he was a spy, why was he not handed over to the *Gestapo* for interrogation?

With the dreadfully persuasive methods that the *Gestapo* had at their disposal, Idzerda might have broken and given the names of his contacts in the local Resistance. It would appear he was executed on the day of his capture, not as spy, but more likely as an example to the local Dutch community. The precise motivation for the actions of both Idzerda and his captors will never be known.

Intensive firing operations by day and night meant that the third *Schießzug* of *Batterie* 444 had to be summoned. This *Schießzug* was sent on 11 November with orders to fire for a temporary period from launching sites at the port of The Hook of Holland, 16 kilometres (10 miles) south-west of The Hague. One of the firing sites used was directly opposite the present day car ferry mooring, which services regular crossings to Harwich in England. Later 1./*Artillerie Abteilung* 485 used these sites. The location, between port buildings and ditches, was very exposed with no natural cover for camouflage, necessitating preparations and firings to take place at night. The FR troops were equipped with shielded lighting, torches and headband electric lamps to help them read instruments in the Rocket and operate support equipment.

Other popular firing sites used by *Batterie* 444, but not exclusively, were the areas around the racetrack of Duindigt, the promenade in front of the sandy beaches of Scheveningen and the Haagse Bos (Hague Wood). It was important that firing sites were sufficiently broad enough to allow easy access for tanker vehicles to fill the Rocket propellant tanks.

The firing sites were used in rotation in order to counter attacks by the RAF who received information from both the Resistance and reports from patrolling Allied fighter pilots. The most popular and most frequently used firing site was the Haagse Bos. The wood, reputed to be the oldest in the Netherlands, is approximately 3 kilometres (1.8 miles) in length and half a kilometre wide and is aligned roughly south-west to north-east. The roads of Benoordenhoutseweg and Bezuidenhoutseweg border its longest sides. Running through the middle of the Haagse Bos and parallel to the roads mentioned, is the cobblestone street of Leidse Straatweg, which gave the FR troops excellent access to firing sites. Located at the most easterly position in the woods and accessible from the Leidse Straatweg is the official residence of the Dutch royal family, the beautiful Paleis Huis ten Bosch. During the war it survived demolition by the Germans, but was seriously damaged in part by the V2 offensive.

The FR troops were equipped with ladders which allowed them to cut back the leafy canopies just sufficiently to allow the Rocket sight of the sky, but simultaneously to give enough cover from patrolling enemy aircraft. In this pursuit of camouflage and concealment the FR troops were extraordinarily successful. As Klein remembered: 'Allied aircraft searched for us but we sawed out just enough from the trees so that they (the RAF) would not recognize us as they flew quickly overhead. The Resistance would have reported our movements and positions, but the FR troops never saw a risk apart from failed Rockets. The aircraft from above would have been the greatest risk. It has always surprised me that we were never attacked and that the woods were not bombed. We were always lucky. It could be that my feelings are different regarding air attacks because I had seen one year of combat in Russia. A less experienced soldier might well have *"Hosen voll"* ['full trousers'] in such circumstances.'

Prior to a Rocket launch, the firing commander, standing at an exposed vantage point, would carefully scan the distant horizon using binoculars and listen for enemy aircraft. When he was satisfied that all was clear he would call out *'Alles ist klar!'* ('All is clear'). Then the command *'Platz räumen!'* ('Vacate the area') would be shouted, the ladder and firing crew vehicles would drive away, and the rest of the personnel would take immediate cover.

Rocket failures were commonplace and on more than one occasion it would be necessary for the firing control officer in the *Feuerleitpanzer* to prematurely cut the engine via a radio signal when he deemed that the Rocket was suffering from insufficient thrust as it sat upon the *Abschusstisch*. This procedure was known as 'Emergency *Brennschluss*'. In the most extreme cases it was necessary to give the emergency *Brennschluss* signal to minimize the danger of a Rocket careering across the sky and threatening either firing crews or local population. It took a very steady nerve to know exactly when in the most severe cases to initiate the command. As Klein recalled: 'One could give *Brennschluss* via radio from the *Feuerleitpanzer* when the A4 either didn't lift or only a weak flame came out or when one saw the Rocket travel in the wrong direction. Although, of course, it was more difficult if the device had a certain height. It was very tricky. If the device was high above and one gave a *Brennschluss* order, the device would come down very quickly. Once, when a Rocket was under my responsibility, it went in the wrong direction. I did not know when to give the *Brennschluss* order and how I could guess where it would come down as it already had enormous speed. The tilt programme began at a height of 400 m. Only then could I see the direction in which it flew. Giving an emergency *Brennschluss* at that height meant that you did not know where it was going to come down. I saw it was travelling in the wrong direction, but the height I could only guess at. I saw that it went off in the direction of Germany. Later I heard from Wernher von Braun that it had fallen in the centre of Osnabrück but, like a miracle, nothing happened. I never heard if the authorities in Berlin wanted an explanation for this failure.'

The reason that the 'authorities in Berlin' never sought an explanation will never be known. The unexpected explosion and resulting crater was just one of many that had occurred and, perhaps in the interest of secrecy, and the fear of handing the Allies a propaganda coup, the incident was hidden away and covered up. It is also interesting to speculate whether the Osnabrück Rocket had been incorrectly placed upon the *Abschusstisch* by 180 degrees. The suggestion is vehemently denied by Klein who commented: 'No way. It was a gyroscope failure! Even if the surveyor had made a mistake, the lowliest soldier would have noticed because fin number 1 was always turned towards the target. That certainly never happened.'

It is possible that the Rocket had been sabotaged during its construction at the *Mittelwerk* but, whatever the reason, if the Rocket had travelled directly the opposite away from Osnabrück, it would have fallen in the area of Chelmsford in Essex, England, 260 kilometres (162 miles) down range of The Hague. Although short of London's northern suburbs due to the lack of range, at least it would have fallen upon enemy soil. During the offensive, several Rockets did indeed fall close to Chelmsford.

In November 1944, *Hauptmann* Müller became the recipient of the prestigious *Deutsches Kreuz* (German Cross) in Gold, an award that (in spite of Klein's reservations) acknowledged Müller's exceptional skills of command. Although billeted at separate locations around The Hague, relationships between the officers and lower ranks within *Batterie* 444 were convivial despite military hierarchy. This was especially so between the officers. Shortly after the award ceremony, *Batterie* 444 enjoyed a brief respite from Rocket-firing duties due to supply difficulties caused by enemy air action. At the officers' billet, Müller entertained himself and fellow officers by playing the piano. Suddenly and without warning, Kammler burst into the room and saw Müller sitting by the piano. The SS officer glared angrily and shouted: 'I can't use battery commanders who play the piano! Müller, you're ordered to Köslin.'

The man who had ignored an order to slaughter 500 civilians was 'undone' for simply playing a piano! It is known that on 10 February 1945 Müller was officially ordered to write training regulations in the use of the V2. Given Klein's recollection of the 'fall from grace', it would seem that Müller no longer played a direct part in the Rocket offensive. This was another example of Kammler's extraordinary and unpredictable nature – a man who was only answerable to Heinrich Himmler and who enjoyed complete overall command of the V-weapons. Müller was posted to the Rocket training school at Köslin to serve as an instructor and the bizarre character that was *Hauptmann* Basse took his place.

Basse's command was to be short-lived. He was completely unknown to the officers in *Batterie* 444. Where Basse had been posted before his involvement with the A4 was never known by his immediate colleagues in the FR troops. He arrived with his adjutant, which was of course perfectly normal. What marked him out as being so different was his entourage: a brass band of six or eight musicians and a personal tailor at a time when fighting men were needed so desperately. For his personal care, not only did he have a 'boy', but also a personal *Oberwachtmeister* (Sergeant Major). Shortly after his arrival in

The Hague, Basse set up a brothel in the restricted zone furnished with local Dutch women. What Klein did not know was whether this was done for the benefit of the troops or whether it was Basse's private harem.

Surprisingly, in spite of his behaviour, Basse was betrothed and the wedding was arranged to take place at Bansin in Usedom about 30 kilometres (19 miles) to the south-east along the coast from Peenemünde. Klein happened to be visiting Peenemünde at this time on official business from The Hague. Basse learned of Klein's presence and ordered him to attend the wedding. Basse suggested in all seriousness that it should be a 'double wedding' and that Klein should marry his girlfriend, Käthchen. This was a ridiculous suggestion as the younger couple were not even betrothed, but nevertheless Klein duly attended the ceremony with the plan to return to The Hague by train. That evening, as the celebrations came to an end, Basse ordered Klein to drive himself, his bride, a friend and his adjutant to The Hague. To make matters worse, he was instructed that the journey would be via Celle near Hannover so that Basse's wife could be delivered to her parents' home. Thus began a nightmarish 880-kilometre (547-mile) journey through freshly bombed towns, cities and villages, with the way lit by shielded car headlamps and with drunken passengers enjoying alcohol and cigars. When Kammler heard of Basse's inappropriate fuel extravagance and other excesses, he demoted him to *Schütze* (Private) and banished him to a penal regiment. His replacement was *Oberleutnant* Böhm who was later appointed to *Hauptmann*.

Beyond the scope of this book are the activities of the Dutch Resistance, and specifically what was known by the German Intelligence services as the *'Englandspiel'* (English Game). To summarize, the British Special Operations Executive's (SOE) attempts to gather intelligence on the German occupying forces had been seriously compromised. In 1942 German military intelligence – the *Abwehr* – had persuaded a captured SOE agent to use his radio set to send misinformation back to London. The failure of the SOE not to realize what was happening and the ignoring of failed security checks in hidden messages from compromised agents, can only be described as crass stupidity and incompetence. The SOE delivered straight into German hands over fifty agents.[16]

By the autumn of 1944 the activities of the *Abwehr* had been taken over by the *Sicherheitsdienst*, the intelligence and security service of the SS. In the employ of the *Sicherheitsdienst* were Dutch agents known to the FR troops as 'V-*Leute*' who had infiltrated some of the Resistance cells in The Hague. Klein was told that 'V-*Leute*' in a local cell had reported that a signal had been sent to London informing the SOE of the billets of *Batterie* 444. At this time *Batterie* 444 was billeted in apartments at Marlot Park Fliet, approximately 3 kilometres (1.8 miles) south of Wassenaar. The accommodation took the form of a large 'U'-shaped building with an inner courtyard. This was a convenient billet as the Rocket-firing sites most frequently used were to be found at the Haagse Bos about half a kilometre away to the south-west. In anticipation of an imminent attack by the RAF, immediate instructions were given that the Marlot Park Fliet was to be evacuated. New accommodation was found at scattered locations in the Scheveningen area. The officers were billeted in attractive villas relieved from their owners and the lower ranks were accommodated in a variety of properties, including some close to the famous Filmstad at Clingendaal. A day or so later on Sunday, 24 December 1944, Spitfires of the RAF's 303, 229 and 602 Squadrons attacked in perfect conditions, dropping 250 lb (113 kg) and 500 lb (227 kg) bombs, completely destroying the accommodation in what Klein described as an '... exact, neat piece of work ... everything was destroyed totally. They [the RAF] did a wonderful job – nothing in the vicinity was damaged.'

What would have been the consequences if *Batterie* 444 had been 'stood down' that morning and in its billets? The elimination of *Batterie* 444 would have dealt a serious blow to the Rocket offensive.

The final days of 1944 ended with a spell of stormy weather that hampered anti-V2 operations by the RAF in and around The Hague. *Batterie* 444 attempted a simultaneous firing of three Rockets to coincide with the 'chiming in of the New Year' of Big Ben in Westminster, London. To see in the New Year with explosions in England's capital would act as a reminder that despite the Allied invasion six months previously, the war was far from over. All three firing *Schießzüge* of *Batterie* 444 were brought into action. The occasional practice of chalked graffiti (doubtless without the approval of the Peenemünde scientists) written by the firing crews on the Rockets bore seasonal greetings to Winston Churchill wishing him a *'Glückliches Neujahr'* ('Happy New Year'). One *Schießzug* was dispatched to the Hook of Holland firing site. Unhappily for the firing crew however, the weather was so stormy that the launching was abandoned due to high winds and the Rocket de-tanked. The two other *Schießzüge* were sent to the V2 launching site of Chateau Bleu, a popular 'cream house' before the war, in the northern edge of the Haagse Bos, a mere half a kilometre north from the Paleis Huis ten Bosch and just a few minutes walk from Filmstad. During the warmer months of peacetime, tables and chairs would be prepared by waiters for strolling visitors to enjoy refreshment in the beautiful gardens adjacent to tennis courts. Klein recalled visiting the building which, during the occupation, was used as a depository for valuable books. The firing troops set their *Abschusstisch* just 200 metres away from one another close to the Chateau. At the appointed time of 2355 hrs, the first of the two Rockets lifted off into a pitch-black sky. Just as the device was about to begin its tilt programme, the thunderous roar ended abruptly and the incandescent light of the exhaust became a feeble glow. The Rocket fell in silence directly onto the Chateau destroying everything. The third Rocket took off and at first all seemed well. However, after climbing sufficiently high enough for the tilt programme to take effect, it too suffered an engine failure, exploded and fell from the sky in a shower of burning debris 2 kilometres (1.25 miles) away.[17] Klein vaguely recalled that this failed Rocket damaged a hospital, but another source indicates that it fell in the area of Waalsdorperweg.[18] The local residents of the Van Voorschotenlann had to be evacuated due to the conflagration. Further research gleaned from Dutch Resistance records indicates that the hospital, known as the Bronovo, lost 2,000 panes of window glass which were blown in by the explosions, caused either from the exploding propellant tanks or from a detonating warhead. Van Voorschotenlann was only 350 metres (1,148 ft) away from the hospital, so not only are both accounts correct, but in all likelihood, the inhabitants that were evacuated were probably the occupying Germans as both the road and the hospital were deep within the restricted zones. The suspicion that sabotage during the manufacture of the Rockets was responsible for many of the spectacular misfires grew stronger with each failure. A report drafted on 15 December 1944 following a spate of tail-end fires in the Rocket indicated that the technical troops were frequently finding pieces of paper in the A-*Stoff* (liquid oxygen) propellant tank as well as in the turbo-pump. The report indicated that the found items would be examined to determine their source. No further comment was noted.[19]

In early 1945, *Oberleutnant* Fredenhagen was seconded to the SS-*Werfer Batterie* 500 which was operating from the Dalfsen and Hellendoorn area against Antwerp. Fredenhagen's experiences are recorded in Chapter Seven. On 26 January 1945, *Batterie* 444 was ordered back to the place of the Rocket's birth, to Peenemünde, to perform a series of tests including some with Leitstrahl (radio guiding beam) to improve target precision. Travelling by train they unloaded at Züssow, 24 kilometres (14 miles) south-west of the Rocket centre, and journeyed in appalling heavy snow to the barrack camp of Buddenhagen close to Peenemünde. The new test-firing positions were already prepared for the trials to begin with *Batterie* 444 under command of *Oberstleutnant* Moser, now of the *Lehr- und Versuchsabteilung z.V. Generalleutnant* Dornberger was said to have regained a degree of control over *Batterie* 444 from Kammler and would have doubtless overseen the tests.

However, the tide of war was well and truly turning, and without a single round fired *Batterie* 444 and its equipment had to withdraw just a few days later due to the proximity of the advancing Soviets. The situation was becoming increasingly chaotic and it was obvious to the rank and file of *Batterie* 444 that the war would soon end. Talk on such matters, however, was restricted to the closest of confidants. The one person who seemed oblivious to the impending disaster was Kammler. As Klein remembered in the final days: 'Crazily, Kammler drove his large Mercedes across Germany and in the occupied areas. He still wanted to win the war. He had so many responsibilities that even Albert Speer, the Armaments Minister, was made a subordinate to him.'

Although Kammler may have been a fanatic, by 14 February 1945 he must have realized that it would be only a matter of time before the FR troops would be overrun. To avoid the capture of valuable equipment, and in order to press the troops into the defence of the Reich, Kammler ordered that preparations should be made to move all FR units back to Germany under the cover name of *'Ziethen'*.[20]

In February *Batterie* 444 was ordered to travel to Rethem in the Lüneburg Heath area, but the planned launches from the German homeland were abandoned. From Rethem the unit travelled to Armsen, 10 kilometres (6 miles) south-east of Verden. From this new location it began to prepare test launches onto the target area of Friesland, 240 kilometres west in northern Holland. Klein recorded in notes following the end of the war that on 5 April 1945, from the woodland of Armsen, the last two Rockets of a total of over 1,000 launched by *Batterie* 444 were fired. One of these was a failure. *Batterie* 444, bereft of any further Rockets, then withdrew from Lüneburg Heath because of advancing Allied troops, to the area of Schleswig-Holstein. It arrived at Steinhorst on 10 April and it was from here, despite the chaos of the final days of the war, that Klein had the very good fortune to meet his future wife who was the secretary of the local *Bürgermeister*. Approximately nine days later, half of *Batterie* 444 moved to the north, arriving at the village of Welmbüttel, near Heide, just 60 kilometres (37 miles) from the Danish border. It had taken with it the special equipment that was unique to the Rocket. Vehicles not taken to Welmbüttel were abandoned in woods at Steinhorst and were later collected by the British Army. At Welmbüttel the newly arrived FR troops were billeted anywhere that could be found – in stables, residential homes and manor houses. On 1 May, some of the remaining men of *Batterie* 444 were ordered to join 5. *Flakdivision* which belonged to Kammler's *Division* and which was used as infantry against the British at Bargteheide/Trittau (between Hamburg and Lübeck). The fate of these men was to remain unknown to Klein. On the same day, and just eight days before the war's end, Klein was ordered to take a small element of the remaining battalion and to hold back the British as an infantry unit. Klein noted that, simultaneously, the remaining troops at Welmbüttel destroyed all remaining special equipment, vehicles and important documents. A comrade of Klein, *Hauptwachtmeister* Pietsch, explained to him after the war that he had personally destroyed *Batterie* 444's War Diaries by incineration.

By now *Batterie* 444 had no heavy weapons and Klein felt that it was a hopeless situation with neither side really wishing to commit to a full exchange of fire with the war so obviously drawing to an end. However one man was killed and several men injured in a futile engagement with the British. Klein and the 'ad hoc' infantry unit rejoined the other troops at Welmbüttel. Three days later dismissal papers were issued with instructions to: '... disappear into the native country.'

Kammler was also to make the decision to disappear. Although his fate is unknown his widow, Jutta, petitioned for her husband to be declared officially dead for legal and financial purposes. The date of 9 May 1945 was proposed and following a sworn statement from a former driver to the SS-*Obergruppenführer*, it was accepted legally. Like many high-ranking Nazis, Kammler was fearful of the treatment he would receive if captured, especially from the Soviets.

He decided to take poison. If some reports are to be believed, however, he ordered an aide to shoot him. No matter the cause of death, it is alleged that Kammler was buried, in an unmarked grave in woods to the south of Prague.[21]

Before the remnants of *Batterie* 444 could disappear, it was decided to surrender to the British. As Klein recalled: 'The companies lined up, having advised their presence to the British. No speeches were given to the unit. Yes, I wept there. We had given a few years of our lives and now it was all useless. Then we climbed into lorries and were taken to the proximity of the canal to a field kitchen of German command, but under English supervision. There was a large zone north of the Kaiser Wilhelm Canal, where we stayed together in our units until we were moved to release camps one by one. We had a pleasant captivity. I did not wish to be taken by the French or the Russians, but the English were real gentlemen. We were dismissed in dribs and drabs, the officers last of all.'

In spite of already being in possession of official release papers, Allied bureaucracy obliged Klein and other ex-prisoners who had stated that their home address was Stuttgart, to be transported by train to a holding camp. The American-operated camp at Heilbronn had a very poor reputation and Klein and the other men were keen to avoid any further confinement. Fortunately, as the train travelled through the suburbs of Klein's home town, he was able to avoid the gaze of the single guard on the carriage, and as the train came to a brief stop, he and several other men jumped. They crouched close to the wheel bogies and when the train eventually pulled off, Klein and the others stood and walked away – to their homes.

Walter Klein, a civilian, arrived at his parents' home amidst the bombed-out remains of Stuttgart in October 1945. He was now twenty-three years of age. He had only experienced childhood, a state education and five years of war wearing the uniform of the *Heer*. What was he to do now? He recalled: 'After the war, "denazification" was introduced and people were classified. Group 1 was the most incriminated; Group 2 for 'fellow travellers'. I was put into Group 1 because I was an officer of the armed forces; this was a crime, as was being a *Hitlerjugendführer* (Hitler youth leader). In the early post-war period, I did not have any chance to be allowed to work. However, to get food cards, one had to work! Therefore, I had to tidy rubble. This situation went on for some time, but an acquaintance of my father, who had been classified as a Nazi opponent and had an insurance office, had sympathy for me. He was not allowed to take me on or he would have run the risk of being considered a Nazi, but I could sell insurance as a free representative. This was far better than tidying rubble, but it did not satisfy me. I felt myself like a hawker. Then one day I met a man on the street to whom I poured out my troubles. He worked in a machine plant in Stuttgart and took me to the staff council. I was asked whether I could use a typewriter, and if so I would be employed as an apprentice. I became a merchant at the completion of my apprenticeship and remained with the company before taking a managerial position in a large machine factory in Westphalia. I retired in 1984 and have lived happily beside the beautiful Lake Constance.'

Following the German defeat at Stalingrad and the bitter fighting elsewhere on the Russian Front, many rocket troops were grateful that the V2 had 'freed' them from the dangers and grim prospects of the East. Here German dead lay buried beside a road in northern Russia. (Barber)

The embankment of the elliptical earthworks known as the 'Arena' at Peenemünde forms a backdrop to an A4 Rocket that has just blasted off the test pad known as *Prüfstand* VII. Frost caused by the liquid oxygen propellant tank is very much in evidence on the black mid-section (Klein)

Taken from a range of 300 metres from the tower of *Prüfstand* I, an A4 takes off from *Prüfstand* VII at Peenemünde in the summer of 1943 and is approximately four seconds into its flight. Note the unmanned television camera building, 26 metres in front of the *Prüfstand*.

Three A4s await final preparations before firing at *Prüfstand* X at Peenemünde. All three Rockets appear to be painted in *Heer* camouflage colours of olive green and black with white tail sections. Note the presence of two Magirus ladders, the use of which required a strong head for heights.

A dramatic time exposure photograph taken from the upper storey of a building showing a typical scene across the night skies over Germany between 1942-45. Anti-aircraft fire traces the sky, targeting RAF bombers. The Rocket development and test establishment at Peenemünde was the target of such a British night raid on the night of 17/18 August 1943. Helmuth Frenk wrote of the attack: 'Every close impact to the bunker felt like an earthquake.' (Barber)

Leutnant Helmuth Frenk of the *Lehr- und Ersatz-Abteilung für Eisenbahn-Artillerie (mot.)* 100 adjusts a *Richtkreis-Kollimator* – a type of artillery theodolite – at Rügenwalde, June 1940. (Frenk)

Leutnant Helmuth Frenk, 1940. (Frenk)

A 6-metre crater on the airfield at Peenemünde marks the end of A4 Rocket, V38, on 29 June 1943. Helmuth Frenk feared that this incident might have brought about his demise. In the background, the runway can be seen, as well as a large piece of the failed A4.

Stefan Blomberg's *'Arbeitsausweis'* (Worker's Card) used whilst serving at *'Rebstock'*, the cover name for the underground factory at Dernau-Marienthal. The name 'J.Geyer u. Sohn' replaced the original Polish-sounding company name of 'J.Gollnow & Sohn'. (Blomberg)

Stefan Blomberg enjoys a moment of relaxation on the beach close to Karlshagen while serving with *Versuchskommando Nord* at Peenemünde in the summer of 1942. (Blomberg)

Stefan Blomberg (lower right) poses for a photograph with his Peenemünde comrades. In back row, second from left, is Schawitzky from Magdeburg and, fifth from left, Alfred Steiner. (Blomberg)

Stefan Blomberg leans out from the cab of a *Raupenschlepper Ost* (Caterpillar Tractor East) or RSO, with unidentified *Heer* comrades at Darmstadt. The tracked, lightweight RSO was used by the *Wehrmacht* as a transport during periods of mud and snow on the Eastern Front. (Blomberg)

Three A4s displaying different camouflage schemes bask in the sun at *Prüfstand* X at Peenemünde. The two closest Rockets show a 'batiked' camouflage scheme of *Heer* cream white, earth grey, oxide red, olive green and chocolate brown. This scheme was relatively short-lived. The Rocket in the background is painted in camouflage colours of olive green and black with a white tail section. The steadying guidelines to protect the Rockets from gusts of wind suggest that they are awaiting propellants. A *Meillerwagen* attends the central Rocket. This was not the only occasion when three Rockets had been set up. An RAF reconnaissance photograph shows a similar view taken in July 1944.

An identification badge allowing the wearer access to *Prüfstand* VII at Peenemünde. This example was discovered after the War in a damaged condition. Note the lettering 'H.A.P. 11' – *Heimatartilleriepark* 11 (HAP 11 – Home Artillery Park 11). (Barber collection)

Leutnant Walter Klein. (Klein)

Leutnant Walter Klein, second from right (foreground), marches in the Honour Guard at the funeral of SS-*Obersturmführer* Hans Lohse, believed to have taken place at Peenemünde. Behind Klein and to the right is Helmut Fredenhagen. (Klein)

Leutnant Walter Klein writes a note at his desk in his quarters at the Heidelager training ground. Note the model of an A4 Rocket on a circular plinth to his left. (Klein)

Below: Officers and NCOs of *Batterie* 444 pose for a group photograph in front of the only 'brick and mortar' building at Heidelager. Identified from l-r: *Inspektor* Zimmermann, *Hptm* Jung, unknown, *Oblt* Fredenhagen, *Major* Jahns, unknown, SS-*Obersturmführer* Hans Lohse, *Hptm* Müller, *Lt* Gauglitz, *Major* Weber, *Hptm* Kühn, *Hptm* Rundeshagen, *Hptm* Böhm, unknown, unknown and *Oblt.* Tanke. (Klein)

Right: *Oberstleutnant* Paul Moser of *Batterie* 444. A veteran of the First World War, Moser served as deputy to *Oberstleutnant* Gerhard Stegmaier. (Klein)

Left: *Major* Wolfgang Weber, the overall commander of the A4 facility at Heidelager. He was known affectionately as 'The Duke of Blizna'. Later he was to command the V2 unit, *Artillerie Abteilung* 836 (mot.). (Klein)

An A4 is fired from Heidelager in June 1944. The camouflage scheme has been applied in the *Heer* colours of cream white, earth grey and olive green. This image shows evidence of considerable doctoring at the Rocket's tail.

Hauptmann Müller, the commander of *Batterie* 444, enjoys a joke with comrades at Heidelager in 1944. Müller was to later ignore an order to execute 500 Dutch civilians. (Klein)

Six officers and a female member of the civilian contingent enjoy the warm July sunshine at Heidelager in 1944. From l-r: *Major* Jahns, *Major* Weber, *Oberstlt.* Moser, *Baurat* Kunze (architect), *Hauptmann* Kirchner, Käthchen (Moser's secretary) and *Oberarzt* Dressel (senior physicist). (Klein)

Walter Klein dines alfresco with an unidentified fellow *Leutnant* at Heidelager. The unknown officer was a surveyor within *Batterie* 444 and was responsible for confirming the vertical alignment of the A4 and orientation of rocket fins to target. (Klein)

Hauptmann Müller cups his hands to take a 'light' from *Oberleutnant* Tanke. *Hauptmann* Kröhn is between the two officers. The men in the background enjoy some impromptu target practice at Heidelager. (Klein)

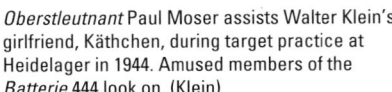

Oberstleutnant Paul Moser assists Walter Klein's girlfriend, Käthchen, during target practice at Heidelager in 1944. Amused members of the *Batterie* 444 look on. (Klein)

The railway carriages seconded to *Batterie* 444 which accommodated high-ranking visitors and guests in comfort while at the cold expanse of Heidelager. (Klein)

Above: *General der Infanterie* Walter Buhle of the Staff of the OKW, *Generalmajor* Walter Dornberger and others await an A4 test-firing from a 'slip' trench at Heidelager, Poland, during the 'Generals' Invasion' in May 1944. (Klein)

Generalmajor Rossmann faces the camera and, with other VIPs, awaits an A4 test-firing from a 'slip' trench at Heidelager, Poland, in May 1944. (Klein)

An A4 Rocket takes off from within the forests of Heidelager during the so-called 'Generals' Invasion'. (Klein)

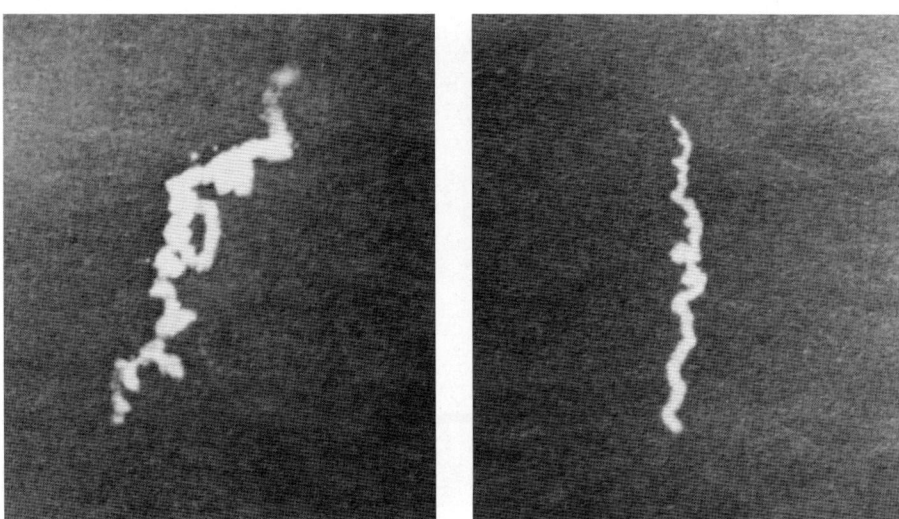
A condensation trail of an A4. Varying air currents shear the vertical trail into the characteristic pattern known as *Gefroreene Blitze* (frozen lightning). (Klein)

The officers of *Batterie* 444 pose for a group photograph at Sandesneben, northern Germany in 1944. Walter Klein is to the extreme left. (Klein)

Walter Klein (centre) stands by a *Kübelwagen* for a snapshot at Heidekraut in 1944. To his left is *Unteroffizier* Berth. (Klein)

Helmut Fredenhagen captured in an uncharacteristically demure mood and photographed while serving as a firing officer with *Batterie* 444. (Fredenhagen)

Eighteen-year old Heinz Wunderlich photographed in 1942 having joined the *Heer*. Later he would be assigned to *Batterie* 444. (Wunderlich)

Heinz Junker's first posting following initial training was to *Batterie* 444. (Junker)

Franz Stolle in the uniform of the RAD *(Reichsarbeitsdienst –* Reich Labour Service) in 1942. (Stolle)

Following his drafting into the *Heer, Gefreiter* Wilhelm Priebe became a member of the *Artillerie Abteilung* 836 security troop. (Priebe)

A troop of the *Reichsarbeitsdienst* (Reich Labour Service) on parade through a German town. Appropriately, spades instead of rifles are carried on the mens' shoulders. (Barber)

A photograph taken from Franz Stolle's album showing a typical moment during his service with the RAD in the spring of 1942. (Stolle)

Franz Stolle in the uniform of the *Heer* some time after March 1942. (Stolle)

Franz Stolle, third from left seated on the ground, poses with unidentified comrades. (Stolle)

Franz Stolle, lower fourth from left, seated on timber, poses with unidentified RAD comrades, probably seen during bridge construction training in Poland in the spring of 1943. (Stolle)

Following his wretched experience serving in the RAD, Stolle and his new comrades in the *Heer* enjoy a more relaxed experience and perform for the camera at their barracks in Poland in 1942. Note the gas masks on the wardrobes in the background of their billet. (Stolle)

Above: A somewhat bizarre photograph: Franz Stolle and comrades participate as extras at the filming of '*Kolberg*' in the summer of 1944. The snow in the foreground is fake. (Stolle)

Oswald Schneider wearing a black *Panzer* crew uniform in 1943. His career with the armoured troops was cut short in September 1943 when he was one of twenty men hand-picked at Kamenz for transfer to Peenemünde and ultimately 2./*Artillerie Abteilung* 485 (mot.). (Schneider)

CHAPTER SEVEN

'WE NEVER THOUGHT ABOUT WHAT HAPPENED AT THE OTHER END...'

HELMUT FREDENHAGEN
Lehr- und Versuchsbatterie 444

ORN in June 1912 in Leipzig, south-eastern Germany, Helmut Fredenhagen was destined to be a career scientist. His father, an educated man and professor, had fought in the Great War and, following Germany's defeat, became politically active in the 1920s. Life in post-war Germany was particularly hard and the situation in Leipzig was no exception. When Fredenhagen was about eleven-years old, his family moved to what he was to describe as the land of 'milk and honey' – the seaside town of Greifswald on the Baltic close to Peenemünde in Usedom. Of common knowledge to the Fredenhagen household, and indeed of almost total disinterest to local people, was the strange activities of young students on the windswept and rodent-infested little island of Greifswalder Oie. Located some 5.5 kilometres from the coast of Usedom and 19 kilometres from Greifswald, the island was used by amateur rocketeers. This isolated location spared the rocketry enthusiasts from the complaints of irate locals, since their many misfires fell harmlessly into the Baltic Sea.

Young Fredenhagen knew the hamlets and villages of Usedom extremely well. Happy family holidays were enjoyed in the home of a farmer and fisherman in the coastal village of Ückeritz in mid-Usedom, south of the Peenemünde peninsula. The area was a perfect setting for a boy with interests in outdoor pursuits and sailing. Fredenhagen spent enjoyable days with his host working in the fields and on sailing trips on the Baltic. It is remarkable that completely unknown to Fredenhagen in 1936, the *Heer*, and later the *Luftwaffe*, acquired and developed Greifswalder Oie and the Peenemünde environs for military research. Later, when he was posted to Peenemünde, he was amazed that such a huge supporting infrastructure had been created to service the Rocket development work that took place there.

Although separated from the economic and political turmoil that affected Germany's towns and cities during the 1920s and 1930s, more rural areas did not evade the political upheavals and both Fredenhagen and his father became members of the powerful paramilitary organization of the *Sturmabteilung* (SA), better known in English as the 'Brown Shirts'. Ernst Röhm (1887-1934), the Nazi leader who co-founded the SA, strove to produce a peoples' militia under his personal control. The struggle for power by the SA within the Third Reich and Hitler's anxiety over its increasing strength, led to the organization's liquidation and the murder of its leaders, including Röhm, at the hands of the competing SS in June 1934. The SS subsequently absorbed the main rank-and-file of the SA. In the early days of Nazi Germany, it was strictly forbidden for a serving member of the independent and non-political *Heer* to also be a member of the SA. Fredenhagen had to prove, in spite of family association, that he had resigned and was no longer a member of the SA when he first joined the *Heer* for one year of artillery service in 1934.

Fredenhagen was scientifically minded and after military service took a doctorate in physical chemistry, becoming an assistant at the Institute of Greifswald. Here he undertook military tests using fluorine to develop poison gas for the *Heereswaffenamt*. He had grave misgivings about this work, and described fluorine as 'one of the ugliest of the elements'. His conscience was so troubled that he volunteered to rejoin military service and left the Institute in September 1939. Now aged 27, Fredenhagen was highly qualified and having already served a year of military service, was a man confident in his abilities and quick to see the shortcomings in others.

With the rank of *Leutnant d.R.* (Reserve) and in command of a measurement platoon of almost twenty men, Fredenhagen served as a mathematician in *Eisenbahn Ersatz-Batterie* 800 (railway reserve battery), determining projectile velocities. His brother also joined the artillery and was destined to survive the war having been taken as POW by the French. Fredenhagen felt that his duties were senseless as no amount of matriculation would increase gun accuracy to an appreciable degree. With the commencement of Operation Barbarossa against the Soviet Union in June 1941, his unit was detailed to fire upon important lines of supply and communication in the Schlüsselburg area on Lake Ladoga close to Leningrad. In spite of wholesale destruction of bridges, Fredenhagen remembered that the Russians had a great talent for improvisation, repairing bridges within 24 hours. The besieged city of Leningrad was only occasionally fired upon.

Life on the Eastern Front, just 20 kilometres from Leningrad, was remarkably comfortable. The supply of food was never a problem and was doubtless helped by the unbroken rail connection behind the railway artillery leading back, ultimately, to Germany. Fredenhagen recalled that 300 men operated two 34 cm guns in an exposed woodland clearing and, later, even larger artillery guns were brought forward. The officers were billeted in comfortable railway carriages and with time to spare, a sauna was built in the nearby woods. Not once did Fredenhagen and his comrades receive any attention from the Soviet air force. However, in spite of his experiences, he knew that the campaign in the East was not necessarily going according to plan: 'Already by 1942 and certainly after Stalingrad, I felt that we really had to end it. It could not go on. If we could not win the war, we should at least try to end it with dignity. But we pursued the war idiotically. For me, Alexander the Great was the most iridescent person, for he quickly made defeated people his friends. If Hitler had said to the Russian people, "We will liberate you from Communism; stay in your homes, work and be peaceful," then we would have marched through. Instead, we did terrible things, especially in Poland. The SS would take no prisoners, and soon the Soviets behaved appropriately. Hitler did not have a care for the *Wehrmacht*, allowing it to march on endlessly without supply. When the winter came, the game was over.'

The Russian climate was far from idyllic. At the height of the summer, temperatures rose to 40 degrees C. In the winter, the thermometer dropped to minus 20 degrees C, and it was common practice for Fredenhagen and his comrades to wear two *Heer* greatcoats to fend off the cold. Whilst suffering from 'Wolhynia fever', otherwise known as trench fever (a disease transmitted by body lice), Fredenhagen was fortunate to be sent on temporary leave from the front to the artillery and proving ranges at Rügenwalde on the Baltic coast of Pomerania. While awaiting new orders, his continued ill health was noticed and he spent a brief period of convalescence during which a Major attached to a team recruiting for a new secret weapon approached him. Fredenhagen was asked if he would be interested in a new posting. The question was asked out of politeness for, of course, it was in reality, an order. As a physicist, chemist and experienced soldier, Fredenhagen was a perfect candidate. He was simply told: "There is a new weapon. You, as an officer, will take a lead in its development. About its function, however, you need to know nothing."

Fredenhagen discovered that his new posting was 'extremely interesting'. However, he felt no sense of gratitude because he was simply following whatever orders were given to him from powers 'on high'. He believed that for the soldier, the most important factor was to survive and 'to come through the time well', irrespective of the duties assigned.

On 26 July 1943, promoted to the rank of *Oberleutnant*, Fredenhagen was ordered to Karlshagen, close to Peenemünde. He was to become a battery officer in *Lehr- und Versuchsbatterie 444* (Training and Experimental Battery 444). After four idle weeks awaiting further orders and becoming increasingly bored, he began to think that his new posting and duties were a nonsense. However, on his own initiative, he began to circulate with other soldiers during training and discovered that many were skilled metalworking craftsmen. His new comrades in the *Batterie 444* impressed Fredenhagen. He recalled that half the men were civilians and unlike others he had served with, they never swore and they earned, in his recollection, the accolade of being 'fantastic'. The senior officers above him, however, impressed him less; he recalled them as being 'stuffed shirts'.

The function of the A4 was explained to him by *Ingenieur* Zeitler. Zeitler was a well-liked advisor who was involved in the introduction and training of the FR troops, not only at Peenemünde, but also later in Poland. At the very top of the Peenemünde hierarchy were Wernher von Braun and Dornberger. Fredenhagen recalled: 'As a battery officer I had frequent contact with both men. Von Braun was very open-minded and I never saw him in a uniform. Not only would he explain but he would also listen if I discussed a problem with the troop. He had an unbelievable ability to coordinate things from all sides. I disagree with the way he is viewed today: he never wanted to build a weapon, but of course accepted the money to do so from the *Wehrmacht*. Where would the funding come from otherwise? Von Braun, like Dornberger, was a very decent man and intelligent. They got along together very well.'

The size of the Rocket impressed Fredenhagen and, given his background in chemistry, he grasped immediately the chemical reactions of the Rocket's fuel system. Of the propellants used, from the point of view of a chemist, he was most intrigued by what was known as T-*Stoff*. T-*Stoff*, otherwise known as hydrogen peroxide, was used to create the steam that powered the fuel pump turbine. In his studies in his previous non-military life, he had been familiar with 40% by volume T-*Stoff* but at Peenemünde it was being used at 80% by volume. How this could be manufactured was entirely beyond Fredenhagen. Liquid oxygen was dangerous, but T-*Stoff* was also very volatile and reactive. Fredenhagen was amazed that the T-*Stoff* was not only decanted, but also transported with relative ease. He wanted to take notes during his time working with the Rocket but, as he recalled, 'I was afraid that this could have been bad for me. We knew that the SS was threateningly behind us.'

However, just knowing the chemical processes of the Rocket could not have prepared him for the spectacle of a launch. Fredenhagen remembered: 'I was astonished as it went up. Every firing was an event in itself.' However he added cautiously: 'How sensational it looked at launch was not important: that was not enough.'

Fredenhagen had grave misgivings about the 'wonder weapon'. He could see immediately that the Rocket could never deliver a serious blow with its diminutive warhead. With Allied bombers attacking the Reich every day with hundreds of tonnes of explosives, how could the Rocket compete?

The Rocket's accuracy was such that it could never be used as an artillery piece to strike specific targets or to be deployed against advancing troops. He recalled: 'We knew that the Rocket wouldn't be very accurate. An integration device was used in most rockets. This calculated the point from acceleration to the time when the thrust had to be switched off. Of course the angle also had to be correct. We knew that this was not quite exact. The *Brennschluss* (close burning) was seldom given by radio signal. However, this meant only another complication. There also was the *Leitstrahl* (guidance beam) procedure. However, this was very seldom used. In addition, at least 100 parts had to work in order for the Rocket to take off correctly. One faulty part would lead to failure. The V2 had a warhead of only a ton and every day some 100 or more Allied bombers came to bomb the Reich. But we knew already that bombing raids could not destroy civilian morale. Englishmen are tough. The Rocket would be of no use and was far too expensive. I never believed that the V2 could help to win the war.'

Fredenhagen was given the task of determining a firing running order for the Rocket and to establish the various protocols that would be used operationally. As he recalled: 'The Peenemünde engineers showed me what had to be done and in what order. Only so much could be done in a set amount of time, but the important thing was that it was done correctly. I studied the information and worked out the procedures. I indicated the 'X-times'. For example, X-10 was the sign for the electricians; it did not mean that the Rocket would take off in 10 minutes. If I saw that a group had finished a task, I gave the next group the new X-time. I told my people: "You can do whatever you want. You can sleep, you can go away but when it is your X-time, you must be here." A supervisor complained about the lack of military drill. So (to appease him) I used a whistle to warn of X-time but I told my people that they could ignore my whistling.'

With the exception of the SS *Werfer Batterie* 500 (SS Launch Battery 500), Fredenhagen was to introduce the Rocket to most other battalions that trained at Peenemünde and later, Heidelager. His experience with the SS was yet to come.

Fredenhagen had only been at Peenemünde for four weeks when, on the night of 17/18 August 1943, the RAF bombed the research centre. Given the nature of the Nazi regime, it is hardly surprising that the foreign workers had no air raid shelters, but this recklessness also extended to the FR troops housed in their wooden billets. At the time of the commencement of the raid, Fredenhagen was quartered close to the railway line that supplied workers from the nearby settlement camp and surrounding area. Looking up into the night sky, he could see the brilliant pyrotechnical display of hanging lights known as 'Christmas Trees' that the RAF used as target markers. He dived for cover into a hole in the ground just half a metre deep and cowered for what little protection there was as bombs exploded around him. He had the uncomfortable suspicion that the RAF was using the railway line as a marker for its bomb runs. He expected that at any moment he was going to be blown up, the detonations taking place just 50 metres away from him. The onslaught lasted for about 45 minutes. A brief lull was followed by a second attack, the bombs falling even closer, perhaps just 30 metres away. Everything around him was destroyed. At first light the following morning, *Batterie* 444 and its mobile equipment were evacuated to nearby villages.

Following the air raid, Fredenhagen became aware that a deliberate attempt had been made to give a false impression to enemy reconnaissance aircraft that Peenemünde was beyond repair and was to be abandoned. This, of course, was partially true because following the raid it was thought that the training of the FR troops should now take place out of range of Allied bombers. Fredenhagen and approximately 200 men travelled from Thurn in West Prussia to the SS *Truppenübungsplatz* (Troop Training Ground) at Heidelager in Poland. The *Batterie* 444 had access initially to only a small fenced area. So segregated was the SS, that the FR troops of *Batterie* 444 had their own railway siding for alighting and delivery of supplies. The accommodation in wooden barracks was comfortable, and the men were fed with good meals. Fredenhagen shared a room with Walter Klein (see Chapter Six) and in the adjacent room was the SS representative, *Obersturmführer* Hans Lohse, who was considered to be *Obergruppenführer* Kammler's 'long arm' and whose primary duty was to counter internal espionage activities. In terms of security, it was Klein's onerous and uncomfortable duty to censor the men's mail. Occasionally Fredenhagen would also be called in to perform the task of opening and reading the correspondence and, in addition, he was given the security task of the final vetting of visitors who wanted access to the Rocket. All visitors with permission to watch a Rocket's preparation and launch were obliged to report their presence to Fredenhagen irrespective of their importance or rank. But Fredenhagen's primary duty at Heidelager was training.

Relocated civilian scientists and engineers from Peenemünde occupied a large part of the accommodation at Heidelager, and Fredenhagen was able to learn a great deal from them as he asked probing questions as to the function of the Rocket. The civilian specialists thought that Fredenhagen was like any other officer and did not appreciate that he had the mind of an experienced chemist. One of the civilians was the likeable engineer, Zeitler, the acknowledged engine expert Fredenhagen had first met at Peenemünde. Zeitler was gradually integrated into the Battery as a private soldier without having received any basic military training. After a few weeks however, he was afforded the special status of *Sonderführer* (Special Leader). This rank indicated that he had the duties of an officer albeit with no military experience but with authority only in the area of his specialized engineering skill. He also had access to the *Offizierskasino*.

For entertainment in the evenings, Fredenhagen remembered playing chess and for troops of all ranks an improvised five-kilometre running track weaved its way through the adjacent woods to the barracks.

Training in the preparation of the Rocket led to innovations from the men. A soldier with an engineering background thought up the idea of using easily transportable metal sheets to make an area 4 metres square under the *Abschusstisch*. The procedure took only ten minutes to accomplish. This practice replaced railway sleepers that could, on occasion, be lifted up and blown away by the Rocket's jet blast. Further field tests showed that the space required to accommodate the Rocket and the service vehicles could be reduced to a square just 10 by 10 metres. Such a small area, it was reasoned, would prevent hostile aircraft spotting the firing site from an oblique angle. Another interesting development designed to assist the Rocket crews was the '*Karussell*' (Carousel). The preparation of the Rocket entailed access via ladders to panels 14 metres above the ground. To speed up the procedure, the Rocket would be rotated upon the *Abschusstisch* turntable. However it was realized that a far better procedure would be to access the panels in situ without any movement of the Rocket. The '*Karussell*' allowed this to happen. It consisted of a metal frame with a supporting floor which sat on the nose of the Rocket. It allowed the firing crew to rotate completely around the access panels. This improvement, however, did require that the technicians had a strong resistance to vertigo and heights. Further changes were made to 'ground equipment' including the complicated 5-metre-long firing control desks that were operated from a slit trench from where soldiers would watch a rocket launch up to the point of *Brennschluss*, when visual contact was lost. Fredenhagen recalled that an Austrian Professor by the name of Wierer from Grönwohl, simplified the controls with redesigned operating panels and that these improvements made their way ultimately into the *Feuerleitpanzer*.

Kammler made frequent appearances at the camp. Fredenhagen recalled: 'Kammler was a swine. He had no understanding of the Rocket. Once he visited us to attend a launching. Walter Klein was the firing control officer. However the firing went wrong and the device flew approximately 50 metres over our heads. Thereafter he [Kammler] never wanted to see another launching again!'

Failed shots were fairly commonplace at Heidelager. On one occasion, following the death of some FR troops caused by a misfire landing close to a slit trench, Fredenhagen remembered that von Braun had explained to him that a serious fault had been discovered with the soldering of an electrical condenser. The solder had broken due to vibrations and so remedies were sought to reduce the fault. The other mysterious failing of the Rocket reported by forward observers in the target area, was the lack of significant impact craters. On one occasion Fredenhagen was part of the search party that went out to try to find the crater from a recently launched Rocket. They drove around the countryside asking the locals if they had seen anything, but nobody had! Fredenhagen recalled asking his driver to stop the car, since he felt nauseous. As he was regaining his composure, a Polish policeman approached and having enquired as to their route, asked for a ride. The FR troops had very little contact with the local Polish community and although hostility was never open, the general attitude to the Poles was such that in acceding to the policeman's request, Fredenhagen unbuttoned his holstered side arm and made sure it was at the ready, just in case...

Again von Braun was to explain to Fredenhagen that the thin, outer steel skin of the Rocket's body was being heated to extreme temperatures during the descent and that the slightest imperfections in the surface of the steel would cause 'burn through'. This, in turn, weakened the Rocket's internal structure causing it to disintegrate.

Following the Allied landings in Normandy in June 1944, the news that the bunkers facing England would never be used came as something of a relief. The destruction meted out upon Peenemünde would surely have befallen the fixed-firing sites. Fredenhagen recalled: 'We did not want to go to France; this would have been a suicide detail. We were certain that the originally planned fixed sites in France would have been quickly located by the Allied forces and destroyed.'

Fredenhagen's fears were well-founded as unbeknown to him the major fixed Rocket sites of Watten and Wizernes facing southern England had already been identified and destroyed by the RAF during their construction. With the benefit of hindsight, Fredenhagen was incredulous that Hitler was reportedly so enthusiastic about the use of fixed-firing sites: 'I just didn't believe it! Hitler couldn't have been so stupid as to have involved himself in this decision. He just wanted Rocket *launches,* but he was not interested in *how* that happened. It was Dornberger who planned the bunkers; he had all these things under his control at that time. Only later was it realized it was wrong.'

The reality, as explained by Dornberger in his book '*V2*', is somewhat different. Sometime shortly after the devastating air raid on Peenemünde, Dornberger met with both Xavier Dorsch, the chief engineer of the *Organisation Todt* and Hitler. The *Organisation Todt* was responsible for the construction of the fixed Rocket firing and storage facilities in northern France. In spite of crippling air raids upon the construction sites, Dorsch remained surprisingly positive, suggesting that the Allies could be fooled into thinking the sites had been abandoned whilst construction work continued. Dornberger was to write: 'He [Hitler] was immediately captured by the grandiose plans Dorsch described ... after which he enthusiastically consented. I could not remain silent.

I considered it my duty to point out that there would be more air attacks ... and [I] described in emphatic terms the advantages of putting the A4 into action from motorized batteries. Hitler heard me out, but gave his decision in favour of Dorsch.'[1]

In Dornberger's assessment, the continued construction work in northern France was 'a faulty decision' that wasted valuable material and labour on projects which would never be completed. Only the very daring would argue against the *Führer*.

The shock of the attempted assassination of Hitler on 20 July 1944 caused widespread revulsion and anxiety in Nazi circles. Following the attempted coup by members of the *Heer*, the normal military salute spontaneously gave way fully to the raised arm Nazi *Hitlergruß* (Hitler greeting) to demonstrate loyalty. This, however, caused much unspoken irritation to long-serving soldiers. In Fredenhagen's experience, National Socialism was never a topic of conversation in either the regular forces, or the reserve, of which he was a member. He considered that being a member of the military gave him the opportunity to live life without ever having to come to terms with politics. The reality was that every action he performed whilst in military service was at the behest of the State.

When the order to commence the operational use of the Rocket came, on 3 September 1944 Fredenhagen found himself at the head of an advance party from *Batterie* 444 advancing across Germany and into Belgium to find suitable firing sites. Driving through the forests of the Ardennes, he and his driver were suddenly fired upon by shadowy figures from a relatively close range of 100 metres. With bullets passing through their vehicle, Fredenhagen recalled: 'Luckily, whoever it was could not aim; it was pure luck that they didn't hit us. My driver and I were alone and deep in the wood; we didn't expect any partisans to be there because who would know we were coming? I yelled out to my driver "*Stop!*" He stopped and bent himself down below the dashboard. I threw myself out and my driver suddenly drove off! He was away and I was left alone in the forest. On my hands and knees, I escaped in the opposite direction to the partisans. For his part, my driver didn't know the way but I had the map. Later, he passed the same place again without incident and together we managed to get back to the convoy. Shortly afterwards a heavily armed German infantry unit arrived at the place of the ambush. Suddenly they noticed a man standing in the forest and drove over to question him. Instead of speaking, the man opened fire and emptied a magazine of bullets into their vehicle. Several men, including *Leutnant* Sauer, were killed before the surviving men shot the partisan dead.'

Fredenhagen appears to have taken the incident in the Ardennes in his stride. He was only seriously alarmed later when the Rocket offensive moved to firing sites in Walcheren in the Netherlands and when the subsequent emergency evacuation took place before the Allies' advance. He was concerned that an enemy bomb could render a bridge impassable or breach a dam, trapping the German troops on the former island.

During Rocket-firing operations in the Netherlands, and in particular when the offensive moved to the suburbs of The Hague, Fredenhagen was aware that the '... Dutch civilian population was not filled with enthusiasm' towards the Germans, but he was nevertheless able to exchange cigarettes for goods and had no difficulties communicating with them: 'We simply had no time to make contact with the civilian population. They didn't need to be afraid of us either though.'

Although Fredenhagen was doubtless thinking of himself and his personal interaction with the Dutch civilians, the locals did have good cause to be afraid. Approximately twenty faulty Rockets exploded in mid-air or in ground explosions in The Hague area during the offensive. Many Rocket misfires brought devices down in the vicinity of the launch sites of the 'Sperrgebiet' security zone – but not all. It is believed that sixty of the local population lost their lives because of misfire incidents.[2]

The only 'local' that he came to know well was, in fact, not Dutch. She was from Austria and was known locally as the 'Viennese'. Remarkably, this woman was allowed to stay in her apartment in spite of being located in the Sperrgebiet in Scheveningen. The relationship between the 'Viennese' and the officers of the FR troop was apparently platonic. As an ally to the Germans, and speaking a common language, she was able to exert an influence upon the occupiers. On one occasion, she spoke out to save a local Dutchman who had been caught by the Sicherungstruppen in the prohibited area while attempting to return to his abandoned home. She asked Fredenhagen if he could intervene in what would automatically warrant summary execution. She pleaded for clemency on the basis that the man had only '...gone to water his garden.' This was granted. Later, however, the 'Viennese' was to cause Fredenhagen an unpleasant encounter with the SS.

Fredenhagen continued with the task of finding new Rocket-firing sites, the criteria being sufficient space free of foliage above the Rocket and access to all sides so that the firing crews could work quickly and in parallel. As he recalled: 'The launching sites were chosen, if possible, in woods or park clearings. We fired many shots from the Hook of Holland where the pier was very suitable because of the solid ground. From Scheveningen we worked undisturbed; the chance of a launch being reported (by the Resistance) by radio was not great because of the prior civilian evacuation (of the Restricted Zone). I was always astonished that we were never attacked from the air, although admittedly we did stay at the firing site for only a short period of time. The time from the arrival of a rocket on site to launch was reduced from two hours to perhaps one-and-a-half hours.

We undertook the work every day and afterwards we would drive to our accommodation and to bed – exhausted. We launched Rockets and never thought about what happened at the other end. But this was also the same for the Allied bombers attacking German cities and fundamentally for every soldier. For the soldier this is a very problematical situation.'

Rockets from Germany arrived in The Hague using the Dutch rail system and the FR technical troops would attend to initial tests and the fitment of the warheads. On one occasion there was a supply problem caused by a new and inexperienced, freshly arrived, technical troop. The FR troop under the control of Fredenhagen discovered that a Rocket had been supplied minus the graphite rudders that were fitted below the engine's venturi and interacted with the flow of the Rocket exhaust giving steering control. Immediately, vehicles were dispatched back to the railway station and the missing parts were found still in their packing boxes, resulting in a delay that lasted two hours. Apart from supply problems, the only other factor that affected the Rocket offensive was stormy weather when the V2 was vulnerable to strong side winds.

During the occupation, it was usual for military personnel to identify themselves at the Dutch/German border. Fredenhagen had heard that an over-zealous border guard had the audacity to stop Kammler's car and to ask for his papers and travel permit. His response was apparently 'acidic' and he handed the guard a document that read:

Generalleutnant of the Waffen-SS and Obergruppenführer of the Allgemeine-SS Doctor Engineer Hans Kammler acts on my order. His orders are to be obeyed.

Signed: Reichsführer-SS Heinrich Himmler.

The impact of this document upon the border guards was such that, from that day, until the end of the offensive, it was only necessary for an FR troop soldier to say 'Unit Kammler' and the soldier would be waved through immediately and without question.

Fredenhagen also recalled a most bizarre and extraordinary incident which, irrespective of its validity, led him to be not only punished by the SS, but seconded temporarily to it. One evening in early January 1945, whilst free from Rocket-firing duties, Fredenhagen and three fellow officers were invited to a soirée at the apartment of the 'Viennese' in the '*Sperrgebiet*' in Scheveningen. The 'Viennese' was apparently disappointed that a *Hauptmann* had declined her invitation as she had also invited one of her friends to the party. In any event, a pleasant evening was had drinking wine and dancing to the sounds of a gramophone. The apartment was warm and Fredenhagen slipped off his tunic jacket and absent-mindedly put it down. Fredenhagen explained that, unknown to him, the 'Viennese' had grabbed his tunic and walked out into the street to his waiting car. She asked the driver to take her directly to the *Hauptmann* so she could invite him personally to the party. To ensure passage past the sentry, she donned the tunic. Sure enough, the car was waved through. The *Hauptmann* was found at *Batterie* 444's quarters but he again declined the invitation. The 'Viennese' returned to her apartment leaving the tunic where she had found it. The following day Fredenhagen was ordered to report to the offices of the local *Hauptamt* of the SS *Gericht* (local head office of the SS Court), an organization responsible for legal affairs and disciplinary matters within the SS. It would appear that either Fredenhagen's driver, or the sentry, had reported the misuse of a military uniform in contravention of military law. In the office of an SS Judge, Fredenhagen was asked to sit upon a chair facing a wall. To add to the tension, the interrogator then sat directly behind and began to question him about the inappropriate use of his uniform by an unauthorized person. Apparently this was the very first time that Fredenhagen realized that his tunic had been stolen, but he gave an explanation to the SS man that appeared to be accepted and he was dismissed.

Several days later when the incident was far from his mind, Fredenhagen received a letter that ordered him 'three weeks confinement to quarters' signed by Kammler. Sitting in his room, well-fed and reading books to entertain him, he thought to himself, 'What a nice war!'

After two days of enforced relaxation, Kammler apparently enquired as to Fredenhagen's whereabouts. Bizarrely, given Kammler's mental acuity, he had completely forgotten the confinement papers he had personally sanctioned. Immediately, fresh orders were given to Fredenhagen. He was to report to SS-*Werfer Batterie* 500 operating in the Dalfsen and Hellendoorn area of eastern Holland and to commence a training programme to improve the unit's efficiency. Fredenhagen remembered his feelings about the SS secondment: 'I was not amused. The relationship between the *Wehrmacht* and the SS was always tense. The SS always claimed to be better than us. If an SS officer sat in a train, then you would find somewhere else to sit. But they were human and didn't have an easy life after the war. My brother-in-law was in the *Waffen*-SS. He had been wounded in action three times. They were employed in particularly dangerous places and never took prisoners. There was a rivalry between Dornberger and Kammler. The SS recognized that in the V2 there was an operational weapon and initially they assumed control over its "protection". This was only the beginning though. What they wanted was to control everything about it.'

Fredenhagen was ordered to report to an SS-*Obersturmführer* for further instructions. Upon doing so Fredenhagen cheerily announced: 'Fredenhagen! Here I am. If I can help you or if I can tell you anything (regarding the Rocket), please let me know.'

However the SS officers did not appreciate his appointment and they had no intention of receiving instructions from a mere 'reservist artilleryman'. He spent the next two days playing chess with an SS officer whom he recalled played better than him. Once again, however, Kammler intervened and, having discovered the resentment of his SS officers and the lack of progress, temporarily replaced those officers who had not already made themselves scarce with lower ranking SS-*Unterscharführer*. Now Fredenhagen was able to take command and the training could begin.

Fredenhagen realized that many of the operational problems associated with SS-*Werfer Batterie* 500 were due, in part, to the non-technical pre-war occupations of the men. In *Batterie* 444 many of the men chosen had had backgrounds in industry or had been metalworkers, electricians, plumbers or locksmiths: in short they already had something of a technical mind. Conversely, as far as Fredenhagen could determine, the SS *Batterie* consisted of 'farmers and bakers' and its personnel were technically inept. It was clear that the SS had not sought skilled professions for its firing battery and, not only that, but the SS-*Oberscharführer* acting as the battery's graduated head engineer simply did not seem to care about the unit's performance. Apparently, it was normal practice for SS-*Werfer Batterie* 500 to send a Rocket back for repair or replacement if it was discovered to have the slightest defect, whilst the firing troops of *Batterie* 444 would attempt – and often succeeded in – 'field' repairs.

Shortly after Fredenhagen had begun training, three Rockets arrived, one for each of the three *Schießzüge* (platoons). In spite of the problems of making good the usual faults, all three Rockets were launched successfully. A few days later two further Rockets were launched, only this time one of them developed an engine fault. Having lifted off, it came crashing down close to a *Feuerleitpanzer*. The propellant tanks ruptured, sending cascades of flame in all directions. Fredenhagen looked up and realized that the top inspection hatch of the *Feuerleitpanzer* had not been closed and was wide open to the sky. Burning alcohol splashed into the tank but quickly burnt out. Fredenhagen waited for the flames of the burning Rocket to subside and then ordered the *Feuerleitpanzer* crew to abandon the vehicle and retreat to a safe distance away from the undetonated warhead. The Rocket safely burnt out and the *Feuerleitpanzer* was recovered undamaged. It is possible that the misfire Fredenhagen recalled occurred on 13 January 1945 as the SS-*Werfer Batterie* 500 experienced two failures on that date with both V2s falling near the launch site at Hessum near Dalfsen. [3]

After just ten unsatisfactory days with the SS *Batterie*, Fredenhagen had finished his penance and was ordered back to The Hague. Although he is unable to remember precise dates, his arrival back at The Hague must have occurred after 28 January 1945 since *Batterie* 444 had already been withdrawn from the Netherlands. Instead of being ordered to rejoin his comrades in Germany, Fredenhagen was ordered to report to *Artillerie Abteilung* 485 (*mot.*). This battery had recently suffered the loss of three of its officers who had been killed in a drunken car crash following celebrations in The Hague earlier in the month.

Fredenhagen's new posting was intended partly to relieve the depleted command structure. On 12 February 1945, he joined the regimental administrative *Stab* of *Art.Abt.* 485 *(mot.)* which was now renamed as *Artillerie-Regiment zur Vergeltung* 902 *(Art.Rgt.z.V* 902 – Artillery Regiment of Retaliation) following the Kammler-induced changes which dictated that Rocket battalions should become regiments.

Towards the end of March 1945 the situation had become critical for the Rocket regiments still left in The Hague. Inevitably they withdrew from the Netherlands back to Germany and on 1 April 1945 *Art.Rgt.z.V.* 902 arrived at Fallingbostel in the Lüneburg Heath area. It delivered what equipment and devices it still possessed to the ammunition store at Leese on the river Weser. The Rocket soldiers were then told that they were now infantrymen and were ordered to march 80 kilometres to defend the River Elbe against advancing American troops. Fredenhagen was simultaneously promoted to company commander and just a few hours later, having crossed the Elbe with his comrades, he found himself in a most extraordinary predicament. In one direction he faced the Americans, and in the opposite direction, the Russians! With the two fronts separated by only 8 kilometres he recalled: 'It was pure madness and chaos.'

In fact Fredenhagen and his men had no contact with either the Americans or Soviets and for reasons unknown, he and his immediate comrades were relieved of their weapons. Now deserted by his 'boy', who had driven off in the unit staff car, he then heard that *Art.Rgt.z.V.* 902 was to have one last assembly prior to surrender. As a pillion passenger on a motorcycle, he travelled to the forest at Ludwigslust. In the general panic of retreat and defeat, and with roads congested with homeless civilians, demoralized troops, vehicles, and horse-drawn carriages, it was perhaps inevitable that, en route, he was involved in a road accident in which he injured his foot. The following morning, on 2 May 1945, the war was over for Helmut Fredenhagen when a fellow soldier informed him that the enemy was very close. His aching foot made walking near impossible, but as luck would have it, he was able to drag himself into a vehicle that just happened to be an American staff car his men had taken as war 'booty' and he made his way to the American line. At first, as he sat in the vehicle unable to move, the Americans paid him very little attention thinking he was one of their own, but it was not long before he was hauled out and taken prisoner. To his enormous relief, he was sent to a British field hospital near Lauenburg, to the west of the Elbe, and his injured foot received basic First Aid. He also enjoyed his first hot meal in days: soup.

Suddenly, from nowhere, a rumour got around that the Russians were coming and panic broke out among the former soldiers of the *Heer* as well as the German civilians in the hospital, who fled to get across the River Elbe using a recently constructed Allied 'sappers'' bridge. Lauenburg was never to fall under the control of the Soviets, but the general hysteria of the moment emptied the field hospital of those patients who were able to move. Fredenhagen, fearing that he would doubtless be taken by the Soviets, could only hobble along when, unexpectedly, he and three or four other injured men were bundled into an amphibious vehicle by the British and taken across the river! Once more falling into the custody of the Americans, he was sent to a hospital at Lüneburg.

From Lüneburg he was sent to a second hospital at Munster–Lager where he was amazed at the standard of care and treatment that he received. After fourteen days, he was deemed to be fit enough to be dismissed. Fredenhagen remembered his feelings as he left the hospital: 'I wasn't a soldier any more, thank God. I had a rucksack and in it were some old drill trousers, a shirt without collars and a billycan. I had nothing, but I didn't have any worries either. I thought, "It's not great, but at least I am well and alive!"'

Fredenhagen's home in Greifswald was now under the control of the Russians and he decided that it would be prudent firstly to keep his wartime experience of the Rocket to himself and, secondly, to lie as to his place of origin. He had heard that there was a great demand for farmers in the Hannover area. He reported to the office of the Hannover Inhabitant Registration Office and was assigned a room and a temporary job – not as a farmer as he expected, but as a factory worker. To supplement his salary he gave tuition in science subjects. Ultimately he was able to return to his previous wartime occupation as a chemist.

Looking back with the hindsight of nearly 60 years, Fredenhagen commented: 'The development of the Rocket was admirable. The chemical workings were completely outside and beyond what we, as students, had been taught. The question is, of course, the military use of the Rocket. We made and used it because it was ordered and what was done cannot be undone. We simply did our duty. And yet still, today, young men must go to war. What insanity!'

CHAPTER EIGHT

'WE SAW THE V2 ONLY AS A WEAPON'

HEINZ WUNDERLICH
Lehr- und Versuchsbatterie 444

IN common with many German veterans of World War Two, Heinz Wunderlich would rarely speak of his wartime experiences. Born in November 1923 in Rudolstadt, Thuringia, in central Germany, Wunderlich was to comment that he had never spoken at length about his service with the *Heer* and the V2 Rocket until he met the authors of this book.

His home town of his youth, Rudolstadt was famed for its manufacture of painted glazed earthenware and Heinz's father was employed as a potter at the Volkstedt factory. Business was good for the porcelain trade during the 1930s as the factory exported its many fine figurines worldwide. However Wunderlich's father was disquieted by the growth of the Nazi Party and remained unsympathetic to the 'new order' when it took power in 1933. Wunderlich recalled that his father would listen to the BBC German service on the wireless and, as the years passed, so the need for secrecy regarding this highly dangerous and clandestine activity grew greater, especially in wartime. Wunderlich recalled that he and his brother or sister would be sent by their mother to fetch their father away from his secret radio listening place for meal times. Other children would, however, denounce their parents to the authorities for such traitorous behaviour. To voice dissatisfaction against the State was of course very unwise and so Heinz's father demonstrated his dislike of the government by other means. In the years of peace before 1939, it was the custom in Germany to unveil the Party flag of the National Socialists from the windows and balconies of ordinary homes during so-called 'Flag Days'. Although not all were declared public holidays, ten such Flag Days commemorated or celebrated events of historical, political or military importance. While most homes flew the familiar red flag with the central white circle and black Swastika, the Wunderlich household did not. This did not go unnoticed and local party officials took note accordingly.

Having left school, young Wunderlich became an engineer toolmaker and produced items for the military. This occupation meant that he was spared the usual mandatory service in the *Reichsarbeitsdienst* and so he entered military service directly on 20 April 1942. To the general surprise of many friends and relatives, Wunderlich's father was unexpectedly drafted the following day! The drafting of a man at the rather advanced age of 43 was unheard of at that time. The State, it seemed, was exacting retribution, for Wunderlich's father joined the *Luftwaffe* as ground crew, based initially at Hannover. Thereafter he was sent to the Eastern Front serving in the Kiev sector before being relocated to Stalingrad to support the ill-fated Sixth Army.

In July 1942, Wunderlich was posted to a Flak unit in Gotha, central Germany, operating in defence of the local aircraft production factories. That summer, nineteen-year old Wunderlich began a year's *Waffenmeisterschulung* (Senior Armourer Training) at Greifswald just 30 kilometres away from Peenemünde in northern Germany. Although enjoying the camaraderie of his unit, and in particular his new friend, Walter Salomon, and another fellow called Mies, the workload was such that only Sundays were free. In the winter of 1943 came the news that Wunderlich's father had been killed at Stalingrad. Wunderlich's mother was visited by a comrade of his father who was returning some personal effects. She was informed that her husband had apparently died in the evacuation of an airfield close to Stalingrad during a failed escape attempt intended to pull back to the inner defensive circle of the besieged city. Her husband's comrade, with little thought as to the impact of his words upon a grieving widow, said that conditions had been so dreadful at Stalingrad that '…rats fed upon the feet of exhausted soldiers.'

It was at Greifswald in July 1943 that the order to report to Peenemünde, fully equipped with front line weapons, was received by Wunderlich's Flak unit. This caused great consternation for Wunderlich and his comrades: they had never heard of Peenemünde before and he remembered that '… we all thought that things were becoming serious.'

Unknown to Wunderlich and his fellow Flak troops, they were to form the first contingent of what was to become the first Rocket-firing battalion, *Lehr- und Versuchsbatterie* 444. Initially, Wunderlich was unsure whether he was happy with this new posting, but it gradually dawned upon him that it was actually very good luck. His father was dead and many of his school friends had been killed on the battle fronts. Luckily for him, he found himself some 1200 kilometres away from the Eastern Front. At first, Wunderlich's unit was given limited access to the Peenemünde research station and its personnel were shown only what they needed to see. They knew nothing of jet- or rocket-powered aircraft, but excited rumours of 'wonder weapons' began to circulate. Eventually, as an introduction to the Rocket, Wunderlich, his comrades and other new arrivals were taken on a tour of two large factory halls close to the proofing test stands. He received his initial technical briefing and saw, for the very first time, the new secret weapon. The experience of seeing the black and white chequerboard-painted Rocket was '... overwhelming and indescribable. But we just couldn't imagine that we would be able to send it up into the sky. We were astonished. I recall thinking that we could still win the war – our Rocket was the wonder weapon.'

The feeling of elation was relatively short-lived however, as he began to realize that the Rocket's aim was far too inaccurate and could be used only against large targets – not against advancing lines of enemy troops. Initially, only Wunderlich and three other team members of identical rank were allowed to be spectators or to help in the preparation of Rocket test launches. It was the 'experts' who continually adjusted the Rocket. Wunderlich had the impression that the officers in the firing crew were scientists and that some had worked as civilian engineers at Peenemünde – indeed, most of the men seen close to the Rocket appeared to be educated civilians who were held in respect. None more so than Wernher von Braun and Wunderlich recalled: 'We respected von Braun; he was only 33-years old and already a Professor [as of July 1943]. He was always very well dressed but we never spoke with him.'

Another well-known character frequently seen in the vicinity of the proofing stands wearing a long leather military coat was *Generalmajor* Dornberger. Often when dignitaries were present to witness launches, they would be 'screened' away from the gaze of the lower ranks.

Wunderlich remembered witnessing his first launch: the Rocket sat silently upon the firing platform, the ice that had formed in the lower section of the Rocket's body standing out in sharp relief against the black of the chequered colour scheme: 'The first launch of a Rocket I saw was incomprehensible to me. At ignition, the flame coming out of the "oven" [nickname for the combustion chamber] was slight. Then the *Vorstufe* and the noise became louder. After four to five seconds, then it was the "*Hauptstufe*". What a noise! Talking was impossible. We could still hear the noise five minutes after the launch.'

Wunderlich recalled that life at Peenemünde was comfortable: no military drill, rustic but dry hut accommodation, and hearty food cooked in large cauldrons. Wunderlich felt that the seldom seen high-ranking officers were enjoying a very comfortable life in the Peenemünde *Offizierskasino*.

All the personnel at Peenemünde had a rude awakening that a 'real' war was being waged on the German homeland when RAF Bomber Command attacked the research centre on the night of 17 August 1943. As bombs exploded nearby, Wunderlich and his comrades escaped from their billets and made off for their lives. With the camp settlement behind them, they ran into the perimeter fence and could go no further. Looking around for cover, Wunderlich saw a pile of rubbish and dived beside it as the bombs fell just 150 metres away. Amazingly, his billet was unscathed and no members of his unit were killed. Following cleaning up duties after the British raid, he and others were evacuated to Posen (now Poznan), 280 kilometres to the south-east of Peenemünde. After a wait of approximately six weeks, while presumably preparations were being made, Wunderlich and the others in his battery then travelled a further 450 kilometres to the south-east to the SS *Truppenübungsplatz* (Troop Training Ground) at Heidelager in Poland.

Accommodation at Heidelager was very rudimentary, with four men to a room and a communal wardrobe, although chocolate and other hard-to-come-by wartime provisions were regularly available. Wunderlich exchanged his 200 cigarettes, a monthly quota, for other goods from men in the battery. From his comrades he heard that a brothel could be found in a nearby village; in this respect, the Heidelager camp was no different to any other *Heer* camp or garrison.

As the firing crews became more familiar with the A4 and its equipment, the Rocket earned the nickname of the 'Cigar'. Wunderlich recalled that the general procedure to launch a V2 was for the *Abschusstisch* to be set up with a pair of surveyors confirming the levelling of the platform. The *Meillerwagen* would then gently raise and then lower the Rocket onto the launch platform and again the surveyors would make the critical final adjustments of the Rocket position and fins relative to the target area. The *Meillerwagen* would then withdraw by just a metre allowing the 'Carousel' to be fitted and the first of the electrical plugs connected. For the purposes of test-firings, the warhead was filled with sand to make up for the lack of explosives. Wunderlich worked directly below the 'dummy' warhead from the upper platform, making adjustments to the equipment in the Rocket instrument compartments and in particular he recalled a device known as the I-*Gerät* (I-Device).[1] The 'I' was an abbreviation for '*Integrationsbeschleunigungsmessgerät*', an integrating accelerometer. The unit would be preset either by controls from the *Feuerleitpanzer* or as was the experience of Wunderlich, manually. An adjustable scale on the I-*Gerät* indicated range to the target. The seemingly simple manner of range adjustment belied a much more complicated means of determining distance. It was, of course, impossible for the Rocket's avionics without radio telemetry to directly determine the amount of ground that had passed under the Rocket following take-off. Instead, the Peenemünde scientists relied upon the physical properties of a gyroscope and a phenomenon known as 'precession'. As a gyroscope rotates (and this is true for other rotating bodies, including the Earth), the axis tends to wobble or precess. This precessional effect, which is proportional to the gyroscope's acceleration, can be very accurately determined. At launch, the I-*Gerät's* gyroscope would be released and the precession revolutions would be counted. Once the correct value had been achieved, determined by the presets, a cut-off signal would be generated to terminate the engine burn and the Rocket would continue to its target in much the same way as an artillery shell.

As Wunderlich worked away at his duties in the control compartments, below him others attended to the fuelling and preparation of the pyrotechnical firework igniter system that lit the atomized propellant flowing from the combustion chamber. Having performed dry checks to ensure the serviceability of the fuelling system and valves, the fuelling process would begin. Constant checks were made to ensure that valves did not freeze as the liquid oxygen passed through supply lines. To reduce the risk of icing, the valves were electrically heated; a faulty or frozen valve could lead to the lengthy de-tanking of a Rocket. With the compartment doors screwed down, Wunderlich would descend to ground level and with the other crew members and vehicles, withdraw as the allotted tasks of preparation were completed. No flare or shouted warning was given to the firing crew of an imminent launch since the procedure became so well known it was unnecessary. However, once the Rocket was filled and ready for launch, a sense of urgency was felt, as the Rocket would lose liquid oxygen at an alarming rate due to evaporation. The crew of the *Feuerleitpanzer* would disappear into the vehicle and this was the sign to seek cover, the firing team members either jumping into slit trenches or standing in the open at a safe distance of 250 metres away.

From the *Abschusstisch* a shower of bright sparks would be seen momentarily just before the gases ignited. This was referred to as the '*Vorstufe*' (pre-stage) and was followed by the '*Hauptstufe*' (main stage) as the Rocket developed full thrust. Simultaneously, the *Abreißstecker* (umbilical) plug connection that ran from the side of the Rocket, down the support tower and on to the *Feuerleitpanzer,* would automatically fall away. If the plug failed to fall, an emergency *Brennschluss* (cut-off) signal could be sent to the Rocket to stop the flow of propellants. However, Wunderlich recalled occasions, both during training and at the front, when errant Rockets would sit on the *Abschusstisch* until all of its propellants had been exhausted in the *Vorstufe* mode. He recalled: 'An emergency *Brennschluss* was not [always] possible and the 8,000 litres of fuel and oxygen would burn out. Inevitably the Rocket would [lean and] crash down to earth because the *Abschusstisch* would [melt and] be destroyed by the heat.'

Wunderlich remembered the failed firing of one device caused by the ground giving way under the weight of the *Abschusstisch* and the Rocket. Mercifully, his comrades sheltering in the trench did not suffer a lingering death, but died immediately in the flames.

Not far away, to the south-west of Heidelager, Wunderlich recalled that the pulse-jet-powered, ramp-launched, Fieseler Fi 103 'Flying Bomb' (or FZG

[*Flakzielgerät*] 76) was being test-launched. As a security measure, the V1 – as the Fi 103 was to be generally known – and FR troops were kept separate from each other. According to British Intelligence reports drafted during the war, test-firing of the V1 took place at Heidelager between 14-18 April 1944.[2] Wunderlich and his comrades were astonished that three pre-fuelled V1s could be prepared and fired in one hour whilst preparation to launch a Rocket would take five, or even up to seven, hours.

Although Wunderlich was never taken into the confidence of either the officers or scientists, he was aware that two problems began to manifest themselves during the Rocket-firing tests at Heidelager in the spring and early summer of 1944. Not only were Rockets breaking up in descent, but also it was subsequently discovered that those that did impact would detonate their warheads deep into the ground and thus minimize the lateral explosive effect. The second problem was only clearly revealed when the first problem of airbursts was reduced. To determine the reason for the airbursts and generally to preserve the secrecy of the Rocket, it was important that as much of the shattered remains of the failed shots as possible were found for analysis. Wunderlich recalled on one such occasion being sent to a target area to search for the remains of an airburst failure that was probably in a region close to the village of Sarnaki, approximately 250 kilometres north north-east of Heidelager. En route, the lorry that carried him and his comrades was shot at by partisans who were hiding in woods. A quick look around revealed no obvious position for the partisans, so rather than stop and become easy victims for snipers, the lorry sped away to the designated search area. Having arrived, Wunderlich recalled seeing Wernher von Braun and *Generalmajor* Dornberger who both joined in the search for metal Rocket fragments. The impact area of Sarnaki was very thinly populated but even so, the activity of the Germans left a clear impression with the indigenous locals. Later the Poles would recount to British Intelligence officers who visited the area not only their observations, but also comments made to them by the Germans. Apparently, the SS assisted the *Heer* with searches for metal fragments, threatening the locals with setting their villages on fire if they did not hand in parts they had found.[3] The Poles, who would frequently confuse the V1 and the V2 during interviews with the British, described Rockets arriving from the south without any noise. However, the resultant explosion was reported to be heard up to a distance of 80 kilometres, which is, in hindsight, perhaps a fanciful comment. However the detonation of the Rocket was described as being 'strong' and 'that all the windows fell out' in a village 500 metres away. A nearby crater, discovered in the forests, was apparently 28 metres wide and five metres in depth, the trees in an area of 300 metres had been burnt, and the ground was cracked in a radius of 100 metres. When Rockets had exploded in the air, the Poles reported that fragments were found over a distance of 3 kilometres. To the locals it was extraordinary that so much damage could occur, but even more extraordinary was that the Germans claimed, perhaps boastfully, that the Rockets were only 'partially' filled with explosives. The Poles also noticed that in the impact area, one soldier appeared to communicate the 'fall of shot' back via radio from a panel-reinforced open hole in the ground, whilst outside, a second man with pen and notepad operated a theodolite type instrument mounted upon a tripod.[4]

From training in Heidelager, Wunderlich was sent to Heidekraut and he remembered that he was given permission to enter the *Feuerleitpanzer* because his duties meant that he was often the last person to be in physical contact with a Rocket prior to launch. This would allow him to observe the Rocket from a range of only 60 metres but he would refuse to do this, as he was anxious that if the device careered out of control towards the vehicle, he would have no chance to escape the Rocket if it landed on top of him!

Wunderlich discovered from the 'rumour factory' that the Allied landings in northern France on 6 June 1944 would mean a change of firing position, but would still allow 'the' target – which everyone knew to be London – to be in range. He was completely oblivious to the support infrastructure that had been built up in northern France and it was only after the war that he was to discover that huge Rocket firing and storage facilities at Wizernes, Watten and other sites had been constructed in vain and abandoned. Still unaware of where the new firing sites would be located, Wunderlich was granted leave and he returned to his parents' home. As usual, he was warned that he was not to discuss any aspect of his work on the 'wonder weapons' with his relatives otherwise he would fall foul of the SS. All outgoing mail was screened by officers to ensure no infringement of security could take place. However his relatives were able to deduce that he had been stationed in Poland from his unit's telltale *Feld Post* (Field Post) stamps. While he was away on leave, the failed assassination attempt on Hitler and the attempted military *coup d'état* took place on 20 July 1944. Upon his return to rejoin his unit at Heidekraut, he immediately got into trouble for the use of the standard military salute. In the post-'bomb plot' period, the Nazi salute was now required to demonstrate both loyalty and obedience.

As the summer of 1944 drew on, Wunderlich and others noticed that men were still being allowed on leave in groups of five, and sometimes tens, and so no sooner had he returned to Heidekraut, than once again, he was sent home on leave! He was mystified: 'We thought to ourselves "Something's up!"' This was extraordinary: Wunderlich concluded that for reasons unknown, the Rocket offensive had been delayed which explained why he was instructed to take a second leave. However, he was not about to complain and thus returned home once more. On 1 September 1944 he received a telegram, issued by the *Heer*, ordering him to return immediately to his unit. He duly travelled east, directly to Heidekraut, to discover that his *Zug* (platoon) and another had already received their orders and had left, travelling west, towards Luxembourg. Although the 3. *Zug* of *Batterie* 444 under *Oberstleutnant* Moser was still present, all that was left behind of his *Zug* were a few individuals, one tent, and some luggage and rucksacks.

Travelling then towards the west he, and the other stragglers, eventually met up with *Batterie* 444 which had reached Belgium on or around 3 or 4 September. Wunderlich heard from other soldiers that a skirmish had taken place between a forward party of *Batterie* 444 and a band of partisans. Of more immediate concern to him was that at around the same time, one of his comrades had been taken away by the SS and never seen again. Wunderlich subsequently learned that the man was either a traitor or spy. In reality, the man was probably arrested for a breach in security. His fate remained unknown. Within the circle of lower ranks, the men all knew each other by their first names which appears to have been a practice fairly unique to the FR troops.

Wunderlich remembers that the first operational firings in which he participated were conducted from Belgium. He recalled that, either because of the speed of preparation, or the lack of *Sicherungstruppen* (security troops), the local inhabitants were able to watch the activities and launches of *Batterie* 444. As Wunderlich recalled: 'When the civilians saw our transports, their eyes bulged and their mouths dropped open. They were astonished that after the launch only the *Abschusstisch* was left.'

The memories of his unit's movements and activities are fogged by the fact that Wunderlich, and his comrades of similar rank, simply did not know where they were unless they passed through a large town or city. Equipment would hurriedly be set up in a clearing in woods, a Rocket would either be launched successfully against an unknown target – or not – and then the equipment was quickly dismantled and stowed again for moving off in canvas-covered vehicles to yet another unknown location somewhere in the Low Countries. The officers had deemed it unnecessary for lower ranks to be informed as to their precise location, whether it be in Belgium, France, Germany or the Netherlands. Additionally the FR troops were always very busy and had no time simply to look around and become acquainted with their surroundings. Temporary tented accommodation was erected beside parked vehicles and close to the firing sites and direct contact with local people would rarely occur. Wunderlich was completely oblivious to the fact that *Batterie* 444 had travelled to the Dutch peninsula of Walcheren, arriving in the small hours of 15 September.[5] Equally, he had not known just how close the unit had been to being captured in its entirety by the Allies before it retreated inland to Germany only to resume operations from Friesland in northern Holland. The lack of knowledge was a common experience for ordinary soldiers in the early days of the V2 offensive.

Batterie 444 moved to The Hague around 20 October 1944. Operating from this area for nearly three months, Wunderlich's recollections and memory improves. He and his comrades were billeted in commandeered villas and apartment blocks in the affluent areas of the pre-war seaside resort town of Scheveningen. The main firing sites to the east were an easy 30-minute walk away. Later *Batterie* 444 was moved to accommodation at Marlot Park Fliet just off the Leidsestraatweg, on the main road between The Hague and Wassenaar. From the ornamental parks and woods, in particular the famous Haagse Bos of The Hague, the firings against London took place in wooded clearings. The forest branches were cut down just enough, but not too close to the Rocket that a fin might strike a bough during the ascent. 'The control of the Rocket was very sensitive,' recalled Wunderlich. 'Since we usually fired from inside the woods, we had to take great care that no branches were in the way. If the Rocket touched a branch, the control would fail. We had an incident, when a Rocket's fin touched a bough of a tree during launch only for it to fly back 180 degrees to crash about 7 kilometres away from the launch site. We drove over in a car to have a look where the Rocket had come down but the building, which had been huge, had disappeared and the crater was slowly filling up with water. The warhead, however, had not exploded because of the safety devices.'

The *Feuerleitpanzer* would be deployed some 60 metres from the *Abschusstisch* and the FR troops would watch the firings from the cover of large trees at a distance of 250 metres. Unlike training operations in Poland, Wunderlich recalled that slit trenches were never dug for firing operations in The Hague. Often an engine would develop a fault just metres off the ground and the device would then fall backwards onto the *Abschusstisch* crushing the fins, then tipping over and exploding. The FR troop watching the unfolding accident would then shelter behind the protected cover of the trees so as not to be caught by the pressure wave from the combusting propellants or from flying shrapnel. On those occasions when the Rocket did fall onto the firing pad, the *Abschusstisch* would be wrecked.

If all went according to plan the crew, emboldened by the Rocket safely ascending into the sky, would stand clear of the trees so the spectacle of the trajectory could be followed; often the condensation trail would be seen to a height of 12 kilometres. Following the success of a firing, apart from feeling a sense of satisfaction and relief, the crews did not engage in any celebration or handshaking. They simply attended to the clear-up procedure before perhaps the delivery of a second device, if not ordered to a new firing position.

On one occasion, Wunderlich recalled that a V2 took off and at first all seemed well as the firing crew took its customary position to watch the Rocket ascend. However as time went by, it began to dawn upon the troops that something was very wrong. The condensation trail was standing perfectly above them as the Rocket continued to ascend but without leaning over towards the target. The tilt programme, which should have taken place automatically four seconds into the flight when the Rocket was 80 metres above the ground, had failed. The FR troops exchanged nervous glances at each other before finally one of the soldiers started to run as quickly as he could away from the launch site into the woods followed by the others. The Rocket continued its path into the sky and quite probably reached an altitude of 96 kilometres. Then in the silent upper atmosphere on the edge of space, the inevitable happened: the V2 began to descend, falling tail first. The device would then have somersaulted around to face the thickening atmosphere and as far as Wunderlich recalled, it did not suffer a mid-air disintegration. Wunderlich reasoned that the chances of the Rocket falling back directly onto the launch site were negligible, so he ran over to the *Abschusstisch* and waited. Sure enough, some six minutes after the Rocket had left the ground, an explosion was heard as the Rocket impacted harmlessly 7 kilometres away in the North Sea. The reality was that it would have been very unlikely for the Rocket to fall back upon the firing site from such an enormous altitude, having travelled 186 kilometres. Forgetting effects caused by the atmosphere and subtle anomalies in the Rocket's aerodynamics, the effect of differential speeds due to the Earth's rotation and that of the airborne Rocket would be significant. The launch site would drift to the east relative to the vertical ascent and descent of the Rocket. The impact site would therefore be west of the firing site as was the case when an explosion occurred in the Sea.

On the rare occasions that a V2 fell at the launch site and injured a soldier, he would be awarded the '*Verwundetenabzeichen*' (Wound Badge) which would be worn on the lower left breast of his uniform and below any other awards if present. Wunderlich recalled that many of the lower rank soldiers would wear the somewhat shapeless, but practical, field grey denim '*Drillich*' (overalls) on firing operations.

Wunderlich recalled that the tip of the Rocket was a glass fuse containing metal strips which would form a circuit as the glass disintegrated when the Rocket penetrated the ground. Apparently the glass fuse was very delicate and he accidentally broke one whilst fitting it to the warhead. Needless to say, the various safety devices prevented premature detonation. Technical faults with a Rocket would often be found during the initial testing of the avionics. If the fault could not be identified, the Rocket would be lowered back down into the horizontal position by the *Meillerwagen* and then given a thorough examination. It was often the case that the firing crews would detect a technical fault in the Rocket but were unable to access the problem in order to effect a repair – assuming that they had spare parts to replace faulty components. Invariably, they only carried enough parts to replace faulty valves and other small items. Sabotage was another problem that affected the FR troops. Screwdrivers, wrenches and other tools would often be found jammed into strategic positions within the Rocket's inner workings. Occasionally small holes would be detected in metal components. Rockets delivered with obvious faults would be rejected immediately. 'Several Rockets had small holes in the outer skin, as if somebody had shot at the Rocket,' Wunderlich remembered. 'Dutch Resistance? Sabotage? I don't know. But in such cases the Rocket had to be sent back to the *Mittelwerk*. I guess two out of ten Rockets were not OK. At least that was what we knew. How many had problems and never reached the target we never knew. We only could change small parts like valves.'

Wunderlich remembered an occasion in which his nerve was put to the test. A V2 had been prepared without incident and with the upper compartments secured, he had dismounted the *Meillerwagen's* ladder so that the vehicle could be withdrawn to a safe distance in anticipation of a launch. Suddenly, smoke was seen pouring from one of the instrument compartments below the warhead, some 14 metres above the ground. Rather than wait for the *Meillerwagen* to be repositioned, a Magirus ladder, was called for. The Magirus ladder was an antiquated, spindly, three-wheeled cart with a telescopic, wire-supported ladder more commonly seen in use with fire brigades. Nervously watched by the officers and men, Wunderlich scaled the ladder ever mindful of the tons of propellant just below him and the warhead just centimetres above his head. He recalled: 'I was ordered to go up there and to see what had happened. I was very nervous! I thought that the Rocket might explode. When I opened the compartment door I saw that a faulty transformer was the reason for the smoke. There was nothing else we could do but take down the Rocket.' Wunderlich was to laugh that he could have been the first man in space!

To increase the chances of a successful launching, the firing crews would work quickly, especially once the Rocket had been fuelled, as this minimized the risk from freezing valves. Wunderlich was also aware that Rockets were being delivered directly to The Hague area from the *Mittelwerk* factory without any transportation stopovers. Even so he remembered that the firing crews never had enough Rockets and delivery delays, whether caused by production difficulties or by Allied air attacks on the railway infrastructure, meant times of idleness. While waiting for a fresh supply of Rockets to arrive, Wunderlich and his comrades would be given permission to walk into The Hague from their billets. It was always advisable for the men to go into the city in pairs or groups – never alone, for he recalled it was not uncommon for a German serviceman to be found murdered in a secluded alleyway.

The German troops were warned by superiors to be very cautious of the local girls, lest they become infected with venereal diseases. It was said that such women had somehow been sent by the enemy to infect the men and to render them useless! Napoleon Bonaparte famously said 'An army marches on its stomach', but from the earliest of times, military leaders realized that men away from home had other basic needs. The *Heer* catered for this as efficiently as possible as men incapacitated by venereal disease were useless for soldiering and were a drain on medical resources. Brothels, administered jointly by the *Feldgendarmerie* (Military Police) and the *Sanitätseinheiten* (medical units) consisted of two basic types: mobile units for operational troops and brothels in garrison towns or other locations where large numbers of soldiers were stationed or passed through. The military brothels were free to use, but regulations and controls to reduce and counter the risk of disease were extremely strict. Not only were the women routinely examined, but also the men would be medically screened and issued a clearance document, a prophylactic and hygiene spray by the *Sanitätseinheiten* prior to using the facilities.[6]

The highly regimented procedures would rob any sense of spontaneity for the more experienced men; local prostitutes were still in demand in spite of the risks of disease and military punishment. Wunderlich recalled that in The Hague separate brothels for the officers and others for the lower ranks had been organized in requisitioned private houses close to the billets and, as was the situation at Marlot Park Fliet, within the billet itself. The girls were Flemish and the 'establishments' had five women apiece. His knowledge of such places was due to the fact that early on during his service in The Hague, he had a played a small part in the initial set-up of the brothel at Marlot Park Fliet by moving furniture into the rooms. Additionally he knew of a comrade who was diagnosed with a venereal disease. Whether the soldier had caught the disease from an official source or not is unknown. Irrespective of this, he had to undertake the dreaded 'cure'. Prior to the widespread use of Penicillin following the end of the war, treatment for venereal diseases such as gonorrhoea and syphilis was problematic. Although mass production of Penicillin was still in its infancy, the Allies had available considerable quantities in time for the D-Day landings in Normandy in June 1944. German doctors did not possess the 'wonder drug' and had to resort to traditional remedies. Gonorrhoea was treated with mercury or colloidal silver nitrate. Early stage syphilis would be treated with injections of Salvarsan containing carbon and arsenic. Either treatment was exceedingly painful and in the case of gonorrhoea, most intrusive upon the victim.[7] Wunderlich's comrade suffered from such excesses of the 'cure'. It was not uncommon for grown men to be brought to their knees, howling like wounded animals, following treatment.

Wunderlich was never aware of any strong resentment against himself by the Dutch. On one occasion of unexpected idleness due to a lack of Rockets, Wunderlich and a comrade travelled into the town and became acquainted with two Dutch sisters who, rather surprisingly, invited them both to their parents' home. Wunderlich was impressed by the friendliness displayed by the parents and he was later to obtain a little food for them.

Firings took place irrespective of the weather; only high winds would stop a launch. Fairly frequently, high winds at the Hook of Holland would prevent a Rocket launching, but Wunderlich recalled that for the FR crews, the least popular weather phenomenon was fog combined with launches at night. Journeying to launch sites in darkness with shielded headlamps would necessitate men having to sit outside on the Hanomag SS100 heavy tractors' or *Feuerleitpanzers'* front wheel fairings to signal directions to the drivers.

The presence of fog, however, added another dimension of difficulty in addition to launching in hours of darkness. The V2, having taken off into the heavily leaden sky, would quickly have its jet flame rendered invisible. The muffled sounds of the Rocket would reverberate all around while the entire sky would flicker with a gradually diminishing, yellowish-red glow. The thought that entered the minds of the FR troops, and that of every terrified inhabitant of The Hague staring into the sky, was that if the Rocket failed, where would it fall? Wunderlich did not envy the officers and crew in the *Feuerleitpanzer* who had poor visibility and restricted escape access so close to the launch site.

Wunderlich recalled that firings took place not only in The Hague and the Hook of Holland, but also at Filmstad in Clingendaal (close to the Haagse Bos) and from locations at Duindigt. Additionally, he mentioned that firings also took place near the famous '*Vredespaleis*' (Peace Palace) and close to the building of the Dutch Ministry of Foreign Affairs. The ministry building had become the headquarters of the local *Gestapo* until it was completely destroyed by a precision attack by RAF Mosquitos in April 1944. It is known that the closest historically recognised firing sites to '*Vredespaleis*' were known as Kerkhofflann and Zorgvliet, a short distance away.[8]

In the field, Wunderlich never saw or had contact with the crews of the other FR batteries as they were spread out over the large area of The Hague. He presumed that this was done to minimize casualties from failing Rockets, but in reality it was probably a measure intended to reduce the risk from air attack. Apart from knowing that three firing crews existed, he never knew exactly how many personnel made up *Batterie* 444 as the unit never had a full 'line-up' of all the men. The preparation of the V2 would require approximately twenty FR troops but he was aware that many more were involved in transportation, fuelling and in the technical troop. The FR soldiers with whom he most frequently came into contact were the *Sicherungstruppen* assigned to *Batterie* 444. These men appeared to be mainly from Silesia, a German province which before 1939 had bordered Poland and Czechoslovakia.

Firing locations would be rotated at random in order to try and thwart Allied *Jabos* (fighter-bombers) which scoured The Hague for mobile V2 units. When a firing took place out of the '*Sperrgebiet*' the *Sicherungstruppen* would cordon off a half-kilometre radius around the launch site area. Wunderlich recalled that the inhabitants were given approximately two hours notice to vacate and were told that, if they so wished, they could gather up a few precious possessions to take with them. Occasionally the Dutch would be told to leave their doors and windows wide open to minimize the effects of blast damage from Rockets taking off. No civilians were allowed to observe or record the firings and the Silesian *Sicherungstruppen* were extremely diligent in their task. The FR troops' motorized convoy would travel from the Rocket supply pick-up points to the firing site, arriving shortly after the area had been secured. Access to the cordoned-off zone would be allowed only once the FR troops had withdrawn.

Although it was to occur infrequently, abandoned wide-open homes were to prove too much of a temptation to some of the troops, in spite of punishment for theft. Wunderlich recalled that bottles of alcohol and pickled food would be stolen from cellars. He admits to once taking a pair of shoes and a highly prized ballpoint pen, an innovation that was yet to be mass-produced, found amongst the burned timbers and smashed masonry of a house destroyed by a failed Rocket. Unlike the situation experienced in Poland during training, Wunderlich was able to take advantage of the lack of mail searches by the officers and he posted the items home. He kept the pen for many years thereafter.

The *Sicherungstruppen* were able to take advantage of their privileged position which made easy access to the B-*Stoff* alcohol propellant. They, like the men in *Artillerie Abteilung* 485 *(mot.)*, had either invented or discovered the technique of filtering the methyl alcohol with their gas masks in an attempt to make it palatable. Wunderlich heard that some of the Silesians had quite literally rendered themselves irreparably 'blind drunk'. The infrequently seen V2 operating manual, the A4 *Fibel* (Primer) compiled during training at Heidelager, carried dire warnings about the abuse of B-*Stoff*. A cartoon image of a gravestone bears the following grim inscription:

Here lies Xaver Willibald.

He is already mouldy and very cold, and after intoxicating himself with B-Stoff he suddenly collapsed. First he drank a small shot of B-Stoff, which caused him to lose his eyesight. Out of grief, he drank two more shots. His whole body shook painfully and his heart started to beat faster and faster until death finally relieved him of his agony. Should B-Stoff tempt young or old, then think of Xaver Willibald!

The precautions taken to avoid detection from Allied air attack were very successful as Wunderlich remembered. V2s were camouflaged in different patterns including mixed drab and olive greens painted in disruptive, curving shapes. With the onset of winter snow, Kammler ordered that the normal camouflage colour scheme was to be replaced with a blue-grey paint. This also had the effect of conserving darker colours that were, apparently, in short supply.[9]

As a result of the different security procedures, Wunderlich recalled that firings had taken place around-the-clock, irrespective of night or day and only subject to the availability of Rockets. In reality however, after the beginning of December 1944, more and more Rockets were launched under the cover of darkness, in the early morning, or during late evening hours to avoid attack from the Allied *Jabos*. The worst incident of aerial attack was when the near empty accommodation of *Batterie* 444 at Marlot Park Fliet was destroyed on Christmas Eve, 1944. Wunderlich recalled: 'When the attack took place on Christmas Eve morning I, and two other comrades, were out hunting rabbits. We got one, but half of the rabbit was missing, because we used normal army ammunition. While we were out hunting, our quarters were attacked by enemy aircraft. Most of the men had already left the buildings, but some of the girls in the brothel were injured.'

Not surprisingly, the official record of this attack makes no mention of the injuries inflicted in the brothel, but instead records that one man, von Löbbecke, died and two others from *Batterie* 444's *Sicherungstruppe* were injured.

To the best of Wunderlich's knowledge, occupied launching sites were only once attacked by Allied fighter-bombers. Firing sites would, however, often be overflown by enemy aircraft and attacked, but invariably one or two days 'late'. Wunderlich recalled that when enemy aircraft were reported to be within a range of 50 kilometres of a site, firing operations would be stopped immediately. It was correctly reasoned that the dusty smoke cloud thrown up by a Rocket taking off lingered for several minutes depending upon the weather and would attract the attention of prowling *Jabos*. Whenever enemy aircraft were known to be operating in an area, it was wise to seek cover until the threat had passed, and this was true for both Dutch civilians and occupiers alike. Anything caught in the open risked being 'fair game', as Wunderlich recalled: 'Those fighter-bombers even shot at cyclists on the Dutch roads. I have seen for myself the corpses and the bicycles lying beside the main roads that led to the forest [of Haagse Bos].' Whether such incidents were accidents or intentional attacks, Wunderlich would not have been in a position to comment.

During his journeys across the grounds of the Duindigt Estate between The Hague and Wassenaar, Wunderlich noticed the bizarre spectacle of animals he had never seen before, grazing and ruminating: Peruvian llamas. Apparently the wealthy owner of Duindigt, Walter Jochems, had imported llamas in 1906 for his amusement and started a tradition that exists today. During the war however, many of the animals were moved to farms in the polders, but some evidently remained. One such llama, a particularly mean stallion, would spend its day running along the perimeter fence screaming and scaring anyone in a field grey uniform who passed by and dared to get too close. This apparently gave some small pleasure to the locals who called the animal's pastime 'badgering the *Gerrie*'. Wunderlich recalled, however, that the llama would only react by spitting at him and his comrades if they had had their sport and teased him. The animal which had made such a memorable impression was called 'Cor' by the Jochems family. When Walter Jochems' son evacuated the herd, Cor determinedly resisted all attempts to be captured and had to be left behind with a herd of Red Deer. Cor was an animal of some reputation, as he was known to suffer from a psychological condition known as 'Berserk Llama Syndrome'. A llama suffering from this condition can perceive a human as a male llama and a territorial threat, or as a female llama and thus it will attempt to mate! The behaviour of a berserk llama can indeed become very aggressive; not only will they spit and bite, but they will also sometimes charge, butting human handlers to the ground. During the long years of occupation, in spite of the deer on the estate, Cor's condition would have deepened in isolation from the herd. As time went by Wunderlich became aware that the number of animals he observed grazing on the Duindigt Estate gradually began to decrease. Later a member of the *Sicherungstruppen*, a fellow German, invited Wunderlich and some comrades to share a meal together and then explained the origin of the meat. Wunderlich was told, jokingly, that llamas were on the menu. In reality however, it was the red deer that the *Sicherungstruppen* used to supplement their increasingly erratic supplies of food. Cor survived the war and was later reunited with the herd, and his descendants today roam the Duindigt estate.[10]

As it has always been for men in uniform, 'fortune favours the brave' and when an unsecured goods wagon was found at the Scheveningen railway sidings, Wunderlich and his friends joyfully helped themselves to a large crate of dairy products. Wunderlich's mother was doubtless delighted to receive, via the post, butter and cheese which her son dutifully sent back home.

Wunderlich also recalled the New Year's Eve triple Rocket-firing operation which is recorded previously in this book (see Chapter Six). He believed that the reason for the coordinated firings (one at The Hook and two in The Hague) was due to a German city being attacked by Allied bombers close to the festive season, but doubtless the attack on the battery's billets on Christmas Eve was another contributing factor. So, on this evening, the V2 was indeed to live up to its name as a '*Vergeltungswaffe*' (Vengeance Weapon). Preparation began in the early evening, but in spite of the determined endeavours of the firing crews, their coordinated attempt was a complete failure. Wunderlich recalled: 'We began the deployment of a Rocket at about 1700 or 1800 hrs. We needed five or six hours. At five minutes to midnight we fired the Rocket against London. But it reached a height of about only 100 metres and came down again. The neighbouring firing crew had a failure too in this "midnight" firing. Hopeless! After the failed launch happened, having walked back to our billets, we got a milk can of about 20 litres capacity full of tea and rum toddy. Of course we were very happy and all 20 of us got one litre each. We were all drunk.'

It was known by the FR troops that the near non-operative *Luftwaffe* could no longer confirm the accuracy of Rocket shots by photographic reconnaissance. However, the troops were under no illusion as to the accuracy of the weapon as it was widely accepted that the 'fall of shot' pattern was an ellipse that was 10 kilometres in length by 7 kilometres wide with an area of approximately 55 kilometres square. In reality, the accuracy was far worse than Wunderlich and his comrades could have imagined. Wunderlich felt that the '*Leitstrahl*' radio-guided (guidance beam) control system might have improved the Rocket's accuracy. The *Leitstrahl* (LS) system used ground-based transmitters to create a radio guide beam that the Rocket was intended to travel along. A pair of aerials in the Rocket's base fins detected the guide beam and the control surfaces of the Rocket would be made to react to correct any deviations. Additionally the Rocket's aerials were able to receive the '*Brennschluss*' command signal that shut down the engine. The first such firing using LS was conducted by SS-*Werfer Batterie* 500 on 4 January 1945 from farmland near Dedemsvaartat, 10 kilometres north-east of Zwolle. It would seem that the SS *Batterie* had sole and exclusive use of LS technology and this was doubtless due to Kammler wanting his own men to have the very best equipment. *Batterie* 444 was not to use LS operationally, but only, however, in tests in the final days of March and early April 1945. Potentially the LS system – which was relatively free from 'jamming' – could have contributed greatly to the effectiveness of the Rocket. According to contemporary research, the V2's accuracy might well have been measured in metres and not kilometres. An important caveat, however, would be if the FR troops had been supported by substantially more accurate geographical positioning intelligence. This always eluded them.[11]

As with many of the extraordinary 'wonder weapons' of the dying Third Reich, it is frightening to speculate what impact the LS system might have had upon the outcome of the war if introduced months earlier.

Wunderlich, whose only source of information was rumour and speculation by comrades, fuelled by the constant official State propaganda, only began to realize that the war was lost when *Batterie* 444 was withdrawn from the Front. Until that time he hoped that perhaps the Rocket, or some other secret weapon, might yet somehow deliver a devastating blow to the enemy. Whatever the future held, in his naivety, he thought operations would be easier being on home ground.

On 26 January 1945, *Batterie* 444 was ordered to Peenemünde and having unloaded its equipment during a blizzard in Züssow, it arrived at an encampment at Buddenhagen, approximately 15 kilometres to the south of the research station and close to Wolgast. It was intended that the *Batterie* would undertake a series of test launches using *Leitstrahl*. In the event, however, and most likely due to the advance of the Soviets, *Batterie* 444 withdrew from the Peenemünde area in early February.

Inevitably, Wunderlich's memories of precise movements are, to some degree, lost in the 'mists of time', but he recalls with confidence a most extraordinary experience that occurred when *Batterie* 444 was in the Hannover area. It is likely that the following series of events took place when the unit moved from Peenemünde to the secluded wooded area of Verden in order to pursue the *Leitstrahl* experimental tests in February 1945. Wunderlich recalled that when *Batterie* 444 was close to Hannover, it was intended that *Leitstrahl* radio-guided shots would be fired at the advancing Allies. Wunderlich and several other men were ordered to deliver an unwanted radio car by train to the *Mittelwerk* underground factory near Nordhausen, 120 kilometres to the south-east. Due to the fractured nature of the German rail infrastructure and because of ever-present Allied fighter-bombers, Wunderlich and his comrades were allowed eight days to perform this duty and to return to *Batterie* 444. In the event they arrived late at the *Mittelwerk* and were greeted by orders to '*Return instantly to your unit!*'; but Wunderlich had other ideas. Always one to take advantage of a situation, he decided to use his non-expired travel permits to visit his mother at Rudolstadt 100 kilometres south of the *Mittelwerk*. His paperwork was examined by the local *Feldgendarmerie* and a note was made as to the expiration of his leave. The very day his leave elapsed, on 23 March 1945, he was immediately arrested at his home and, in spite of protestations, he was sent to a military prison garrison at Gera 55 kilometres to the east. He and other arrested soldiers were confined to a riding stable with straw for bedding. Wunderlich explained to the interrogating officers that he was not a deserter and that a call to his unit would surely explain. As the confinement grew into days, soldiers at morning 'roll call' would be picked and then rushed directly to the front line.

During the first week of his imprisonment, the end of March 1945, the Western Front lay 285 kilometres from Gera, but the Eastern Front was 220 kilometres away, so more likely than not, he would have been sent to fight against the Soviets and his prospects of a new posting would have been, in reality, a death sentence. Fortunately for Wunderlich the confirming call from his unit spared him and with a feeling of great relief, he made his way back to *Batterie* 444 and his *Zug* (platoon), which had now moved from Verden. Almost certainly, if Wunderlich had been apprehended under similar circumstances just a month later, when the fronts were separated by only a few tens of kilometres, the outcome of this adventure would have been very different. In the final days of the war, the slightest suggestion that a soldier was a deserter would mean summary execution, which more often than not was by a hanging beside the road as a warning to others.

Batterie 444 was pulled back 270 kilometres north to the area of Flensburg in the state of Schleswig-Holstein. The remnants of the unit arrived at the hamlet of Welmbüttel, just 67 kilometres from the Danish border, on 19 April 1945, to find whatever quarters they could. Wunderlich recalled that perhaps some 20 to 30 vehicles in total arrived in the centre of the village, including the mobile field kitchen unit – increasingly important for the ordinary rank-and-file troops. From here, the vehicles proceeded to nearby marshland and were parked up tightly in four groups. Demolition charges were fitted and detonated, reducing the equipment to scrap metal. The notion that *Batterie* 444 might have fired Rockets from Welmbüttel is dismissed by Wunderlich, but he offers the suggestion that the demolition explosions might have given the locals the impression that devices had been fired. Whatever the truth of precisely 'when' or 'which' was the final V2 fired, Wunderlich was told (albeit incorrectly) that *Batterie* 444 had the honour of firing the last Rocket at the enemy. On 5 May, the unit was dissolved. Flensburg being so far to the north had yet to be occupied by the Allies and Wunderlich remembered being warned to avoid being picked up by German combat units who would probably 'press-gang' him as an infantryman.

Whilst pondering what to do next, Wunderlich discovered that the mobile field kitchen was still parked up in the village. From its stores he 'liberated' food coupons and 1,500 Reichsmarks. Having commandeered a half-track vehicle with six other men, he decided to drive to the Kaiser Wilhelm Canal (now the Kiel Canal or *Nord-Ostsee-Kanal*) located between the North Sea and the Baltic Sea. The hope was to ultimately continue the journey home by foot to the south. However whilst attempting to cross the Canal, they were stopped by an advance party of American soldiers, taken prisoner and delivered to a temporary internment camp.

The Reichsmarks were soon frittered away in gambling with other POWs to relieve the tension and boredom of captivity. The camp held some 50,000 men, but Wunderlich was relatively comfortable, living in a barn with three others and fed daily with bread, corned beef and soup. Wunderlich was warned by his comrades that it would be advantageous to keep the experience of serving in a V2 Rocket Battalion very quiet. It might delay his return home or, if he was to be handed over by the Americans to the Soviets, result in a far worse fate. Under interrogation, Wunderlich maintained that he had been an ordinary infantry soldier and gave as his home address that of a relative whom he knew lived in the American zone.

When an appeal for farm labourers was made by the Americans, Wunderlich and doubtless many others saw their chance and claimed farming experience. The Americans believed his story and he was eventually dismissed with papers to report to farms in the Hannover area. In the days that followed, while toiling away under the sun in the fields, he had a most extraordinary experience. He looked up from his labours as his attention was drawn by the sound of heavy transport vehicles moving along the road to either Hamburg to the north, or Bremen to the north-west. The vehicles were carrying three V2 Rockets. What this could possibly mean, he had no idea. It is likely that these vehicles were being driven the 160 kilometres north to Cuxhaven to participate in 'Operation Backfire'. In August 1945, the British began a programme of interrogating German personnel associated with the development and deployment of the V2 under the codename 'Backfire'. Additionally, 'Backfire' evaluated and documented the V2 and its support equipment. The culmination of this investigation was three test-firings of the Rocket from Cuxhaven, over the North Sea, in early to mid-October 1945. Equipment and personnel for the tests had to be gathered from around Germany, and it is conceivable that Wunderlich saw early mobilization in anticipation of 'Backfire'.

After a few weeks of working the fields, Wunderlich made his way to his parents' home in Leipzig, which was now in the Soviet zone. Wunderlich was given the chance of starting his life anew in the United States when his paternal uncle sent him two tickets to travel to America. His uncle had made a new life for himself when he emigrated to America in the early 1920s following the end of the First World War. The uncle had very nearly returned to Germany in 1936 as the country's affluence began to increase. However, news of the outbreak of the Spanish Civil War, and Hitler's entanglement with that conflict, convinced Wunderlich's uncle that a war in Europe was imminent and he wisely abandoned his return to the Fatherland and remained in Philadelphia. Wunderlich, however, had hopes of betrothal to a girl, later to become his wife, who wanted to stay in Leipzig. Plans for America were therefore dropped. The necessity of maintaining silence about his wartime experience took on a very serious importance: 'The first years after the war were very hard. We did not have enough to eat and worried about other problems. At first, we didn't dare to speak about our wartime experiences. Any people who had a connection with the Nazis or the war were sent to Siberia by the Soviets, especially during Stalin's time. Many people disappeared. In the past sixty years I have never spoken of my experiences – not only because of the Soviets, but because nobody was interested. I never knew of the V2 firings by the British and the Americans because I lived behind the Iron Curtain.'

Wunderlich joined the Leipzig Fire Brigade and retired from the service in the early 1970s. His feelings about his wartime experience with the Rocket are summarized as follows: 'We just wanted to survive the war. We young people had no thoughts for future space travel. We saw the V2 only as a weapon. You ask about the moral perspective of the Rocket? I was only twenty-years old. We didn't think about it. So many fellows lost their homes and families in the bombing of German cities too. It was war!'

CHAPTER NINE

'IT WAS VERY LOUD...'

HEINZ JUNKER
Lehr- und Versuchsbatterie 444

HEINZ JUNKER was born in 1925 and, having left school, worked as an apprentice electrical engineer at the famous Carl Zeiss factory in his home town of Gera, 40 kilometres east of Jena in Thuringia. Zeiss was a well-established manufacturer of precision optical devices and Junker worked on mechanical computers which aided the firing accuracy of anti-aircraft guns. Fired anti-aircraft shells would detonate via one of several methods: either using altitude barometric settings, time delay or proximity fuses. No matter what method was used, it was shrapnel that damaged and destroyed aircraft but only if the shell was sufficiently close enough to cause damage. The mechanical computers were able to predict the position that an aircraft would occupy so that the course of its flight would intersect that of an exploding shell. The device was known as a '*Flakvisier*' and several different types existed. In its basic form as Junker recalled: 'All the data needed to fire an anti-aircraft gun effectively was entered into this device and everything was calculated mechanically – height, speed and direction of the aircraft, wind speed and the location of the gun.'

In practice an anti-aircraft team would use a stereoscopic range-finder to determine distance to the target and this would be called out to an operator who would enter the range and other basic information into the *Flakvisier* which, in turn, automatically adjusted the telescopic sights on the anti-aircraft gun. To place this in context, the Allies had a very similar device known as a 'Predictor' for obvious reasons.

Like many of his generation, Junker was called to serve in the *Reichsarbeitsdienst* in the spring of 1942. Having been dismissed from the service on 19 April 1943, he returned to his parents' home to celebrate his eighteenth birthday on 21 April and discovered that his call-up papers were already waiting for him. The following day he made his farewells to his family and set off to Wetzlar in Hessen to join a *Fernmeldeeinheit* (signals unit). Although Junker considered himself not to have had an engineering education, he had served an apprenticeship with Carl Zeiss and this made him a perfect candidate to be trained as a *Fernmelder* (signaller) and technician for radio installations. He also underwent training in the use of mobile field telephone exchange systems. At this stage of his military experience however, Junker would have been totally unaware that a rocket 'wonder weapon' was undergoing development in the Reich.

The barracks at Wetzlar had been divided into two separate entities; one was for the training of infantry, the other for *Fernmelde* troops. A sense that the communications troop were something special and different to the ordinary soldiers was brought home to Junker when on one occasion he had to report to the infantry barracks. The strictness and harsh atmosphere of the infantrymen's quarters struck him as a great deal more unpleasant than the more comfortable environment he and his comrades enjoyed. He was very pleased to leave and return to his more familiar surroundings.

With training complete and with the rank of *Gefreiter* (Lance Corporal), Junker awaited orders for his first posting. It was perhaps something of a relief that he discovered in January 1944 that he was not to be sent to the front line, but instead dispatched to the *Fernraketen* (FR – long-range rocket) troop training grounds at Heidelager near Blizna in Poland. His only anxiety stemmed from the fact that he had heard that the troop ground was in some way connected to the SS, but during his time at Heidelager he never saw one SS man nor indeed their parade ground or billets which were located very close to the A4 training operations. He was to join the *Fernmeldeeinheit* of the ever-growing ranks of *Lehr- und Versuchsbatterie* 444. With his technical background, his opinion as to why he had been selected was very straightforward: 'Well, I assume they needed signals people and drew them from the reserve batteries accordingly.'

For some of the men at Heidelager, the posting seemed to be entirely random. Nevertheless, Junker and many of the other young men called into this special service appeared to have been carefully chosen. He arrived without any forewarning or knowledge as to the activities carried out at the camp. He was billeted close to the camp where conditions were spartan but comfortable: 'The barracks were huts which accommodated ten to twelve men, two of whom were technicians who worked directly with the Rocket. These men talked about the problems [of the Rocket], of course, but at that time, it wasn't of interest to me. But barrack life wasn't so bad; there weren't any excesses imposed by the military regime. No drill... but sometimes you were called to order. You had to wash your own laundry and, of course, catering was according to the prevailing situation. Sometimes we would barter deals for food, dealing sugar with the Poles, with whom I remember we had no problems.'

Junker and the other 'new faces' were quickly integrated into the signals training programmes being conducted at Heidelager. He had the feeling that approximately 150 men were under the command of *Batterie* 444 and recalled that one officer was '*Oberstleutnant* Steffenhagen', but in reality, this was probably *Oberleutnant* Helmut Fredenhagen (see Chapter Seven) who was one of three firing officers. The majority of men seemed to range in ages from their late twenties to their early forties and so he considered himself to belong to the youngest group. Typical of men of his rank, he was not privy to the structure of *Batterie* 444 or the other Rocket units. It would seem that contact with men other than those in the *Fernmeldeeinheit*, and those whose training he shared, was not encouraged – a restriction which may have been a further extension of security measures.

Junker's perception of the Rocket was remarkably astute given his age and lack of combat experience. The first launching he witnessed he described as: 'A beautiful and interesting experience. The noise played a great role in impressing me because it was very loud. The exhaust jet was very sharp and clearly defined. I was, however, skeptical as to whether it would be a success and at that time the dangers, which were already there, were not clear to me at all.' It had occurred to Junker that despite his enthusiasm over the technical qualities of the A4, the Rocket required an enormous team of men and equipment to prepare and fire it. The scale of effort required for its construction he could only imagine, but with his experience working with precision equipment, he believed that it too would be considerable. The balance between effort and effect was seriously at odds. The dangers all too soon manifested themselves in one failed Rocket launching incident, which, for inexperienced men, was terrifying. The sirens had sounded to alert the various groups of technicians and trainees of an impending firing. The snaking, one-metre deep, shelter trenches that had been dug into the ground facing the launch site quickly filled. The Rocket lifted off but, as frequently happened, the engine lost thrust. As Junker recalled: 'Sometimes misfires would come down no more than 50 metres away from the *Abschusstisch*. On this occasion, the Rocket fell into the shelter trenches. The oxygen and alcohol fuel exploded at once. It was an enormous explosion. I think there were four dead bodies. For me, at 19–years old, this was a very shocking experience.'

The frustration of misfires was keenly felt by everyone, but men like *Major* von Plötz knew that failures would ultimately delay the weapon's deployment. His anger was plain and he sought scapegoats from the ranks of the FR troop: 'There were two respected sergeants, really old battle horses, who had helped conduct the firing. When the Rocket came down, *Major* von Plötz had them arrested! I didn't know whether he [von Plötz] was part of the FR troop. He probably had not the slightest (technical) knowledge about it.'

The two sergeants briefly endured von Plötz's wrath and were soon back at their posts. Von Plötz was later appointed commander of *Gruppe Nord* (Group North) on 9 September 1944 and was responsible for approximately 60 per cent of the entire FR force. *Gruppe Süd* (Group South) was under the command of *Major* Weber.

The *Fernmeldeeinheit* expanded its knowledge with training exercises that would have been fairly unique in the *Wehrmacht*. In addition to the normal field operations of radio, telephone and Teletype writers, the trainees were introduced to the *Feuerleitpanzer*. One of the *Feuerleitpanzer's* control desks was designated specifically for radio communications. Junker would relay information and orders to the Firing Officer who would stand, exposed, with the heavy metal inspection hatch on top of the vehicle open.

During his training exercises, Junker recalled that a mere 30 metres separated him and the other crew members of the *Feuerleitpanzer* from the *Abschusstisch*. He was always fearful that the Firing Officer might have to suddenly drop down, slamming the hatch behind him as a wayward device careened towards the *Feuerleitpanzer*. The memory of the recent accident was not far from Junker's mind.

Dangers also existed 'down range' of the Rocket as men were detailed to the predicted impact zones. The wreckage of failed devices and the shrapnel of successful tests would be gathered together not only for analysis, but also to prevent Rocket components from falling into the hands of the Polish Resistance. Junker vaguely recalled that a comrade of similar age to him was shot and killed by the Resistance as he searched the remote countryside for Rocket debris.

As previously mentioned, the Heidelager camp was also used by the *Luftwaffe* to test its Fi 103 flying bomb (V1). When the test was imminent, the *Heer* camp was notified. As the camp had no internal perimeter fence, Junker and some comrades wandered across with other troops to see the preparation and test launch. Like Heinz Wunderlich (see Chapter Eight), Junker was surprised that after only an hour or so of preparation, the V1 was ready for launching. For a V2 it could take a whole day. The V1's engine started with a staccato roar, and the bomb rapidly ascended along its gently climbing launching ramp timed with a 'chase' aircraft flying above. The aircraft was quickly overtaken as the V1's speed increased. Both machines disappeared into the distance. The *Luftwaffe* ground personnel quickly made good their clean-up operation and vanished. The test was an obvious success and to the best of Junker's recollection, it was not repeated.

After serving with *Batterie* 444 for nearly nine months, Junker and his comrades moved off to begin the Rocket offensive. Accommodation for the battery in The Hague was even more dispersed than it had been in the wooden barracks of Poland. The sense of isolation the *Fernmeldeeinheit* experienced in Poland continued in the Netherlands, and indeed became greater as the soldiers were found accommodation in permanent housing rather than grouped together in wooden huts. However, they enjoyed the comfort of requisitioned, solid brick houses. But the isolation was such that Junker had even less contact with the Rocket than he had before. As an example, he never met a member of the *Sicherungstruppe* and this would explain why he and his comrades had no contact with pilfered alcohol. However, Junker was well aware that Rocket alcohol could be filtered using the standard issue gas mask. *Sicherungstruppen* were always an excellent source of such 'contraband'! There was, however, an occasion when the alcohol was to prove useful: 'I had to go on guard duty with a fellow who didn't like such duty because it was cold. We fetched a bucket of spirit and then climbed into a lorry. We lit the alcohol fuel and then fell asleep.'

Unlike the men in the FR troop, the *Fernmeldeeinheit* already had a high degree of security clearance because they had access to very secretive material; therefore it was not necessary to issue them with any special papers to aid quick passage at national frontiers.

Junker remembered that the signals department was set up in a small room (the precise location has been forgotten over time). On one occasion at least, the *Fernmeldeeinheit* of *Batterie* 444 was known by the cover name '*Tigerburg*' (Tiger Castle) as the use of specific names would have seriously compromised security. '*Tigerburg*' was manned by eight personnel known as *Funker* (radio operators) and *Fernmelder* (telephonists). The commander of this small unit was the Communications Signal Officer, *Leutnant* Liske, who was Junker's direct superior. Most of *Batterie* 444's communications with the military 'outside world' were handled by '*Tigerburg*' and the methods used included messenger courier service for the most sensitive communications (with which Junker had no involvement), radio, telephone, and Teletype writer. Most communications were between *Batterie* departments and the *Division zur Vergeltung* (*Div.z.V.* – Division for Retaliation) under the command of SS-*Obergruppenführer* Kammler. The manual telephone exchange system used a device known as a '*Klappenschrank*' (flap box): 'We had a drop-type switchboard,' Junker recalled. 'This was a message table where the appropriate flaps would make a noise when a message arrived. When I was on duty I had to be at this switchboard and my comrades were in a neighbouring room.'

It is perhaps ironic that this type of telephone exchange system, which was invented in the 19th century, was involved with a weapons system that many at the time perceived as being very much of the 21st century. The *Klappenschrank* was so called because a small flap would drop down under a predetermined number indicating the source of the incoming caller. The *Klappenschrank* operator would plug a 'request wire' into the revealed socket and enquire of the caller to whom he wished to be connected. The operator then plugged a 'call wire' into the exchange whilst turning a hand crank to ring the requested recipient. If the recipient answered, the operator would make the connection. The operator would be informed that the call had ended when one of the two connected parties would briefly turn the crank on his telephone as he placed the receiver back onto the cradle as this operated an 'end flap' on the exchange. It was the practice to eavesdrop to make sure that either the connection had been made or that the call had finished when the operating procedure had been forgotten by the user. The tiring monotony of operating manual telephone exchanges was, however, occasionally punctuated by calls from high-ranking personnel and Junker recalled one particular occasion in the small hours of 1 January 1945: 'I was on duty, but had celebrated New Year's Eve with two or three colleagues. Then the flap fell on the *Klappenschrank* and I had a conversation with SS-*Obergruppenführer* Kammler – not that I knew the name at that time. He wanted to know about the two Rockets launched from The Hague just before New Year by *Batterie* 444. Kammler was informed that there hadn't been a firing because of technical reasons. I didn't know any more than what I told him!'

The notorious failure of the New Year's Eve Rockets appears to have been very well known by every man in *Batterie* 444, no matter what position they held. Junker heard that both of the two Rockets that had failed in such a spectacular way had chalked upon them caricatures of the British Prime Minister, Winston Churchill. For his part, Churchill would most probably have been highly amused to hear that both devices carrying his image had misfired!

Another important means of communication used by the *Fernmeldeeinheit* of *Batterie* 444 was via the Teletype writer machine. The machine, in common use with the *Wehrmacht*, used the *Feld-Hell* system and was known as the *Feldfernschreiber* (Field Text Writer). It was manufactured by Siemens & Halske and was the forerunner of the modern day Facsimile machine. The *Feldfernschreiber* was based upon an earlier machine known as *Hellschreiber* (Bright Writer) and was capable of sending, via radio or telephone, a digital representation of a character broken down into an array of seven x seven image elements or, as they are known today, pixels. A receiving *Feldfernschreiber* would receive and reinterpret the signal and output the message onto paper. A skilled operator would have been able to 'key' 2.5 characters per second, which was the maximum speed the machine could work at. The receiver section of the *Feldfernschreiber* used a tiny hammer to tap the back of continually moving paper, momentarily bringing the front surface of the paper into contact with a special surface coated in ink. The taps of the hammer would leave on the paper a series of inky marks in the form of ticks that would build up to form the character. The font used was specially designed to increase legibility. The *Feldfernschreiber* system was rugged, dependable and offered immunity from interference. It was in use for many years after the war.[1]

Junker remembered that 'rest and recreation' in The Hague was a great improvement upon Heidelager, and he felt the Dutch town was no different to any other garrison town he had experienced. Although Junker had very little contact with the Dutch, the local people seemed to be indifferent to the presence of the Germans. Admittedly, however, he did not know what they were thinking when he did speak with them, but it was always without problem. He felt genuinely that the differences between the Germans and the Dutch were very little. It was usual for he, and his comrades, to have local Dutch girlfriends. In contrast to the experiences of fellow *Batterie* 444 member, Heinz Wunderlich, it is Junker's memory that threats from the Resistance and attacks from the air were minimal. He recalled: 'True – aircraft did appear and we German anti-aircraft crews opened fire on them – but they were German machines! We were not used to seeing German aircraft in the skies!'

An activity that Junker had enjoyed before his enlistment, and one he was able to pursue in The Hague, was hunting fowl for the table. The ornamental parks and woodland close to where he was billeted and in particular areas within the restricted zone, proved to be rich in pigeons. Junker would visit the parks and woods with a rifle and the 'bagged' birds made a pleasant change to the normal military diet. On New Years Eve, 1944, he found himself close to the launch sites used by his comrades of *Batterie* 444, near the former coffee house of *Chateau Bleu* on the northern edge of the Haagse Bos. It was here that he had an odd encounter: 'I always went on the hunt for pigeons and had already shot a few that morning. A park attendant came up to me and said, "Please move away from here quickly: this land is the property of *Generalfeldmarschall* of the *Luftwaffe* Milch!"'

The Milch to whom the park attendant was referring was none other than *Generalfeldmarschall* Erhard Milch (1892-1972), deputy to *Reichsmarschall* Hermann Göring, the supreme commander of the *Luftwaffe*. It would seem, however, that the park attendant was perhaps having his own 'sport' with the young German who was creating a noisy disturbance with his rifle. Milch had been in the Netherlands with Albert Speer to witness the *Wehrmacht's* successful counter-attack upon the Allies' tenuous position at Arnhem in September 1944. On 1 October, whilst returning to Germany, Milch's vehicle crashed at high speed and the Field Marshal was to spend in excess of four months recuperating from serious injuries in Germany.[2] As *Batterie* 444 had left the Netherlands by the end of January 1945, it seems highly unlikely that Milch would have had a residency in The Hague. Junker, however, was not aware of this and decided that his best course of action was to take no chances with the situation in case he was disturbing the early morning quiet enjoyed by the *Generalfeldmarschall*. He left the park, never to return again with his hunting rifle.

Batterie 444 fired its last Rocket of the offensive on 26 January 1945 and moved off to continue experimental test-shots from Peenemünde. However this did not occur due to the advance of the Soviets and test launches were organized elsewhere. The new operating status meant that the unit had men who were surplus to its new requirements. The *Fernmeldeeinheit* was reduced in strength and Junker was informed that his services were no longer required; in February 1945 he was ordered to be trained as an infantryman. The news from both battlefronts was grave, but the East gave the greatest concern. Junker was ordered to the western side of Berlin in anticipation of the Soviet attack against the capital. Mercifully, and much to his relief, Junker was withdrawn from Berlin and sent 200 kilometres to the west to face the Americans on the River Elbe. It was here, close to Dömitz, 55 kilometres east of Lüneburg, that he was taken into captivity on 3 May 1945.

No sooner had he been taken POW by the Americans, than he and thousands of other prisoners discovered that they were to be handed over to the British who were to be responsible for that sector. Conditions in captivity were a great deal more comfortable than many others had to endure, but Junker felt that the food rations were 'meagre' – although, equally, conditions were hard for all Germans following the end of hostilities.

Upon his release from captivity in June 1945, he returned to his parents' home. Eventually he was able to renew his education and career in the ever-growing electronics industry.

Looking back to the deployment of the V2 Rocket, Junker made the following observations: 'Michael Neufeld in his book, *The Rocket and the Reich*, writes about a missed opportunity.[3] He says that for the cost of the V2 some 22,000 fighters could have been built. If Germany had built 22,000 fighters, in my opinion the course of the war probably would have been different.'

In the aforementioned book, author Michael J. Neufeld argues that the money expended on both the V1 and V2 as well as four types of experimental anti-aircraft missiles, could have been used to greater effect elsewhere in military equipment procurement. He notes that the US Strategic Bombing Survey of 1944/45 claims that 24,000 fighter aircraft could have been built for the same cost. Neufeld wrote: 'In short: as predicted by the supporters of the rocket program, the rocket development shortened the war greatly, but in benefit for the Allies.'

The implication (conveniently forgetting the dire lack of aircrew and dwindling fuel facing the *Luftwaffe* during the second half of the war) is that the extra aircraft available to the *Luftwaffe* would have enabled the *Heer* to hold on to occupied territories and to defend its airspace more robustly, and that the *Kriegsmarine* could have maintained more effectively the naval siege of the Atlantic. However, this assessment might be considered an over-simplification, because no matter what resources were made available to Germany's war industry, at the top of the Reich's command structure was one man, Adolf Hitler.

CHAPTER TEN

'A HORDE OF TANKS WOULD BE NOTHING AGAINST THIS!'

WILHELM PRIEBE

Artillerie Abteilung 836 (Motorisiert)

WILHELM PRIEBE was born in October 1924 in the rural environment of Wutzow, Pomerania, in what was then north-eastern Germany, 35 kilometres south of Köslin. He was, apparently, a good student and was advised to attend senior school, a *Gymnasium*, which would make him eligible for university. However, he was a farmer's son and the demands of the land kept him from furthering his education. His father, who was also the village *Bürgermeister* (Mayor), had hoped that his two sons would continue to work the family farmstead and, indeed, young Willi Priebe thought that one day he would become an overseer of a large farm. The responsibilities he craved would have led to a more interesting life than simply toiling on the land as an agricultural worker. However, the outbreak of war brought about a complete change of direction for him. Like so many of his peers, he was reluctantly drafted into military service.

On 9 December 1942, Priebe joined an infantry battalion at Elbing, 90 kilometres south-west of Königsberg. During basic training, he contracted the highly contagious disease of diphtheria and was confined to an isolation bed in a military hospital. Meanwhile his comrades, having completed their training, were dispatched to the Eastern Front to fight at the besieged city of Stalingrad. Priebe envied his friends going off to fight, but little did he know as he lay fevered in bed, that his newfound comrades were doomed never to return from Russia.

As his health returned, he was allowed a period of convalescence at home before returning to service. In November 1943, following a full recovery, Priebe was ordered to travel from Stettin in north-eastern Germany (later known as Szczecin, Poland), to join 92. *Infanterie-Regiment* which formed part of 60. *Infanterie Division* based at Greifenberg. From the division, Priebe and approximately 40 men were picked out for secret duties yet to be revealed. One of these men was Fritz Meibert who was to become a lifelong friend. This new unit was the *Artillerie Abteilung* 836 (*mot.*) and was sufficiently important to be given its own unique Field Post Number. The men of the *Art. Abt.* 836 (*mot.*) were given strict instructions not to reveal movements or unit change in correspondence to family or friends. The rumour began to circulate that they were going to be deployed into the service of secret weapons. Despite a growing desire for action, time seemed to drag on interminably, with constant drill practices, while other units received their postings. Priebe recalled: 'As young men we just wanted to go, voluntarily, to the front. Instead we were always drill marching. We became very impatient.'

Then, just before Christmas 1943, Priebe and his comrades were sent to the troop drill camp at Groß Born in Pomerania and billeted in isolation. Inside the camp, the accommodation was divided into those who slept under canvas and others who lived in vacated properties in the former village of Westfalenhof. The men were fed predominantly cold meals from the unit's own field kitchen. Soldiers from other units at Groß Born were strictly prevented from entering the area.

Following another frustrating period of inactivity, in the late spring of 1944, the men were sent urgently to Heidekraut in the Tucheler Heide, 110 kilometres (68 miles) to the west. In July, or possibly August, Priebe and the other forty or so men were ordered to the *Truppenübungsplatz* (military training camp) at Baumholder some 50 kilometres north-east of Saarbrücken. Again, they were separated from the other troops already massed there who were awaiting orders to move off to firing positions to begin the V2 offensive.

Quarters at Baumholder were found close to and, in some instances, beside the parade ground in abandoned houses. These houses, although not quite derelict, often needed the floorboards replacing to make them safe for habitation. Simple cloth mattresses filled with straw were used for bedding. Once again, with so much free time available, the unit leader, *Leutnant d.R* Waldemar Utpadel, ran extra exercises to keep the men active and occupied. Priebe and his comrades also worked in the fields bringing in the harvest with the local farmers. He remembered, with a smile, that all the farmers had daughters!

It was here that *Gefreiter* Priebe and his immediate comrades were, at last, assigned *Sicherungstruppe* (Security Troop) duties in *Art. Abt.* 3./836 (*mot.*) in support of the V2 offensive. And why had he been chosen? 'I have no idea. I had no technical experience; perhaps it was my face!'

Officially, the duties of the Rocket *Sicherungstruppen* were to secure and cordon off launch sites in anticipation of firings. Priebe recalled their tasks:

'When told of a rocket-firing position, we had to protect the surroundings so that nobody disrupted the work there. Our task was to keep civilians away. We were equipped with machine guns and also small armoured vehicles. We would patrol the area and streets for a few hundred metres away from the firing position.'

Evacuations from a cordoned zone were to be made with no regard to the civil population. They were instructed that no one would be allowed to observe any of the equipment or the preparation of a launching. It was deemed that a small, tight area was easier to secure than a large, rambling one. In the Netherlands, the *Sicherungstruppen* also had the responsibility of securing supply lines. This task became unnecessary when devices were launched from Germany.

In comparison to the technical and firing troops more directly involved with the Rocket, the responsibility of the *Sicherungstruppen* was relatively straightforward and required no great investment in time for training. The long periods of inactivity, Priebe remembered, were, in reality, an indication that he and his comrades had been called to Rocket security duty too early and thereafter had to endure boredom and isolation from other soldiers in order to preserve the secrecy surrounding the V2.

Because of the isolation and lack of contact with other, more established members of the battalion, Priebe and his new comrades in the *Sicherungstruppe* had no knowledge of the activities of *Artillerie Abteilung* 836 (*mot.*) during its early stage of operations. Fortunately, it is possible to glimpse what had occurred following the *Abteilung's* formation thanks to the interrogation of a former member of the unit following his surrender to British forces in September 1944.[1] The prisoner, whose identity is unknown, was a clerk to a technical officer. The clerk arrived at Peenemünde in the autumn of 1943 to discover a state of unpreparedness and was temporarily posted to Groß Born before returning to Peenemünde around mid-December. By now, preparations were in hand for training and the clerk and some 25 members of *Art. Abt.* 1./836 (*mot.*) received an introductory lecture and initial training. From the very beginning of his exposure to the Rocket, the trainees were under no illusion as to what was to be the target: London and coordinated with that of the V1. Seven different courses of instruction associated with the Rocket were being performed; for example, general engineering, surveying, power plant and electrical studies. The clerk attended the surveying course which was conducted in the large workshop located south-west of Proof Stand VII. During mid-January 1944, the entire *Artillerie Abteilung* 836 (*mot.*) moved to Heidelager to continue instruction and firing practices. Conditions at Heidelager must have been somewhat crowded, for the clerk was aware that the *Abteilung's* sister unit, *Artillerie Abteilung* 485 (*mot.*), as well as *Lehr- und Versuchsbatterie* 444 were also present. During the six week course, the clerk recalled that his unit had fired four Rockets: only one was successful. One of the aforementioned tests took place on 29 January 1944 and the *Kriegstagebuch* (War Diary) of *Artillerie Abteilung* 2./836 (*mot.*) graphically captures the atmosphere and spectacle of the event.

'*The Generals (Dornberger and Metz) definitely want to see a launch today, it simply has to work and an A4 has to perform. But up to now the A4 sits tight on the firing table and it eagerly gulps A, B, T and Z-Stoff into its belly. Everything works, even the fuelling. We are again very optimistic. Finally at 2200 hrs, V105 stands ready for launching. 2200 hrs is X-time, and everybody seeks the shelter trenches. Air is ventilated from the A-Stoff tank; the Vorstufe takes place but something is wrong. Then the Hauptstufe begins. It seems to take an eternity until the device lifts off, but nevertheless it flies with much jubilation and hurrahs from the ground!*

'*Unfortunately our delight is short-lived. After about 4 to 6 seconds and at 300 metres, the exhaust jet switches off and the Rocket falls back into the woods about 50 metres from the launch site with a tremendous noise. Even the most fearless crouch down in the trenches. Tree trunks fly through the air; a massive blast strikes the Feuerleitpanzer standing 100 metres away. Rocket parts hurtle through the air. It's scary! The blast pushes out the windows of the test vehicle and the walls of the compressor trailer.*

'*At the impact site the B-Stoff burns. Throughout the woods are small "will-o'-the-wisps". So "lived, suffered and died" Rocket V105. Luckily nobody was hurt. Only the removed coats, bread bags etc., of a few comrades have been atomized or hang 15 metres up in the trees. When we went to bed that night we were still very much impressed by such energy. Even the most inquisitive and courageous among us went to bed with trembling knees.'*[2]

The clerk told his interrogators that there were three separate stages in the selection of a Rocket-firing site. Firstly, a special *Vermessungs-Batterie* (Measuring Battery) would establish trigonometrical points from which coordinates would be determined for ranging the Rocket. The *Vermessungs* detachment would drive a stake into the ground to show the intersection of the diagonals on the *Abschusstisch*, while a second stake placed 10 metres away indicated the base line whose continuation was the distant target. The ultimate setting up of the Rocket and its critical ranging was determined from mathematical tables known as the BWE *Tafel* (*Besondere Witterungs Einflüsse* – special weather influences) Table. The clerk recalled that a *Hauptmann Dr.* Schwartz, a ballistics expert attached to the *Rechner und Auswerter* (Computation Section), had been responsible for the production of these tables and had had to take into account the curvature and sidereal rotation of the Earth, gravitational effects and retardation due to the atmosphere.

The second stage in the selection of a Rocket-firing site involved the *Erkundungsstab* (Exploration Staff) who would make a topographical survey to determine the practical viability of the site. Thirdly, the *Erkundungsstab* would assess the preparation time each site required to enable easy vehicle access as well as studying the natural camouflage with which to protect the site and determining if the ground was sufficiently stable enough to allow the Rocket and its equipment to be safely operated. In training, it was envisaged that three firing sites would be operational, either in an equilateral triangle pattern or in a straight line. No matter what pattern was selected, the firing sites were to be separated by 80 to 100 metres.

Great emphasis was made in training exercises to determine the best possible way to protect firing sites from detection from the air. Natural cover was used whenever possible and firing sites were chosen when the tree canopy was at least 15 metres above the ground. Experiments were conducted with a perforated ring that fitted over the nose cone through which natural foliage was inserted. To test the various experiments and techniques of camouflage, the firing sites would be photographed from the air using a Fieseler Fi 156 *Storch* light observation aircraft on loan from the *Luftwaffe* and for night exercises photoflash bombs would be used to illuminate the darkness. Failures or successes in hiding firing sites were assessed in the resulting photographs and eventually a standard approved practice was adopted.

Artillerie Abteilung 836 (*mot.*) and its batteries had code names. For example:

Artillerie Abteilung 836 = *Falkenhorst* 1 (Falcon's eyrie 1)
1./836 = *Falkenhorst* 2
2./836 = *Falkenhorst* 3
3./836 = *Falkenhorst* 4

Similarly, *HARKO* 191 was known by the code name '*Vogelweide*' ('bird pasture'), The V2 Rocket was known as '*Hanswurst*' which, in German and Austrian dramas of the 18th century, was a popular, clown-like puppet character.

By early March *Artillerie Abteilung* 836 had returned to Groß Born where handling exercises were performed on a dummy V2 using different vehicles. Some of these exercises took place at night and the work of the surveying unit was helped by the presence of a small lamp held at the tip of the practice Rocket. It was rumoured that the activities of the FR troop were attracting too much attention from enemy agents, of whom at least five had been caught. Perhaps due to security concerns, *Artillerie Abteilung* 836 (*mot.*) moved off in May 1944 to the area of Baumholder. Apparently the military facilities at Baumholder were not prepared for continued training and some 90 soldiers of *Art. Abt.* 836 (*mot.*) were obliged to lend a hand in the building of practice sites. In the middle of July, the clerk parted company from the rest of his battery and joined a *Tarn- und Nebeltrupp* (Camouflage and Smoke Detachment) and reported to the headquarters of the *Erkundungsstab 'Lindemann'* close to Saint Omer in north-western France. His unit, under the command of *Major* Lindemann, was tasked to perform a general environmental survey of established, and also proposed, Rocket-firing sites in the Pas-de-Calais area. The principal concern for the survey was concealment of the vulnerable fixed sites from aerial attack. According to the captured clerk's understanding, the original plan was for the Rockets to be fired from within underground bunkers, but these locations had been detected by the RAF, destroyed and abandoned.

At around the time of the fall of Paris in the third week of August 1944, the contingent *Artillerie Abteilung* 836 in France was ordered to withdraw back to Germany with *General* Richard Metz leading the retreat via Ypres to Turnhout in Belgium and on to Dongen near Tilburg in the Netherlands. The aforementioned British interrogation report stated that following a journey of approximately 240 kilometres, the former clerk, '...finally severed his connection with the unit and was given shelter by a patriotic Hollander who eventually handed him over to the British forces.' It is believed that the British interrogated him before or just after the V2 campaign began. The dossier by the Intelligence Officers was deemed to be of such importance that it was distributed to no fewer than 59 military offices and commands. This included the cabinet member Lord Cherwell the principal scientific advisor to Winston Churchill, Duncan Sandys, M.P., Minister of Supply and Chairman of the War Cabinet Committee for defence against German flying bombs and rockets.[3]

Priebe recalled that from Germany he and his comrades in *Artillerie Abteilung* 836 were moved to Poland. He remembered that a full complement of V2 equipment was available for training purposes at Heidekraut and it was here that he saw the Rocket for the very first time. He remembered his feelings of astonishment, 'The Rocket stood in front of us on the *Meillerwagen* which seemed somewhat primitive. Although stable, the *Abschusstisch* was simply a square table. My comrades and I thought "*My God, will this work?*" I wanted to see the very first firing and although I was 150 metres away from the firing position I was very frightened! The yellow-red jet flame was five to 10 metres in length. A horde of tanks would be nothing against this!'

Priebe's assessment of the *Abschusstisch* and its apparent simplicity confirms the notion that the training of the *Sicherungstruppen* did not require them to be familiar with the technical aspects of the Rocket's firing equipment. The *Abschusstisch*, like much of the Rocket's ground equipment, was highly innovative and sophisticated.

Shortly after having seen the Rocket for the first time, Priebe was granted 'leave'. The atmosphere at home was gloomy as his father reflected upon the reversals suffered by German forces on the Southern and Eastern Fronts and the continuous Allied air raids over the Reich. His father would lament to his son, 'My boy, how is this all going to end?' With the impression of the Rocket still very much etched upon his mind, Priebe replied reassuringly, 'Just wait: the V-weapons are so nearly ready. They will help us!'

Because of the great secrecy, he could say no more about the Rocket to his father. Superiors had told the soldiers of Priebe's unit that the explosive effect of the V2 was huge and that tall buildings and factory stacks would be particularly vulnerable to the blast effect of the shock wave. It was thought by Priebe and his comrades that the exceptionally advanced technology seen in the V2 Rocket would eventually allow future infantrymen to be able to carry in their rucksacks the fire power of heavy artillery! Rocket-propelled, hand-held weapons with a range of a kilometre would transform the battlefield of the future. At that time in the *Heer* a very similar weapon already existed, the rocket-propelled '*Panzerschreck*' (tank terror) anti-tank missile. Although modelled closely on the American Bazooka, the *Panzerschreck* had a range of only 150 metres and required a crew of two to operate. Thinking back to that dark and desperate time, Priebe commented: '*Perhaps we were blind, but we believed*'.

Back from leave, Priebe recalled that *Art. Abt. 3./836 (mot.)* left Baumholder in early September 1944 to travel to Belgium to begin the V2 offensive. He further recalled that in spite of supply problems caused by the Allied advance and the enemy parachute landings near Arnhem, the *Batterie* arrived at a place called 'La Rochelle'. More likely, however, was that the *Art. Abt. 3./836* arrived at La Roche-en-Ardenne as no place with the name of La Rochelle is believed to exist in Belgium.

The situation in the Low Countries was at that time very fluid and volatile. Following the Allied landings in France as well as the more recent liberation of Antwerp on 4 September and Luxembourg on 10 September, the occupying German forces began a retreat back behind the Siegfried Line into Germany. In Belgium, in particular, the Germans made good use of the natural cover afforded by the Ardennes region that extends across not only Belgium but also France and Luxembourg. Travelling routes identical to those taken during the heady days of the *Blitzkrieg* offensive in 1940, the German armed forces had many encounters with the emboldened Resistance. The Resistance, armed by secret parachute drops made by the RAF, was encouraged to harass the fleeing Germans as frequently as possible. This was to have a sapping effect upon morale. The Germans were not able to turn to defend themselves and take on the Resistance as the delay might mean engagement and capture by the Allied main forces. Simultaneously, as the general retreat took place, the V2 batteries were moving into forward positions in order to gain range on their targets. The quiet of the forested Ardennes was frequently shattered by the sounds of gunfire as the Resistance attacked not only German forces travelling east to the Fatherland, but also the FR troops travelling in the opposite direction. The Resistance, which wrongly sensed an irretrievable collapse of the enemy armed forces, vented its full fury. After more than four years of occupation, the Resistance gave 'no quarter' and exacted revenge on small units of Germans travelling on foot or in motorized cavalcades. Priebe recalled what happened having arrived in the area of La Roche-en-Ardenne: 'We did not fire any Rockets there [La Roche-en-Ardenne] because of supply problems. We had no *Feuerleitpanzers*. At that time there had already been a lot of sabotage [of equipment]. Our forward scouts close to us met the partisans. Three or four of our soldiers were killed. After this, we went immediately to a nearby village and fetched the parish priest. The priest then summoned the whole village, but no one identified themselves or others responsible. Punishments were then imposed – however my comrades and I had nothing to do with the shootings.'

Research to determine precise information about reprisal actions taken by the FR troops have not confirmed any of Priebe's recollections and therefore it is impossible to confirm the shooting incident. It is however known that the Germans would react quickly to attacks made upon them by those they considered to be 'terrorists' and it would be the local civilian population who would suffer. The Resistance further provoked the viciousness and hatred of the Germans by maiming prisoners they caught by the severing of leg tendons and, if anecdotal evidence is to be believed, mutilation of the dead. In one instance, on 9 September 1944, near the village of Marcourt, 5 kilometres north-west of La Roche-en-Ardenne, using a captured *Panzerfaust*, the Resistance attacked a German armoured unit. The Germans were advancing to engage Americans at Hampteau near Hotton, 9 kilometres north-west of La Roche. The lead armoured vehicle was destroyed and the Germans initially turned back to La Roche-en-Ardenne. Later that same day the Germans returned to the scene of the ambush and retribution was exacted upon the villagers of Marcourt. Nine civilians died.[4] Perhaps Priebe had heard of this incident and confused it with security operations at La Roche-en-Ardenne?

After three days *Art.Abt.* 3./836 (*mot.*) temporarily withdrew and, having been supplied with *Feuerleitpanzers*, the offensive began in earnest – but from Germany. Priebe and his comrades were aware that the war situation was changing dramatically and that facilities prepared for V2 operations in northern France had been abandoned to the Allies: 'We now had to fire from out of Germany. No one had expected this, and therefore no positions were prepared; but we couldn't change things.'

From 15 September 1944, *Art.Abt.* 3./836 (*mot.*) began firing Rockets from Euskirchen in the beautiful countryside of the low mountain area known as Eifel, 35 kilometres south of Cologne. Priebe recalled that targets were initially Paris, London and Antwerp. In reality it would have been impossible for the Rocket to strike at London as England's capital lay approximately 130 kilometres beyond the Rocket's normal range of 370 kilometres. The targets actually fired upon in mid-September 1944 by *Art.Abt.* 836 (*mot.*) were Arras, Cambrai, Lille, Mons, and Tourcoing in France and Charleroi in Belgium. *Art.Abt.* 836 (*mot.*) continued the offensive until 22 September when it withdrew to the Westerwald area a further 60 kilometres east into Germany. By 23 September the command headquarters *Art.Abt.* 3./836 (*mot.*) was located beside the newly established firing sites in the Rossbach forest, the soldiers being billeted in and around the surrounding countryside of Rossbach. Priebe recalled being billeted in the homes of civilians at Merkelbach, Hütte and Mündersbach – all within 10 kilometres of Hachenburg.

Accommodation with local people was very comfortable and in stark contrast to the time spent in military camps where the food was often served cold. When the soldiers returned from duty, the owners of the property were quick to make them coffee, and hot dinners would be prepared. Secrecy was still of paramount importance, although the locals knew only too well what the soldiers' duties actually were. Once a Rocket was airborne it was impossible for secrecy to be maintained, so casual conversations about the 'wonder weapon' would take place. Priebe and his comrades gave the Rocket the nickname of 'Cigar', but more frequently on operations, simply called it 'A4'. Detailed discussions with local residents about the Rocket and the unit's duties had to be far more circumspect. Priebe recalled a conversation he and his comrades had with the locals when they enquired what sort of unit they were with: *'We told them:* "We're engineers. We fell trees for the construction of bridges." The following day (after a night of firings) when we returned to our accommodations they said to us, "You are fine engineers!" The locals were astonished with the first Rocket launchings and proclaimed, "We finally have the miracle weapon!" – but not all of them 'believed'!'

The residents were not oblivious to the dangers of the Rocket and the misfires that took place literally over their heads. Priebe remembered an occasion when a Rocket lost power on take-off and came careering down close to Hachenburg. It flew low over a group of farm labourers toiling with the potato harvest. Showering the area with dirt, shrapnel and the odd uprooted potato, the Rocket to the amazement of the uninjured farm workers left a crater 20 metres in diameter and 8 metres deep. The FR soldiers would have felt some small irony, as they surveyed the crater and collected metal shards; they knew that the alcohol carried as propellant in the V2 was derived from potatoes.

In fact, it would appear that it was the presence of alcohol rather than the technology of the Rocket that seemed to create the greatest interest with the local civilians. As Priebe recalled: 'Pure alcohol was used for the Rockets. The farmers in the surrounding area noticed this very quickly and would approach us with milk cans wanting alcohol. We had to drive around on motorcycles laying camouflage smoke to hide the area. We also drank this alcohol.

Later the alcohol was coloured and denatured. You could no longer drink it so easily. However, soldiers are rich in the ways of invention! We would pass the alcohol through our gas mask filters three times. Then it was drinkable!'

To safeguard against possible attack from the air on an active firing site, the sky was constantly monitored. From positions on high ground, observers would scan the horizon for possible aerial activity and alert the FR crews by field telephone if they needed to throw camouflage netting over their equipment. Priebe recalled: 'Once I was based on the hillside as a look-out for enemy aircraft. I recall that this was at Hachenburg. We were on the telephone to the FR crew. The time ran, X–20 minutes to launch… X–19… X–18 minutes… We had to confirm security for every minute. Then at X–5 minutes, enemy fighter-bombers suddenly appeared! The countdown could not be stopped after X–5 minutes and the fighter-bombers just passed by when the Rocket quite slowly lifted out of the woods! We all thought: "They'll bomb us tomorrow!" But nothing happened. Perhaps the fighter-bombers were too far away. If they had seen us, they could have simply fired at the Rocket. It was pure luck that we were not attacked then, or during the campaign.'

Normally, however, Priebe and the other *Sicherungstruppe* soldiers patrolled the firing site from a distance of a few hundred metres. He recalled: 'Everything was very primitive. Everyone withdrew from the launch site. Only the *Feuerleitpanzer* was directly in the firing position. We fired at night and once I was 150 metres away from a launch. It was so bright – like daylight! I sheltered by a tree and thought that the world was coming to an end! Sometimes the devices would fall back onto the firing position and we would 'salute shoot' – that meant we'd have to fire a volley of rifle rounds over the coffins of comrades.'

Priebe remembered that his immediate comrades in the *Sicherungstruppe* were '… quite a good crowd and behaviour to one another was good.' The technical men who prepared and fired the Rocket, however, were not known to him and the others in his detail. Many of his comrades had seen action: these men were easily distinguishable from those like himself who had seen none, for they carried on their tunics awards for campaigns, or wound badges. Most had the '*Ostmedaille*' (East Medal) for the winter campaign in Russia 1941–42. Most of them were of his age and it was joked: 'The men born in the year 1924 were Adolf's secret weapon but the weapon was used up at Stalingrad!'

Priebe remembered that his superiors, for example *Leutnant* Utpadel, were older men. He also recalled that the platoon leader was *Oberfeldwebel* Möhs and that a *Feldwebel* Schulz was also with *Art.Abt.* 1./836 (*mot.*), albeit briefly.

The officers told the men that intermittent messages were being received about the accuracy of the 'fall of shot'. They were told that reports were compiled by occasional aerial surveys conducted by the *Luftwaffe* and, more frequently, by spies operating in Antwerp in particular. The soldiers of *Artillerie Abteilung*

836 (*mot.*) were not oblivious to the consequences of their Rockets. As Priebe recalled: 'We once had a report of an impact in Antwerp. This must have been terrible. The Rocket hit a market place – and it was market day. People were slapped to the walls of the houses by the pressure and were left hanging there.'

This incident, in all likelihood, relates to a Rocket fired by the *Art. Abt.* 1./836 (*mot.*) on 27 November 1944.[5] It exploded above the crossroads of Teniers Plaats a few minutes past midday. Although not a market place, it was, in fact, a very busy road and tram intersection, over which a British motorized convoy and civilian trams happened to be passing. The Rocket detonated above the ground as it struck cables or stanchions for the trams and exaggerated the blast effect mentioned by Priebe; no impact crater was found. The full force of the air burst Rocket turned the scene into a charnel yard of unimaginable horror. One hundred and fifty-six people died, twenty-six of whom were Allied soldiers, and nearly 200 others were injured. Although this was not the worst incident to befall Antwerp (this grim accolade fell to the Rex Cinema explosion of 16 December 1944, resulting in 296 dead with 291 injuries), the Teniers Plaats is the most infamous as photographers were immediately on hand to record the carnage.

Appalling and unquestionably dreadful as the effects of the Rocket were, Priebe heard from his comrades that attempts were being made to increase its destructive power. It was said the explosive content of the warhead was being replaced either fully, or partially, with phosphorus. He was further told that reports indicated that large areas in the target zones were being incinerated. In reality, this modification to the warhead was never actually undertaken. Assuming that it had been used, and that the effect of phosphorus was not nullified in the impact, it is debatable if the V2 as an incendiary weapon would have been worthwhile. From a propaganda point of view, however, it may well have been.

Completely unknown to the vast majority of the men serving in the FR units, SS-*Obergruppenführer* Hans Kammler initiated a reorganization and streamlining of the V2 Rocket battalions in January 1945. In reality, Kammler may have wanted simply to massage his own ego by being able to boast to his fellow SS officers and superiors that he had command over regiments rather than just battalions. *Artillerie Abteilung* 836 became *Artillerie Regiment* z.V 901 (*mot.*) and took over the functions of the former *Gruppe Süd* headquarters which at that time had three complete battalions under its command. *Artillerie Abteilung* 485 (*mot.*) became *Artillerie Regiment* z.V. 902 (*mot.*). The SS *Werfer-Batterie* 500 was reassigned as a fourth Abteilung of *Art.-Regt.* z.V. 902 (*mot.*). *Lehr- und Versuchsbatterie* 444 became *Lehr- und Versuchs Abteilung z.V.* To the continued chagrin of Dornberger, Kammler's influence over the secret weapons strengthened to cover V1 as well as V2 operations. Not only was he Special SS

Plenipotentiary for all V2 matters, but he was also commander of the entire V2 *Division z. V.* The Battalion changes amounted to nothing more than a bureaucratic paper exercise and the original Battalion and Battery designation continued to be used in the field. For the sake of simplicity, the authors also use the original unit numbers.

By mid–February 1945, supplies of oxygen were becoming desperately short and this affected the ability of *Art. Abt.* 3./836 (*mot.*) to maintain what had been a successful period of launches. In the first 18 days of February, a total of approximately 55 devices are known to have been fired.[6] From 19 February until 1 March there appears to have been a hiatus in launches. At around this time it is possible that members of Priebe's unit were posted to the anti-tank company, *Panzer-Jagd-Kompanie* 836 (*Pz.Jg.Kp.* 836), to defend the 'wonder weapon' known as the V3 or 'HDP' at Hermeskeil some 13 kilometres south-east of Trier.[7] This weapon used multiple high-pressure charges to accelerate a 140 kilogramme projectile of 15 centimetres calibre along a length of angled pipe towards the target. Having gained sufficient velocity, the shell would travel to the target on its momentum. Simultaneously however, it is also possible that some of the *Sicherungstruppe of Art. Abt.* 3./836 (*mot.*) were used to defend the oxygen plant of Wittringen, close to Saarbrücken. By this stage of the war only one or two factories were capable of producing liquid oxygen. Whatever the actual postings and the disposition of the men, American troops were very close and by 15 February 1945, it would appear that Priebe's unit returned to Hachenburg in the Westerwald.

Art. Abt. 3./836 (*mot.*) continued firing only intermittently due to supply problems until 16 March 1945 when it fired its sixteenth Rocket of the month. As the final and fourth Rocket of the day lifted off from its *Abschusstisch* at approximately 1500 hrs, the unit's offensive operations ended. Some ten days earlier, the Americans had taken the last German-held crossing over the Rhine, the Ludendorff Bridge at Remagen, which lay just over 40 kilometres to the west of the *Batterie* position. The Americans were now dangerously close and so the unit withdrew further into Germany.

If the situation in the West was bad, the situation on the Eastern Front was critical. *Reichsführer*-SS Heinrich Himmler who, from December 1944, had been appointed Commander-in-Chief of *Heeresgruppe Oberrhein* (Army Group Upper Rhine) and later *Heeresgruppe Weichsel* (Army Group Vistula), ordered that the increasingly irrelevant V-weapon *Sicherungstruppen* be detailed as infantrymen in defence of the approaches to Berlin. Priebe and his comrades had always dreaded the perpetual rumour that ultimately the SS would take control of the Rocket and all of the personnel in the FR batteries. Now, in the final stages of the war, Priebe and his friend Meibert did indeed find themselves under the control of Himmler in a combat unit known as the *Kampfgruppe Heistermann*. This unit, operating within the combat group known as *Marchregiment* 2, took all of its fighting men from the *Division z. V.* As Priebe recalled: 'We were given new kit and weapons and ordered to the *Kampfgruppe Heistermann* at Berlin-Bernau, [22 kilometres north-east of central Berlin], and then to the Oderbruch area and Seelow-Golzow, [70 kilometres east of Berlin.]'

The 'Battle of the Seelow Heights', as it became known, was a titanic and bitter four-day assault in which the Germans defended 'The Gates of Berlin' from the onslaught of the Red Army. The battle raged from 16 to 19 April until, eventually, by 23 April 1945, the German capital was encircled and the 'Battle of Berlin' began. Priebe was in action before these fateful dates – as he recalled: 'The Heights were important because whoever held them checked the access to Berlin. There was very bloody fighting. We took and lost the Seelow Heights three times. The Soviets then fired so many 'Stalin Organs' (*Katyusha* rockets) at us that we had no chance. I was wounded, so, thank God, the war was over for me.'

A hand grenade had exploded very close to Priebe and a hail of shrapnel hit his right leg and calf, seriously wounding him.[8] It was, indeed, merciful that he received a life-saving wound which brought about his withdrawal from the front line. In the great and decisive battle that was to take place 20 days later, 12,000 Germans and 33,000 Russians were to die. From the Battle of the Seelow Heights, survivors claim that only 1 in 15 German soldiers survived. In later life Priebe very rarely spoke of his memories of the desperate final battle, but did confide to his family of his great fear as he lay in the mud, seeking shelter from the fearful Soviet artillery barrage.

Having been withdrawn to the west with other injured soldiers, his wounds were treated as well as the very difficult circumstances allowed. Eventually, the Americans took him and the other casualties as prisoners. Shortly afterwards however, the sector was taken over by the Soviets who, surprisingly, allowed the injured Germans to quickly withdraw further to the west behind the Allied line. During the move, Priebe was able, for the first time, to see the enemy, the Red Army, at close quarters and he was astounded by how simple some elements of the Soviet military machine were. He noticed that the Red Army in common with the *Heer*, relied upon horses for much of its transport, but that the Soviet wooden wagons were drawn along by specially bred 'Panji' horses that were dwarfed by the German equivalent. Priebe was sent to a military hospital in Apolda, 40 kilometres east of Erfurt, and after eleven months of treatment and recovery, he was discharged from hospital.

It was impossible for Priebe to return to his home of Wutzow in Pomerania, for not only was his family about to depart forever, but Pomerania had ceased to exist, now no longer part of Germany. The 'Big Three' of Churchill, Roosevelt and Stalin had decided at the Yalta Conference of February 1945 that this former German territory was now to be integrated into greater Poland. His parents had lived there until the war's end, working the family farm. Unfortunately, at the very moment that the Soviets were taking power, an acquaintance of the family decided to settle an old score and denounced Priebe senior to the authorities for a fictitious crime against the new masters. Priebe's father was arrested and transported to work as a forced labourer in Russia. For Priebe's father, a man who had enjoyed the 'outdoor life' working on his farm, this was especially cruel, for he was to spend two years working in a Soviet mine. Meanwhile the situation for Priebe's mother worsened even further. German-speaking residents were no longer welcome in their former homeland and an exodus of displaced refugees trudged to the west and an uncertain future. [9]

Having left Apolda, Priebe travelled to a refugee camp at Osterode, 50 kilometres south-east of Hannover, with the hope of finding employment. From the refugee camp he and many other former soldiers were dispersed into the community. The reception for Priebe from the local people of the rural village of Förste was less than friendly: they resented having to feed and take on lodgers. However, as good fortune would have it, Priebe met some relatives who were able to secure him employment as a carpenter, making picture frames and furniture for a local company. Life for Priebe, and for many like him, was fairly wretched. Germany was in ruins and there was very little prospect of finding satisfying work. The Priebe family was dispersed, with the old homestead abandoned to new Polish owners. Priebe and a former comrade decided to make plans to leave Germany and to emigrate to Argentina where the prospects of a new life seemed good. Word of the proposed plan reached Priebe's father in the Soviet Union, and he wrote back to his son reminding him, '*When you emigrate, what will become of us?*' Reluctantly, Priebe changed his mind and eventually moved to Berlin to be with the rest of his family. In 1947 the Priebe family was briefly reunited when Priebe senior was released from captivity, but they had to endure further heartache when he died almost immediately from pneumonia brought about by the harsh conditions and heavy work in the Soviet mines. [10]

In time, Priebe took a job in a civil engineering company and worked his way up from an assistant into a managerial position. He worked as a site overseer and consultant on major pipe-laying construction work which took him and, following his marriage in 1952, his family, to nearly every continent of the world. The past, however, caught up with him, for in the 'Seventies his old injuries caused his doctor concern. The wounds in his leg had to be opened to remove highly corroded metal shards. [11]

As often happens with old soldiers, his dreams in his twilight years were troubled by memories of the 'old days', but he enjoyed a happy family life and many years of retirement after a successful career as a civil engineer. Willi Priebe died in 2005 aged 81 years.

CHAPTER ELEVEN

'A VIOLENT EXPERIENCE...'

FRITZ MEIBERT
Artillerie Abteilung 836 (Motorisiert)

FRITZ MEIBERT was born in Kassel in western Germany in 1924. He was the youngest of three children and his father owned a construction business. Young Meibert had hoped to join the family business at the end of his schooling; however, as was so often the situation for his generation, the war intervened. No sooner had he finished his basic education and become an apprentice builder, than he was called into the service of the *Reichsarbeitsdienst* in March 1942. For the Nazis, in peacetime, the *Reichsarbeitsdienst* (RAD) had been a means of reducing unemployment and its recruits would often work in civic, agricultural and military construction projects. In wartime, however, the RAD became more of an auxiliary to the German military, undertaking construction work on fortifications, roads and airfields. Later, in 1943, and as a prelude to absorption into the German armed forces, the RAD was to become fully militarized and undertook mine-laying, anti-aircraft and anti-tank duties often with front line troops. More than one RAD unit was to serve as infantry on the Eastern Front and it was here, eventually, that Meibert first saw combat. In common with many who had served in the RAD, having left the comforts of home, the experience for Meibert was a shock. He recalled the gnawing pangs of hunger: 'The worst (aspect) was the food. The "Lords" (the RAD chiefs) got quite good food, but we who always had to work, got very little in spite of special rations for us younger people.'

In May 1942 and after a short period of 'leave', Meibert was instructed in the use and maintenance of rifles, which he took to with ease as he had enjoyed competition shooting before his call-up.

Some time during the summer of 1942, Meibert and the Third *Zug* (Platoon) of his RAD unit were ordered directly to the northern sector of the Eastern

Front around Poloz-Witebsk (today in northern Belarus) and constructed anti-tank defence ditches. A sense of urgency was spurred on by the fact that the front line was a mere 30 kilometres away. In spite of occasional interruptions from local partisans, in a period of just four weeks the Third *Zug* had constructed by hand, and without mechanical aid, a complete anti-tank defensive network out of the soft sand.

In October 1942 Meibert and his comrades were discharged from the RAD and immediately became soldiers of the *Heer*. They were ordered to travel to Latvia, approximately 750 kilometres to the north-east to begin basic military training. Thereafter, without any intervening home leave, they were ordered to the Eastern Front. If nothing else, the food was better and its distribution appeared fairer: 'When we joined the army all of the officers and lower ranks got the same meal from the field kitchen. That impressed us.'

As a concession, as Meibert was still just seventeen-years old, he was not sent to the front line. Instead, during the winter of 1942–43, he was ordered to protect local railway supply lines from sabotage by the partisans in a relatively quiet area behind the German lines in the Northern Sector of the front which Meibert referred to as a 'Russian Kindergarten'. Of this less than enjoyable duty, he recalled: 'Every five kilometres was a wooden tower and at night we had to guard the line. We had to go once, or sometimes twice, along the tracks to the next tower and back. One *Gefreiter* would go ahead and two soldiers would follow five metres behind, one on the right track and the other on the left track. Luckily nothing ever happened.'

To protect the transport of troops and supplies by rail in hostile country, a simple technique was used by the railwaymen: 'Ahead of every train were two empty, but damaged, coaches. If ever a mine was hit, the coaches would blow up, but not the locomotive.'

The bitter cold of the Russian winter was infamously as dangerous as any partisan, and clothing sent from home would be worn underneath standard issue winter garb. Living in cramped wooden bunkers in forward-firing positions, other hazards revealed themselves: 'The worst were the lice. One evening I "murdered" eighty-eight of them and my hands were as bloody as if I had slaughtered a pig. They had got into the pullover which I had received from my mother. One night I hung out my pullover outside thinking that the temperature of minus 43°C would kill the lice. Next morning the lice were gone, but so was my pullover!'

With no direct access to a water supply, Meibert and his comrades would walk the 200 metres or so to fetch water from the Tisza River and when the warmer weather of spring arrived, they would have their daily high spirited 'early morning sport' as they performed their ablutions. Even during lighter moments of relief from combat, the fear of capture, especially by partisans, remained high and Meibert and his comrades always made sure that they each kept in reserve at least one *Eierhandgranate* M-39 'egg' hand grenade to avoid being taken alive. Meibert recalled that throughout the war he had no thoughts of 'destroying the Bolsheviks' and generally, he and his comrades gave such considerations scant regard: 'We didn't think too much about it [the invasion of Russia or politics]. Our aim was simply not to be taken POW – it was better to be dead. Once we found a dead Partisan in a nearby village; we didn't know who had killed him but we took his body with us and as a reward 'for killing him' we got a bottle of sparkling wine for the group. We sometimes worked in the wheat fields harvesting with horse-drawn machinery. I enjoyed the work and it was better than being at the front! But then, after two weeks, we had to set the fields on fire because the Russians came too close. I often had tears in my eyes.'

From the banks of the Tisza, Meibert was sent to the southern sector of the Eastern Front, to Orel in the Ukraine and over a period of several weeks he and other reserve troops were selected for service with combat units. Like many other young men, he quickly became a seasoned front line soldier, and was to spend (without ceremony) both his 18th and 19th birthdays at the front. His requests for leave, so that he could see his family, were continually denied. Meibert knew that the fortunes of war were turning against Germany and that the days of moving ever east had ended. The notion of a 'front line' in some particularly fragmented sectors was very much an abstract notion as Meibert recalled: 'With five other men I spent three days behind the front on the Russian side. We sat in a forward position and didn't know where the nearest Germans might be. I went behind the house in which we sheltered to fetch a few potatoes and butter and to prepare a fire. From this side the Russians could not see us, or so I thought! Suddenly I heard a sound like "*ping!*" and I was hit by a bullet in the thigh. It was then I realized that the Russians had broken through and that I had been wounded by a bullet, which had been shot from behind. I had already put out the fire when, thankfully, at that moment, a motorcycle and sidecar approached ridden by a *Leutnant*. The *Leutnant* noticed my blood-soaked trousers and I told him that the shot had come from what had been a safe direction. He went into the house, fetched my clothes, took me with him in the sidecar, and back to a rear position. That was my 'home shot'! I arrived at the assembly ground in Karashev [today Kazakhstan]. On 14 August 1943 Mongols who served as helpers loaded me onto a hospital train. I asked them to place my jacket under my head because I wanted my head to lay on something soft for the journey. When I awoke, I was already in Warsaw and my jacket, with all my papers, had gone. In Warsaw, I received new papers, and was given extended home leave [to recover from wounds]. I had already been de-liced in Russia, for the *Wehrmacht* offered very good health services – like saunas, for example. My parents were just happy that I was still alive.'

Meibert's name had already been put forward for military awards, not only for his wounds, but also in recognition of his successful 'break-out', in spite of injuries, from behind enemy lines. Thereafter, on 23 October 1943, following a near complete recovery, he was ordered to report to Stettin. However his travel plans by rail were thrown into chaos as he witnessed at first hand the effects of a major air raid by the RAF on his home town of Kassel. The 1800 hrs train to Stettin via Hannover was delayed by four hours because of the raid and Meibert left the railway station and walked into the flaming town. Battle-hardened though he was, the sight of so many suffocated civilians laid out upon the pavements was worse than anything that he had seen at the front. The RAF had attacked Kassel with an exceptionally accurate and concentrated force of 569 bombers. The resultant firestorm, although not as intensive as the fate that befell Hamburg earlier in July of the same year, killed 10,000 people and destroyed 90 per cent of the city.[1]

Meibert's journey was again disrupted by the RAF at Hannover where he and other fellow travellers had to seek shelter from the bombs. He eventually arrived at Stettin at 1800 hrs the following day. There, for the first time in his life, he saw German military barracks, despite having joined the *Heer* the year before! He was anticipating a posting as a replacement to cover the heavy losses on the Eastern Front. Naturally enough, given his experiences to date, he was extremely anxious about the prospect of fighting the Red Army again and so it was with relief that he soon discovered that his orders were to report to a special command at Greifenberg in Pomerania (now Gryfice in Poland) approximately 90 kilometres east of Peenemünde. It was here that he met, for the first time, Wilhelm Priebe. Meibert remembered the resentment he felt, that in spite of his battle experience and wounds, he still held the lowest possible rank in the *Heer*, a '*Schütze Bumm*' (slang for a private soldier). Men such as his friend-to-be Priebe, who had not seen combat, already held the higher rank of *Gefreiter*. He was also resentful of others who appeared to have enjoyed a comfortable and easy military career: 'He (Priebe) had arrived before me. While most of the others already wore medals, he still had nothing. Because he was a farmers' son, he had been held back. They [the other soldiers at Greifenberg] were mostly sons of wealthier people – like farmers and so on. To be honest, I was angry...'

In reality, Priebe's respiratory illness of diphtheria contracted during basic training and a lengthy period of convalescence was responsible for him being 'held back' and not sent to the Front.

Meibert's late arrival at Greifenberg had been noted, and the excuses he offered about air raids apparently did not impress his superiors who assessed that the young man who stood before them was a liar. Adding to what appears to have been a mutually developing atmosphere of animosity, Meibert's replacement jacket, following its theft from his stretcher in Warsaw, was at least one size, and perhaps more, too small for him. The rest of his uniform was worn out. Meibert recalled: 'I arrived at Greifenberg wearing what was left of my uniform. I went to the office and asked a non-commissioned officer for a new uniform. The NCO there had the '*Gefrierfleischorden*' [slang: 'frozen meat badge'] from the first Russian winter campaign of 1942. As he didn't want to give me one, I became impudent. It was said that I shouted at him. The NCO reported me to the *Hauptmann*, our company commander who did not believe my combat record because I was so young. He said: "I should lock you up for three days! But instead, for the next three days, you will take your lunch breaks in solitary confinement with only a cup of water as your meal." But just three days later I was ordered to step forward from morning line-up to be presented with the *Eisernes Kreuz* [Iron Cross] Second Class, the *Verwundetenabzeichen* [Wound Badge] and was promoted to *Gefreiter*. Everyone apologized to me. That's how it works in the army!'

The distinctive, and much prized, Iron Cross was the most famous German award that acknowledged personal bravery and notable military achievement. The medal would be formally awarded with a coloured ribbon of red, white and black, hung from the second buttonhole of the recipient's tunic. Thereafter, just the ribbon would be worn. Less well known was the *Verwundetenabzeichen*. This was awarded in black or silver, depending upon the severity of the wound, or in gold if awarded posthumously. The award was given to the members of the armed forces, and increasingly to civilians towards the end of the war. The oval metal pressed badge was outlined with laurel leaves enclosing a pair of crossed swords upon which was superimposed a German helmet seen in profile. It was worn on the lower left breast of either a tunic or uniform. During the Second World War it is estimated that over two million awards of the Iron Cross Second Class were issued, while the Wound Badge had over five million recipients.

The relief brought about by Meibert's new posting was short-lived as rumours circulated that his group was to join a *Panzer* unit in Russia. The mystery of this 'special command' deepened as he was then dispatched with forty others to the training camp at Groß Born in Pomerania. His white infantry shoulder straps were exchanged for the bright red of the artillery. He and the others were informed that they were now members of a new unit, *Artillerie Abteilung* 836 (*mot.*). It was only now that he started to hear stories of a new 'wonder weapon' and, for the first time, while on duty guarding a large barn that contained a Rocket, the term 'A4'. He was one of four guards posted at each corner of the barn with strict instructions not to peer in! Why he had been chosen to serve with the Rocket force was, at first, unknown to him, but as time went by he learned that men who had experienced warfare were considered an asset. This was especially true given that his duties concerned the security of Rocket operations. It was only much later that he heard the Rocket title of 'V2' while listening to the radio, for it was the custom to refer to the device as simply 'A4'.

Meibert was under no illusions as to the 'usefulness' of the Rocket. Even with the war some seventeen months away from its end, his view was firm: 'There was no way it could work as a weapon. Initially, we had no idea as to its effect on the enemy. We then heard that it flew up to 88 kilometres and impacted vertically. We were told that an impact in the area of the River Thames in London would cost many lives, but its accuracy was only 70 per cent. The whole thing was senseless anyway as the war was already lost. We just thought that hopefully it would all be over soon.'

This pessimistic view was doubtless the result of Meibert's experience of combat on the Eastern Front and is very much at odds with the views of inexperienced soldiers. Men like Priebe had great faith in the Rocket as a decisive weapon capable of turning the tide of the war.

As far as Meibert was aware, training at Groß Born was similar to that given to ordinary troops although he did notice that much energy was expended in exercises in defence against an attack by airborne troops. Unknown to Meibert, it is conceivable that personnel higher up the command chain of *HARKO* 191 (*Höh.Art.Kdr.*191 – High Artillery Command 191) anticipated that the Allies would use parachute troops to attack and destroy mobile Rocket units. Meibert was grateful that his unit never had to put into practice what it had learned defending the V2 troop from parachutists. The *Sicherungstruppen* of *Art. Abt.* 2./836 (*mot.*) spent several months at Groß Born billeted in either tents or houses. Although well fed, the inexperienced men started to grumble at the inactivity. Meibert, however, was pleased to enjoy the extended period of non-combat duties as he regained the strength in his injured leg.

A distraction from the training, and one that was reported by many who served at Groß Born prior to orders to move off for the start of the V2 campaign, was the participation as extras in the production of the film *Kolberg*. Meibert recalled the costumes and the shouted instructions from the directors during outdoor filming: 'It was a very hot summer but we had to wear thick coats and hats. The worst aspect was the constant order to move "uphill" then "downhill"! We thought it was madness as it was 1944! We worked on that film for four to five days. We never saw any actors but we all got a photograph of the starring actress, Kristina Söderbaum [1912-2001]. Later the film was shown to us. It was ridiculous, to make such a film so late in the war.'

Ridiculous indeed. *Kolberg* opened officially on 30 January 1945, just fourteen weeks before the war ended. Hardly anyone saw the production, as by late January 1945, Allied air raids by day and night had already reduced many cinema theatres throughout Germany to rubble. The propaganda value therefore was nil, in spite of costing eight million Reichsmarks. Contrary to much that has been written about *Kolberg*, no front line soldiers were withdrawn to participate as extras. The directors Veit Harlan (1899-1964) and Wolfgang Liebeneiner (1905-1987) took their 'direction' from Dr. Joseph Goebbels, the *Reichsminister* for Propaganda and Public Enlightenment. The film portrays, inaccurately, the siege and defence of the Baltic city of Kolberg which was threatened by occupation by the army of Napoleon in 1807. Between the exciting battle scenes (which cost the lives of two extras), the propaganda message would have been plain to any German. Those in the *Volkssturm* would have been left in no doubt as to what was expected of them in the defence of the Reich. In a scene set in a square in central Kolberg, filled with local defenders, a principal character, Count August von Gneisenau, played by Horst Caspar (1913-1952), addresses the masses:

'Citizens of Kolberg! Prussians! Germans! A heavy fate hangs over your city and our unfortunate country. Stronger than fate is the courage that bears it... No love is more sacred than love for one's country. No joy is sweeter than that of freedom. You know our fate if we do not win this battle. Regardless of the sacrifice each individual must make, what matters is the sacred trust for which we will fight and win, unless we wish to cease being Prussians and Germans. Citizens and soldiers, from servants to generals, you don't wish to be less than your fathers. You have their example. Now forge another. The best defence is attack!'

This stirring eulogy is doubtless straight from the pen of Goebbels. Historically, although the siege of Kolberg failed, thanks to fresh defenders landed by sea, the city was peaceably occupied following the signing of the Treaty of Tilsit in July 1807. Kolberg in 1945 was not so fortunate. The city fell to Polish and Soviet forces after ferocious street battles on 18 March. Kolberg was all but destroyed, but was rebuilt after the war and is now known as Kołobrzeg.

Following the experience of '*Kolberg*', Art. Abt. 2./836 (*mot.*) and 3./836 finally received orders to move off from Groß Born. Meibert recalled that they arrived in the area of La Roche-en-Ardenne in Belgium in early September 1944, not far from the front line of the advancing Allies. The campaign did not begin auspiciously however. Equipment supply problems caused by a lack of *Feuerleitpanzers* meant that they were unable to fire any Rockets. Additionally, one battery's cars failed to return from a forward reconnaissance mission. It was presumed that the men had either been taken prisoner or killed by the Allies. It was also possible that they may have fallen foul of the Resistance. During the three days they spent in the Ardennes, the FR troops had several contacts with the Resistance which led to skirmishes. Meibert recalled that after one such encounter, properties in the village of La Roche-en-Ardenne were searched extensively. Germans, in small groups of two or three, attempted to find the weapons, and in particular the rifles, of the Resistance. They found nothing. Meibert has no memory of any punishment or reprisals being handed out to the local people in La Roche-en-Ardenne. Enquiries made during the research for this book confirm his memory to be correct.

Meibert's unit was withdrawn from Belgium and resumed its firing offensive from the area of Merzig, close to the border of Luxembourg. A standard practice carried out by all *Schießzüge* (launching platoons) was to rotate launching sites to avoid the risk of air attack. The greatest threat from the air may well have occurred sometime between 5 and 13 October 1944 when both *Art. Abt.* 2./836 (*mot.*) and 3./836 were operating from firing sites close to Losheim. Meibert was part of a security observation group which, from the vantage point of a high hill, was keeping a watchful eye for enemy aircraft near Losheim, and close to Merzig. Below, the firing crews were busy preparing a Rocket for launching. With just four minutes left before launch, a group of '*Jabos*' were spotted on the distant horizon. The firing crew were alerted to the potential threat. They responded that the countdown had already begun and would not be halted. With seconds left to launch, the '*Jabos*' suddenly turned toward the direction of the launching site, flying at low altitude. From their vantage point it seemed to Meibert and his comrades that a disaster was about to befall the firing crew: 'We thought that we were all done for.' Meibert, in contradiction of contemporary accounts, recalled that *Art. Abt.* 2./836 (*mot.*) had no Flak guns and would have been defenceless if it had been attacked by Allied fighter-bombers. Meanwhile, the Rocket lifted off the *Abschusstisch* at its characteristically ponderous pace and from the higher viewpoint it appeared that the device travelled straight up and *through* the group of aircraft. Remarkably it seemed as if none of the enemy pilots had noticed the spectacle! They continued on their course, without turning back to attack the woods where smoke was still clearly rising. Instead they disappeared towards the horizon. As far as Meibert was aware, enemy aircraft had little direct effect upon the V2 offensive.

In the early stages of the offensive, Paris was one of many targets fired upon, until as Meibert recalled: '... this was stopped very quickly because of the important monuments in the city.'

The order to stop the offensive against the French capital would have doubtless rankled with the men of the FR troop as they knew only too well that Germany's towns and cities were being systematically reduced to rubble by the combined aerial operations of both the RAF and USAAF. The apparent mercy extended to monuments of stone and marble seemed ridiculous to them, but the firings were halted as per Hitler's orders. The last Rocket known to have fallen on Paris was on 5 October 1944, fired by either *Art. Abt.* (*mot.*) 2./836 or 3./836.[2]

The *Art. Abt.* (*mot.*) 2./836 and 3./836 then moved to Burgsteinfurt on the 28 and 26 October respectively to join with *Art. Abt.* (*mot.*) 1./836. Shortly afterwards 2./836 and 3./836 returned to the Merzig area. After firing against

Antwerp on 3 November 2./836 was temporarily withdrawn for testing duties. The *Art. Abt. (mot.)* 1./836 and 3./836 continued the offensive operating from firing sites in both the Merzig and Hachenburg area, until 1./836 fired its last V2 on 25 February 1945.[3] Throughout the V2 campaign it would appear that the men of the *Sicherungstruppen* were shared out depending upon the requirements of *Artillerie Abteilung* 836 (*mot.*).

Unlike the reception meted out by the Belgian Resistance groups in the Ardennes, the *Sicherungstruppen* of *Art. Abt.* 2./836 (*mot.*) were made to feel very welcome by the German civilian population of the Westerwald in whose homes the men were accommodated. However, as time went by, the locals became increasingly concerned about the many misfires that threatened life, limb and property. Meibert recalled that on at least one occasion, he and the other men were ordered to put right the damage made to a house by replacing the blown off roofing tiles caused by a Rocket that had exploded nearby.

As the local menfolk were away from home, the troops would help in the fields as farm labourers. There was very little in the form of entertainment for the men, but the boredom was relieved somewhat by the abundance of alcohol and the numerous romances that took place with the local women. After the war, some of the men settled in the area and married their former girlfriends. The abuse of alcohol was fairly widespread, but so was the knowledge that it could not be drunk directly because of the risk of blindness or death. The main difference between the FR batteries was the way the alcohol was made safe and palatable. Meibert recalled that, in his unit, the favourite technique was not to distil the liquid but to filter it. This process involved pouring the alcohol through carbon ash. This would absorb the coloured dye but without reducing the percentage of ethanol. It was perhaps fortunate that so much alcohol was available as apparently the filtering of five litres of alcohol would only return half a litre of drinkable and colourless, but highly intoxicating, liquid.

Meibert recalled that subject to supply, Rocket-firing operations took place no matter what the weather and the risk of aerial attack at night was apparently considered to be very low. When Rockets arrived by rail, the *Sicherungstruppen* would be available for safeguarding the transport to the firing site. Local people interviewed by British Intelligence officers in early April 1945 reported that Rockets would be delivered by night.[4] No advance notice was give to the Stationmaster, nor any detail as to the source of the transports or their final destination. Additionally, the railway station staff would be sent home and the local people would be confined to their homes during a delivery. Once the Rockets and ancillaries were unloaded, a cavalcade consisting of an armoured scout car, with an officer and a pair of soldiers leading the *Meillerwagen*, would set off into the darkness, its cargo hidden by tarpaulins. The *Sicherungstruppe* members not already at the cordoned-off restricted area would make up the rearguard and follow in a lorry, fully armed. If it was necessary for the motorized cavalcade to pass through a village, a smokescreen would be laid in advance to hide the transport from prying eyes. The Rockets would be delivered to the centre of a circular, cordoned-off area. The perimeter would be perhaps a kilometre away from the launch site and the *Sicherungstruppe,* in groups of four, would monitor lanes and roads that entered the restricted zone. Across open land and pathways, signs would be erected proclaiming: '*NO GO AREA, WE SHOOT WITHOUT WARNING!*' As the *Sicherungstruppen* conducted their patrol, they heard the sounds of the unseen support vehicles moving backwards and forwards. The reverberating roar of the pumps dispensing propellant into the fuel tanks would join the sounds of the diesel-powered electrical generator vehicles. The soldiers of the *Sicherungstruppe* could gaze through the foliage of trees and see the bright lights of the erected lamp gantries shining in the darkness. Small moving lights swept the darkness from the hand-held battery pocket torches and headband lamps used by the FR crews. The ending of the incessant noises of the pumps indicated that a launch was imminent. Support vehicles would pass along the access lanes and the quiet of the forest would return before the combustion chamber suddenly erupted. Meibert recalled: 'First the ignition, then the *Vorstufe* and then the *Hauptstufe.* We would then see the Rocket climbing slowly above the trees, vertically to the sky. We would hear a rumbling sound for a very long time. At night a weird droning sound could be heard. We were always glad when the Rocket had gone and didn't "come back".'

The men of the *Sicherungstruppe* were discouraged from getting too close to the Rocket, not for reasons of security, but for their own safety. However, on more than one occasion, curiosity would get the better of Meibert and he would leave the other three men at the perimeter cordon and walk towards the epicentre. The pumps had already finished and only one vehicle, the *Feuerleitpanzer* was left behind facing the Rocket as it stood on its *Abschusstisch*. Looking carefully for the sparks of the rotating pyrotechnic lighter Meibert recalled: 'I was once standing 80 metres away when the Rocket took off. The exhaust stream was tremendous. It beat around the *Abschusstisch* and around the trees. I put my hands over my ears as eardrums could burst and hid behind a tree. It was a violent experience!'

Misfires were a common occurrence. Rockets would sometimes fall back onto the *Abschusstisch* or career above the trees. Even Rockets that had gained height and speed would unexpectedly fail. Meibert remembered that only one in three launches was a success. Like Wilhelm Priebe, he remembered the occasion when a misfired Rocket exploded in a field of potatoes. He recalled that the device suddenly lost control and tipped over so that it was horizontal, some 14 metres above the ground. Remarkably, the Rocket stayed at this meagre height and, at full tilt, disappeared into the distance, falling to the ground some six kilometres away near Hachenburg. The *Sicherungstruppe* made its way to the distant smoke on the horizon to discover farm labourers gazing into a huge crater. The V2's warhead had not detonated and was dispensed of with an explosive charge. During the clean-up operations, the *Sicherungstruppen* found a dead wild boar that had been killed by the blast. That evening Meibert and his comrades enjoyed a hastily prepared boar roast.

The *Sicherungstruppen* had very little contact with the other FR crews and were not even billeted together. Whether intentionally or not, Meibert had no idea where these men, who he considered mainly to be engineers, were housed. Nevertheless, stories would permeate from the launch site to the men on the cordon: 'If a Rocket could be prepared in a short time, the troop would be praised, but often preparations would last for a whole day. There was already much sabotage.'

Meibert was appointed as batman to *Leutnant d.R* Waldemar Utpadel, a security *Zug* leader. In the German military, a batman was referred to as '*bursche*' meaning a 'lad' or 'young boy' and Meibert, who looked upon his duties as a great honour, would clean Utpadel's kit, including his boots. Although he never cooked for him, he would fetch Utpadel's breakfast and coffee. By midday however, Meibert was excused from further batman duties unless called upon.

Before being assigned to *Art. Abt.* 836 (*mot.*) on 9 December 1943, Utpadel had served in the *Grenadier Ausbildungs Battaillon* (Grenadier Training Battalion) 92. Utpadel, who had responsibilities other than the V2 *Sicherungstruppe*, was seldom seen by Meibert and his comrades in the afternoon or evening. He was, however, very much liked and respected by those under his command. His demeanour was the very opposite of the more Prussian officers Meibert had met in his early days in the army. *Oberfeldwebel* Möhs, a platoon leader, and *Feldwebel* Schulz, a senior NCO, were also viewed with respect and fondness. Both were in their early thirties and were thought of as kindly father figures by the younger men in the unit who would seek their advice as substitutes for family, far from home. Curiously, both Möhs and Schulz were from the island of Rügen, just 60 kilometres to the north-west of Peenemünde in the Baltic Sea. Utpadel, a teacher in civilian life, who had been called to duty very late in the war, was to later fall in active service. Möhs was to survive the conflict, but the fate of Schulz is unknown.

Apart from the fact that *Art. Abt.* 836 (*mot.*) had some 160 vehicles at its disposal, Meibert knew nothing more of the structure and organization of the V2 units or the effort expended in preparing sites in northern France for the offensive against England. He had never visited Heidelager or Heidekraut in Poland during his training. He recalled that neither he, nor any of his immediate comrades, had ever heard of Peenemünde. Only after the war did he hear of the Rocket development centre and its importance. Of the personalities associated with the Rocket, he had never heard of the names of von Braun or Kammler, nor was he aware of the omnipresence of the SS during the V2 offensive. As contact with the non-security men in *Art. Abt. 2./836 (mot.)* was hardly encouraged, it is easy to understand his lack of knowledge. The men were told only what they needed to know in order to perform their tasks. If the men of the *Sicherungstruppe* had possessed more information, then they themselves might have been a threat to the security of the campaign if they had been taken prisoner by enemy troops or commandos/parachutists. It was the men of the *Sicherungstruppe* who would have faced the enemy to protect not only the Rocket, but the FR troops responsible for its deployment. The *Sicherungstruppe* was doubtlessly considered to be 'dispensable' and if the worst had ever happened, they would have been expected to die in the defence of the preservation of the secret that was the V2.

Christmas 1944 saw Meibert on active service in spite of hoping for leave to return home to celebrate festivities with his family. On the evening of Christmas Day, Meibert was part of a security group guarding a convoy of vehicles of *Art. Abt. 836 (mot.)* crossing the Rhine at Koblenz en route to the Westerwald area. Having been dropped off by a lead vehicle, he shared his duty with three comrades, two at either end of the bridge across the river. The night was thoroughly miserable and Meibert remembered drawing his '*Zeltbahn*' (waterproof triangular cape) even tighter to fend off the bitterly cold rain that turned to ice, making the bridge hazardous. As the night drew on, hundreds of soldiers and vehicles from other units passed by in both directions until, at last, the final vehicle in his unit's column collected him. He was dropped off at his billet in a family home. Meibert, like many others in the *Sicherungstruppe*, was billeted comfortably with a civilian family. His night duty meant he was an unexpected arrival on Boxing Day morning, and he discovered that the woman of the house was temporarily using his bedroom for the family laundry. Scattered across his room were wooden trellises upon which were drying clothes and bed linen. Not wishing to impose further upon the household, Meibert said that the laundry could stay where it was to dry overnight. However the next morning when he awoke: 'I was not able to speak and could hardly breathe. I had an abscess in my throat! A military doctor arrived, dressed in formal parade uniform for a Christmas party. He lanced the abscess and from there I was sent to the hospital in Hachenburg. It seems sleeping in a room with wet laundry is very dangerous...'

Although sleeping in a damp room is not conducive to good health, the reality is that the chronic abscess, caused by a streptococcal infection, had taken root in a person whose immune system was still poor and recovering from the injuries sustained on the Eastern Front. Meibert was able to quickly return to his duties.

After 1./836 fired its last V2 on 25 February, no further Rockets were launched from the Merzig and Hachenburg area until *Art. Abt. (mot.)* 2./836 returned to combat duty on 28 February, resuming firing operations upon Antwerp from Hachenburg. The *Art. Abt. (mot.)* 3./836 rejoined operations on the following day. The two Batteries remained operational around Hachenburg and Helferskirchen until the advance of Allied troops in the Remagen area forced Batterie 836 to cease operations on 16 March 1945, with *Art. Abt. (mot.)* 3./836 firing the final shot from Hachenburg at 14:58 on that day.[5]

As supplies ran out and the threat from the Soviet advance on the Reich grew stronger, the *Sicherungstruppe* was dissolved into fighting units operating in the defence of Berlin. Prior to the official disbandment of the FR troop, on 31 March 1945, the commanding officer for *Gruppe Süd* (Group South) *Oberstleutnant* Wolfgang Weber, sent what was perhaps his final communiqué to his officers in the *Art. Abt.* 836 (*mot.*):

'My Comrades!

'Our enemies – filled with hatred – are in the east and in the west, and have pushed deep into our Fatherland. Our homeland and our most loved ones face being overwhelmed by enemy troops. The hour has come, my comrades, when we must become active fighters. Fighting with a gun in our hands, side by side with other Wehrmacht soldiers, Waffen-SS and those old and young, to fanatically defend our native soil.

'When you were ordered into your present position, you will have witnessed the failings of many cowardly soldiers who have irresponsibly left their posts, enabling the enemy to penetrate deep into our homeland. I know you will think the same when I say, that to continue with our orders [of conducting the V2 offensive], when we also wish to hold back the enemy at the front line, is difficult for us as soldiers and Germans when we are burdened with our valuable equipment.

'The figure of the dishonourable soldier is not a reflection of the fighting troops, who fight like heroes while being overrun by enemy tanks and infantry. They will always bitterly oppose the next assault.

'The special operation [the V2 offensive] is temporarily cancelled. Its success is undoubted. It is at this serious hour, that every courageous and fit man should be sent to the front. We conducted our operations in difficult situations, often under enemy threat; but then we were not a fighting troop. The achievements of the fighting troops are incomparably greater than ours. Our preparations to do the same must be undertaken with urgency and devotion, to enable every one of us to do his duty. Every one of us has to prepare himself mentally to hold his own. The FR soldier will be a good fighter.

'My comrades! The present situation has to be mastered. Maybe we have to become fanatic fighters, if we are willing – and believe – that we can improve the situation. The weaklings among us will be eliminated! Our families and our dead demand *this attitude from us, even if we do not recognize this ourselves. Onwards, my comrades, we have no time to lose! The sun does not set for us.*

Hail our Führer!' [6]

Weber obviously intended that his communiqué should be read to the FR troops at the last roll call of the *Batterien*. It is not known if it was actually delivered to the men, but if it was, its effect must have been a confirmation of their worst fears. The end was approaching – and it was approaching quickly.

Meibert and many of his comrades, including Priebe and Möhs, joined a *Kampfgruppe* commanded by *Hauptmann* Heistermann. *Kampfgruppe Heistermann*, and many other units drawn from every quarter, were used to reinforce the Ninth Army under the command of *General* Theodor Busse. The Ninth Army formed part of Army Group Vistula, and defended the escarpment of the Seelow Heights to halt the advance of the Red Army. The battle that ensued was to see some of the bitterest fighting of the entire war and raged for four days until the last defensive line that lay between the Russians and the capital was breached. On 19 April the Soviets started to break through, taking the Heights and advancing virtually unopposed as fractured German units attempted to halt them. Tens of thousands of civilians rushed in blind panic to the west. Meibert and his comrades were held back in reserve and were ordered forward to the Seelow Heights on 20 April to form a defensive position between Lebus and Küstrin, 29 kilometres west of Berlin and close to the Oder River.

On 24 April, Meibert's unit advanced under the cover of darkness, but yet again the uncompromising geography of the huge battlefield conspired against the defenders as the soil made it impossible to dig a firing position deep enough to escape the relentless rain of Russian bullets and shells. As Meibert recalled: 'We advanced at 2200. I tried to dig a hole but it was sand. Suddenly, I felt pain in my arm and blood ran down my sleeve. The arm became numb because of the loss of blood. We had to retreat at 0200.'

Meibert's memory is hampered by the loss of blood he experienced, for he has no recollection as to how he left the battlefield. Nevertheless, he became aware that he had arrived at a First Aid Station at Fürstenwalde, 32 kilometres south-west of Seelow. Some grenade shrapnel was extracted from his arm, and his wounds were cleaned and dressed. Upon discharge, a medical orderly presented Meibert with a grim souvenir: the near fatal shrapnel in an empty wristwatch box. As Meibert contemplated his fate, he had the good fortune to see a familiar face: *Oberfeldwebel* Möhs, his former comrade from *Art.Abt.* 2./836 (*mot.*), who had been wounded in the shoulder. Möhs had some lifesaving advice: 'Möhs offered me the tip of reporting as fit as possible as early as possible for combat duties, because I would then be sent to the west and away from the Russian advance which was like a steamroller.'

The situation was now very grave and the Russians occupied the eastern side of Berlin. Fürstenwalde must have been a small salient, protruding into the front line that had not been taken in the Soviet dash for the main prize – the German capital. Möhs had heard that men of the Combat Group Heistermann were being rushed to a defensive position at Eisenach, 275 kilometres to the south-west of Berlin. Demonstrating a remarkable degree of faith in his comrade's suggestion, Meibert duly reported himself as fit with every expectation of being dispatched to Eisenach. However, his destination was to be much further afield: Austria – 1200 kilometres away. He recalled: 'From the Berlin area we drove to Magdeburg, but the Americans were already there. We were ordered to Bayreuth. Then a *Leutnant*, myself and another soldier were ordered to guard a lorry travelling to Innsbruck, where a second lorry joined us. Then we continued to Reichsstadt, near Graz. There we met *Hauptmann* Heistermann and were then dismissed on 10 or 12 May 1945. We wanted to drive to Frankfurt, but we were captured by the Americans at Hüttau, near Salzburg. We were then taken to Ruhpolding and were released shortly after as free men.'

After a period of just under a month as a prisoner of the Americans, Meibert returned to his parents' home in Kassel on 15 June 1945. Eventually, he was able to rejoin his father's construction business after continuing the apprenticeship that he had abandoned three years earlier. His skills as a time-served craftsman were very much in demand as Kassel was rebuilt from the rubble of the air raids. In the spirit of the new Germany (albeit a divided one), Meibert destroyed the photographs of his military past and the old wristwatch box containing the shrapnel extracted from his arm was similarly discarded. Of his old comrades he kept in contact with Willi Priebe, but the last time he had physical contact with Möhs was on either 26 or 27 April 1945 at the First Aid station at Fürstenwalde. Meibert did, however, communicate via mail with Möhs who had returned to his home which now lay behind the 'Iron Curtain' in the German Democratic Republic. Möhs would joke that he had somehow 'retained' a V2 Rocket on the isle of Rügen! Although Meibert had always wanted to visit him and to perhaps talk about the 'old times', the political situation prevented him from doing so.

Only very rarely, and with some reluctance, will Meibert reminisce upon his former military service, but occasionally when hearing the distant deep rumble of a jet aircraft, his thoughts take him back to his youth and the woods of the Westerwald.

CHAPTER TWELVE

'SOMETHING VERY SPECIAL TO SEE...'

FRANZ STOLLE
Artillerie Abteilung 836 (Motorisiert)

FRANZ STOLLE was born in October 1924 in Ketten in the Sudetenland of western Czechoslovakia, 85 kilometres north-east of Prague. The Sudetenland has gained its place in history as one of the pivotal territories to lead to the most appalling catastrophe to befall the people of Europe in the 20th century.

The history of the Sudetenland is complex and is beyond the remit of this work. However, it is necessary to outline its history briefly so as to understand its effect upon the Stolle family. Franz Stolle's father, a baker by trade, had been called up to fight during the First World War and he did so against both the Russians and the Italians. Even before the end of the War, the Stolle family homeland which had been part of the Austro-Hungarian Empire, was broken up in accordance with formal and controversial agreements made in Paris during September–October 1918 between the Allies, most notably the Americans and the Czechs. At that time the Sudetenland region was inhabited mainly by ethnic German-speaking people in a land that, historically, was composed of Bohemia, Moravia, Silesia and other territories. Nevertheless, in spite of the majority of the Sudeten Germans, the new multi-ethnic nation of Czechoslovakia was forced into existence.

Unfortunately, long-term conflicts between the German and Czech-speaking population, that stretched back in time to the Habsburgs of the 17th century, came to the fore. The civil unrest that occurred was observed by the American Ambassador, Archibald Coolidge (1866-1928), who had been sent as an emissary by President Woodrow Wilson (1856-1924). Coolidge witnessed the deaths of over fifty apparently peaceful Sudeten protesters, including children, at the hands of the Czech police. The emissary made the suggestion that the German-speaking areas of western Czechoslovakia should be ceded to Germany. The tone of the Paris conferences was such that no matter how small their number, the unity of the Czechs was crucial and the proposal was dismissed. The seeds of festering resentment were sown, to be harvested some twenty years later by Nazi opportunists.

In common with so many other men who had left the Kaiser's army, Stolle's father found that employment in the 1920s was scarce. The decade that had started so badly ended with the disastrous 'Wall Street Crash'. Stolle recalled: 'A huge tide of bankruptcy arrived from America in 1929. Companies closed everywhere, and there was no work. There were food [ration] cards for the unemployed. Germans still had to pay taxes but later it came to light that the Czechs paid none. This led to argument and hatred.'

Stolle's father was able to find employment working in the woollen industry as a spinner and later in a confectionery factory. Young Stolle began his six-year state education schooling in 1930. Stolle, his sister, and their fellow German-speaking friends, were strictly forbidden to speak their own language at school, but instead they were taught how to read and write in Czech. Stolle recalled that German schools were closed down. With a less than adequate education, it is perhaps not surprising that Stolle became a bricklayer in the construction industry. Although the ban on German speech at school must have rankled with the Sudetens, this was not, as Stolle recalled, a cause for great distress: 'When [Thomas] Masaryk was Prime Minister everything was OK, but when [Edvard] Beneš took over, it became bad – he hated Germans. We suffered. The Czechs themselves didn't like him. We wanted autonomy, but Beneš refused it.'

Thomas Masaryk (1850-1937), who became the first President of Czechoslovakia, was considered by many to be an authoritative statesman who was also sympathetic to the separatist movements. He was destined to win several re-elections during his political career until his retirement due to ill health in 1935. His presidential successor, Edvard Beneš (1884-1948), however, was opposed to any of the claims of the German-speaking Sudetens and especially those of the increasingly ardent and vocal leadership of Nazi Germany. In 1938 the Nazis demanded that the Sudeten Germans must be freed from 'oppression', and the situation became so dire that many European statesmen feared a renewed war on the Continent. The British Prime Minister, Neville Chamberlain (1869-1940), in particular desperately wanted to avoid a return to conflict after a respite of just twenty years of peace in Europe. A hastily convened meeting took place in Munich between the principal antagonist, Germany, and the former Allies of the First World War, France and Great Britain. The policy adopted was famously that of appeasement. With the intervention of the Italian Prime Minister, Benito Mussolini (1883-1945), the 'Munich Crisis' was seemingly resolved and Chamberlain famously announced on the doorstep of 10 Downing Street in London, 'Peace in our time!' It should be noted that the agreements were decided upon without any reference to Edvard Beneš or the Czechoslovakian government. Not one Czechoslovakian was invited to participate at Munich or the subsequent meetings held at Hitler's mountain-top retreat at Berchtesgaden. Germany's demand to annex the Sudetenland was sanctioned on the understanding that the Nazis would make no further claims of territory.

Hitler was concerned that although the Czechoslovakian authorities had been urged by Britain and France to accept terms, the Czech army might yet mobilize and the *Wehrmacht* was ordered to act quickly. The cession began on 1 October 1938, Beneš was obliged to resign on the 5th and, by the 10th, the cession was complete. Of those tumultuous times, Stolle remembered: 'In September 1938 we experienced curfews from six in the evening until eight the following morning. Radios had to be handed in. What few newspapers existed were censored, schools were closed and many other repressive measures occurred that I find hard to remember, as I was fourteen at the time. On 1 October the infantry of the German *Wehrmacht* marched in – I saw no tanks, only an artillery battery, which had its headquarters close to our home. My family accommodated two soldiers from Saxony but they left after eight days. There were ethnic areas of different languages being set up (by the *Wehrmacht*). New laws and the Reichsmark were introduced but the exchange rate was poor. The sense of jubilation was quickly over. Then came the miserable war.'

Stolle reluctantly had to accept that his destiny as a Sudeten German was to serve the Greater German Reich. From his point of view however, it seemed logical: Germany needed men and from where could they obtain them? The Sudetenland was one option.

From the construction industry Stolle was compelled to join the *Reichsarbeitsdienst* (RAD) in early March 1942. He and his fellow workers were put to work in support of the *Heer*. His time with the RAD was, by all accounts, a thoroughly miserable experience, with outrageous demands upon order and cleanliness: 'In the RAD we never walked, we only ran. When we left the barracks we had to run. Making beds was a nonsense for they would be intentionally spoilt [by superiors] and our punishment would be guard duty. At 2100 hrs there would be a Roll Call followed by a barrack heater examination to check for any remains of burnt-out ashes, no matter if the temperature was minus 30°C, then to bed. If your shared locker failed a check, it would be thrown down a 50-metre hill into the snow. We were always hungry but there was always enough for the bosses. Alcohol misuse was widespread. We were still children, less than eighteen, but we suddenly had to become men!'

Fortunately, Stolle's time with the RAD was a mercifully short four weeks as he was then called into the *Heer* and began basic infantry training. Training in Poland no longer involved spades, but rifles, machine guns and grenades.

Although the training was hard the treatment from superiors involved less sadistic bullying and Stolle built up friendships which had been impossible in the RAD. In the barracks, which were inspected less frequently than those of the RAD, the men would engage in high-spirited antics by wildly abusing *Heer* dress regulations to much raucous laughter.

Then in June 1942 with the rank of *Schütze* (Private), Stolle was posted to the southern sector of the Eastern Front to join an infantry *Pioneer* replacement unit. Operating in the Astrakhan region between the Azov and the Caspian Sea, he worked on road construction and the 'cleaning of positions.' Stolle recalled what this entailed: 'Following their advance, German motorized units rushed off and we, as the pioneer service, had the assignment of searching positions and taking prisoners. In reality, in such a huge area, many more soldiers were needed.'

Stolle's unit was to support the forthcoming '*Unternehmen Edelweiss*' (Operation Edelweiss) which was to be launched on 23 July 1942. The objective of the operation was to take control of the Caucasus and thereby deny the Soviets access to the lifeblood of mechanized warfare: the oilfields of Baku. From the Astrakhan area, Stolle was relocated as part of the support for the battle of Stalingrad, where he was assigned to the western side of the Don River. From his position he could look across the seemingly endless plains towards the source of the constant distant thundering that marked the position of the city. Of the war on the Eastern Front Stolle recalled: 'We felt that we were intruders: I had often thought that. We had little contact with Russian civilians and at the front there was none at all. The children could speak a little German, and with my Czech, I could understand them: for example, they told me that "a quick move to the west" was planned by the Soviet Army. We felt that their weapons were very good although our own side often told us differently. Supplies were the problem: there was very little drinking water, perhaps 1 litre daily, and food seldom arrived. The bread would be green because it had been stored for so long. Hunger and thirst prevailed. Hygiene was zero, but we would collect the Russian propaganda leaflets for toilet paper! The mood among the soldiers was mixed. Many of us were not even 18 years of age, and we wondered whether the Generals lived as spartan a life as us.'

Then, in October 1942, Stolle fell ill and the field doctors decided to evacuate him. 'It was my luck to have tropical malaria. From 41.5°C to 42°C fever to being cold within a few hours. I was flown directly to Berlin and celebrated my 18th birthday in hospital.'

Indeed, it *was* luck, for during Stolle's recovery the desperate battle of Stalingrad, one of the bloodiest battles in history, raged on without him. The battle finally petered out with the near annihilation of the German Sixth Army in early February 1943, marking the first disaster for the *Wehrmacht*. One-and-a-half-million German servicemen and their allies were either dead or wounded, whilst the Soviets incurred slightly fewer casualties at just over one million, one hundred thousand. Civilian casualties remain unknown.

Following complete recovery from his malaria, Stolle was sent for further *Pioneer* training in Dresden. A skill he learned, and hoped he would never have to apply, was that of being a *Gasspürer* (gas-finder): 'Gas-finders were trained for gas warfare. We were to give the alarm at once if we noticed the strange smells of *Gelbkreuz* (yellow cross), the old World War One recognition name we gave to mustard gas, and other substances. Every *Pioneer* had to do the training course. It was not a nice thing to do.'

From Dresden he was sent to Radom in Poland for further training, this time in bridge construction. From Radom, once again he was sent off to the Eastern Front and at the beginning of July 1943 he began a journey of over 1000 kilometres flying east in a Junkers Ju 52. Stolle remembered that the three-engined transport aircraft flew very low, 'hedge-hopping' to avoid Soviet anti-aircraft fire. The Junkers' low cruising speed of just 211 km/h made it very vulnerable not only to AA fire but also to small arms fire at lower altitudes. After a nerve-sapping flight, the Junkers arrived at an airfield in the area of Orel, 320 kilometres south of Moscow. No sooner had Stolle and the other passengers disembarked, than injured men were quickly loaded on board and the aircraft took off for the west.

Stolle participated in the last ever significant offensive action mounted by the *Wehrmacht* in the East: *Unternehmen Zitadelle* (Operation Citadel). Following the battle of Stalingrad, a salient or 'bulge' had appeared in the German line. *Zitadelle's* objective was to encircle the salient in a pincer movement and then to eliminate the remaining Red Army and its military hardware taken within. The aims of the operation were considered so important that Hitler allocated one-third of Germany's total military strength for the mighty battles that were to take place. This crucial and decisive action saw the famous tank battles at Prokhorovka and Kursk. Stolle recalled: '2,000 German tanks against 3,000 Russian tanks.'

Stolle remembered that during the battles of Kursk, a *Panzer* crewman whom he had known had a remarkable escape from death. Apparently, the man had been struck by a bullet that had entered the front of his helmet. Having passed through the thin metal, miraculously the bullet then orbited the man's head, scraping the metal and exiting at the rear, leaving a gaping hole! The lucky soldier was fortunate to escape with just a headache. But Stolle, too, was to have his own near encounter with death. He recalled vividly one particular engagement with the enemy on the last night of August 1943: 'I was a member of a listening post down at a small river and the Russians were uphill of us. When we wanted to move, we would firstly lift our steel helmets on the end of our rifles. I was on the outer side of the barbed wire and we noticed that Russian shock troops were moving towards us. It was very dark and my comrade called out: "Franz, come back. The Russians are coming!" Then our men opened fire and the Russians started shooting back. They were already very close to me and as I pulled back, I got stuck in the barbed wire. Suddenly a hand grenade exploded very nearby and I could see the sparks where the grenade splinters had hit the metal of the barbed wire. A lot of splinters had hit me and I was wounded in the neck. How I got away I cannot remember because of gaps in my memory, but my steel helmet, which we forward listening posts men were not allowed to wear, was full of blood.'

Stolle was again evacuated from the front line to a military hospital at Gomel in Belarus across the border from Russia. His injuries and his confinement to bed were fortuitous, as he recalled: 'I knew that only injured men treated to the west of Russia would go home; those who were treated at the front went back to the front!'

The shrapnel was dug out of his neck and, with great anxiety, Stolle contemplated where his military masters might send him to next. He did not have to wait very long to find out. As a precursor to a return to combat duty he was posted to Stettin in Pomerania. Stolle knew that the disaster at Stalingrad had been a turning point in Germany's war effort, but he was not aware that following the failure of the summer campaigns against the Red Army, the *Wehrmacht* could only react to the Soviets and would never again be able to dictate military offensives in the east. Stolle remembered his feelings and those of his comrades of impending doom: 'After 1943 and Stalingrad we knew something was up but we never spoke about it in case the 'wrong ears' might have overheard it. We often thought that the fortunes of war would change for us. All the time, transports carrying soldiers left Stettin for the east. It was October and I certainly did not want to go to Russia again! I then heard of transports going to France. I had never been to France, so I volunteered.'

Stolle's hopes of serving in France were, however, dashed; from Greifenberg in Pomerania, he and fifty other men were picked out and sent to Groß Born to join the third Battery of *Artillerie Abteilung* 836 *(mot.)*. At that time he knew nothing of the A4 Rocket, but assumed that whatever his duties were to be, he had been chosen because of his combat experience and *Pioneer* training.

Stolle arrived at Groß Born in the late autumn of 1943. He began training as a member of the *Sicherungstruppe* (security troop) of the *Art. Abt.* 836 *(mot.)* in anticipation of the start of the A4 offensive expected to commence in early 1944. However the start of the offensive was delayed and the months dragged by for the FR troops. In the early summer of 1944, Stolle and his comrades had an experience that can only be described as surreal. One morning he and a crowd of other soldiers were ordered into the backs of lorries and transported to nearby fields. They joined several thousand similarly mystified men from the training grounds. They, like Fritz Meibert (see Chapter Eleven), were all to participate as extras in the production of the propaganda film *Kolberg*. Wearing heavy greatcoats and period helmets of the Napoleonic wars, they were organized into groups identified by large signs carried aloft by a standard bearer. When 'Action!' was called by megaphone, the instructed group would then break formation and run down the slope brandishing weapons that had either been made as film props or borrowed from museum collections. Having been ordered to stop, they would then wait patiently before being ordered to run up the gradient again, waving their weapons, and back to the original starting position. This bizarre activity went on for two to three days. Stolle recalled with much understatement: 'It was different!'

Another oddity that could also be similarly described as 'different' was the high level of security Stolle experienced. He gradually began to realize that his new unit was something out of the ordinary, as he recalled: 'I began to grow aware about the kind of unit I was now in. Taking photographs was forbidden, and I have always liked to have photos of my life. Every week we had to sign a paper that we would maintain strict secrecy. Nobody was interested in being punished. We all conformed because we wanted to get home safely again.'

The first time he saw a Rocket it was erected on a *Meillerwagen*: 'It was 1944 and I was one of the security guards. It was finished in green shades of camouflage. We could not understand how it worked. It was something very special to see.'

Stolle's commanding officer in the *Sicherungstruppe* was *Leutnant* Utpadel, whom he remembers as a man of gentle appearance with a thin aquiline face. In character too, he was a gentleman and much respected as an 'all-round good guy'. On one occasion Stolle had made the mistake of force drying his wet boots by placing them too close to an open fire. The leather surface was burned in the process and Stolle expected a punishment from the battalion's *Stabsfeldwebel* (Sergeant Major) for damaging *Heer* issue equipment. However Utpadel intervened and Stolle was saved from a reprimand. Possibly Utpadel was more concerned with the change from training to operational security duties for *Art. Abt. 836 (mot.)*. By September 1944 training was well and truly complete, the V2 offensive was about to begin. Burnt boots paled into insignificance!

From Groß Born *Art. Abt. 3./836 (mot.)* moved to Baumholder in western Germany in anticipation of moving into forward-firing positions. Travelling by rail with its equipment, the unit's destination was Venlo in the Netherlands, but the *Batterie* was ordered back to Germany and arrived briefly at Bonn. It then travelled to Euskirchen in the area of Eifel. The constant changes in destination may well have been due to the pressure on the front by the advancing Allies. Eventually *Art. Abt. 3./836 (mot.)* disembarked to the sounds of distant American artillery at the strategically important rail and road junction of St. Vith, near Bastogne in Belgium, and after a few days (presumably awaiting more supplies) the unit started to move through the woods of the Ardennes to forward-firing positions on 7 September 1944.

It was here that Stolle first came into contact with what was known as the '*Weiße Garde*' ('White Guard' – the Resistance). He had no idea, however, how the expression, *Weiße Garde,* had been coined. It is possible that he had heard this term from a comrade who had served in Slovenia where the Slovene *Domobranci*, or 'White Guard', was a sizeable home defence force of Nazi collaborators which never adopted a uniform and was impossible to distinguish from the similarly dressed Resistance.

On one occasion, two men from the battery had been sent forward on a reconnaissance patrol. They were captured by the *Weiße Garde* and as Stolle recalled: 'They (the 'White Guard') had cut the popliteus tendons behind the knees of two soldiers. As a result of this barbarity, the men were unable to walk so both literally crawled back to the safety of the *Batterie.*'

It is probable that the two men had also been beaten to extract information that the Resistance would have passed on to the Allies. Thereafter the Resistance might have contemplated killing the men but perhaps decided that to do so would bring about retaliation upon the local community. Crippling the men, although barbaric, would not necessarily encourage retribution and would also have the effect of allowing the Resistance to melt away into the countryside before the position was reported by the injured soldiers. A deep wounding of popliteal muscle would cause massive blood loss as the artery would also be cut. In the woods of the Ardennes, so many kilometres away from medical aid, the injury would have resulted in death. The cutting of the knee tendons is the more likely injury that the men suffered. Modern surgery can repair such a serious injury, but in the conditions of September 1944, it would have been very unlikely to have been possible. The injured men would have had to come to terms with walking with braced, locked knees, but nevertheless they would learn to walk again with difficulty.[1]

To the ordinary German soldier the activities of the Resistance were an anathema; civilians who could suddenly pull out a knife or machine gun and who laid landmines earned the highest revulsion. Stolle had seen for himself the effects of a Resistance landmine on a German lorry whose shattered hulk, together with its occupants, had careened down a steep hill into a stone wall.

Stolle recalled what happened when his two wounded comrades crawled back to the wooded bivouac and how the experiences of fighting on the Eastern Front were brought to bear: 'Instantly a search action was put under way, but it was dark. The villages were far apart and surrounded by woodland. It could only have been done by the people from the village and they must have been hiding in the woods. We went to the nearest village.'

Members of the V2 Technical Troop hoist and lower the Rocket onto a *Vidalwagen* Road Transporter using a *Strabo* 15 tonne Portable Gantry Crane. This standard issue crane could be set up in 30 minutes. The supply railway carriage has already moved off. (NARA/USAF)

The Technical troops manhandle the '*Elefant*' (warhead) within its transit-packaging container onto the Rocket's body using a small portable crane assembly. (NARA/USAF)

With the warhead secured by the crane, the Rocket is now transferred from the *Vidalwagen* Road Transporter (left) onto the *Meillerwagen* before delivery to the firing site. The *Meillerwagen's* adjustable clamps can be seen clearly. (NARA/USAF)

The *Feuerleitpanzer* approaches the launch site towing the *Abschussplattform*. (NARA/USAF)

The rear of the *Feuerleitpanzer* showing the inspection hatches used by the firing crew to monitor the launch of a V2. The *Abschussplattform* will be carefully positioned on a surveyor's mark and then the trolley removed. Each leg of the *Abschussplattform* is adjustable for levelling. (NARA/USAF

The *Meillerwagen* is hand-hauled and winched into position prior to the V2 being raised onto the *Abschussplattform*. (NARA/USAF)

FR crew fix a version of the 'Carousel' to the nose cone of the Rocket. When elevated into the vertical position, the Carousel will aid quick access to the A4's upper instrument compartments. (NARA/USAF)

A convoy of FR support vehicles: closest is a Hanomag SS-100 *Schwerer Radschlepper* (Heavy Tractor) which appears to be towing a *Luftwaffe B-Stoff* Alcohol Bowser; then a Kfz.385 *Flugbetriebsstoff Kesselwagen*; a second Hanomag SS-100 *Schwerer Radschlepper* tows the *A-Stoff Betriebsstoffanhanger* Liquid Oxygen Bowser, and at the rear, an Opel *Blitz T-Stofftankwagen*. (NARA/USAF)

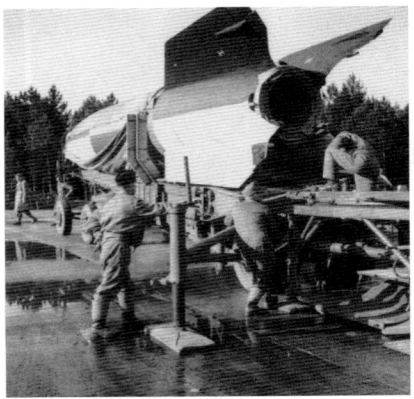

The final delicate adjustments are made before the *Meillerwagen* begins to elevate the Rocket onto the launch table. (NARA/USAF)

The V2's fins (1 and 3) are aligned precisely towards the target. Fin 3 is closest to camera and furthest from target. Below the *Abschussplattform,* the thrust deflector plate can be seen. This was known as the 'lemon squeezer' by Allied troops. The delicate and easily broken graphite rudders will be attached following the end of the levelling process. (NARA/USAF)

The surveyor calls out corrections to the firing crew who vertical-align the Rocket upon the *Abschussplattform*. Note that an upper compartment hatch is open as final adjustments are made. (NARA/USAF)

The Rocket is now in the vertical position and the technician on the *Meillerwagen* access ladder makes adjustments to the fitted gyroscopes. He is approximately 14 metres above the ground. Shortly, the propellant bowsers will arrive to commence fuelling. (NARA/USAF)

The *B-Stoff* bowser, a Kfz.385 *Flugbetriebsstoff Kesselwagen*, pumps alcohol to the Rocket closely observed by a technician. In the background can be seen the buildings and masts of Altenwalde, the gun-firing test range satellite station to the much larger *Kriegsmarine* base of Cuxhaven. (NARA/USAF)

Right: The alcohol (*B-Stoff*) propellant tank is being filled by the technician on the ladder. Below, technicians prepare to fill the liquid oxygen tank. Note one of the upper compartments is open which was standard procedure on warm days to prevent the avionics becoming too warm. (NARA/USAF)

The business end of the bizarrely shaped *A-Stoff Betriebsstoffanhänger* (Liquid Oxygen Towable Bowser). The inlet for filling the bowser is seen at the top of the tank. Once fuelling was completed, frozen pipe unions would have to be 'knocked off' using wooden mallets. (NARA/USAF)

A Magirus ladder allows a technician access to the mid-section joint that separates the *Mittelteil* (Middle Fuselage) from the *Antriebsblock* (propulsion block). As the A4's weight increases during fuelling, adjustments are made to reduce stress. The photographer's back is towards the target. (NARA/USAF)

A technician uses a field telephone to communicate with the crew of the *Feuerleitpanzer*. To his right, the fuelling control valves are clearly seen in the top of the Propulsion Test unit. (NARA/USAF)

The continuity of the V2's plumbing was tested using compressed air. The results of a test were read from a pressure gauge. (NARA/USAF)

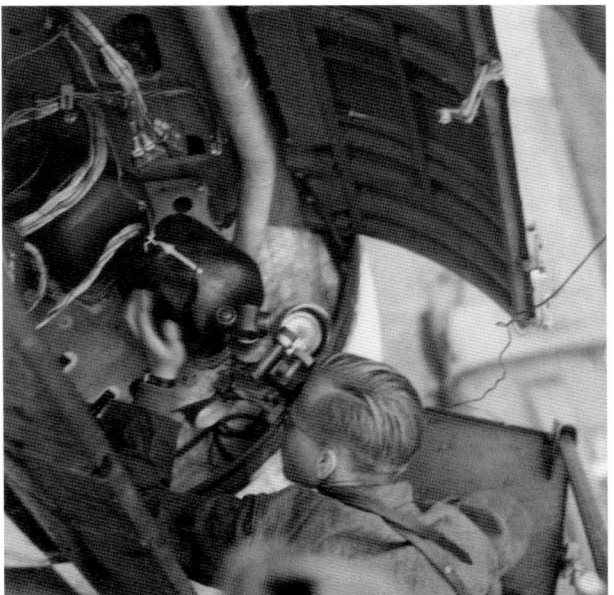

The V2 seen during the fuelling process; the *A-Stoff* tanker is to the left, the *B-Stoff* is seen on the right. The *Stotz Stecker* has been attached just below the warhead. Note the cylinder halfway up the *Meillerwagen* arm. This would be filled with *T-Stoff* (hydrogen peroxide) and would dispense a measured quantity into the *T-Stoff* tank on board the V2. (NARA/USAF)

The alignment between a gyroscope and fins 1 and 3 was critical for the accuracy of the V2. An FR soldier carefully checks the position of the gyroscope using a Bunker collimator. This was a procedure determined by *Leutnant* Helmuth Frenk. (NARA/USAF)

An Opel Blitz *T-Stoff* (Hydrogen Peroxide) tanker.
(NARA/USAF)

Below: V2 support vehicles, bowser and ancillary
equipment gather around the V2. Soon all vehicles
will be ordered away in anticipation of firing.
The central bowser carries the *T-Stoff* (Hydrogen
Peroxide). Shortly, a simple wooden frame will be
placed under the venturi. This will hold the rotating
pyrotechnical lighter that will ignite the engine.
(NARA/USAF)

A technician using a 'dial sight' orientates the V2's
position with reference to a tripod-mounted
collimator that has been accurately positioned above
a 'Trig Point'. In the background, steam from liquid
oxygen is caught by the wind. The *Meillerwagen* was
equipped with mounted pipes to aid the fuelling
process. (NARA/USAF)

An A4 Rocket rises into the sky. The black and white paint schemes aided observation of roll. The white band in front of the tail is frost caused by the liquid oxygen propellant tank. This Rocket is believed to have been photographed at Peenemünde. (Klein)

Above: 'An incident somewhere in southern England': civil defence personnel work to clear roof timbers and pipes from the scene of a V2 impact in the southern Home Counties in the autumn of 1944. (Getty Images)

Below: Damage to houses caused by a V2 Rocket at Blake Hall Crescent in Wanstead, East London in October 1944. This Rocket was fired by *Batt. 2./Art. Abt.* 485 on the night of 3 October from The Hague. Five properties were demolished and eight people killed. (Getty Images)

The cartoon character of the Rocket soldier 'Xaver Willibald', as seen in a guidance booklet for A4 personnel, contemplates the merits of drinking V2 Rocket propellant as an alcohol accompaniment to his meal.

Xaver Willibald, having not heeded the dangers of drinking methanol alcohol, rests in peace. A light-hearted, but dire warning to all Rocket personnel of the dangers of consuming V2 propellant.

Henricus Schotanus à Steringa Idzerda, a pioneer radio broadcaster, was to pay with his life for collecting V2 shrapnel in The Hague in November 1944. (Archief Beeld en Geluid, Cat. No. 84615/ Photo No. 297)

A llama of the Duindigt Estate, close to The Hague. A relative of the particularly aggressive stallion, Cor, is fed a treat by a member of the Jochems family. (Jochems)

Residents are guided to safety across the rubble from the remains of a building struck by a V2 in East London in late November 1944. The job of the fire and emergency services was made extremely dangerous by structurally damaged buildings and, by the following year, the use of specially trained tracker dogs was authorized by the government to aid search and rescue. (Getty Images)

Wilhelm Priebe, to the extreme right, and fellow members of the security troop of *Artillerie Abteilung* 836 line up in winter smocks in late 1944. (Priebe)

Members of the security troop of *Artillerie Abteilung* 3./836 (mot.) gather around their commanding officer, *Leutnant* Waldemar Utpadel (standing in leather coat and with field glasses), for a photograph at a forested operational position. The photograph captures a rare occasion when most of the troop were present. Below and to the left of Utpadel is *Oberfeldwebel* Möws, while Fritz Meibert, with a boyish smile, is seen diagonally to the right and three rows behind Utpadel. Wilhelm Priebe and Franz Stolle are also believed to be in this group. The man to the far right in the front row was a dispatch rider and wears a leather map and document case on his belt. (Stolle)

Wilhelm Priebe and members of *Artillerie Abteilung* 836 wearing full battle gear pose for a quick photograph before moving off in an Opel *Blitz* 3-ton truck in late 1944/early 1945. (Priebe)

Men of the *Artillerie Abteilung* 836 security troop clad in typical late-war camouflage smocks and kitted out with field glasses, pistols and ammunition pouches, prepare to move off aboard an Opel *Blitz* truck. (Stolle)

Left: A severely damaged property on Van Voorschotenlaan in The Hague caused by one of the two V2 misfires fired by *Batterie* 444 in the evening of New Year's Eve 1944. The nearby Bronovo hospital was also damaged in the same blast when it lost over 2,000 window panes. No civilians died in this incident. (Beeldbank Haags Gemeentearchief)

A bleak photograph showing the once beautiful coffee house, '*Chateau Bleu*', on the northern edge of the wooded Haagse Bos in The Hague. An anti-tank ditch can be seen in place of the Benoordenhoutseweg (a road). On New Year's Eve, 1944, a V2 fired 200 metres away from *Chateau Bleu*, lost power and fell onto the building, completely destroying it. This was the second misfire *Batterie* 444 experienced that evening. (Beeldbank Haags Gemeentearchief)

In a rare photograph of the third most important Nazi during the late stages of the war, SS-*Obergruppenführer Dr.-Ing.* Hans Kammler, seated on a deckchair, enjoys a moment of relaxation with coffee and unseasonably warm winter sunshine. The location and date are unknown. (Heiko Petermann)

Riouwstraat in The Hague. This street was destroyed by a V2 misfire that occurred on 25 January 1945, killing ten and injuring 45. It is possible that this is the same incident recalled by Eduard Jericha of *Art.Ausb.Abt.* 271: 'A nearby row of houses had simply fallen down and it resembled a doll's house. The crater very quickly filled with water.' For scale, note the figures centre and to the right. (van Vleuten via Beeldbank Haags Gemeentearchief)

A stairway close to the junction of Indigostraat and Kamperfoeliestraat in The Hague leads to nowhere. A V2, probably fired by *Art. Abt.* 485 (mot.) misfired in the late afternoon of 1 January 1945, killing 38 civilians. If the V2 had fallen behind the photographer's position, it would have fallen harmlessly in a cemetery. Approximately 60 citizens of The Hague lost their lives due to misfires. (Beeldbank Haags Gemeentearchief)

An artist captures the moment a V2 takes off from Scheveningen, close to the Nieuwe Badkapel church at the crossroads formed by Nieuwe Parklaan and Nieuwe Duinweg in The Hague, February 1945. The launch site appears to be from the wooded, ornamental Westbroekpark. No photograph is known to exist of a V2 firing at such close quarters and the penalty for either an FR soldier or a Dutch citizen taking one would have been death. Members of the V2 *Sicherungstruppen* stand passively as the Rocket gathers momentum. (Dirk van Rijn, 1980/Beeldbank Haags Gemeentearchief)

Eduard Jericha of *Art.Ausb.Abt.* 271; he was to witness an RAF Spitfire attacking an ascending V2 Rocket over The Hague in 1945. (Jericha)

Flight Lieutenant Raymond Baxter of 602 (City of Glasgow) Squadron, RAF, in his beloved clipped-wing Spitfire Mark XVI. Note Baxter's non-standard leather jacket, a gift from his girlfriend and wife-to-be, Sylvia. Post-war, Baxter became a noted TV/Radio broadcaster. (Baxter)

An RAF photo-reconnaissance photograph of 18 March 1945. To the top right is the imposing building of the Bataafsche Import Maatschappij (Shell Building) and the St. Paschalis Baylonkerk. One block in front, and again in the top right, is the wooded area of Haagse Bos. (Baxter)

Hofstede Farm off Leidsestraatweg in Duindigt from where Oswald Schneider of *Art. Abt.* 2./485 (mot.) collected fresh milk. The farm was destroyed accidentally by the RAF in an anti-V2 attack in March 1945. (Beeldbank Haags Gemeentearchief)

Along this lane, known as Leidsestraatweg, in Duindigt, FR *Meillerwagens* would carry their deadly cargoes to launching sites situated close to the protective cover of trees. The area was attacked several times by the RAF. (Beeldbank Haags Gemeentearchief)

Local workers carry an injured colleague to safety while a fireman prepares to dampen out flames amid the smoke-blanketed wreckage of Smithfield Market off the Farringdon Road, close to the City of London, which had been hit by a V2 Rocket fired by *Batt.* 3./485 from Wassenaar on the morning of 8 March 1945. (Getty Images)

'The receiving end': a bewildered and bloodstained Londoner sits forlornly amidst the debris following a V2 impact in central London on 8 March 1945. (Getty Images)

Right: The casualties resulting from the attack on Smithfield amounted to 110 dead, 123 seriously injured and 243 with lesser injuries. Here, injured workers have been lifted aboard a horse-drawn market trailer to be taken to the casualty department of one of several London hospitals. In total, 2,754 people were killed by V2 Rockets in England, with another 6,523 seriously injured. V-weapons also accounted for 3,515 people killed in the district of Antwerp in Belgium, with 5,824 seriously injured. (Getty Images)

The scene of devastation left by the V2 fired by *Batt.* 3./485 (Art. Reg. 3./902) at London on 8 March 1945. The official damage report stated that the Rocket '... had penetrated two-storey shop and fishmarket buildings at NE junction of Charterhouse and Farringdon Road and detonated at a lower level than the roadway of Farringdon Road.' The blast from the V2 was violent enough to bring down the concrete and iron vaulted floor and the lattice-framed roof of the fishmarket. (Getty Images)

As recalled by Stolle's comrade, Wilhelm Priebe (see Chapter Ten), the *Sicherungstruppe* fetched the local parish priest who in turn summoned the entire village. Demands were then made that those responsible for maiming the two Germans should be identified. Stolle recalled: 'As had been the practice in Russia, thirty men were taken as hostages. The local people were told, "If another one of our men is injured, the hostages will be executed." This proved to be the best way to stop ambush attacks. Pressure creates contra-pressure – a physical law that was proved in Russia. It was the best method with which to protect ourselves. As far as I know, we [the V2 *Sicherungstruppe*] never shot hostages, although with the continual movement of our unit, they would have been in the way. It might be that executions happened elsewhere though.'

Whilst this drama unfolded, Stolle remembered a comrade who could not resist an opportunity of petty thievery: 'One of our soldiers who had been sent to the church stole a jar of jam from the priest.' The *Sicherungstruppe* detachment of *Art. Abt.* 836 *(mot.)* then made its way back to the others waiting in the nearby woods. Stolle recalled: 'As we drove back we saw a man with a rucksack running across a field. It was obvious that something was going on. One of our men shot at him and hit him in the leg. We cared for his wound. This man was aged about 30 or 40 with a rucksack full of food, as well as maps, but no weapons. What were we to do with him? Shoot him? We didn't want to kill him. An old *Obergefreiter*, who already had the Gold Wound Badge [awarded in recognition of being wounded five or more times in action], suggested, "Take him to the next village, and for ten bottles of Cognac they can keep him!" It was a fair trade and it worked.'

The village from which the hostages were taken was, in all probability, La Roche-en-Ardenne. Stolle recalled that a rumour began to circulate that members of *Art. Abt.* 836's other *Sicherungstruppen* may have fired an anti-tank weapon into a village – again possibly La Roche-en-Ardenne – in an act of retaliation. However, no confirmation of this event has been discovered.

Stolle never saw the preparation of a Rocket for a launch, but instead would see a V2 rising from the canopy of the forest from whatever position he had been ordered to: 'As guards at the look-out posts, we were not too close to the launch site, and we the *Sicherungstruppe* could never understand how the thing could be launched. The sound of the V2's engine was heard first, then the jet and blast of the flame, as the Rocket rose into the sky. A certain amount of fear and caution was always present during Rocket firings. We could tell from the sounds of the V2's engine whether it was a good launch or not. With experience we grew to know whether all was OK or not.'

Misfires and explosions when Rockets were still on the *Abschusstisch* were a common occurrence. Stolle vaguely recalled that the *Art. Abt.* 3./836 would attempt to fire Rockets that had failed to be successfully launched for technical reasons by the other two batteries: 'They either worked or blew up, these were the only two options.' From his position on guard duty, Stolle witnessed a Rocket take-off only for it to crash to the ground, exploding into three fiery sections a relatively short distance away. Other Rockets would lose thrust and then fall complete into the forests around the launching sites or into nearby fields. Failures, he believed, were the result of sabotage by concentration camp workers and POWs who constructed the Rocket. The worst incident of a misfire he was aware of took place at Hunsrück in the Westerwald area, when a Rocket fired by 3. *Batterie* crashed upon another unit of *Art. Abt.* 836 *(mot.)* some distance away, killing several soldiers. Strangely, the war diary of *Art. Abt.* 836 *(mot.)* does not record an incident of a Rocket falling onto an adjacent firing position and causing fatalities.

In recent years, an account of a bizarre V2 incident has surfaced in the same vicinity that might partially explain Stolle's recollection. A Rocket launching performed by *Art. Abt.* 836 *(mot.)* had apparently failed and the device toppled to the ground beside the *Abschusstisch*. Local residents reported that the frustrated soldiers, who presumably did not wish to abandon a 'live' Rocket, decided to destroy it by scuppering the propellant tanks. Armed with pickaxes, they set about puncturing the thin, outer steel skin, hacking into the aluminium tanks of liquid oxygen and alcohol propellant. Local people claimed that the resultant – and inevitable – explosion not only destroyed the Rocket but also, simultaneously, dispatched many of the soldiers involved, and those witnessing the spectacle, to a fiery death. However, Stolle is doubtful that such an incident could have occurred as it would suggest crass stupidity on the part of his fellow FR troops: 'I cannot imagine such a thing happening at all. There are a lot of fairy tales told about the V2.'

It is known, with certainty, from the recorded entry in *Art. Abt.* 836's *(mot.)* war diary that on 10 December 1944, a very serious event *did* occur, resulting in casualties. Rocket No. 20471, destined for Antwerp, failed to reach its full 25-tonne thrust and, having momentarily lifted off the *Abschusstisch*, it completely lost power and settled unevenly upon its tail fins. The Rocket was tilted over at what must have been a very precarious angle and the FR troops then moved forward to pull the device away from the platform. During the attempt to de-tank the propellant tanks, the B-*Stoff* (alcohol) tank exploded without warning, killing three men and injuring two others.[2] It is interesting to speculate whether the local people and the recorded entry in the *Art. Abt.* 836 *(mot.)* war diary are recalling the same event! The war diary of *Art. Abt.* 836 *(mot.)* does not record any unorthodox procedures to de-tank a Rocket, although if this had happened, it would suggest a level of ineptitude that is difficult to believe given that firing crew were chosen for technical ability and, invariably, had combat experience. The 'pickaxe' story has now become part of the local folklore for the region. Whatever the reality, the Rocket soldiers remained stoic in the face of death and injury – as Stolle recalled: 'These sorts of accidents always had to be expected. Even today, such tragedies happen. In those days though, from a technical viewpoint, the Rocket was still in its infancy and it was war and we just had to keep going.'

Operating from forested launch sites in and around the forests of the Westerwald, Stolle remembered that the security posts would be located at the edge of the woods or in the hidden parking areas for the support vehicles. The *Sicherungstruppen* would man three sentry posts with five men apiece. The posts were connected to one another by field telephones as no post had sight of the others, or indeed of the launch site. Although signs warning locals to keep away were posted in the area and on the edges of woods, the *Sicherungstruppe* would frequently find curious children from the nearby villages, oblivious to the dangers, within the security zone. The *Sicherungstruppen* were ordered to fire upon adults without warning, although Stolle cannot recollect any occasion of this actually happening.

Occasionally Stolle would man an observation tower equipped with field telephone and binoculars from which he would scan the distant horizon for approaching enemy aircraft. The towers, which had been built before the war for fire-watching, proved to be very useful for the *Sicherungstruppe*, although on occasions rather dangerous for those on duty in them. Stolle recalled that on one occasion a manned observation tower was spotted by low-flying enemy fighter-bombers which swooped down raking the tower with blazing machine gun fire. The *Sicherungstruppen* on duty managed to escape under the cover of the trees as the tower was reduced to wooden splinters. Stolle also heard that on a German-speaking BBC radio broadcast it was reported that Allied pilots would be rewarded with a large farm in Canada if they found and destroyed a V2 site! He recalled: 'Whether this was true, I don't know; you would have to ask the other side! Although strictly forbidden to listen to enemy radio, this is what we heard. Of course, a lot of propaganda was always in the game.'

The *Sicherungstruppen* were under no illusion: the threat of attack from the air was real and was taken very seriously. If a single aircraft was spotted, the preparation to launch a Rocket would continue, but if '*pulks*' (formations) of low-flying fighter-bombers appeared, an emergency signal would be sent to the launch site and all preparation would stop. The *Sicherungstruppe* had its own anti-aircraft guns and to reduce the risk of detection, most movement of equipment and Rockets would take place at night. Stolle recalls vividly an instance during the potato harvest when he and his comrades were helping to gather in the crop and in doing so they came to the notice of prying *Jabos* looking for targets of opportunity. Stolle and his comrades were wearing '*drillich*' (fatigues) of a muted green military colour, but the civilian women toiling in the fields were wearing bright coloured clothing, which the fighter-bombers had seen. As the aircraft began to turn sharply to bring their guns to bear, the experienced soldiers urgently told the women, one of whom was pregnant, to lie on the ground whilst they covered them with hessian sacks to hide them. In spite of the obvious dangers, Stolle recalled an incident near Euskirchen when the *Sicherungstruppe* attempted to snare unwary enemy fighters' pilots: 'One day we tried to make a trap for the *Jabos*. We drove with a car along a road several times. Enemy aircraft soon arrived and we opened up with our 2 cm *Flakvierling* (four-barrelled combination gun). Although we didn't hit them, they never came back to bother us!'

The men of the *Sicherungstruppe* were billeted with local people in and around the forest firing sites of the Westerwald, and Stolle resided with a family in the village of Hütte, 50 kilometres east of Bonn. Relationships with the families and local people were good and food was exchanged between the soldiers and the civilians. Stolle recalled a general feeling of war weariness and anxiety that pervaded the locals. Everyone seemed to be aware that the war would soon end and in ending, would bring an uncertain future.

Stolle and his comrades would be available for duty for 24 hours 'on' followed by 24 hours 'off'. He recalls that alcohol abuse did occur during free time in spite of constant warnings of blindness. Such habits feature little in his memory, as he did not enjoy drinking. Although Stolle was acquainted with his fellow *Sicherungstruppe* soldiers, Wilhelm Priebe and Fritz Meibert, they were simply 'faces' seen occasionally because they were members of the other two firing batteries. It was only very rarely that all of the *Sicherungstruppe* would be together. During their free time, the soldiers would train the local *Volkssturm* in school classrooms. The local men received instruction on tactics, how to clean, service and use rifles, a pursuit made the more difficult as only one rifle was available to some thirty men! They also received training in the use of the *Panzerfaust* anti-tank weapon. Stolle viewed them as 'old men'.

The people and the mainly forested low-lying mountain area of the Westerwald left an indelible impression upon Stolle's mind. Tranquil villages set on either side of undulating hills were a stark contrast to the countryside of endless plains on which he had served in Russia. And, unlike the forests of the Ardennes, no '*Weiße Garde*' The Westerwald, although without mountain peaks, reminded him of his home back in the Sudetenland, 400 kilometres to the east. By late 1944, it was with regret that he realized that his time in the Westerwald, and the local friendships he had made, was drawing to a close. Stolle remembered that by Christmas, *Art. Abt. 3./836 (mot.)* had launched about 200 Rockets in spite of increasingly erratic supplies of liquid oxygen. By the end of January 1945 the supply problems, coupled with the pressing need for troops to defend the Eastern Front, meant that the

Sicherungstruppe of 3./836 *(mot.)* was disbanded and assigned to ordinary infantry units. Stolle and many of his comrades were transported to Selters in south-eastern Germany, some 40 kilometres north-east of Frankfurt, and then, on 15 February, via Berlin to Briesen, and ever closer to the Red Army. From Briesen, Stolle was moved into the district of Lebus located on the Oder River, 10 kilometres north of Frankfurt. Then he was moved forward to engage the enemy in the vicinity of Oderbruch. He recalled: 'The Russians already were west of the River Oder. The Easter week of 1945, in the evening of Monday, 2 April, it started. Our engineer troops and tanks should have been there. They eventually arrived but in the swampy area of the Oderbruch, the water was just below the ground level. Digging in it was impossible and the area was full of mines. Our *Kampfgruppe* (Battle Group) had about 1,000 men. Most of our casualties were due to the mines. I used to walk only on the tank tracks, but the tanks that had moved ahead of us then pulled back. From 0200 in the morning, right through to midnight, we didn't win one metre of ground. We were near the village of Zechin [10 km north-east of Seelow and 15 km west of Küstrin]. At night I laid down on the soggy ground to snatch some sleep near a shed. Suddenly there was an explosion from a mortar shell. I got a punch to the head and felt my steel helmet; it had two holes, one small and one large. I had a thumping headache and felt like I was drunk. That was on Wednesday, 4 April 1945. Only 100 of our men [of the one thousand] were now left. The tanks had driven away again. I said to myself: "This is madness. Enough's enough!" But the order to retreat had already been given. I remember that during our retreat, two kilometres from the front a comrade, a machine gun operator, was shot dead in the stomach. I suppose it was from a sniper.'

Although Stolle remembers clearly the actions he took part in against the Soviets, some specific dates elude him. However, he was engaged in combat with the Red Army a week or so before the famous Battle of the Seelow Heights which was to occur between 16-19 April. This Battle was one of the last major Russian assaults that secured the advance to Berlin.

Stolle and the remains of his *Kampfgruppe* were withdrawn to Berlin and, having eaten for the first time in days, they were ordered the next morning to Roßlau, beside the River Elbe, 100 kilometres south-west of the doomed capital. Moving yet again, they travelled 120 kilometres to the south, arriving at the strategically important motorway junction of 'Hermsdorfer Kreuz' where the Frankfurt-Dresden autobahn crosses the Berlin-Munich autobahn. Already however, the Americans were very close by and the air was full of Allied fighter-bombers which attacked ceaselessly the long columns of German soldiers caught in open countryside. The movements of the German troops reflected a desire not to engage the enemy, but rather to withdraw, for Stolle was then ordered further south and east to Bavaria. He and his weary comrades arrived at Bayreuth, (famed for its Wagnerian music festival), during a major air raid. Stolle was sure that some 300 aircraft were involved, but assuming that the date of his arrival was 11 April it was in fact an attack of one-hundred and twenty-two RAF bombers upon the Bayreuth railway yards. Although the official RAF record indicates it as a '…good attack without loss', Stolle saw several destroyed houses but no casualties to the withdrawing troops.[3] He was later to discover that he and Fritz Meibert were separated at Bayreuth and Meibert disappeared to the south. The two men would not meet again for 63 years. Shortly afterwards, Stolle and others were ordered to engage the enemy, he recalled: 'We were ordered to Bamberg, 48 kilometres to the west of Bayreuth, to stop three or four American tanks. At night the Americans would never move very much, but in the morning of 14 April, it all started! Three or four tanks? We realized we needed to add two zeros to that figure! It was more like 200 tanks… We managed to destroy one, and a second suffered track damage, but then we became encircled and that was it – we had to surrender.'

Stolle and his comrades had fought against, and been taken prisoner by, General Patton's US Third Army, fighting its way towards Bayreuth, which would fall just two days later. Unknown to Stolle it was elements of the Third Army that had liberated the infamous Buchenwald concentration camp some 118 kilometres to the north on 11 April. Word of what had been discovered there had travelled very fast and, as such, the Americans' attitude to German prisoners was to prove to be uncompromising.

Having been disarmed by the Americans, Stolle and hundreds of very fearful prisoners were herded, under a fusillade of fist blows and kicks, into a large two-storey barn for the night. Conditions were extremely crowded and because no thought had been given to sanitation, a foul rain perpetually fell in the darkness upon the unfortunate men, including Stolle, on the lower floor. The following morning of 15 April, the prisoners were ordered out of the barn and marched in the direction of Bad Kissingen. En route some liberated Yugoslavians – former prisoners of the Germans – fashioned whips from lengths of rope and vented their hatred by mercilessly lashing out at their former masters to the general amusement of the American soldiers.

The escorted prisoners arrived at Bad Kissingen in the evening, and as they did so, suddenly from the sky an unfamiliar and extraordinary sound was heard, as a *Luftwaffe* jet aircraft attacked the local area having spotted the flames of American camp fires. The flames were quickly extinguished and the jet disappeared into the night. Whether the aircraft was a Messerschmitt Me 262 or the less well-known Arado Ar 234, Stolle would never know. Similarly, although he heard clearly the sound of gunfire, he could not tell how many casualties had occurred during the brief attack.

Having covered 220 kilometres under armed escort in the three days since capture, the long line of prisoners arrived at Böhl-Iggelheim beside the Rhine and close to Haßloch, approximately 80 kilometres south of Frankfurt. Böhl-Iggelheim was one of nineteen American *Rheinwiesenlager* (Rhine meadow camp) transit camps that held, in total, about one million former German combatants as prisoners. Many of the prisoners had originally been detained by the British but were now given over to the Americans. The conditions at Böhl-Iggelheim were appalling as Stolle recalled: 'It was farmland; an open naked field, no tents. We wore only our light uniforms as our coats had been taken away. We had very little food – only a few biscuits, a slice of white bread and a plate of soup that had three peas in it. The water from the river Rhine was white because of the chlorine mixed in it because of disease. On 20 April, I still remember very clearly, the camp commander announced: "Today there is an extra meal." We were looking forward to it, but we didn't get it. Next day the Americans told us that the extra meal was due to Hitler's birthday. It rained, and rained, sometimes as snow showers. I wonder how many died? In the morning there was always the removal of dead bodies and among them many Hungarians, who couldn't stand the climate. They all must have been buried nameless. In the camp there was a wire – some metres before the barbed wire: if you crossed it, you would be shot instantly.'

Stolle and the other detainees wondered why they were being treated so poorly. The reason, in part, lay in the official classification that was used by the American authorities. Instead of being considered as 'Prisoners of War' ('POWs') they were described as 'Disarmed Enemy Forces' ('DEF') and, less frequently, as 'Surrendered Enemy Forces' ('SEF'). The subtle change in terminology came about in 1943 when the Allied Commander-in-Chief, General Dwight D. Eisenhower, decided that following victory in Europe, it would be impossible to feed vast numbers of German prisoners. Rather than consider other possibilities, a legal expedient was implemented to change the status of the expected German prisoners from POWs to DEFs, meaning a reduced obligation to feed the prisoners was required. Additionally, the Geneva Convention of 1929 would not protect the DEF prisoners, nor would the International Red Cross have any jurisdiction. Legally, the prisoners had no rights. It should be mentioned that the reappraisal of prisoner status was also carried out by Germany to exploit Italian prisoners as slave workers, for example in the production of V2 support equipment.

The American guards at the *Rheinwiesenlager* were made up of men from the famed 106th Infantry Division that had held Bastogne courageously during the Ardennes Offensive in December 1944. The legal distinctions between POWs and DEFs would have been completely unknown to the guards of the 106th. Instead, they would have viewed the treatment of the prisoners as a justifiable consequence of the treatment that the Germans had meted out upon the victims of the concentration camps and the death camps to the east. At a local level, the mistreatment of the prisoners was carried out with zeal by the Americans, as in the case of extra rations that were cruelly promised but never given. The enforced starvation rations forced the men to eat any vegetation they could find including grass, and their only shelter from the elements was holes and ditches dug with bare hands.

It is not known how many DEFs died as no accurate statistics were ever compiled and only estimates are available more than 65 years after the event. One estimate places the figure at 6,000.[4] It is worth noting that the altered Third Geneva Convention of 1949 was, in part, intended to outlaw both DEF and SEF statuses by clearly stating that soldiers who fall into the power of an enemy are protected, as well as those taken prisoner in combat. The question of the legal status of prisoners has recently taken on a renewed significance since the campaign of America and her Allies against international terrorism following the 11 September 2001 attacks against the United States by al-Qaeda.

Stolle and thousands of others endured the *Rheinwiesenlager* of Böhl-Iggelheim until 5 May when many were transported to a camp at Barberey airfield, 2 kilometres north-west of Troyes and 150 kilometres south-east of Paris. Conditions were as bad as those at Böhl-Iggelheim for the prisoners were still not allowed to shelter in tents. The late winter of Germany gave way to the heat of a French summer and the men, still denied the use of tents, now began to die from heat stroke. In August 1945, Stolle was taken from Troyes to a camp near Reims, 110 kilometres to the north, and was then sent to work clearing and repairing canals which supplied food and equipment for the garrisoned Americans. New American guards who had recently returned from the east from Soviet zones of occupation, treated the DEFs more humanely. Food was still scarce however, but entrepreneurial Polish workers and German prisoners would barter on the understanding that neither side would denounce the other to the authorities for stealing.

In February 1946, the promise of freedom was dashed; Stolle recalled that the Prime Minister of the Provisional Government of the French Republic, Félix Gouin (1884-1977), called for the continued detention of 50,000 prisoners to work in France as reparations. 'We had been dismissed by the Americans to the camp of Stenay near the Belgian border. We had to wait until a transport was full. Then one day they called a line-up for examination: all those over 40 years of age and disabled men went to the right, while all the others got a stamp on the hand and were sent to the French.'

Stolle and many other DEFs had to accept that they would not become free men for another three months and were then sent to Mulhouse in the Alsace region of central eastern France. Having arrived at their new camp, they were ordered to 'line up' and were then given a stark choice by their new captors: '"Who wants to die for France?" They were looking for soldiers for Indo-China.

One-third of our group volunteered and was removed immediately. I never heard anything about them ever again. The others that were left went to the potash mines.'

Stolle and the others resigned themselves to labour in the mines, but he then heard some news that perhaps saved his life: 'They (the French) were looking for construction craftsmen. I reported myself and became a bricklayer. Houses had to be repaired.'

Stolle worked in the building industry repairing war-damaged workers' 'tied' properties owned by the French potash mining industry. Each German slave worker was twinned with a Frenchman who acted as a guardian. The potash mine settlements each had four to five hundred properties and Stolle recalled that there was a sense of great urgency to finish one house and move on to the next. The imperative to restart French industry and the French economy was strong, but the government's sense of obligation towards the DEFs remained unchanged. As Stolle recalled: 'In the camp the food was very bad. In the summer, spoilt fish smelt of mildew, and the corn bread was so hard it had to be cut with an axe. In the winter we had frozen potatoes. Then there were the rats: they crept over us at night. Bread had to be eaten immediately, otherwise it would vanish. But I never drank so much wine as there! Every morning we were picked up (for work) and my "guardian" would give me half of his breakfast although he and his family had rationing. I had regular contact with my guardian until his death and even today with his family. We also had contact with the local people. Half were nice to us, the other half would rather have us liquidated! We got to find out later that many of them, as well as our guards, had been partisans.'

Stolle witnessed that it took a brave man to complain about conditions in the camp. One man he knew did so and was slapped and threatened with a gun by the camp commandant, a Swiss called Weilenmann. On one occasion there was a brief respite from the appalling food with the unexpected and unofficial arrival of a Red Cross delegation at the camp. However, once it had left the food worsened just as suddenly as it had improved.

Because of constant and intentional procrastination by the French authorities to extract as much as they could from a cheap labour force, three months became three years, until, at last, Stolle was given his freedom at Christmas 1948. However Stolle's homeland, the Sudetenland, no longer existed. The Potsdam Conference of late July 1945, held between Prime Minister Winston Churchill, General Secretary Josef Stalin and President Harry Truman, had agreed to reverse the annexations brought about by the Nazis, including that of the Sudetenland. They also agreed upon the forced migration of German nationals and ethnic Germans from these areas to greater Germany. The Sudetens, however, were to feel the full wrath of the Czechs who had endured the Nazis since the annexation of 1938 and the occupation of Czechoslovakia in 1939.

Acting on behalf of the victorious powers, the Soviets implemented the expulsions. The dispossessed Sudetens had to 'run the gauntlet' of the locals in their immediate neighbourhoods and also of those encountered throughout long marches to the west. The immense hatred held by the Czechs was fuelled by memories of the occupation and the behaviour of SS-*Obergruppenführer* Reinhard Heydrich (1904-1942) who had been appointed *Reichsprotektor* of Bohemia and Moravia. His cruelty knew no bounds and he had pursued his murderous career in the former Czechoslovakia with great enthusiasm before dying of injuries in June 1942 following an assassination attempt. In death his legacy was to become infamous through the eradication of the village and the people of Lidice at Hitler's behest as a reprisal for killing the man who would have become the *Führer's* successor. It is believed that between 700,000 and 800,000 Germans were expelled and that 15,000 to 30,000 died in massacres, single murders, suicides and natural causes exacerbated by the circumstances.[5]

Stolle knew that a return to his home of Ketten, now renamed Chotyne, in Czechoslovakia, would be impossible, so he took the decision to return to the Westerwald and to the village of Hütte where he had once been billeted. He eventually settled in a village nearby, married a local girl and, using the skills he had acquired rebuilding houses in France, he returned to his pre-war occupation as a builder until his retirement.

In spite of all that had befallen him, Stolle has a philosophical attitude towards his own stolen youth and the loss of his homeland: 'After the war [local] people said to me: "Go back to where you come from!" We were Germans, but we heard over and over again, that we were '*Beutegermanen*'. With time one gets used to it.'

The derogatory expression '*Beutegermanen*' for the former Sudeten soldiers implied a stupidity for allowing their loyalty to be abused by a regime that cared very little for them and then in peacetime, to be ignored by the new Germany.

Stolle laments that the youth of Germany today does not understand and does not care to understand what has happened during the last war. He believes, for example, that the bombing of Dresden in February 1945 should be examined and questioned without the risk of the accusation of being called a Nazi sympathizer. He commented that it was his wartime generation that 'had the guilt of the murder' but added, cynically, that given the present state of world politics '… this is demonstrated to us every day.'

'Oh yes, we have been betrayed of our youth, but I did not want it to get me down. I couldn't change any of it. I was 17 when I left for war, and 24 when I came back. Did we get compensation? No. I was happy that I had not been captured in Russia. I know Russia! I was there in 1942 and later 1943. In 1942 we were at the Don and the road that led to Stalingrad. The Allies allowed the Russians too much after the war. They should have set them more limits.

It's history now, and one doesn't speak about it often any more. I wish that Germans would learn more of history from Bismark to the present day. There is one lesson we should learn from history: every war is the beginning for a next war and not every winner is in the right. Surely only the stronger one is right.'

Regarding his involvement with the V2 Rocket, Stolle concluded: 'It was an interesting time to be in such a unit, but it was all too late!'

CHAPTER THIRTEEN

'LIKE A BLOWTORCH'

EDUARD JERICHA
Artillerie Ausbildungs Abteilung 271

ALTHOUGH perhaps a cliché, it could be said that Eduard Jericha was something of a Renaissance man. In the telling of his account of his experiences, we discover that he possessed a technical background enabling him to understand the complexity of aircraft construction, and yet he enjoyed an artistic temperament. Never slow to voice his abilities and insight in a wide range of topics, he was able to turn his hand to an eclectic mix of activities, whether the use of a slide rule, puppetry or, predominantly in later life, a paintbrush. A flaw in his character was, perhaps, his apparent lack of political correctness, a trait that was either completely innocent or used possibly to take a quiet delight in the reaction of his listeners. The writers believe that his views, although perhaps occasionally misguided, give a flavour of the attitudes and feelings that were prevalent in the dark days when Germany was at war. Many of his recollections have been confirmed and are important as they touch upon the memories of others.

Eduard Jericha was born in 1913 in Ribnitz, near Rostock in Mecklenburg, northern Germany. Ribnitz lies approximately 88 kilometres west of Peenemünde and is located on the mouth of the River Recknitz that flows into the Bay of Saal and in turn into the Baltic Sea. The area of his birth became synonymous with aircraft manufacture following the establishment of the Heinkel Flugzeugwerke at Warnemünde in 1922. Heinkel was to become an industrial colossus along with other well-known German aircraft manufacturers of the 1930s and 1940s such as Messerschmitt and Junkers. The skies of Rostock reverberated to the sounds of seaplane engines and young Jericha became fascinated by flight. So it was that he became an enthusiastic member of a local glider-flying club. Between the wars and especially after the Nazis came to power, flying clubs flourished throughout Germany, allowing young men to pursue an exciting hobby that would lead many of them to join the fledgling *Luftwaffe*. The flying clubs were the '*Kindergarten*' for the *Luftwaffe*. Many of the young glider pilots were to later perfect their flying skills as members of the *Legion Condor* dispatched by Hitler to aid General Francisco Franco's (1892–1975) Nationalist forces in the fight against the Republicans during the Spanish Civil War from 1936 to 1939.

Jericha was apparently an excellent pupil and was to join a glider construction company where he became a site supervisor. He later completed his formal education at the Vienna University of Technology in Austria were he was single-mindedly devoted to his studies. Following the annexation of Austria by the Nazis in March 1938, Jericha recalled his desire to return home: 'I was married to work and never had time for other things. After the annexation I said to myself: "This is enough. I am doing nothing more here." I was already 25 or 26 years old and wanted to get married and have a family. I wanted to get out and to do something else.'

Having returned to Ribnitz, Jericha was able to indulge his interest in gliders by rejoining the local Aero Club and out of necessity contacted the employment office. He was flattered to discover that his skills as an aircraft constructor were very much sought after. He joined the local manufacturing company of Walter Bachmann Flugzeugbau KG of Pütnitz, a few kilometres away from Ribnitz. Bachmann, like the aircraft manufacturer Heinkel, had a reputation for constructing seaplanes before the war, but both were later to be pressed into essential war production work. The Mecklenburg area became an important centre for aircraft production: in addition to Bachmann and Heinkel, the factories of Arado, Fokker and Dornier were also established there. The local populace, which traditionally had a background in agriculture and fishing, demonstrated its ability to take on new skills as aircraft technicians. When the labour force began to fall behind schedule as the demands of the war industry increased, the manufacturers increasingly used foreign and eventually slave workers. Typically, at the start of the war, Heinkel at Warnemünde employed more than 9,000 employees but this was to swell to over 16,000 workers by the end of 1944. Jericha was involved in the manufacture of both Heinkel and Arado aircraft types. Heinkel's Rostock factory worked on the construction of the Heinkel He 111 medium bomber and approximately 7,000 such aircraft were produced. Perhaps the most technologically significant aircraft produced by Heinkel, and unbeknown to Jericha, was the He 176. This remarkable, but diminutive liquid-fuelled rocket aircraft first took to the air from the *Luftwaffe* airfield at Peenemünde on 20 June 1939. Powered by hydrogen peroxide and the catalyst calcium permanganate, this one-off prototype was the world's first aircraft powered solely by a rocket engine. However, and much to Heinkel's chagrin, the project was abandoned and its rival manufacturer, Messerschmitt, having gained Hitler's favour, developed the first operational rocket-propelled interceptor, the Me 163 *Komet*.

Although Jericha was not aware of the emergence of rocket aircraft, he did have an inkling that something extraordinary was being developed not too far away from his home town. He recalled: 'I was travelling home from work one night. It was dark and I saw this orange point climbing up very fast from the direction of Peenemünde. Others did not know what it was, but I knew. I saw the first Rocket from Ribnitz.'

Jericha believed earnestly that this event occurred in 1940, but it is a matter of historical record that the A4 Rocket which was to become the V2 was not launched successfully until 3 October 1942. Although an earlier test-firing did take place that might conceivably have been seen from Ribnitz, this too occurred much later than 1940, on 13 June 1942. The question therefore remains, if not an A4, what did Jericha see? A possible answer might be that he had seen the predecessor to the A4 Rocket, the A5. The *Aggregate* 5, was 5.8 metres in length and was slightly less than half the length of the famous A4 (V2) Rocket whose basic proportions it shared. It too used liquid oxygen and alcohol as a propellant. With a launching weight of 900 kg, it was able to reach altitudes of 12 kilometres. From Ribnitz, Peenemünde is 88 km to the east and the A5 could have been seen approximately 8 degrees above the horizon at maximum altitude. It is known that in 1940 eight A5 test launches were conducted by the Peenemünde scientists.[1] In 1940, however, Jericha would not have known specific details of the devices fired from Peenemünde; the important issue for him at the time was that German technology was moving forward assuredly. Wisely, Jericha kept his thoughts to himself and forgot about the experience until much later in the war and, when he did eventually see the A4 Rocket, it simply confirmed his faith in his nation's scientific abilities. Unfortunately, it has not been possible during the preparation of this work to confirm whether any of the A5 launches took place at night.

On occasions, in the early part of the war, Jericha found himself seconded temporarily to other factories and he worked for a time at the Volkswagen plant in Wolfsburg. He recalled that forced-labour convicts worked harmoniously with the factory staff in the production of aircraft for Junkers. This observation served to convince him that all forced-labour prisoners enjoyed a similarly pleasant experience. He recalled: 'There was a large room at the Volkswagen factory in which the female forced labour convicts worked while they sang and talked. A floor below, the male prisoners worked hand-in-hand with German workers. They did not suffer in any way.'

At the time of being interviewed by the authors, Jericha was aware that, following the war's end, the brutality of the Nazi regime and the exploitation of forced labour in German industry were exposed, but he believed this to be an exaggerated deception.

Repeatedly, Jericha was 'called up' for pilot training, but his employer was always able to refuse the request. Eventually however, an irrevocable order arrived in early October 1944 instructing him to join, not – surprisingly – the *Luftwaffe*, but the *Heer*. Unbeknown to Jericha, this was to be a precursor to participating in the V2 offensive that had begun a month before. He was ordered to report to *Artillerie Ausbildungs Abteilung* 5 (AAA5), an artillery training department at Schneidemühl in western Pomerania. Now known as Piła in north-western Poland, Schneidemühl was a Prussian garrison town set in deep woodland. The historical connection with forestry and woodcutting gave the town its name, meaning 'saw mill' in German. Jericha arrived at the camp towards the end of November 1944 and was transferred to 4. *Artillerie Ausbildungs Abteilung* 271 (4. AAA 271 – the prefix '4.' indicates the fourth troop of the battalion). Jericha was now part of a supposedly efficient and well-structured training programme in which he and his immediate colleagues would be used as replacement personnel for the Rocket-firing battalions who were taking the war direct to the enemy. The optimistic training programme developed the previous year and the reality experienced by Jericha were, however, very different.

The background of the training organization of V2 personnel had begun in Peenemünde the previous year in early June 1943 with the formation of *Lehr- und Ersatz-Batterie* (*mot.*) 93 (Motorized Demonstration and Depot Battery 93) commanded by *Oberstleutnant* Stegmaier. A sense of urgency must have prevailed as it was hoped that the V2 offensive would begin in January 1944. During that summer, *Artillerie Ersatz Abteilung* 271 (*Art.Ers.Abt.* 271), an artillery replacement battalion, was also formed at Peenemünde: although officially a depot battery, this unit was, in fact, a training and replacement resource unit for the FR troops. Stegmaier's training programme, however, was disrupted by the RAF attack on Peenemünde on 17/18 August 1943 and the units had to be dispersed. Indeed, Jericha discovered that his training should have taken place at Peenemünde, but the damage sustained in the air raid made that impossible. By September, *Art.Ers.Abt.* 271 was dispatched to Schneidemühl to begin initial training and orders were issued that saw the establishment of *Kommando-Stelle* S at Köslin (V2 Training School).

In December 1943, *Art.Ers.Abt.* 271 had been expanded and divided falling under the control of Dornberger. The *Abteilung* then contained one component which continued to be assigned as a Depot Battery (*Artillerie Ersatz Abteilung*) whilst the other became a Training Battery (*Artillerie Ausbildungs Abteilung*). This basic structure was to remain intact until January 1945.

The *Art.Ers.Abt.* 271 consisted of three troops: a cadre troop (*Stammbatterie*) of raw recruits, a march troop (*Marschbatterie*) and a convalescent troop

(*Genesenenbatterie*) of either wholly or partly trained men. Conversely, when Jericha first joined *Art.Ausb.Abt.* 271, it consisted of five troops: a *Lehrbatterie* (demonstration troop), two *Ausbildungs Batterien* (training troops) for training launching personnel, an *Ausbildungs Batterie* (*Flak und Pak*) (anti-aircraft and ground protection troop) and a *Nachrichten Ausbildung Batterie* (signals training troop). Later, a sixth troop of men was formed at Peenemünde as a technical troop and a seventh became a motor training troop (*Kraftfahr Ausbildungs*) for the training of drivers for the different vehicles used in the field.

Suitable candidates to join the training programme were drawn from artillery depot units within Germany by Dornberger, Stegmaier and other officers from Schneidemühl. The selected men were often young soldiers with some technical or educational qualification and were drafted to the 271 Depot and Training Battery (*Art.Ers.u.Ausb.Abt.* 271). Men with military experience were sent directly to field units, for example the *Artillerie Abteilung* 485 (*mot.*) and the *Artillerie Abteilung* 836 (*mot.*), both of which had existed from August 1943. When Köslin became operational, the V2 school was able to draw upon a sufficient supply of students from both the field units and the *Art.Ers.u.Ausb.Abt.* 271 to begin specialist courses.

Jericha recalled that his comrades at Schneidemühl were mainly technicians and engineers, many of whom had served at Peenemünde. The officers in charge were frequently young, but highly decorated former front line soldiers who had served on the Eastern Front. One such officer whom Jericha recalled was a *Leutnant* Kurt Titze who had been similarly called to Rocket duty at Schneidemühl. Jericha was never aware who had specifically singled him out for V2 duties but, without any modesty, commented that: 'I was a specialist in all subjects. I think that this was important.'

All training at Schneidemühl was intended to be very elementary so as not to compromise the security of the Rocket and for expediency each man was to be trained to perform just one task. However, an initial training instruction was intended to give every man an overview of the entire Rocket. It was initially believed that it would take five to six months to train an inexperienced man but in reality this was an underestimation. Of the training time, it was envisaged that two months of initial instruction was to take place at Schneidemühl with *Art.Ers.u.Ausb.Abt.* 271 (Depot and Training Battery 271) followed by one month at the V2 School at Köslin. This was to be followed by approximately two months of practical work, including firing with field units. It was also hoped that the student would participate in perhaps six to seven launches at Heidelager, but the lack of equipment for training and the delays in the Rocket's development scuppered this plan. Irrespective of supply problems, it became evident that at least a year would be needed to train an inexperienced man.

Not only was it becoming clear that the Rocket offensive could not possibly begin in January 1944 but it was dawning upon the V2 hierarchy that firing operations would have to be conducted by mobile units. In April 1944 *Generalleutnant* Richard Metz of *Höh.Art.Kdr.* (*HARKO*) 191 was to report not only his lack of confidence in the battery commanders, but that, in his opinion, even if the Rocket was immediately available, he doubted if any of the FR troops would be available for operations. The situation was to worsen when the predicted Allied invasion of France occurred in June followed by the Soviet advance in the East, forcing the evacuation of Heidelager in July 1944.

When Jericha arrived at Schneidemühl in November 1944, it was amidst this upheaval and a failing command structure. Jericha and the other new recruits were billeted in strict isolation from other students undertaking Rocket training and they commenced basic military training. Full security measures were in place and photography was strictly forbidden. Jericha and his comrades spent the next three to four weeks in complete ignorance as to their ultimate postings. The large reserve of men at Schneidemühl was part of a Dornberger contingency plan: it was envisaged that the FR troops would experience a high rate of attrition from air attacks and the estimated 'wastage' anticipated was 20 per cent of the FR troops per month.[2] However, the perceived threat from Allied air attacks had been greatly exaggerated. The strategies of using camouflaged firing sites intentionally close to civilians in The Hague, or in forest locations elsewhere, all reduced FR troop casualties to a minimum. The introduction of night launches also reduced the threat of air attack. So successful were the FR troops in tactics, guile and deception, that not one demand was ever made on reserves, although it is believed that the combined units had 5,000 men available. Jericha was just one of their number.

Although the Rocket offensive had already begun, Jericha's memories confirmed that the negativity reported in the spring by *Generalleutnant* Metz had not improved by Autumn 1944. Jericha recalled: 'There was very little training, only in the basics such as how to salute and to stand to attention.' In spite of the training syllabus so carefully planned, Jericha further commented: 'We learned only in the Netherlands that we had joined a V2 troop.'

The reserve of men did not remain static for long as the Russian advances in January 1945 were to cause the evacuation of personnel from Schneidemühl, Köslin and Heidekraut. Naturally this caused great upheaval. *Art.Ausb.Abt.* 271 was moved to Neustrelitz, 240 kilometres to the west in Germany and reorganized. Ultimately the reserve troops were quickly absorbed into infantry regiments and thrown into action against the Soviets in defence of the Reich. Schneidemühl itself was declared a '*Festung*' (fortress) by Hitler and after two weeks of heavy fighting against Polish and Soviet forces, the city (and not for the first time in its long history) was destroyed.

Fortunately for Jericha, his destiny was not to face the Red Army. Instead, on 14 December 1944 he was one of 120 men of *Art.Ausb.Abt.* 271 sent as part of a security command to the Netherlands.[3]

During the research for this book, Jericha did recall his membership of *Art.Ausb.Abt.* 271: 'We did very little really. We were completely on our own in The Hague and could do what we wanted. However we did have a unit leader and company commander.'

Jericha and his comrades were expecting to be given specific duties with the forming of a new battery. He believed that the new unit would fire Rockets against the Soviets from East Prussia. However, despite Jericha's recollections, it is difficult to conceive a large group of able men being so idle at a time of such great military adversity. The explanation is likely to be quite prosaic.

It is known that some of the men called for Rocket duties were often dumbfounded that their proven technical abilities were not fully exploited. An excellent example of this was the experience of Oswald Schneider whose military service is recorded in Chapter Fourteen. Schneider was a skilled engineer who had worked in the armaments industry and yet, bizarrely, his duty in support of the Rocket offensive was as a motorcycle dispatch rider! Schneider, however, was resigned to this knowing, as he did, that after a full year of being in the *Heer*, it was pointless to question such illogicality. Men drafted directly from industry to support the Rocket would have been affronted and dismayed that their skills and abilities were ignored. This doubtless rankled with many men during the war and in the years after, it coloured their attitudes. During the interview and subsequent correspondence for this book, Jericha never admitted that he was part of the security personnel. Nor does he appear to have admitted this to his family either. It was only when he mentioned the title of his troop that the writers discovered the nature of his involvement with the Rocket. He perhaps never came to terms with his posting given his technical abilities.

Jericha was billeted at a large property along Benoordenhoutseweg in The Hague. The Benoordenhoutseweg borders the length of the Haagse Bos for a distance of nearly 2 kilometres and runs north–eastwards towards Wassenaar. During the occupation, properties along this road provided billets for the *Heer* and also a wide range of SS security personnel, specifically the *Polizei-Waffenschule* (Police Weapon School), *Waffen*-SS, *Germaanse* SS (Dutch SS) and the *Hauptwirtschaftslager der Waffen*-SS (Economic Department of the *Waffen*-SS). The SS personnel were partly responsible for the protection of The Hague and formed a link in the Reich's 5300-kilometre defensive '*Atlantikwall*' that ran from Norway to Spain. The *Polizei-Waffenschule* was predominantly the main resident along the Benoordenhoutseweg and its presence reflected the anxiety of the police commander, Johann Baptist Albin Rauter (1895-1949). Appointed as *Generalkommissar für das Sicherheitswesen* (Commissioner of Security Forces) and *Höhere SS-und Polizeiführer* (Higher SS and Police Leader), Rauter was paranoid that The Hague and his headquarters, based in Clingendael, might be targeted by Allied Commandos.[4] The presence of so many SS personnel gave Rauter 'peace of mind'. After the war he was executed for war crimes by a Dutch firing squad in the city.

In spite of descriptions and drawings furnished by Jericha, it has not been possible to determine the precise location of his billet. Jericha recalled: 'We stayed in a first-class hotel, three or four soldiers to a room. Before us, the German police had occupied it. All of this was in the restricted area and we had to safeguard the building. The street led up to the church about 500 metres away. When we had to go to the Haagse Bos, we turned left and over a bridge. There must have been trams in former times. On both sides of the road there were V2 Rockets lying under the cover of trees.'

Clearly the hotel was located facing the famous Haagse Bos. With somewhat less certainty, the church may have been the Roman Catholic St. Paschalis Baylonkerk, and the connecting road, the Neuhuyskade. One final piece of evidence relates to an incident that occurred on New Year's Eve 1944 and this suggests that the billet used by Jericha and his comrades was either Huize Boschzich or Van Bylandt Huis at 24-39 or 46 Benoordenhoutseweg, respectively. Both are imposing five-storey buildings with commanding views over the Haagse Bos. Importantly, and with regards to the incident on New Year's Eve, the St. Paschalis Baylonkerk can be sighted from the upper storeys, approximately 400 metres to the north-west. The Huize Boschzich is of historical and architectural importance being the first residential hotel built in the Netherlands in 1920. During the occupation, it was the billet of the *Polizei-Waffenschule* III, an SS organization which specialized in advanced training for officers and enlisted men from any of the military services.[5]

Although impressed by his new accommodation, Jericha remembered that the arrangements for providing meals for the new 'residents' of Huize Boschzich were decidedly 'ad hoc': 'There was no cook. Those of us who had worked as cooks before did the cooking. I had a go at it. We had to shop for ourselves and obtained eggs and milk from smallholders. In the cellar, we peeled potatoes and the more we peeled, the more we had to eat. I shot (and cooked) rabbits. A *Leutnant* who visited us found the rabbit so good that he didn't want to leave! In gratitude he gave us a bottle of Cognac with which I made egg cognac.'

It is believed that Jericha and his comrades assisted 3./Art.Abt. 485 (*mot.*) in security operations. Jericha saw the Rocket for the first time at close quarters in the Haagse Bos, which by the late autumn of 1944 was a thinly wooded cratered area within the Sperrgebiet. He recalled that his comrade's reaction to the Rocket was typical: '*It's fantastic!*' – but Jericha took the experience with a calmness that would have seemed extraordinary to those around him, primarily because he was already aware of the existence of rocket technology. Four years previously, as already mentioned, from Ribnitz he had observed, in the direction of Peenemünde, a rocket's rapidly ascending orange thrust flame upon the distant horizon. Later, from the grounds of his quarters, he saw many Rockets launched from the Haagse Bos. The Rockets were painted in green and brown *Wehrmacht* camouflage. He recalled: 'We were not positioned that close to the V2s. When the fuel vehicles came, we had to leave the area. Only the specialists were allowed to stay. When launched, the Rocket sounded like a blowtorch. The thrust jet was like fire and about half the length of the Rocket. We launched about twenty in The Hague, but four or five of these failed as misfires. Photography was strictly forbidden although we didn't have the opportunity to take pictures anyway.'

Jericha recalled that relations with the local Dutch population were apparently good and with few conflicts. Many of his comrades had local girlfriends but, as he was a married man, he did not pursue further relationships. For recreation, he played chess and became his company's 'master'. In small groups, he and his comrades would visit the nearby cafés, where, either at the instigation of the local residents, (although more probably from other relaxing German soldiers), the topic of conversation would invariably turn to the V2 Rocket and Jericha recalled exchanges with the Dutch: 'They often asked us how the V2 worked. We told them that the V2 had been developed for space travel, but since the British had not stopped bombing our towns, the V2 had to serve as a weapon. The Dutch were enthusiastic about it; the Rocket was seen as a kind of scientific miracle.'

It is difficult to reconcile this recollection since the Dutch had been subjugated and denied their freedom by an occupying military force for over four years. For the locals it was most probably a situation of smiles and platitudes through gritted teeth! As Jericha recalled tellingly to the authors: 'The civilian population was very "quiet"...'

Alcohol for some of Jericha's comrades was a release from the boredom and monotony of service in The Hague. The consumption of Rocket alcohol was strictly forbidden and although Jericha never drank filtered B-*Stoff*, he was aware that a few men did – predominantly those who had easy access to the V2, for example the transport teams who had a reputation as frequent abusers. Instead, Jericha and his friends became acquainted with the crews of an anti-aircraft battery positioned on the beach at Scheveningen who secretly produced palatable schnapps from their own still. Whether from the schnapps or tampered B-*Stoff*, high-spirited behaviour on New Year's Eve, 1944 nearly caused a disaster for some of Jericha's comrades. That evening, as the men of *Lehr- und Versuchsbatterie* 444 were occupied preparing for multiple launches aimed at London, Jericha and some of his comrades were off-duty celebrating the approaching New Year in their billet. As the evening progressed, the drinking increased until it was suggested that it would be entertaining to use the nearby St. Paschalis Baylonkerk church for some target practice. Two of Jericha's comrades picked up their standard issue *Karabiner* 98k rifles and from either the roof or the upper floor of the Huize Boschzich fired off a few rounds towards the steeple.

From the direction of the church, German voices rang out from the darkness: '*What the Hell are you doing?*' In their intoxicated state, the men of *Art.Ausb.Abt.* 271 had forgotten that there was an SS sentry post down at ground level close to the church. The post had steel shutters that could be dropped down to protect the occupiers in the event of an emergency. The SS sentry post may well have been tactically positioned because in front of the church were the former offices of the Bataafsche Import Maatschappij (Batavian Import Company), on the Wassenaarseweg road. This imposing building was used during the occupation by more than one German organization, some of which may well have been connected with the V2 offensive. Known locally as the Shell or BIM Building, it was later to come to the attention of the RAF when it was bombed on 18 March 1945 by Spitfires of 602 Squadron.

Jericha recalled that an SS-*Obersturmführer* duly arrived on the scene and a heated conversation took place with the commanding officer of the drunken soldiers (possibly *Leutnant* Kurt Titze). Jericha was not privy to the exchange, but the outcome was that the SS officer was appeased and the two men were spared any punishment. If the incident had occurred on any night other than New Year's Eve, the drunken soldiers might well have faced a stiff reprimand. It would appear, however, that this incident of firing weapons into the night sky to usher in the New Year was not an isolated case. Interestingly, Jericha recalled of that evening: 'A patrolling soldier was shot in the head on a bridge inside Haagse Bos. It was said to have been the work of partisans. However, [in his experience] there weren't any partisans in The Hague. It was New Year's Eve and other soldiers somewhere else had shot into the air and he must have been hit.'

Of the four or five Rocket misfires that Jericha witnessed, one in particular was memorable: the V2 suffered an intermittent fault with its engine and it fell to earth within the Sperrgebiet: 'I remember that the Rocket climbed up and then came down flying over the roofs of The Hague. It went up again, and then finally came down and struck a suburb. We immediately went over. When we arrived, the police were already there and had turned all the services off. The Rocket had impacted into some allotments. The walls of a nearby row of houses had simply fallen down and they resembled a doll's house. The crater very quickly filled with water. Otherwise, nothing else was damaged. There were no people there as everyone had already been evacuated from the area. The senior Dutch police officer made a report to our officer. We had no problems with the Dutch civilian population. When a Rocket went up it seemed as if the whole of The Hague stood still and the people looked up in astonishment.'

Again, Jericha's recollection of the attitude of the civilian population of The Hague is at odds with accepted historical record. Even Rocket launches conducted from within Germany caused enormous fear and anxiety among civilians. Apart from the frightening sound of the roaring combustion chamber, the Rockets could suddenly explode mid-air, veer off course or simply fall back to the ground in a cataclysm of fire. Indeed, the inhabitants of The Hague probably did look up in 'astonishment' but this was more likely due to self-preservation rather than admiration.

The greatest danger that Jericha experienced during his service in the Rocket offensive came from Allied fighter-bombers which harassed not only V2 deployment, but also interrupted the supply of essential propellants and equipment. One incident in particular left a deep impression upon his mind. It occurred in February 1945 in the Haagse Bos. Jericha was observing the preparations for a Rocket launch; the *Abschusstisch* was practically opposite his quarters at Huize Boschzich. The fuel bowsers, followed by the *Meillerwagen*, had withdrawn leaving just the *Feuerleitpanzer* connected umbilically to the Rocket. The FR troop soldiers sought shelter behind trees as the final tests took place prior to firing. The pyrotechnic igniter placed within the combustion chamber then burst into life producing a shower of incandescent sparks. Then, in sequence, the spray of propellants flowing under the influence of gravity ignited, producing an exhaust thrust of about eight tonnes. For the firing crews and observers, the roar of the Rocket suddenly increased to an excruciatingly painful volume as the final command was issued from the crew of the *Feuerleitpanzer* to engage the steam turbine pump and the thrust increased to 25 tonnes. At just about the same time as the Rocket was leaving the ground, Jericha's attention was drawn towards a fast moving silhouette which he had spotted from the corner of his eye. An enemy fighter-bomber was flying directly towards the launch site above the trees, but the sound of the approaching aircraft was inaudible above the ear-splitting scream of the Rocket. Nevertheless, he could see bright gun muzzle flashes along the aircraft's leading edges. He recalled: 'We had just completed the launch preparations; everybody had moved away. At that moment a *Jabo* began circling above in the sky. I was standing in front of the Rocket just as it lifted into the air. The enemy pilot opened fire on the Rocket but didn't hit it. But as I moved back into the shadow of the trees, our officers ordered us away, because the situation was too dangerous.'

As Jericha and his comrades ran for cover, the Rocket continued its ascent unhindered towards its target of London and the enemy aircraft disappeared into the distance. Jericha reflected that, not only must the Allied pilot have been completely surprised by his encounter, but also that both he and the men on the ground had been fortunate that the rounds fired by the aircraft had not found their mark. Strangely, neither the Germans nor the Allies officially recorded the extraordinary event of a V2 Rocket being attacked in flight. Therefore, only the combined interpretation of the official records, anecdotal evidence and eye-witness statements made many years after the war can be cited to tell the tale.

The attempted shooting down of the V2 was kept a secret by former members of the RAF's Second Tactical Air Force for nearly thirty years. The keepers of the secret, the pilots of 602 City of Glasgow Squadron, were held together by a relationship that one of them, Raymond Baxter, was to describe as, '... a close brotherhood in the squadron. The kind of friendship that you only get in wartime. Blood brothers if you like.'

Raymond Baxter (1922-2006) was well known and much admired in the United Kingdom for his television and radio work from the 1950s to the 1970s. He was renowned for stirring commentaries during many live broadcasts of sporting events and state ceremonial occasions, most notably the Coronation of Queen Elizabeth II and the funeral of Winston Churchill. His easy manner and authoritative television presence came to the fore, however, presenting the BBC's technology news programme 'Tomorrow's World' for twelve years until his retirement in 1977. During the war, he had served as a fighter pilot in 602 City of Glasgow Squadron. Flying clipped-wing Spitfire Mark XVIs armed with .303 Browning machine guns, 20 mm Hispano cannon and bombs, Flight Lieutenant Baxter and his comrades were part of the Allied response to the V2 offensive known as 'Operation Big Ben', the purpose of which was to harass and disrupt the Rocket-firing infrastructure. One of Baxter's fellow 'brothers' in 602 Squadron was Thomas L. Love (1923-1997), otherwise known as 'Cupid'.

Tommie 'Cupid' Love, a Scotsman from Rutherglen, Glasgow, joined 602 Squadron and began flying operations on 9 February 1945. He had previously flown Hawker Typhoons with 145 Squadron but his short stature, by his own admission, did not suit such a large aircraft. He was far more comfortable in Spitfires in which he had previously flown combat missions in Italy with 154 and 43 Squadrons. With 602 Squadron, he was to fly as Baxter's number 'Two' or 'Four' in sorties over occupied Europe. Baxter recalled the incident over the woods of The Hague: 'It was pretty much a routine attack, a dive-bombing attack... Four of us... I was leading and we dive-bombed this wood, a designated target, and there was an exceptional amount of light Flak. There was nearly always light Flak and if there wasn't any we knew we were wasting our time. We always got shot at on the way in, but anyway there was an exceptional amount of light Flak so, very foolishly, after we had dropped our bombs, I called the boys and we turned at nought feet and at very high speed, and came back to do the place over. There was an Oerlikon-type gun firing at me which I could see, so I engaged it, together with my number four who was out there somewhere, to my right and perhaps slightly behind, who was a little fellow called Flight Sergeant 'Cupid' Love, and suddenly there appeared this bloody great V2 looking like Nelson's Column. We were absolutely flabbergasted by the size of the thing and it came up so slowly and right through Cupid's gunsight, so he fired at it. But he didn't hit it, because he had no chance of hitting it and so that was that!'

Love and Baxter were both interviewed in 1980 for BBC Radio Scotland by Douglas Roberts for a programme entitled '*Beware the Crossed Lion – the Story of 602 Squadron*' during which Cupid Love recounted: 'I remember the V2 coming out of the woods certainly, and I can remember exactly what was said to bring everybody's attention to it. Just as I was pulling out, I heard a voice saying "*Kee-rist!! Would you look at that!*" I was still firing...' [6]

It is curious that Jericha did not recollect that the four Spitfires had already passed over the launch site whilst dive-bombing nor that the aircraft had then subsequently returned, passing over the target area to strafe the anti-aircraft position. Baxter commented: 'The battery was on the edge of a wood and unless he [Jericha] was in the open he would not have had a good view. The guys who would have had a good view were the ones shooting at me... but they were under camouflage netting and I did not see them until I came around again!'

Another noteworthy aspect of the incident was the assumption by Jericha and the RAF pilots that the Rocket launch could not be interrupted. The launch could almost certainly have been delayed long enough for the RAF to leave the area and for the firing officer in the *Feuerleitpanzer* to be informed by either radio or field telephone that the area was free from enemy aircraft. In the short term, the only item on the Rocket that would suffer from a delay would have been the gyroscopes in the control compartments as these had been designed to run for one hour for preparation, adjustment and one minute in flight. [7]

Long term, the anxiety for the firing crew would have been the excessive loss of liquid oxygen through evaporation. The firing officer would have had to weigh up the possibility that the Rocket might be struck either by shrapnel or from a direct strike by a cannon shell if the Spitfires returned for another pass. He would have judged that the Rocket and its preparation time would be lost in addition to concerns he may have had for the safety of his comrades and himself. In the forty or so seconds it would have taken Baxter and his colleagues to orbit and return to the target area, the fire control officer took the bold decision to launch as soon as possible. By the time he had pressed the final button in the launch sequence, the four Spitfires had returned to observe the extraordinary spectacle of the Rocket lifting off and for Love to be unofficially accredited as the only person to have attacked a ballistic missile in flight.

Baxter commented during the aforementioned radio broadcast: 'Thank God he didn't hit it – he'd have blown us all up!'

This would have been a sentiment doubtlessly felt by Jericha and his comrades as they ran for their lives. However, the assumption that the Allied pilots would all be killed by the exploding Rocket was perhaps incorrect.

Firstly, Love and the other Spitfire pilots were not aware of the diminutive size of the warhead. Just 4% of the physical surface area of the Rocket (26 m² in total) presented to Love's gunsight formed the actual warhead, making the chances of a direct hit slim. Secondly, a direct hit from a Browning .303 machine gun bullet would not have caused the warhead to detonate. Nor indeed would a direct hit from a 20 mm cannon shell. Instead, the effect would cause a 'low order deflagration' as opposed to detonation, and the high explosive content of the warhead would burn unevenly. Additionally, if the warhead's casing had been split by the cannon shell, such damage would have weakened any explosive effect. Although shrapnel could pose a serious risk, the shockwave produced by the incomplete deflagration would be subsonic.[8]

If a bullet or cannon shell had struck the Rocket, it would more likely have hit the main body. Although the Rocket's propellants were highly inflammable (especially the oxidizing agent liquid oxygen), the Rocket's propellant tanks were only lightly pressurized, so the risk of the explosive effect may again have been exaggerated. If the propellant tanks had been penetrated by a semi-armour piercing incendiary round, the fireball would have been most spectacular, but it definitely would not have ignited the warhead. Baxter recalled that the Rocket had passed directly through the middle of Love's gunsight, and so it is just possible that his range to the target was so close that his rounds would have passed either side of the target. In any event, when Love, Baxter and the other pilots landed, an excited conversation ensued, but to the surprise of his comrades, Love made it plain that he was not going to report the incident, nor did he wish the other three pilots to discuss it further. This conversation apparently took place as the pilots walked away from their aircraft to be debriefed by the Intelligence Officer whose responsibility it was to record anything exceptional or important that, potentially, could be of value. Love was later to comment that he could not report the Rocket to be damaged let alone destroyed. Baxter related: 'Cupid went very funny about it and would not tell anyone for years and years and years. So we kept it secret.'

Perhaps the real reason that Love did not wish to discuss the incident was because he was acutely embarrassed that he believed that his instinctive firing at the Rocket could have killed his comrades. Whatever the reason behind the secret, neither Love, Baxter nor the other pilots recorded the incident in their flying logbooks, nor was it recorded in the Operations Records Book of 602 Squadron. Consequently, information that may have been of value to the No. 105 MARU (Mobile Air Reporting Unit) which was attempting to pinpoint V2 launch sites, was lost.[9] Additionally, it has proved to be very difficult to determine with absolute certainty when the actual event took place! In this regard however, Baxter was quite certain: 14 February 1945. This date coincided with damage sustained to Squadron aircraft from AA fire whilst overflying a target area for the second time. Reading from his own logbook Baxter recalled from his cryptic handwriting: 'It's very simple. It says that on 14 February, I was flying a Spitfire XVI, 'G' for 'Golf'. 1000 lb [ordnance payload]. I was flying as Number 4. Pretty good bombing on Hague Bosch, a lot of light Flak and then went in again strafing. Hole in cockpit.'

This date 'fits' with the War Diaries of *Artillerie Abteilung* 485 (*mot.*) which noted an engagement with Spitfires at a V2 launch site, one of which was incorrectly reported as shot down. Unfortunately, it would appear that on that date, Love, although flying, was not yet operational with 602 Squadron. His logbook records that he had only one flight that day in Spitfire LO-K for a duration of one hour for the purposes of 'formation, tail chase, cine gun' practice.[10]

Love believed incorrectly that the incident had occurred on 22 March 1945. For Love, the date was indeed memorable for he nearly drowned returning from operations over the Netherlands. He was to recall the experience as his 'second birth'. Love's Spitfire had been damaged by light Flak in the target area and the aircraft's Packard-built Merlin engine became very rough. Returning to base, the engine stopped and he had to parachute into the North Sea approximately 65 miles from the coast. Suffering from hyperthermia, Love was rescued by a Consolidated PBY Catalina flying boat and, having spent a night at the hospital at RAF Haleworth, he continued his recovery at RAF Beccles. Subsequently he was to suffer from cervical spondylosis (degenerative arthritis of the neck vertebra) attributed to the incident.[11] Having made an apparent recovery, he duly returned to his base and flew an 'air test' on 2 April before returning to operations.[12] Baxter recalled the event and the conversation he had with Love on his return: 'He got shot down and baled out just off Southend. I stayed with him, and I later asked him, "How far did you go down, do you reckon?" He said, "I don't know, but it was bloody dark!"'

It is possible that the attempted air attack on the V2 took place on the afternoon of 21 February. Both Love and Baxter flew that day and the 602 Squadron Operations Record Book records the attacks on The Haagse Bos as having: '…*continued throughout the day, a total of 28 sorties being flown. All operations carried out by four aircraft each of which carried 2 – 250 lbs bombs fused airburst. As the aircraft pulled out of their dive they all strafed the length of the wooded area with cannon and machine gun fire, and in many cases the aircraft went down to deck level.*'

Unfortunately, the RAF Form 541 (a daily summary of sorties including take-off and landing times) fails to record that Baxter and Love actually flew together on 21 February. Strangely, it indicates that the two pilots only flew together once during the V2 offensive. This occurred ('officially') on 15 March 1945 when the weather was so poor, the mission to The Hague had to be aborted and the bombs jettisoned into the sea. But this record is an error and cannot be correct. It is known categorically that Love flew frequently with Baxter either as his 'Number Two' or 'Number Four'.[13] The errors are not necessarily attributable to failures in memory, but a reflection that the records were often compiled under hectic circumstances with aircraft operating from more than one airfield during a day of missions. In some instances the details would be chronicled long after the event they referred to by squadron staff with a poor understanding of operational flying.

However German records do tend to support the hypothesis that Spitfires may have been active during the V2 firing operations on 21 February 1945. The war diary 3./Art.Abt. 485 (mot.) indicates launches at 1249 hrs and 1620 hrs. The accompanying handwritten notes detail that two Spitfires had been engaged by the battery's anti-aircraft unit and that many enemy fighter-bombers were in the area. Perhaps, however, the entry in Love's logbook for that date is significant: 'Dive bombing and straffing Ockenburg. Ockenburg (house in the wood). Bit intrepid to strafe nowadays; Heinie [Germans] throws kitchen sinks up.'[14]

Could it be that Love was referring to his attack on the V2 and that the expression 'kitchen sinks' could be a mnemonic to later remind him of the event? We will never know and this is precisely what Love would have hoped for.

Jericha also recalled that he attended firings conducted from the intersections of tramlines in the vicinity of the Haagse Bos as these afforded a very stable ground platform from which the Abschusstisch could be set.

The firing offensive from The Hague continued up until 27 March 1945. The following day, the V2 firing batteries began to withdraw. However Jericha recalls that he and his unit were ordered to withdraw by their unit commander at the beginning of the month. Irrespective as to exactly when the unit pulled out, Jericha recalled that Art.Ausb.Abt. 271 was intended to be involved in the testing of new artillery ammunition at Lüneburg Heath. This was not to happen. Following a rendezvous with other units at Nijkerk, 80 kilometres east of The Hague, the retreat continued into Germany. Most of the soldiers apparently used bicycles, but Jericha used a horse and cart. His hay seat was made of the animal feed! Along the route, suspicious SS guards carefully examined the soldiers' papers, but seeing that the unit was connected with the Division z.V. (zur Vergeltung), [Division for Retaliation], it was quickly allowed to go on its way.

Jericha's memories as to his precise movements from this time are, at best, sketchy as Germany began to disintegrate as the Allied armies advanced in the West and the Soviets from the East. However, he recalls that he crossed the River Elbe (possibly in the area of Hannover and Lüneburg Heath) and was supposed to make his way towards Perleberg. Rumours spread amongst his comrades that an escape with what equipment they had was to be made by rail. This was a somewhat forlorn hope and Jericha decided he had a stark choice: to continue the journey with a very uncertain outcome or to desert. He recalled:

'Everyone knew that the war was lost. Standing on the bridge over the Elbe I wondered what should I do. If I went back, I would end up with the Americans. However, I had family. My family lived in the area that was later to be the Soviet occupied zone. So I went over the bridge to that side. The Russians hadn't reached the Elbe by that time, and I threw my papers into the river.'

With the horse and cart he simply headed off toward his home town of Ribnitz near Rostock, some 160 kilometres to the north-east. It was inevitable that Soviet soldiers would capture him. On 1 May at Lenzen, close to the River Elbe, 20 kilometres north-west of Wittenberge, he was caught and put into a camp with thousands of other prisoners. At a time of great anxiety, Jericha had some luck as he struck up an unlikely friendship; he remembered: 'The Russians then sorted us, first the pilots, then V1 and V2 (crews). I didn't report myself, however. Nobody knew me or recognized me there. We V2 boys only had simple artillery uniform. I then slipped into the [Russian] equine hospital. I found I got on well with the Russians.'

As a reflection of the trust he had quickly acquired with the former dreaded enemy together with the general hunger of the Soviet troops, he recalled: 'The Russians pushed a weapon into my hands one day. I was to watch the horse pasture. They said to me, "If Ruski comes – *Zap* – *zap!*" This meant that if other Russians attempted to steal horses, I was to shoot at them!'

Jericha remained with the Red Army Equine Hospital until late September when he was released from captivity and was admitted to the military hospital in Perleberg suffering from jaundice. However he made a full recovery and on 10 November 1945, he returned to his home in Ribnitz and a joyful reunion with his wife who shortly afterwards celebrated her birthday.

The years following the war's end were difficult for Jericha, but for a brief period he found an extraordinary outlet for the artistic side of his personality. He operated a travelling '*Kaspar und Grete*' (Punch and Judy) show for a few months in 1949. Thereafter he had numerous occupations. He recalled the uneasy relationship he had with the socialist masters of Eastern Germany. He recalled: 'The Russians wanted me to start a gliding operation. I didn't do it. Then they wanted me to work in the shipyard. I didn't do that either. They then wanted me to work in aircraft repair. I didn't do it. I wanted to do something for myself. I then opened my own workshop and produced different things. We produced fifteen to twenty weighing scales employing twenty people every week. The company was nationalized in 1953. Within ten days I sold my house and fled to the West.'

Before the laying of the barbed wire and concreted Berlin Wall in August 1961, Jericha escaped with his wife and three young children. Although potentially dangerous because of the communist border control guards, they caught a tram and journeyed from the Soviet occupation zone to West Berlin and then by air to a refugee camp at Stammheim near Stuttgart. Just ten days later, Jericha repeated his journey from East to West Berlin, but this time he was alone. He was smuggling the proceeds of his house sale: 140,000 GDR-Marks were hidden in his pockets. As the tram made its way to the sector border, three East German security guards were conducting 'inspections', gradually making their way through the carriage towards Jericha. In his mind, he chanted the mantra, 'turn around... *turn around...*' again and again. To his relief, they did and he made the crossing successfully unchallenged.

Ultimately the Jericha family settled in Tauberbischofsheim, north-east of Baden-Württemberg. In the early 1960s, he rekindled his childhood interest in art and following retirement from the electronics industry as a technical clerk in 1976, became a noteworthy local artist and frequently displayed his work at public exhibitions.

Looking back to the 'old times', Jericha reflected: 'It was clear from the moment England stepped in, that the war was lost. We couldn't win it. It was the same in the First World War. The British colonies joined in. Therefore, Hitler had to react. We say today: "Hitler wanted to dominate the world." All this is untrue.'

Regarding the Rocket: 'Von Braun is depicted as a war criminal today. But he never wore a uniform and was always a civilian. It was a fine thing that von Braun did. We hoped that the V-weapons could prevent an Allied invasion, but it was too little, too late.'

Eduard Jericha died in 2006.

CHAPTER FOURTEEN

'WHEN DO YOU START FIRING AT ENGLAND?'

OSWALD SCHNEIDER
Artillerie Abteilung 485 *(Motorisiert)*

O SWALD SCHNEIDER was born in Mühlhausen, 25 kilometres west of Stuttgart, in September 1924. Having left school, his chosen profession was that of a precision engineer, an occupation that was much sought after by the armaments industry. Working in one of the many factories at Pforzheim in south-west Germany, he produced igniter fuses for the famous 88 mm anti-aircraft gun. In peacetime, Pforzheim had an established workforce experienced in the mass production of delicate sensitive devices and a reputation for making excellent clocks, chronometers and jewellery. Schneider was conscripted in October 1942 and just before his departure for military life, his mother gave him a St. Christopher talisman which he was to keep with him throughout his service. He had been ordered to report to a *Panzer* unit at Böblingen, near Stuttgart. In addition to being a training ground for *Panzer* units, Böblingen was also a proving ground for tanks produced by Porsche. In mid-January 1943, his detachment was moved to the proving ground at Milowitz in Czechoslovakia, and then to Kamenz, 38 kilometres north-east of Dresden in Saxony. The rumours started to circulate that his group was due to be posted to North Africa. The speculation was quashed however when Axis forces in North Africa surrendered on 13 May 1943. Then, on 27 September, without warning, officers picked twenty men from several companies, of whom one was Schneider, and he was sent to the growing concentration of men at Peenemünde awaiting assignment to new units. His stay at Peenemünde was short. Having arrived in the evening, he left the following morning as his group was dispatched to Greifswald. Here he was billeted temporarily at a nearby farm along with hundreds of other soldiers waiting to be assigned to the newly-formed V2 Rocket units.

Eventually, he was posted to join 2./*Artillerie Abteilung* 485 (*mot.*). The figure 2 indicates the second Battery and '*mot.*' is a shortening for (*Motorisiert*) indicating that the Artillery Battalion was motorized). The *Artillerie Abteilung* 485 (*mot.*) had been newly formed that November at Massow in Pomerania, 60 kilometres east of Peenemünde, to commence training with the A4.

It would be logical to assume that Schneider, who by this time held the rank of *Gefreiter* (Lance Corporal), would then be pressed into service as either a technician or as a member of a Rocket-firing crew given his engineering background. Instead, he was assigned to be a motorcycle dispatch rider! The bewilderment as to the 'whys' and 'wherefores' of Rocket postings was felt by many soldiers. As Schneider was to recall: 'Yes, our officers probably looked for metalworking professionals, but as it is in the forces, one never does what one is professional at!'

Under the utmost secrecy, the first test Rocket was delivered to *Art. Abt.* 2./485 (*mot.*) in November 1943. Schneider was assigned to be part of a two-man night guard, patrolling in stints of two hours duration the perimeter fence at the edge of the forest which held the device. The A4 and its *Meillerwagen* were parked beside a woodman's lodge, which also served as accommodation for Schneider and his comrades. In daylight, *Art. Abt.* 485 (*mot.*) used the equipment for familiarization and training exercises in general handling. There was also an opportunity to test the electrical functions of the Rocket having ridden the V2 on the *Meillerwagen* along the unmade roads and lanes that criss-crossed the forests.

Schneider's very first impression of the Rocket was the diminutive size of its warhead. As he was to comment to the authors: 'What was this against so many Allied bombers?'

He did appreciate, however, given his experiences in engineering, that the Rocket was, technologically, a marvel and he recalled that it incorporated a considerable amount of electrical equipment. One of his colleagues, another *Gefreiter*, was an electrical engineer who had acquired a wiring diagram for the whole Rocket. Unfolded, the plan filled half the accommodation in which the unit was billeted at Massow. Apparently, an older *Oberleutnant* in the unit took a dislike to the electrical engineer as he knew more about the weapon than he did!

The *Art. Abt.* 2./485 (*mot.*) moved to Heidelager in early to mid-May 1944 to intensify training with the A4. The accommodation in wooden barracks was now completely taken up and so the lower ranks were quartered in tents. Large enough to sleep six to eight men, the tents were pitched in the forests. Schneider's comrades were mainly from Hamburg and Saxony. He noticed that not one of the new men came from the German-speaking areas that had been 'introduced' into the greater Reich following 1937, for example the Sudetenland. He presumed that the Sudetens had been deemed to be less trustworthy and had been excluded during the selection process to join the *Fernraketen* troop. As has been related in Chapter Twelve, Sudeten Germans did serve in the V2 offensive, and in particular, in the *Sicherungstruppen* of *Artillerie Abteilung* 836 (*mot.*).

With hundreds of soldiers in the process of being trained, Heidelager was an extremely busy place. The use of the *Feuerleitpanzer* and *Meillerwagen* was standard practice. As Schneider was to recall: 'An extra railway line was built to deliver the rockets. I was in a firing battery. The technical battery, based a couple of kilometres away, would complete preparation for the Rockets by mounting the warheads. Every two days a Rocket would be launched. There were three *Schießzüge* (launching platoons) for each battery. The *Schießzüge* trained one after another. We used two launching sites and each had its own *Feuerleitpanzer*. The tyres of the *Meillerwagen* were often burned by the A4 exhaust jet. Later the extra length cables were extended, looping them away from the platform, rather than being laid straight, in order to avoid this.'

Those troops who were not technically minded soon developed an 'ear' for hearing if a Rocket firing was to be a success or a failure. If the tone or consistency of the thrust was heard to be uneven or interrupted, they knew it was best to quickly ascertain if the Rocket was already airborne or not. The incident when members of the *Lehr- und Versuchsbatterie* 444 had been incinerated by a crashing Rocket failure was, by now, well known. Many of the troops who witnessed Rocket launches would frequently decide to take their chances and remain out of the slip trenches where quick escape would not be impeded. By watching the launches out in the open, it was always possible to run away from a careering Rocket rather than risk the slip trench becoming a fiery grave. Occasionally the Rocket would simply burn out on the *Abschusstisch*. The frustration of Rocket failures was bad enough, but when support equipment also failed, it was humiliating. Schneider remembered one particularly frustrating incident: 'A General wanted to see a firing and the engine of the *Meillerwagen* refused to start. The General was extremely angry and demanded "What do you *do* all the time?" The General sarcastically answered his own question, '"Just practise military drill!"'

One incident of special note was the occasion when a Rocket that had developed a fault could not be de-tanked. Schneider recalled that the valves which controlled the fuelling process relied not only upon electric heating elements, but also the passive effect of rising heated air to prevent seizure by freezing caused by the liquid oxygen held in one of the propellant tanks. This process of keeping the extreme cold at bay and preventing the ice from condensing out of the air could only be maintained for a mere two hours.

Difficulties in this particular Rocket's preparation had extended well beyond this time and it became impossible to open the valves and de-tank the propellants. Rather than abandon the Rocket to be a hazard for Heidelager personnel and a security risk, a platoon commander, *Leutnant* Behrens, took the extraordinary decision to destroy the Rocket where it stood. He armed himself with a *Karabiner* 98k bolt-action rifle loaded with tracer shells and then proceeded to fire into the propellant tanks until the Rocket burst into flames. Behrens, a technician, was regarded as a skilful man, unlike another platoon commander whose peacetime occupation was that of a butcher.

The woods surrounding Heidelager were a rich source of yellow chanterelle mushrooms and Schneider, unperturbed by the presence of partisans, would gather a crop to be cooked in the field kitchen. During his wanderings, he came across several craters made by earlier failed Rockets, the largest being a staggering 12 metres in diameter and 6 metres deep. Although the larger pieces of wreckage, including combustion chambers, had been cleared from the craters, he remembered seeing parts from the propellant tanks including the curiously shaped elliptical T-*Stoff* (hydrogen peroxide) fuel tank. The woods supplemented the troops' rations not only with fungi, but also occasionally with venison, although the majority of the red deer had been frightened away by the noisy activity associated with the A4. Travelling further afield on his motorcycle, Schneider was able to buy fresh eggs from local Polish farmers.

During his training, Schneider began to hear disquieting reports about the Rocket tests that had apparently been *successful*: 'We heard from the firing crews of the big problems that arose because of airbursts.'

Schneider and his comrades never knew if the airburst problems were resolved. However, after a stay of just eight weeks, *Art. Abt. 2./485 (mot.)* was ordered to leave Heidelager; the Red Army was coming ever closer.

The unit travelled to Tuchel Heide and the camp known as 'Heidekraut' to continue training in early to mid-July 1944. The train transporting the *Abteilung's* Rockets arrived at Lindenbusch and they were then delivered by road to Heidekraut, 3 kilometres from the firing sites. The Lindenbusch sidings also accommodated the staff railway coaches of both *Art. Abt. 485 (mot.)* and *Batterie 444.* This time Schneider did not have to sleep under canvas, but in the relative luxury of railway carriages. The high standard of provisions and hearty meals that he had enjoyed at Heidelager continued at Heidekraut.

At Heidekraut, Schneider met for the first time *Hauptmann* Neusch from Breslau (now Wroclaw, Poland) who was placed in command of his battery. Schneider recalled that his *Unteroffizier* (Sergeant) had already served with Neusch on the Eastern Front and had a tale to tell. Apparently Neusch had, for many years, been friendly with a fellow Silesian who was the battalion's war diarist. The sector of the front in which the men had served was under regular artillery attack. During one Soviet barrage, a shell struck the bunker in which the diarist was sheltering and he was killed instantly. But Neusch refused to attend the funeral ceremony for his friend, preferring to remain in the safety of his bunker! Whatever the truth was, Neusch had an unpleasant reputation which preceded him and it was wise to stay 'on his right side' rather than earn his disfavour. Schneider and his comrades disliked Neusch enormously and he recalled that a well-liked soldier, who served as the paymaster's driver in *Art.Abt.* 2./485 (*mot.*), was to feel the full animosity of Neusch for no other reason than the fact that he did not like his face. After persistent hounding and haranguing in front of his comrades, the man was later to shoot himself in the forests close to Heek and was buried at nearby Nienborg. It was also learned that another contributing factor which may have led to his suicide was that he had been ordered to the *Schießzug* (firing platoon) as the worsening fuel situation meant that he had lost his driving job.

Schneider had heard a rumour that *Art.Abt.* 485 (*mot.*) would be redesignated as a '*Lehr- und Versuchs Batterie*' like *Batterie 444*. Neusch, who was apparently an ambitious man, seeking action and acknowledgement, resisted the change. He had already received the prestigious *Deutsche Kreuz in Gold* which recognized repeated acts of extraordinary bravery or exceptional command skills. Many of Schneider's comrades, however, presumed that Neusch's decoration was not for bravery, but for his perceived command skills, yet Schneider was firmly of the opinion it was simply an acknowledgement of his length of service. Whatever the reason, it was generally believed that Neusch did not wish to be bogged down with the long-term testing and evaluation of the A4 – or any other weapon for that matter. He wanted to *fire* Rockets offensively!

By August 1944, the men of *Art. Abt.* 485 (*mot.*) were impatient for action and the local people living around Heidekraut sensed the air of anticipation. Schneider recalled that the locals frequently asked the Rocket troops, 'When do you start firing at England?' The answer was 'Not long!'

Having stayed at Heidekraut for only six weeks *Art. Abt.* 485 (*mot.*) moved via train back to Massow for a two-day stopover. The unit was then loaded onto railway carriages and travelled to Kleve on the German-Dutch border, the ultimate goal being Antwerp in Belgium from where the firing offensive against London was to begin. From Kleve they travelled by road in a fifty-vehicle convoy and arrived by night in Breda, just 50 kilometres (31 miles) north of their destination.

Schneider recalled that he and his comrades had not been issued with any ammunition or reserves of fuel. Their situation was desperate with many vehicles near empty; the thirsty 8.5 litre, six-cylinder Hanomag SS100 *Schwere Radschlepper* (Heavy Tractor or 'heavy motorized towing vehicles') tractors used to trail either the *Meillerwagen* or the liquid oxygen bowser were very vulnerable as they consumed a litre of diesel for every 2.5 kilometres travelled.[1]

At one location en route German infantrymen called out to the FR soldiers and asked where they thought they were going! Upon hearing the reply, 'Antwerp', Schneider recalled that infantrymen responded: 'No you're not. We're the last to leave. We're blowing up the bridges in a few minutes.' It is believed that it was the impending destruction of the bridges over the Schelde River and canal that would impede *Art. Abt.* 485's (*mot.*) progress.[2]

Schneider recalled: 'We had to turn around. Travelling through a small Belgian town at five in the morning, the Belgians greeted us with bouquets of flowers. They thought we were the British and had come to liberate them! The situation was made worse as we had run out of petrol. The big Hanomag tractors needed a huge amount of fuel. We had to abandon the vehicles with no fuel and they were captured. Our '*Alte*' [nickname for commanding officer: 'the elder one'] would look into everyone's fuel tanks and send back the vehicle with the least empty one to collect the men who had abandoned theirs. On my motorcycle, I would dash backwards and forwards collecting stragglers.

The hope of using Antwerp as a launching site against London was dashed when, on 4 September 1944, the British 11th Armoured Division liberated the great city port. Travelling via Utrecht, *Art. Abt.* 2./485 (*mot.*) reached The Hague on 8 September and commenced firing immediately. Although delayed by early poor weather and equipment problems, two firing positions were assembled in Wassenaar, a leafy suburb just 5 kilometres to the north-east of The Hague. Two *Abschusstischen* were set just under 190 metres away from each other. One *Abschusstisch* was located on the small road of Koekkoekslaan where it was intersected by the Konijnenelaan and Lijsterlaan. The second and slightly more easterly firing position was at the crossroads of Koekoekslaan and Schouweg. The 'X-times' for the two Rockets were synchronized and at 1836 hrs local time, the two V2s took off and thundered into the sky. At 1843 hrs both Rockets impacted in southern England; one fell at Staveley Road in Chiswick, West London, killing three and seriously wounding 17 others, while the second Rocket fell at Parndon Wood, Epping, in the east of the capital causing only light damage and forming a crater, still visible today. The V2 offensive against London had started and would not end for another 202 days.

Schneider and his comrades had no idea what happened at the receiving end of their Rocket firings although it was often said in the battery that the *Luftwaffe* would send reconnaissance aircraft over London to report on targeting accuracy. He never knew if this was actually carried out or not. Schneider recalled that the opening salvo firing two synchronized Rockets was attempted again but never achieved the dramatic success of the very first of the offensive.

Schneider's battalion had a complement of six 250cc DKW motorcycles and two BMWs with sidecars. One of Schneider's duties in addition to local couriering was to carry messages and reports from the battalion, either from launch sites or from the billets, to the Battery HQ which was located at Burgsteinfurt, 205 kilometres to the east of The Hague. A report was generated for every Rocket launch, irrespective of whether it had been a success or failure. He never saw the content of the report as it was sealed and stamped 'Geheim!' ('Secret').

Schneider remembered that a lesson quickly learned in the early days of the offensive was that firing sites on old cobbled streets such as those in The Hague and Wassenaar area were to be avoided. The blast of the Rocket's exhaust would rip the stones from the road surface and send them flying in all directions. During the day it became normal procedure to leave vehicles close to firing sites, but under the protective camouflage of tree-lined lanes and roads. This was a particular feature of the firing sites located in and around the estate and horse racing track at Duindigt. This location offered many firing points in a relatively small area with good access. The only vehicles that would need to leave the area would be the propellant tankers and the *Meillerwagen* to collect Rockets. Schneider recalled that vehicles would be left parked under trees on a small track that was between Wassenaar and the Leiden road (in all probability the Leidsestraatweg), and the racetrack. On a regular basis Schneider and his comrades would collect milk from a nearby farm on the Duindigt estate.

Firing continued from the Wassenaar area uninterrupted until 17 September 1944 when the men of *Art. Abt.* 2./485 (*mot.*) saw an aerial armada of towed gliders filling the distant horizon towards the east. This was the start of the Allied airborne landings at Arnhem, Nijmegen and Eindhoven known as Operation 'Market Garden'. The emergency caused all of the Rocket Battalions to retreat from The Hague as a precaution against ensnarement. To underscore this expectation of danger, Schneider recalled that later the RAF attacked the Rocket-firing positions. Indeed, the British Air Ministry War Room Daily Operational Summaries state:

27 Lancaster bombers and 3 Mosquitos, acting on a tip from the Dutch underground, attacked the surrounding area near Beukenhorst between Raaphorstlaan and Eikenhorstlaan. The attack took place between 18.38 hrs and 18.48 hrs. 169 tons of Brisant high explosive bombs and twenty-four 250-pound marker-bombs were dropped. Sighted visually, the target was well marked and the attack was concentrated with many bombs falling directly on target. These heavily wooded areas southeast of Wassenaar were suspected as V-2 supply depots but in fact were not.' [3]

What struck Schneider was that before the attack it was discovered that the farm that normally supplied milk had been abandoned without explanation. 'It was striking that a nearby farm had been left by the inhabitants that morning. They probably got a warning. The Resistance must have informed them. The firing position, 150 metres away from the road was destroyed.'

It is likely that the farm on the Duindigt estate from which Schneider remembered collecting milk was called, 'Hofstede'. It was accidentally destroyed by 602 Squadron RAF during an anti-V2 raid on either 13 or 14 March 1945. The foundations of the farm are still visible.[4]

Art. Abt. 485 (*mot.*) moved rapidly north the following day, along the coast to Amsterdam, then inland to Zwolle and then to Heek close to Burgsteinfurt, in Westphalia. From this new position, the battery began firing onto Louvain, Tournai, Maastricht and Liège.

Schneider recalled that each of the three Batteries of the *Abteilung* had its own infantry, Flak and anti-tank platoon which he considered as being something of a waste of time since these units were never really deployed. However, during the 'Market Garden' emergency, he recalled that to support the German forces facing the Allies at Arnhem, *Art. Abt.* 485 (*mot.*) sent in its anti-tank platoons. Arriving at night in the battle zone, the crew in the lead vehicle saw a swinging signal lamp ahead of them. Thinking that they were to be directed to the front line positions, they approached the signalman to gain directions, only to discover they were surrounded by British paratroopers and were immediately taken Prisoners of War. Without relief however, the Allied position around Arnhem became untenable and the captured men of *Art. Abt.* 485 (*mot.*) were eventually liberated and returned to rejoin their unit at Heek. On 30 September, they were ordered back to The Hague. *Art. Abt.* 2./485 (*mot.*) started its return journey on 1 October and had several overnight stops en route including a temporary billet close to the spectacular 12th century De Haar Castle to the west of Utrecht and close to the village of Haazuilens. Schneider recalled that he and his comrades were told that the Castle and grounds, the property of the Rothschild family, were strictly 'out of bounds.'

Arriving on 2 October at The Hook of Holland *Art. Abt.* 2./485 (*mot.*) recommenced the offensive on London on the night of 3 October 1944. From here, the local Dutch inhabitants were evacuated every evening for security reasons. How the nightly dispossessed Dutch found shelter was not known and was of no interest to the FR troops. Because many launches took place under the cover of darkness and the inhabitants of The Hague lived under nightly curfews, it is hardly surprising that Schneider recalled that he and his immediate comrades had very little contact with the Dutch. The temporarily abandoned homes in the Hook of Holland and the empty premises in the restricted areas proved to be too much of a temptation and, in spite of punishment and the watchfulness of the officers, looting did take place. No matter whether the stolen item was of value or not, the punishment was often harsh. Schneider recalled an incident during operations in The Hague area: 'On one occasion we had pinched cake from a hospital. *Hauptmann* Neusch heard about this and had every vehicle searched.

A colleague of mine had also stolen some silver cutlery. He was demoted and sent off to serve in a penal battalion in Russia.'

Service in a penal battalion would last for one to perhaps three months. Irrespective of the length of the sentence, such a punishment was often a death sentence as soldiers in such units were considered highly expendable.

Although Schneider was aware that behind the scenes the SS were attempting to take over the entire V2 firing offensive and the FR infrastructure, he felt none of the pressure. The one high-ranking officer whom he and the others did know of was Kammler. Schneider recalled: 'I saw Kammler once. We had our battery command post based in a hotel in the middle of The Hague. A comrade of mine was ordered to collect and escort Kammler with a motorcycle from the motorway to the command post. On the return, he lost his way! Fortunately, Kammler, in his sports car, had not noticed this. Everybody was always very anxious when his visit was announced and for the officers, naturally, it was red alert. I personally had no direct contact with him.'

Art. Abt. 2./485 (*mot.*) then moved from The Hague to the Burgsteinfurt area at the end of October to support the Rocket offensive against Antwerp and began operations in early November. An air raid ensued shortly afterwards upon the town of Burgsteinfurt and there were several direct hits on the vehicle maintenance shop. Several of Schneider's comrades died including Schöppingen the battery diarist, and others including *Feldwebel* Sotta, were wounded. Fearing further attacks by the RAF, the staff of *Art. Abt.* 485 (*mot.*) moved from their location in the civic finance offices of Burgsteinfurt around 15 December 1944, a short distance away to the ornamental grounds of Bagno Park. Schneider recalled that the park and its ruined castle had a connection with the royal family of Bentheim-Tecklenburg and in common with European royalty, the family was related to the House of Windsor. It was considered unlikely the RAF would countenance an attack on such a location and it was thus hoped that the new headquarters would be safe from a raid. The connection with the British royal family was very tenuous and the truth of the matter was that after five years of brutal warfare, the Allies were probably above such niceties. If the RAF had received intelligence as to the location of the staff headquarters of *Art. Abt.* 485 (*mot.*), it would not have hesitated to attack the area.

From mid-December, *Art. Abt.* 2./485 (*mot.*) had returned from the Burgsteinfurt area to The Hague. Local residents in The Hague had by now grown familiar to the sound of the V2s but the level of fear remained. Misfires could entail mid-air detonation with metal parts falling over large areas. The more dangerous situation was when a Rocket lost thrust or guidance and would crash, exploding in a fireball. Schneider remembered: 'The launch sites were always chosen in inhabited areas. The use of Rockets brought tremendous fear to the inhabitants of The Hague. The sudden noise of a Rocket at launch was so tremendous that the inhabitants were terrified and would drop down in the street as they had no idea what was happening.'

Strangely, Schneider recalled very few incidents of misfire. It was said that those that did occur were due to sabotage during the Rocket's manufacture at the *Mittelwerk* underground factory. It was also rumoured that another cause of failure was excessive over-testing of components whether they be combustion chambers or small electric devices. Much of the delicate equipment of the Rocket had extremely short operational life expectancy.

Schneider recalled that launches took place at different locations including the compound and grounds of the Bloemendaal Psychiatric Hospital off Monsterse Weg in Ockenburgh. This mostly uninhabited wooded location was just outside the '*Sperrgebiet*' security zone and was ideal because of the natural cover and easy access for vehicles. He recalled: 'I was based at the mental home where we launched several Rockets from the yard. At that time no patients were there of course. We had two misfires and maybe a few tiles were damaged.'

In fact, the hospital was destroyed and the nearby church was almost demolished by misfires: the scars are still visible today. In the nearby woods close to the hospital it is possible to see the best-preserved V2 misfire crater that still exists in The Hague over sixty years after the event.

Whatever the reason for the failures, Schneider recalled that his comrades in *Art. Abt.* 2./485 (*mot.*) took a particular pride in their Rocket-firing programme and considered themselves to enjoy a higher degree of successful launches than *Batterie* 444 which often launched A4s, which it was said, were outside manufactured tolerances. To the best of his knowledge he could recall only one occasion when the battery had to abandon a Rocket because of iced propellant valves and only a few occasions of low-altitude misfires causing minor damage on the ground. The greatest contempt for lack of aptitude, Schneider remembered, was reserved for the SS *Werfer-Batterie* 500 which was said to be 'good for nothing!'

Rocket firing took place irrespective of the weather. The most serious problems encountered in the preparation of the Rockets as far as Schneider was concerned were the use of liquid oxygen and the threat from the air. The extreme cold of the liquid oxygen necessitated the use of asbestos gloves, but nevertheless he recalled only one case of frostbite. The loss by evaporation from the liquid oxygen bowser frequently meant that the fuelling process would be delayed whilst a fresh bowser was called for. The normal procedure at the start of the campaign was for Rockets to be launched at the beginning of the day, but delays would push the firing time later into the morning. Aesthetically, for the firing crews, the launchings that took place either side of sunrise or sunset were the most spectacular. The V2, having left the dark ground, would pass up through the Earth's shadow, and the condensation trail would suddenly appear in mid-air, arching across the sky. At the peak of the white trail, the glistening Rocket would be bathed in sunlight with its thrust flame clearly visible. Over a period of time, the varying winds at altitude would distort the contrail into a characteristic lightning or zigzag shape. Night firings naturally meant that the only visual impression of the Rocket was the thrust flame becoming smaller and smaller until it was extinguished after about sixty seconds from launching. Night preparations saw the firing crews using electric torches and Schneider recalled the numerous times he would be sent to the stores to collect fresh cells.

Daylight launches, although easier to prepare, brought about the added risk of air attack from enemy aircraft. The Rocket contrails could be seen from great distances and enemy aircraft operating in the area would circle around them trying to spot the location of the firing crews. The increasing numbers of enemy aircraft forced the firing batteries to complete the entire process of preparation and launch under the cover of darkness. Rockets which could not, for whatever reason, be fired before dawn were simply launched when ready.

The supply of Rockets on railway wagons, their preparation by the technical troops, and collection by the firing troop became a routine procedure. Schneider recalled a perfect location of sheltered assembly halls used by the technical troop of *Art. Abt.* 485 (*mot.*) for the fitment of warheads and for field repairs; this was commonly known as Filmstad. It would appear that just one technical troop of *Art. Abt.* 2./485 (*mot.*) following the end of October 1944 had the overall responsibility to supply Rockets not only to its own comrades but to the other batteries operating in The Hague.[5]

Unknown to Schneider, the tired and abused buildings of Filmstad once had a glittering past. Hidden away in the woods of Clingendaal and close to the Benoordenhoutseweg, the film studios had been established by the 'rags to riches' film entrepreneur, distributor and producer, Loet (Lou) Cordell Barnstijn (1880-1953). Having bought land in 1935 from the Oosterbeek estate, he built two large well-appointed studios which he called 'Filmstad' (Film City) and began a period of successful film production. However, with the outbreak of war and fearful of the Nazis' anti-Semitism, Barnstijn had to abandon his 'dream factory' and flee to the United States. The Nazis then seized Filmstad and the famous German studio of Universum Film AG (UFA) acquired the empty buildings and began its own film production. Doubtless to Barnstijn's great personal disgust, UFA, under the overall leadership of the *Reichsminister* for Propaganda, Joseph Goebbels (1897-1945), began the production of anti-Semitic films.

At the beginning of the V2 offensive, the Rocket technical troops, and in particular the men of *Batterie* 444, used two large halls at Filmstad to prepare Rockets. Once the warheads had been attached and other procedures carried out, the Rockets would be collected by the launching crews for the short journey to firing sites situated nearby in the Haagse Bos, Duindigt and other locations scattered across The Hague.

The preparation of Rockets by the technical troops appears to have been very well coordinated and organized as indicated in the following observations made by *Sonderführer* (Specialist Officer) Krause from the test centre at Karlshagen, who visited the V2 facilities in the Netherlands in appalling weather between 26–31 December 1944. He travelled to The Hague from Berlin via Hannover, Münster and Burgsteinfurt. His difficulties, however, began in earnest as he approached Utrecht.

'Report on the Official Visit to Gruppe Nord

'...*Very dense fog, which forces the driver to drive slowly in the dark. Before Utrecht, it is impossible to proceed since the roads are icy and misty. Continue at night. Only by 2 o'clock arrived at base (code name) Ursula in Utrecht. On 28.12.44 continue on to The Hague. Very icy roads make driving almost impossible. Improving weather at about 10.00 o'clock brings better opportunity to travel and thus the first enemy fighter-bombers. Gradually, the route becomes ice-free and allows higher speeds. Two kilometres from the end of the journey, our vehicle is overturned through carelessness on the part of the driver and the occupants are ejected or partially buried [in the snow]. Result of the accident: car (Volkswagen) badly damaged. After brief repairs to the car, I was able to continue...*

'...*The morning brought a visit to the T.B., [Technical Battery] in Filmstad. The battery is well camouflaged and housed in partially bombproof bunkers and small forts. Testing and compressor cars are available in the two movie halls where also the Rockets are tested. The work of the battery could not be ascertained, but as a result of a meeting with the platoon commanders it was learnt that an average of one to one-and-a-half hours is (required for preparation) per Rocket. This indicates that the two test centres can prepare around eight to twelve Rockets in one night. The (covered) halls allow work in the light.*'[6]

Krause also recorded that the technical troops were preparing Rockets not only for *Batterie* 444 but also for the launching sites operated by 1. and 2./ *Art. Abt.* 485 (*mot.*).

In February 1945, Filmstad came to the attention of the RAF and to deny the Germans the use of the buildings for the preparation of V2s, an attack was ordered. Spitfire Mk IXs of 453 Squadron, RAAF, carried out six 'armed reconnaissance' sorties over The Hague on 22 February. The first sortie was recalled due to poor weather, but the second mission of 12 aircraft dive-bombed Filmstad with each aircraft dropping two 250 lbs bombs. Eighteen bombs struck the target area and the pilots observed that '...*bombs hit buildings with very good result*' and that there was '...*one very large explosion from the easternmost building.*' Although no official confirmation exists, it is possible that the large explosion observed might have been due to a V2 warhead detonating in the intense heat.

All 12 Spitfires returned safely to RAF Swannington in Norfolk at 1215 hrs after a mission of 85 minutes. Following three further sorties, 453 Squadron summarily reported '*large fires…burning furiously*' at Filmstad with smoke drifting nearly as far as Leiden – a distance of 12 kilometres.[7] Shortly after the raid, pilots of 602 Squadron, who attacked targets nearby, observed the towering column of smoke. The spectacle was deemed so impressive that it was even commented upon in the 602 Squadron 'Operational Record Book'.

The Australians had successfully destroyed the buildings used by the *Art. Abt.* 2./485 (*mot.*) technical troop and erased the final vestiges of what had once been 'Film City'.

Schneider recalled that Filmstad had been *destroyed* from the air. However, in spite of the great success of the attack, it did not, at first, thwart the V2 offensive significantly: 12 firings against London occurred the day after the attack. However, once the supply of prepared V2s had been used, a significant fall-off occurred. Only one known V2 was fired towards London over 24 and 25 February.[8] The technical troops soon pressed other buildings in The Hague area into service to prepare Rockets for firing. As long as the supplies were maintained, the offensive carried on. As one Rocket hurtled into the stratosphere to fall upon an unseen target far away, another device would be waiting its turn close by under the cover of trees. Schneider recalled: 'When the Rocket was launched, the work was done. We didn't care what happened at the other end. It was war, but what was this against all the Allied bombers? We knew that civilians were hit in London and we were aware that there wasn't any warning for them.'

On two separate occasions however, the near regular routine of Rocket-firing activity was suspended by the actions of the FR troops themselves. On Christmas Eve, 1944 the ever ambitious Neusch wanted to fire Rockets and in doing so 'send greetings over'. The men, however, had other ideas and wanted to celebrate Christmas Eve their own way, either among themselves or with the few local families they had established relationships with. Schneider recalls that Neusch was told that supply problems were such that 'there was no fuel' and therefore no launches occurred. Neusch was unaware of the deception. On another occasion towards the end of the offensive, Schneider recalled another extraordinary event. It occurred at the end of an inactive day when supplies had unexpectedly arrived, but the men had been granted evening leave: 'Then the order came to launch. Neusch asked his staff who was available, but the answer was "Nobody!" Neusch turned to me and said, "You know where they are! Go and fetch them!" I went to the local inn and the men were all there with prostitutes, even the *Feldwebel*. Reluctantly, I announced, "Get up and get out! We're launching"! But they just replied, "No way. Sit down and have a drink." So I sat down and from under the table, one of the girls handed me a piece of paper with her address on it! I never 'went' with her, but a friend of mine did and this was a person who had a wife and six children waiting for him at home. Fortunately, there was no trouble for not launching. This was towards the very end of the offensive and at that time everything was out of control!'

Members of *Art. Abt. 2./485 (mot.)* were also billeted in the restricted area of the seaside town and resort of Scheveningen. The beach huts had long since disappeared and been replaced with barbed wire and anti-amphibious defence systems. The sand dunes further along to the north-east concealed machine gun nests. The town's large houses stood empty – their owners, under the orders of the German forces, had been forced to vacate. Owners of non-German occupied properties were allowed to pass the security perimeter and visit their homes every eight to ten days. In spite of resentment and distrust, occasional romances took place between the soldiers and the local girls. As is often the situation with men of arms away from home the services of prostitutes were in demand by some of the men. Schneider recalled a friend, Hans Cieslar, who was not only something of a prankster, but also an insatiable lothario. Of Cieslar, Schneider recalled: 'Hans was so clever and was always good for a joke. He had served on the Eastern Front. One day in Heek, an Allied bomber crashed and five or six crew came down by parachute. Neusch told Hans to drive one of them to headquarters and to shoot him on the way! But Hans did not do this. Hans had told me that once he had killed an unarmed Russian soldier and had said, 'It affected me deeply. I can't do that kind of thing anymore.'

Of Cieslar's predilection, Schneider recalled that his friend had slipped a local girl past the security guards into his billet. He had used his motorcycle sidecar combination and dressed the girl in a field grey greatcoat and steel helmet. She was smuggled out before first light. Apparently, this activity was not restricted to just *Gefreiters* but to men of all ranks; the guards would invariably and obligingly 'look the other way'. Schneider recalled that several different billets were used in and around The Hague, including those of Wassenaar further along the coast but the aforementioned incident with Cieslar apparently took place at the Villa Maria on Hogeweg facing the beautiful Scheveningen Bos. If this was the case, then there is perhaps some small irony inasmuch as the Villa Maria, used as a billet for the Rocket soldiers, was later destroyed by a Rocket misfire.

As mentioned in previous chapters, another activity when not on duty, and one that was peculiar to the firing units, was the procurement and distillation of Rocket propellant to make drinkable alcohol. When the FR troops were first introduced to the Rocket, they quickly realized that one of the two principal propellants known as B-*Stoff* was, in fact a mix of ethyl alcohol and water. The abuse of this crystal clear alcohol mix would appear to have been fairly widespread with the FR troops, but Schneider recalled that it never led to discipline problems with the soldiers. However, after reported incidences of theft, steps were taken to denature the alcohol into methyl alcohol. Schneider recalled that the methyl alcohol had a purple colour, which was probably caused by aniline in addition to other chemicals to make the alcohol unpalatable. As he remembered: 'We were told that the alcohol was dangerous and we could become blind. However, we filtered the alcohol through our gas mask filters three times. Our field kitchen cook would distil it on the stove. We drank the stuff from billycans and this was bad, as we got very intoxicated. One of my comrades and a fellow Swabian, *Hauptfeldwebel* Patriz Schmidt, wanted a handgun and an *Unteroffizier* who had a spare weapon wanted to barter for schnapps, but he didn't want B-*Stoff*. We filtered our B-*Stoff* and added peppermint to make three bottles. He didn't seem to notice! We also once tried to make Genever [Dutch gin].'

The abundance of so much B-*Stoff* led the ever practical and experimental soldiers to think of ways of using the alcohol beyond its normal use as a propellant in addition to simply drinking it. They would wash their clothes, cook and, during cold weather, light fires with it. Ultimately the soldiers became blasé about the alcohol and Schneider recalled that one soldier made an error, confusing the alcohol with similarly 'borrowed' petrol, whilst relighting a reluctant fire in a cold billet. The sudden whooshing ignition set fire to the straw bedding mattresses. The windows were quickly thrown open and the burning bedding hurled into the street below. Neusch was to hear of the incident. Although he wanted to establish who was responsible for nearly destroying the billet, he apparently was told a tale so convincing that he was placated and no punishments were imposed!

Having withdrawn from The Hague on or around 12 or 13 December 1944, Schneider recalled that *Art. Abt.* 2./485 (*mot.*) returned yet again to the area of Burgsteinfurt, 20 kilometres south-east of the Dutch town of Enschede. From nearby Heek, the Battery began to use the *Leitstrahl* (LS, radar guide beam system) to improve the V2's accuracy. Although it may have been planned to use LS, no evidence from the *Art. Abt.* 2./485 (*mot.*) War Diary supports Schneider's memory. Intriguingly however, the War Diary does mention LS on 16 February 1945 but not necessarily in an operational sense.

Schneider recalled that at Heek he came into contact with *Führungsoffizier* Biwack. This non-commissioned political officer held the full title of *Nationalsozialistischer Führungsoffizier* (National Socialist Leadership Officer – NSFO). NSFOs came into existence in late 1943 on Hitler's orders and, like the security-minded SS officers, they were embedded in the V2 batteries and throughout the *Wehrmacht*. Biwack's mission was to make fanatical Nazis out of the men, who would then be prepared to die for the *Führer* without question. Biwack, who on all accounts was not over-zealous, was considered to be an 'OK' individual by Schneider and his fellow FR troops. Biwack took it upon himself to perform a security check on the local inhabitants of Heek to test their knowledge of both the FR troops and the Rocket. During the interviews he conducted, he discovered that the 'locals' were very well informed and in some instances better informed on Rocket operations than Biwack himself and the Rocket soldiers! He discovered that information had come from the loose tongue of just one officer. The consequences of this disclosure are not known.

Some time later Schneider was instructed by his *Hauptmann* to take a pillion passenger to the Battery HQ at Burgsteinfurt. The man he saw awaiting transportation was dressed as a civilian, but as he turned his head Schneider realized it was Biwack. Later Schneider heard that Biwack was one of the first men to go into captivity, possibly after deserting.

The *Art. Abt. 2./485* (*mot.*) continued firing, in spite of increasing supply problems, until 28 March 1945 when the last V2 was launched towards Antwerp at 0849 hrs.[9] Schneider recalled that from Heek, the unit travelled to Osnabrück, 68 kilometres to the north-east, and henceforth part of the Battery travelled on to the Munsterlager where the *Art. Abt. 2./485* (*mot.*) was to be re-equipped with heavy artillery guns. However, in the event, this did not happen and the troops were ordered to deploy as infantry to defend the Fatherland. Now that Schneider and his comrades were no longer involved with the 'wonder weapon' the special Kammler pass card was permanently revoked.

Schneider was ordered to drive his motorcycle the 165 kilometres from Munsterlager to Osnabrück under the cover of darkness to pass new orders on to the remnants of the unit who waited by their vehicles. The journey was made difficult because the *Volkssturm* had built anti-tank defences on the roads. En route, and briefly resting during the journey, he was approached by a soldier who asked where he was going and whether it would be possible for him to ride as pillion passenger; Schneider agreed to do so. Continuing to travel through the night and approaching Minden, 60 kilometres from Osnabrück, Schneider suddenly became aware of an urgent tapping on his shoulders from his passenger who shouted, '*Stop here please, I'm home*' and with that the man deserted the *Wehrmacht* and disappeared into the darkness.

Having made contact with his comrades at Osnabrück he made his return journey stopping briefly at a *Wehrmacht* security road-check. Beside the road lay a large pile of *Panzerfaust* anti-tank ammunition. Schneider showed his paper to the officer who whispered, 'Everything is lost – it's all over…'

Schneider nodded his agreement. The officer then said, 'Make yourself scarce!'

Ignoring the advice, Schneider decided to continue his journey back to his comrades at Munsterlager. The unit then moved to Hohenziethen where he received his final military order. He and his comrade, *Leutnant* Happel, were ordered by the deputy Battery commander, Bilge, to Braunschweig on a reconnaissance mission to search for ammunition supply vehicles to equip

Art. Abt. 2./485 (*mot.*) – a forlorn hope as they had no idea as to the exact position of the advancing enemy. During the journey, Schneider and Happel had the misfortune of running straight into an American tank unit on the approaches to a road junction that was piled with supplies. Schneider did an immediate turn and opened the throttle. The motorcycle, however, was too slow and American soldiers in a jeep quickly caught up with them and opened fire with machine guns. The safety of the woods was too far away and the two men were caught out in the open. Happel and Schneider were both hit in a hail of bullets as the careering motorcycle pitched the two men to the ground. A single round struck Schneider in his upper right leg, but the bullet glanced off some coins held in a small purse in his trouser pocket, just missing the St. Christopher's talisman given to him by his mother. It travelled the length of his upper leg, exiting by his kneecap. The bullet passed through clear air until it eventually came to a stop having entered his left ankle. Schneider recalled: 'After we had been hit, we sat at the side of the road. I pulled off my boots and saw the wound to my ankle and my thigh. Happel, who sat about two-and-a-half metres away, shouted to me: "*Oswald! Oswald!*" When I tried to stand up to go over to him, one of two black American soldiers who had in the meantime caught up with us, aimed his machine gun at me and I thought it was all over. Why would they not act as we had done? What would they do with us? We would only be a burden for them. Instead, the Americans disarmed me of my 7.65 mm pistol. Very soon, an ambulance truck appeared and we were loaded on board and driven to a First Aid station. We were then separated. Sometime later, I asked one of the Americans about Happel. He said he had died.'

Meanwhile *Hauptmann* Neusch, still in search of medals and with nothing more to lose, ordered the battery to cross the River Elbe to face the Russians. The fate of Neusch and the others remains unknown. Schneider was to hear later that many died in futile actions against the Red Army and that Neusch may have drowned in the Elbe whilst attempting to flee to the west. The one survivor of the carnage was Schneider's comrade, Patriz Schmidt. In the evening of the day that Schneider was injured, Schmidt was riding his 750cc BMW motorcycle in support of Neusch when a Russian mortar shell suddenly exploded in a flash of light in his path and threw him from his mount. Lying on the ground with his face covered in blood, Schmidt was aware that a Soviet soldier was approaching and was about to administer the *coup de grâce*. Under his coat Schmidt quietly reached for the handgun that he had bartered for three bottles of 'V2 schnapps' months earlier. Pulling the trigger the bullet passed through his coat and killed the Russian who fell at his feet. Schmidt survived the war to tell Schneider of his escape years later.

Immediately following the end of the war, the Allied powers divided Germany into zones of occupation either because of positions held at the end of hostilities or due to agreements between senior leaders. Schneider recalled that order dissolved and it was a case of 'every man for himself'. German servicemen attempted to travel home, but most did not get far before being taken prisoner. Those ex-servicemen who were quick-thinking were able to save themselves from an uncertain future and a lifetime under Communist rule, but the situation for wounded men was desperate. Schneider knew of an *Unteroffizier* who had been seriously wounded and, as a Russian prisoner of war, found himself on a hospital train travelling into the feared Soviet zone. Fortunately, the train happened to stop in the siding of a railway station beside a train travelling in the opposite direction. Summoning his strength, the *Unteroffizier* quietly crept from one train into the other, avoiding the guards and was eventually able to make it to his home.

Having received First Aid from the Americans, Schneider was handed over to the British authorities who were in command of the area. He was sent with other injured men to the local hospital in Salzwedel. Shortly afterwards the Salzwedel area fell to the jurisdiction of the Soviets. The Russians assessed that the injured men were useless to them as they could not be put to work, so the British were called to remove them. The British sent him and three or four other moveable casualties by hospital train to a civilian hospital in Munsterlager.

The hospital, unlike the well-supported military field hospitals, was poorly equipped to handle such seriously injured men and because of this, Schneider was to lose his left foot. He remembered that of the 80,000 prisoners of war at Munsterlager, 1,800 of them, including himself, were amputees. In anticipation of his release, the British authorities asked him which unit he had served with. Taking very special care not to mention 'wonder weapons' he calmly answered 'Artillery 485' which was a perfectly reasonable answer, but one that had been carefully calculated to garner no interest whatsoever. Schneider had heard from his fellows in the hospital that his home was in an area close to, or in a zone controlled by, the French and not the Americans. He also knew that the French had a poor reputation regarding their treatment of POWs and that newly released prisoners were being transported to work in France. This he wanted to avoid at all costs if only so his wounds could heal. Schneider predicted correctly that he would be asked as to his place of residence before his release. His answer was prepared. When asked, he replied 'Mühlhausen', knowing that this place name could either be taken to be his actual home of Mühlhausen, near Stuttgart, or mistaken for several other towns of the same name throughout Germany. He could decide at his convenience which location was appropriate once he knew the actual position that the French controlled. It was with good reason that members of his family respectfully referred to him as a 'sly fox'!

After five weeks of hospitalization, Schneider was allowed home and making the best progress that he could on crutches, he arrived in Mühlhausen on 15 August 1945. It was not until Christmas Day four months later that he received his first artificial limb. On 1 April 1946, he returned to his peacetime profession of a precision engineer, which he subsequently developed into his own business.

In 1947 Schneider contacted the *Einwohnermeldeamt* (Inhabitants Office) and was able to find the address of his deceased friend, *Leutnant* Happel, who had died just before the war's end. He wrote to Happel's widow who resided in Marburg, to simply state that he had been his friend and that they had served together. A letter arrived very shortly from *Frau* Happel asking if Schneider knew of her husband's whereabouts: '*Had he been captured by the Soviets*?' She explained that for the last two years following the end of the war, she had been looking desperately for him and that, officially, he was posted as 'missing'. Schneider wrote a poignant letter telling her that the sad search had come to an end.

Looking back at his wartime experiences Schneider commented: 'I can only say that I hated military service, but nevertheless tried to get the best out of my stolen youth. I was not a typical sample of a soldier. I acted so I could survive. Today, one would do things differently: but then today is so different to the old days. I managed to survive and did not give in, although I suffered damaged health. When one has the mental and physical condition of my age, then not only cleverness, but also luck and contentment are important. Unfortunately the senselessness of war has changed little.'

Oswald Schneider died in February 2008.

A4/V2 ROCKET – TECHNICAL SPECIFICATIONS, DIMENSIONS AND PERFORMANCE

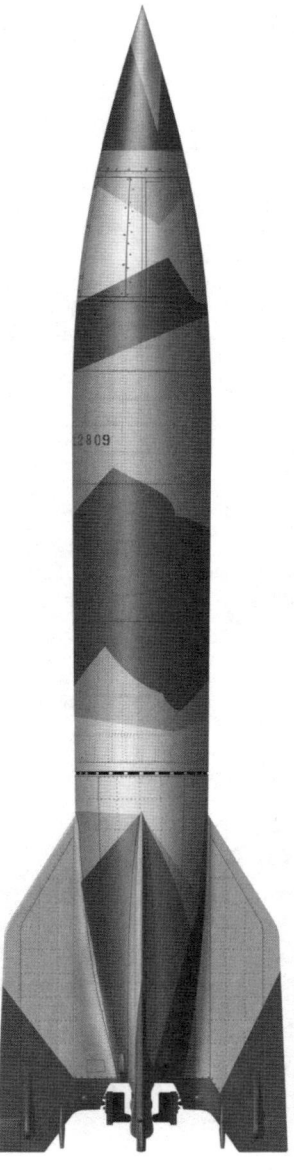

Length 14.036 metres (46 feet and ½ inch)

Width 1.651 metres (5 feet 5 inches)

Fin to fin 3.564 metres (11 feet 8 inches)

Dry weight 4008 kg (8,838 lb)

Launch weight 12873 kg (28,380 lb)

Fuel weight 9 tonnes

Overall operational launch weight 13.5 (12.8) tonnes (13000 kg)

Warhead weight 1 tonne (60% Amatol and 40% Ammonia Nitrate)

Range 370 km (maximum)

Altitude prior to *Brennschluss* 28 km (17 miles)

Maximum altitude of the A4 B 80 km (50 miles)

Fuel consumption rate 134 kg/second (295 lb/second)

Fuel Consumable Requirements:

    Alcohol (75% ethyl and 25% water) 3710 kg (8179 lb) (*B-Stoff*)

    Liquid Oxygen 4900 kg (10802 lb) (*A-Stoff*)

    Hydrogen Peroxide 129 kg (285 lb) (*T-Stoff*)

    Sodium Permanganate 15.8 kg (35 lb) (*Z-Stoff*)

    Nitrogen 13.6 kg (30 lb)

Turbo-Pump 47 cm (18.5 in) diameter turbine developing 675 hp

    at 5000 rpm

Maximum speed 5760 km/h (3,580 mph)

Velocity 1585 m/sec (5,200 ft/sec) approximately

Terminal speed 1100 m/s (3,600 ft/sec)

Maximum operational altitude 96 km (60 miles)

Combustion Chamber temperature (maximum) 4890 F / 2700 C

Thrust at lift-off 25 tonnes 25,000 kg (55,116 lb)

Fuel consumption 130 kg/s (286 lb/s)

Burn time 65 seconds

Combustion Chamber pressure 15 Bar / 217 lb/sq inch

Combustion Chamber temperature 4890 F / 2700 C

Acceleration 0.9 g rising to 5 g

Warhead/Launch Weight Ratio 0,075:1

External Temperature of Rocket body

during re-entry 649 deg C (1200 F)

254

APPENDIX 2

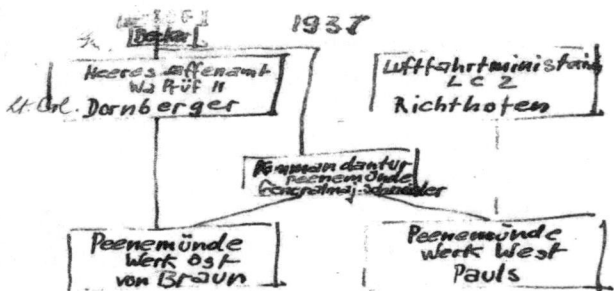

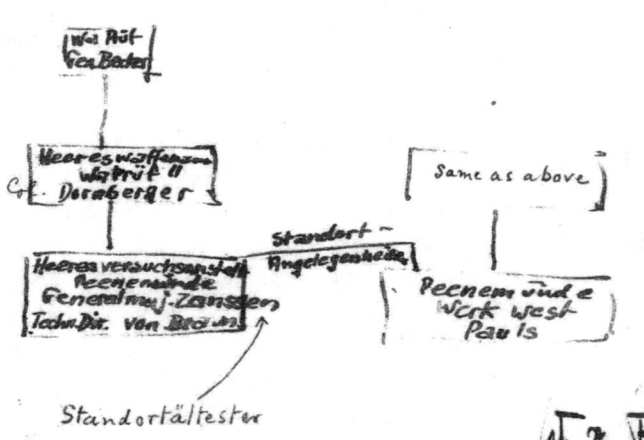

A diagram on the German rocket development organisation drawn by Wernher von Braun
during his interview with the Special Investigations Field Information Agency at the Headquarters
of the U.S. Forces European Theatre, Frankfurt, 1947.

W.v.Braun   8/3/47

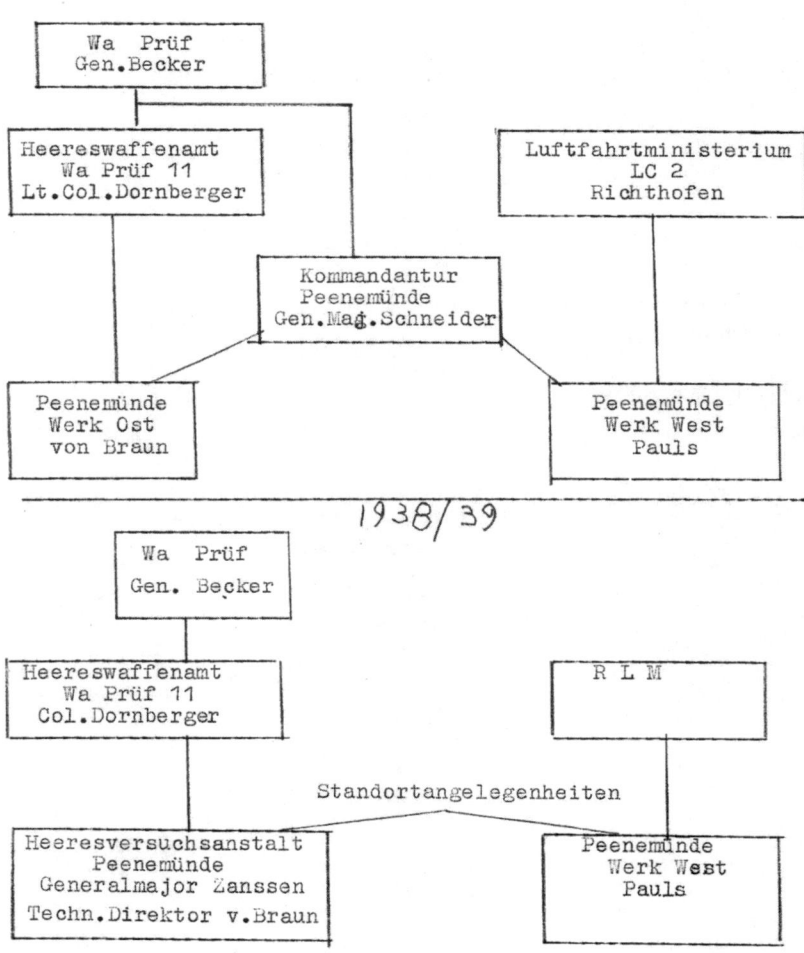

For clarification, an English interpretation of the previous diagram.
Chain of Command at Peenemünde 1937/38.

APPENDIX 3

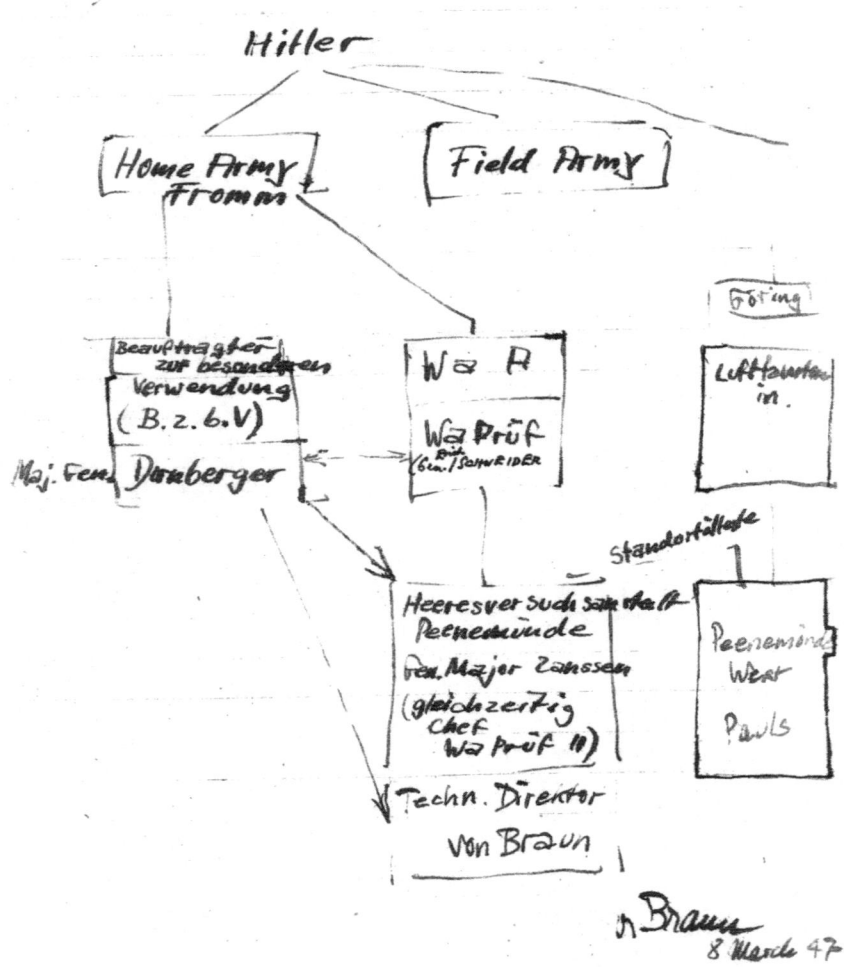

A diagram partly in German and English, drawn by von Braun recollecting the Chain of Command of 1942 from Adolf Hitler down to the staff at Peenemünde.

APPENDIX 4

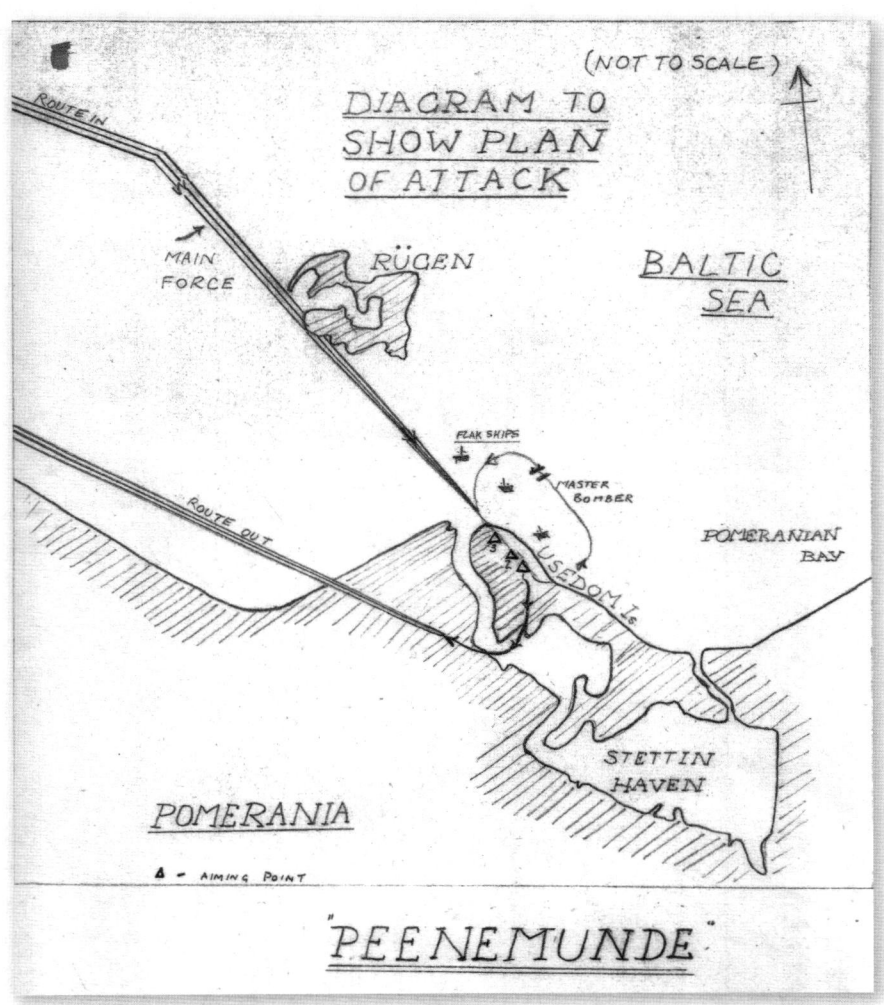

Peenemünde attack map of 17/18 August 1943 as recalled by Master Bomber
and Pathfinder for the attack, Group Captain John H. Searby, D.S.O., and D.F.C.,
83 Squadron RAF in December 1948.

APPENDIX 5

A4/V2 ROCKET WARHEAD NOSE FUSE　　SECRET

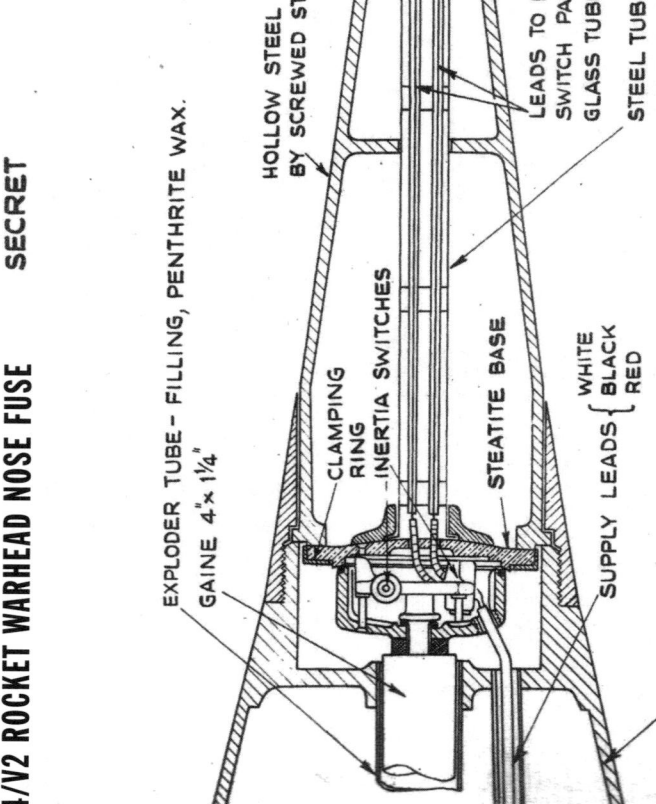

EL. REP. 1362
FIG. 1

SCALE:- HALF FULL SIZE.

GLASS INSULATION AND FAIRING.

COLLAPSIBLE METAL DOME FORMING NOSE SWITCH

HOLLOW STEEL NOSE HELD BY SCREWED STEEL RING.

LEADS TO NOSE SWITCH PASS THRO' GLASS TUBES.

STEEL TUBE CARRYING NOSE SWITCH LEADS.

EXPLODER TUBE – FILLING, PENTHRITE WAX.
GAINE 4" × 1¼"

CLAMPING RING

INERTIA SWITCHES

STEATITE BASE

SUPPLY LEADS { WHITE, BLACK, RED

WARHEAD 994 KG. AMATOL {60% T.N.T. 40% AMM. NIT.

APPENDIX 6

A4/V2 GLASS DETONATOR/NOSE SWITCH   SECRET

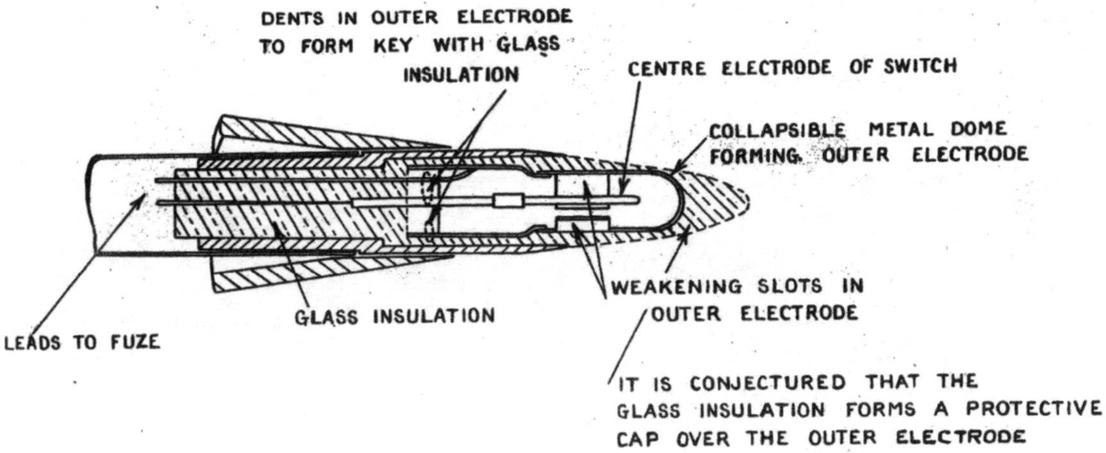

DENTS IN OUTER ELECTRODE
TO FORM KEY WITH GLASS
INSULATION

CENTRE ELECTRODE OF SWITCH

COLLAPSIBLE METAL DOME
FORMING OUTER ELECTRODE

WEAKENING SLOTS IN
OUTER ELECTRODE

IT IS CONJECTURED THAT THE
GLASS INSULATION FORMS A PROTECTIVE
CAP OVER THE OUTER ELECTRODE

SCALE:- FULL SIZE

GLASS INSULATION

LEADS TO FUZE

APPENDIX 7
ORGANIZATION OF *DIVISION* z.V.

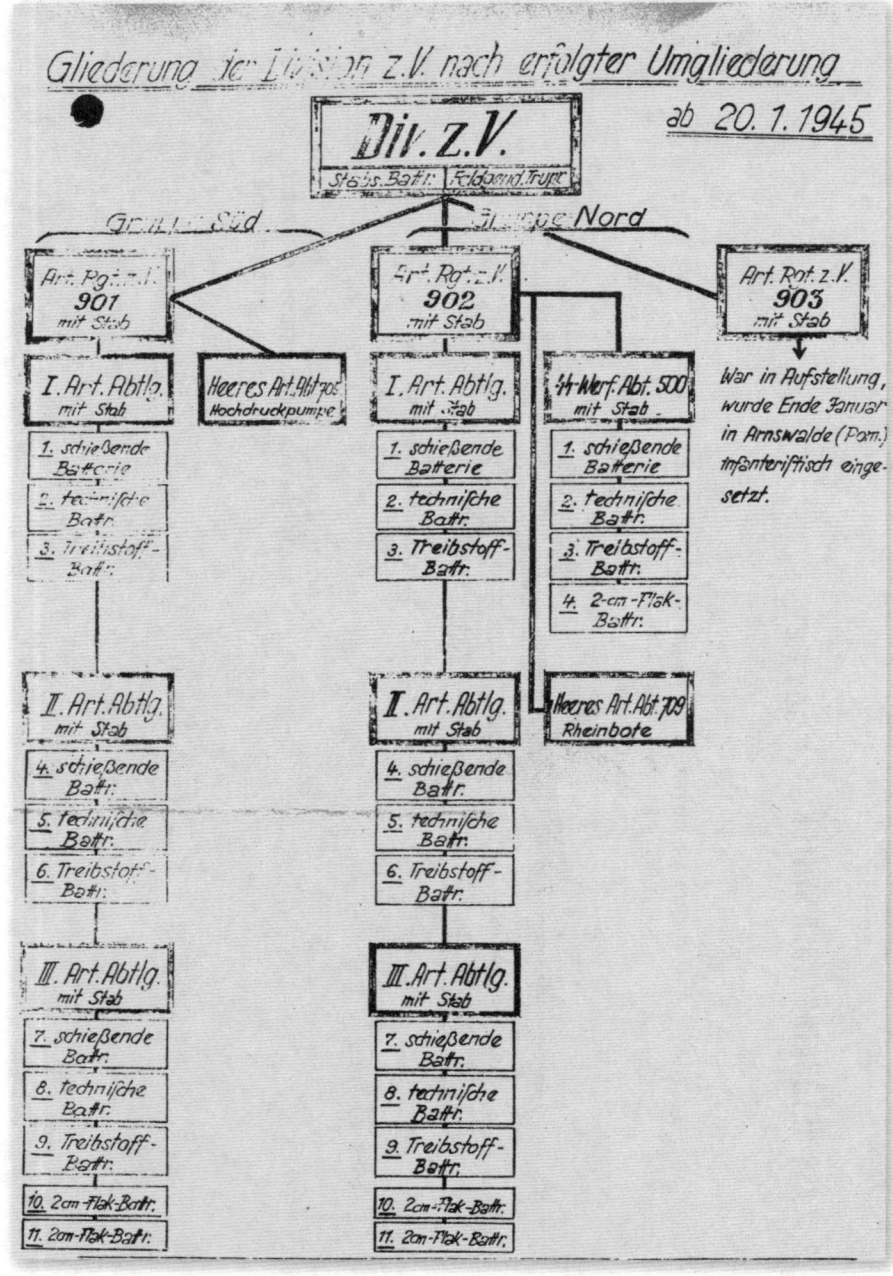

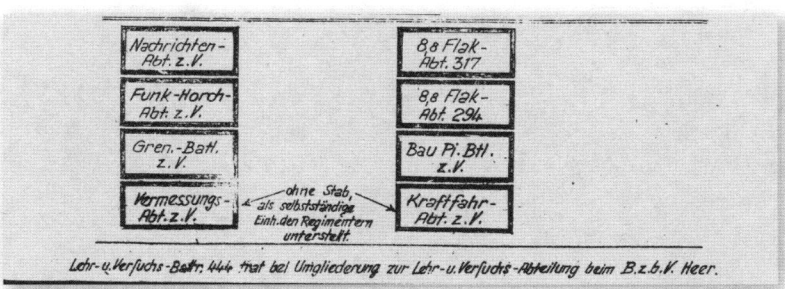

Nachrichten-Abt. z.V.
Funk-Horch-Abt. z.V.
Gren.-Batl. z.V.
Vermessungs-Abt. z.V.
8,8 Flak-Abt. 317
8,8 Flak-Abt. 294
Bau Pi. Btl. z.V.
Kraftfahr-Abt. z.V.
ohne Stab, als selbstständige Einh. den Regimentern unterstellt.
Lehr-u. Versuchs-Battr. 444 trat bei Umgliederung zur Lehr-u. Versuchs-Abteilung beim B.z.b.V. Heer.

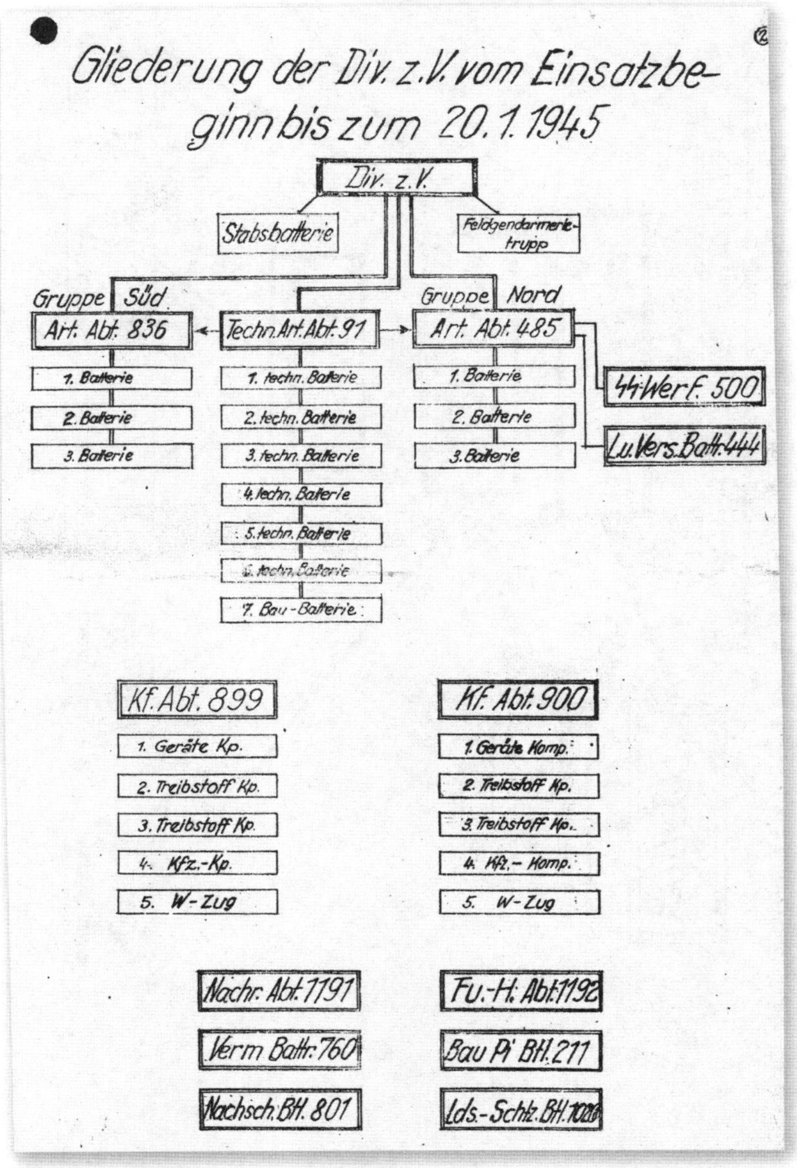

Gliederung der Div. z.V. vom Einsatzbeginn bis zum 20.1.1945
Div. z.V.
Stabsbatterie
Feldgendarmerie-trupp
Gruppe Süd
Art. Abt. 836
1. Batterie
2. Batterie
3. Batterie
Techn. Art. Abt. 91
1. techn. Batterie
2. techn. Batterie
3. techn. Batterie
4. techn. Batterie
5. techn. Batterie
6. techn. Batterie
7. Bau-Batterie
Gruppe Nord
Art. Abt. 485
1. Batterie
2. Batterie
3. Batterie
SS-Werf. 500
L.u.Vers. Battr. 444
Kf. Abt. 899
1. Geräte Kp.
2. Treibstoff Kp.
3. Treibstoff Kp.
4. Kfz.-Kp.
5. W-Zug
Kf. Abt. 900
1. Geräte Komp.
2. Treibstoff Kp.
3. Treibstoff Kp.
4. Kfz.-Komp.
5. W-Zug
Nachr. Abt. 1191
Fu.-H. Abt. 1192
Verm Battr. 760
Bau Pi Btl. 211
Nachsch. Btl. 801
Lds.-Schtz. Btl. 1020

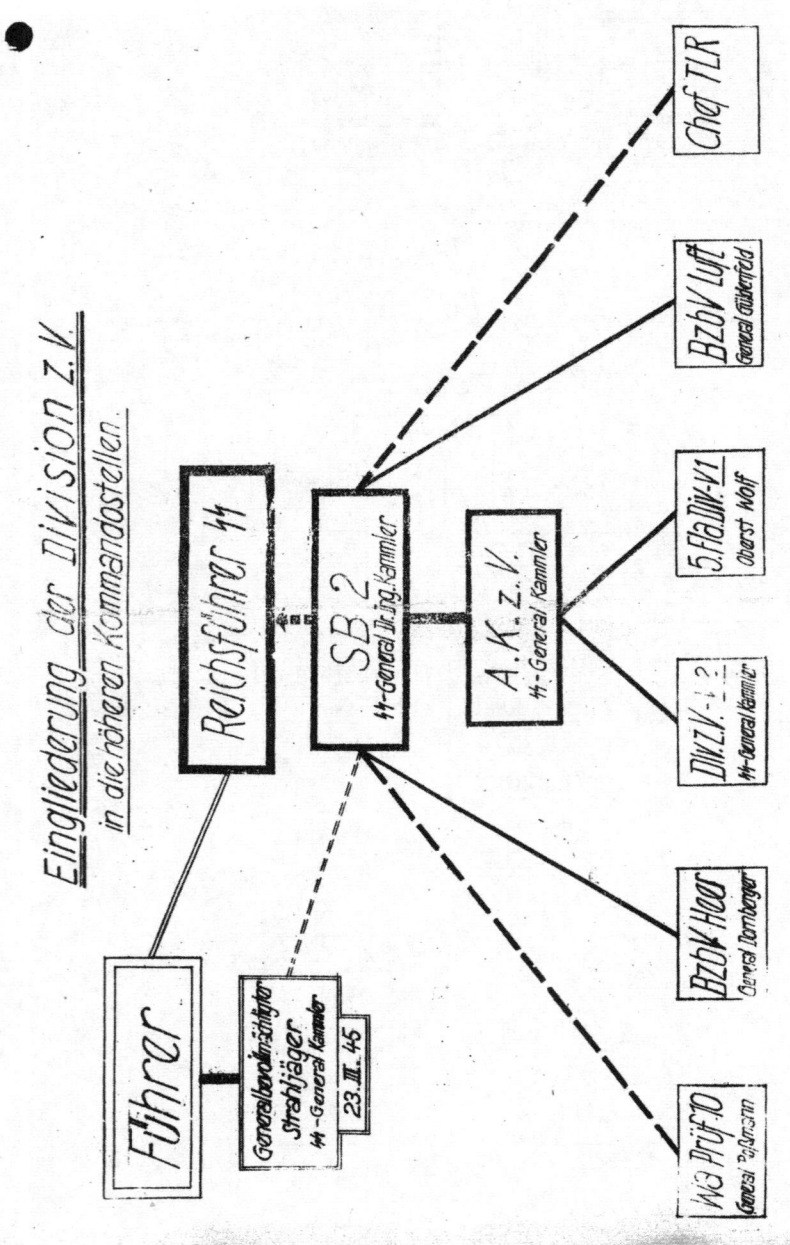

Eingliederung der Division z.V. in die höheren Kommandostellen.

APPENDIX 8
ORGANIZATION OF *FERNRAKETEN* BATTERY

KEY TO DIAGRAM ON FOLLOWING PAGE

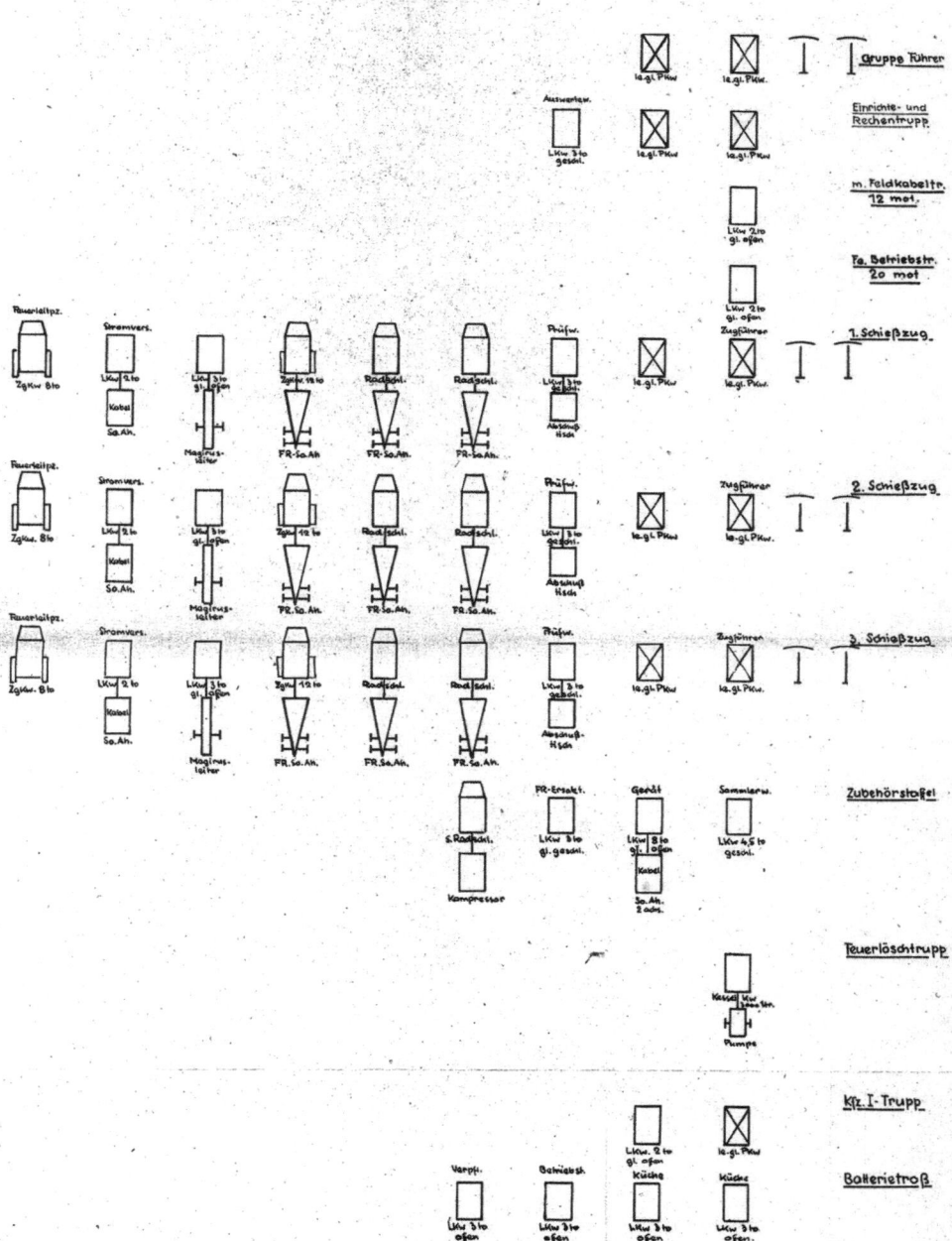

KEY TO DIAGRAM ON PAGE 259

Gruppe Führer	Group Leader
Einrichte- und Rechentrupp	Set-up and Computing Unit
m. Feldkabeltr. 12 mot.	Medium Field Cable Unit 12 mot.
	[Note:12 is a type code, mot. is motorized]
Fe.Betriebstr. 20 mot.	Telephone, Building and Operating Unit 20 mot.
1. Schießzug	1st Launch Platoon (plus Nos. 2. and 3)
Zubehörstaffel	Accessory Squadron
Feuerlöschtrupp	Fire Extinguisher Unit
Kfz.I-Trupp	Motor Transport Maintenance Unit
Batterietroß	Battery Baggage Unit [Field Kitchen etc.]
Auswertew.	Evaluation Vehicle
Feuerleitpz.	Fire Control Vehicle
Stromvers.	Power Supply
Prüfw.	Inspection Vehicle
Zugführer	Platoon Leader
FR-Ersatzt.	FR-supply parts
Gerät	equipment
Sammlerw.	Ferry vehicle ['hack']
Verpfl.	Food supply
Betriebst.	Works/Maintenance Unit
Küche	Kitchen
le. = leicht	light
gl. = geländegängig	cross-country
Pkw = Personenkraftwagen	Motor Car (normally max 5 persons)
Lkw = Lastkraftwagen	lorry
to	tons
geschl.	closed
offen	open
ZgKw 12 to	Towing Vehicle 12 tons
Radschl.	Wheeled Tractor
So.Ah.	Special Trailer
Magirus-leiter	Magirus Ladder
FR.So.Ah	FR Special Trailer [Meillerwagen]
Abschusstisch	launch table
So.Ah 2 achs.	Special Trailer with 2 axles
Kessel Kw 3000 ltr.	Boiler Vehicle 3000 litre
Pumpe	Pump
so: le.gl.Pkw	Light cross-country vehicle

APPENDIX 9

SURVEY OF V2 LAUNCH PROCEDURE FROM ARRIVAL OF ROCKET TRAIN TO LAUNCH

(BY *OBERSTLEUTNANT* WEBER, *VERSUCHSKOMMANDO ALTENWALDE* [AVKO])

Confidential

ALTENWALDE.
Experimental Station   5. September 1945

Survey of the Principal Operations
on the Rocket (V2) from the arrival of
Rocket train at Railhead until the launching
of the Rocket.

A field demonstration of the operations detailed below can be carried out by
the Versuchskommando ALTENWALDE after training of suitable personnel, on receipt
of supplies enumerated in the "Deficiency" column. Necessary transport is
required also, for rendering detachments mobile.

Serial No.	Operation	Requirements a) Personnel b) Materials	Troop employed	Deficiency a) Personnel b) Materials
1	Erection of the Strabo-crane at Railhead.	a) Transloading Section for Unloading at Railhead. 1 Section Commander (Sgt) 1 2 I/C (NCO) 1 Crane driver (Pte) 1 Crane mechanic (") 6 Crane personnel (") 1 Driver (") 1 Spare driver (") b) 1 Strabocrane, complete, with support for Rocket without war-head. 1 Wheeled tractor with cable winch 1 Electric Power Set 220/380V, 15 KVA	Technical Troop	a) See Intro-ductory note b) 1 Electric Power Set
2	Removing tarpaulin covers from rocket train.	a) Transloading Section as above b) ./.	Technical Troop	a) See Intro-ductory note b) ./.

-2-

Serial No.	Operation	Requirements a) Personnel b) Materials	Troop employed	Deficiency a) Personnel b) Materials
3	Transfer of Rocket to Vidalwagen.	a) Transloading Section as above, plus:= 1 driver of the Rocket Platoon of the Fuel and Rocket Troop and 1 spare driver b) in addition to requirement under serial No 1(b) 1 Vidalwagen 1 Wheeled tractor	Technical Troop and Fuel and Rocket Troop	a) See Introductory note b) 1 Vidalwagen
4	Moving rocket to the site of the Technical Troop.	a) As serial No 3 plus Sgt of the Transloading Sec of the Technical Troop as responsible for taking rocket over. b) 1 Vidal truck 1 Wheeled tractor	Fuel and Rocket Troop and Technical Troop	a) See Introductory note. b) as for Serial No.3.
		a) 1 Driver 1 spare Driver b) 1 Wheeled tractor 1 Test tent.	Technical Troop	a) See Introductory note b) 1 Test tent
		a) 1 Testing Section of the Technical troop, see Serial No.7. b) ./.	Technical Troop	a) See Introductory note b) ./.

-3-

Serial No.	Operation	Requirements a) Personnel b) Materials	Troop employed	Deficiency a) Personnel b) Materials
7	Overall funct-ional tests of the rocket while in a horizontal position, including general test (Generaldurchsch-altversuch)	a) Testing Section Section Commander (s/Sjt) NCO for Rocket motor " " Steering control " " Wireless and T-Geräte 4 men for Rocket motor (rank & File) 2 " " Rocket circuit (rank & file) 1 man for Steering Con-trols (rank & file) 1 man for Wireless (rank & file) 4 men for Electric Power and Transformer Sets 1 Compressor mechanic (Rank & file) 1 Clerk (" ") b) 1 Test truck, complete 1 Cable " " 1 Electric Power Set 220 /380V 15 KVA 1 Transformer Set 27V = 100 Amp 1 Compressor 230 atms. together with electrical measuring instruments, tools, and general eqpt	Technical Troop	a) See intro-ductory note b) 1 Test truck 1 Cable truck 1 Electric Power Set 1 Transformer Set
8	Repair of imperfect rocket by Repair Sec	a) 1 Repair Section 1 Sec Commander (Armd) 1 2 i/c (NCO) 5 Mechanics (men) 1 Turner (") 1 Welder (") 1 Aluminium welder (") 1 Electrician (") 1 Carpenter (") 1 Tail Removal Sec 1 Sec Commander (NCO) 5 Mechanics (men) b) 1 Wksp Lorry with compl-ete tools & machinery. 1 Test Tent 1 Electric Power Set 220 /380 V 6 KVA.	Technical Troop	a) See intro-ductory note b) 1 Workshop lorry 1 Test tent 1 Electric Power Set

-4-

Operation	Requirements a) Personnel b) Materials	Troop employed	Deficiency a) Personnel b) Materials
	1 Vane Test Box 2 Hot air blowers 1 Tail removal unit		
8A	Repair of imperfect rocket by Repair Sec	a) 1 Electrical spare parts Lorry. 1 Mechanical spare parts lorry.	Technical Troop	b) 1 Elec spare parts lorry 1 Mech spare parts lorry
8B	Putting cover on rocket found to be in working order, and moving rocket to warhead mntg point.	a) Testing Sec as Ser No 7. 1 Driver 1 spare driver b)1 Wheeled tractor	Technical Troop	a) See introductory note b) ./.
9	Mounting of warhead, installation of fuses, screwing in igniters and connection of Sterg unit.	a) Warhead mounting Sec 1 Sec Commander (TCO) 1 2 i/c (") 6 Mounters (men) b)1 Mounting block 2 Blocks and Tackle each 1 ton Tools for warhead mounting	Technical Troop	a) See introductory note b) Mountingblock 2Blocks and Tackle
10	Move to Meillerwagen Loading Point	a)1 Driver 1 spare driver b)1 Wheeled tractor	Technical Troop	a) See introductory note b) ./.
11	Transfer of rocket from Vidalwagen; to.., Meillerwagon; and, simultaneous receipt of launching eqpt by Launching Troop	a) Transloading Sec for Transfer of rocket from Tech to Launching Troop 1 Sec Commander (Sgt) 1 2 i/c (TCO) 1 Crane driver (man) 1 Crane mechanic (man) 6 Crane Personnel (man) 1 Driver (man) 1 spare driver (man) 1 Electrician from Charging Station b) Strabocrane complete with support for rocket with warhead. 1 Wheeled tractor with cable winch. 1 Charging lorry with heating apparatus 1 Meiller wagen	Technical Troop and Launching Troop	a) See introductory note b) 1 Strabo crane with support 1 Charging lorry with heating apparatus

-5-

Serial No.	Operation	Requirements a) Personnel b) Materials	Troop employed	Deficiency a) Personnel b) Materials

12	Move of Rocket from Technical Troop to launching point.	a) 1 Transport Sec
		   1 N.C.O.
		   1 Man
		   1 Driver
		
		b) 1 Meillerwagen
		   1 Tractor
			Launching Troop	a) see Introductory Note
				
				b) ./.

13	Driving rocket on to Launching Point, uncovering rocket erecting it, & placing it on launching platform	a) 1 Truck Sec
		   1 NCO
		   7 Men
		   1 Driver
		b) 1 Meillerwagen
		   1 Tractor
		   1 Launching platform
			Launching Troop	a) see Introductory note
				
				b) ./.

14	Levelling rocket in vertical position.	a) 1 Laying Sec
		   1 N.C.O.
		   2 Men
		   1 Truck Sec, as Serial No 13.
		
		b) 2 Collimators with stands
			Launching Troop	a) see Introductory note
				
				b) 2 Collimators with stands.

15	Opening rocket hatches, connecting electric cables and pnuematic leads to rocket.	a) 1 Rocket motor sec
		   1 N.C.O.
		   5 Men
		   1 Electrical Sec
		   1 N.C.O.
		   6 Men
		   1 Fire Control Sec
		   1 N.C.O.
		   2 Men
		   2 Switch - N.C.O's.
		
		b) Complete Ground installations
			Launching Troop	a) see Introductory Note
				
				b) 1 Relay Box, complete ground cables.
				1 Rocket motor Panel
				1 Steering Control Panel
				1 Vane Locator Battery
				1 Stotzplug Battery
				1 Control Battery

-6-

Serial No	Operation	Requirements a) Personnel b) Materials	Troop employed	Deficiency a) Personnel b) Materials
16	Rocket tests including general test	a) as for Serial No 15 b) as for Serial No 15	Launching Troop	a) see Introductory note b) as for Serial No 15
17	Driving fuelling trucks to Launching point. Fuelling of rocket with : B-Stoff(alcohol) A-Stoff(liquid oxygen) T-Stoff(Hydrogen Peroxide) Z-Stoff(Sodium Permanganate). Tankers depart.	a) 1 Rocket Motor Sec 1 N.C.O. 5 Men Fuelling party will be provided by Fuel & Rocket Troop 1 N.C.O. 7 Men. b) Fuelling trucks with accessories.	Launching Troop and Fuel & Rocket Troop	a) see introductory note b) 2 B-Stoff (Alcohol) tankers 1 T-Stoff (Hydrogen Peroxide) tanker, Indicator fluid for contents indicator.
18	Closing of hatches and departure of Meillerwagen.	a) 1 Rocket Motor Sec 1 N.C.O. 5 Men 1 Electrical Sec 1 N.C.O. 6 Men 1 Truck Section 1 N.C.O. 7 Men 1 Driver b) Meillerwagen Tractor	Launching Troop	a) see Introductory note b) ./.
19	Laying rocket	a) Rocket Motor Sec 1 N.C.O. 5 Men Laying Section 1 N.C.O. 2 Men b) 2 Collimators with stands 1 Director	Launching Troop	a) see Introductory note b) 2 Collimators with stands 1 Director

-7-

	Operation	Requirements a) Personnel b) Materials	Troop employed	Deficiency a) Personnel b) Materials
20	Final testing of rocket	a) as for Serial No 15 b) as for Serial No 15	Launching Troop	a) see Introductory note b) as for Serial No 15.
21	Clearing of Launching Position	Launching Platoon Commander	Launching Troop	./.
22	Launching of Rocket	a) Launching Platoon Commander 2 Switch N.C.O's b) as for Serial No. 15	Launching Troop	a) see Introductory note b) as for Serial No. 15

The following are at the disposal of the Launching Troop for supervision of work and assistance in the event of difficulties.

1 Chief Engineer
1 Rocket Motor Engineer
1 Electrical Engineer
1 Steering Control Engineer
1 Wireless Engineer

Draft signed

WEBER
Obstlt (Lieut-Col)

Checked by :

von CHLINGE'SPERG
Hptm. u. Abteilungsleiter

(Captain and Battery Commander)

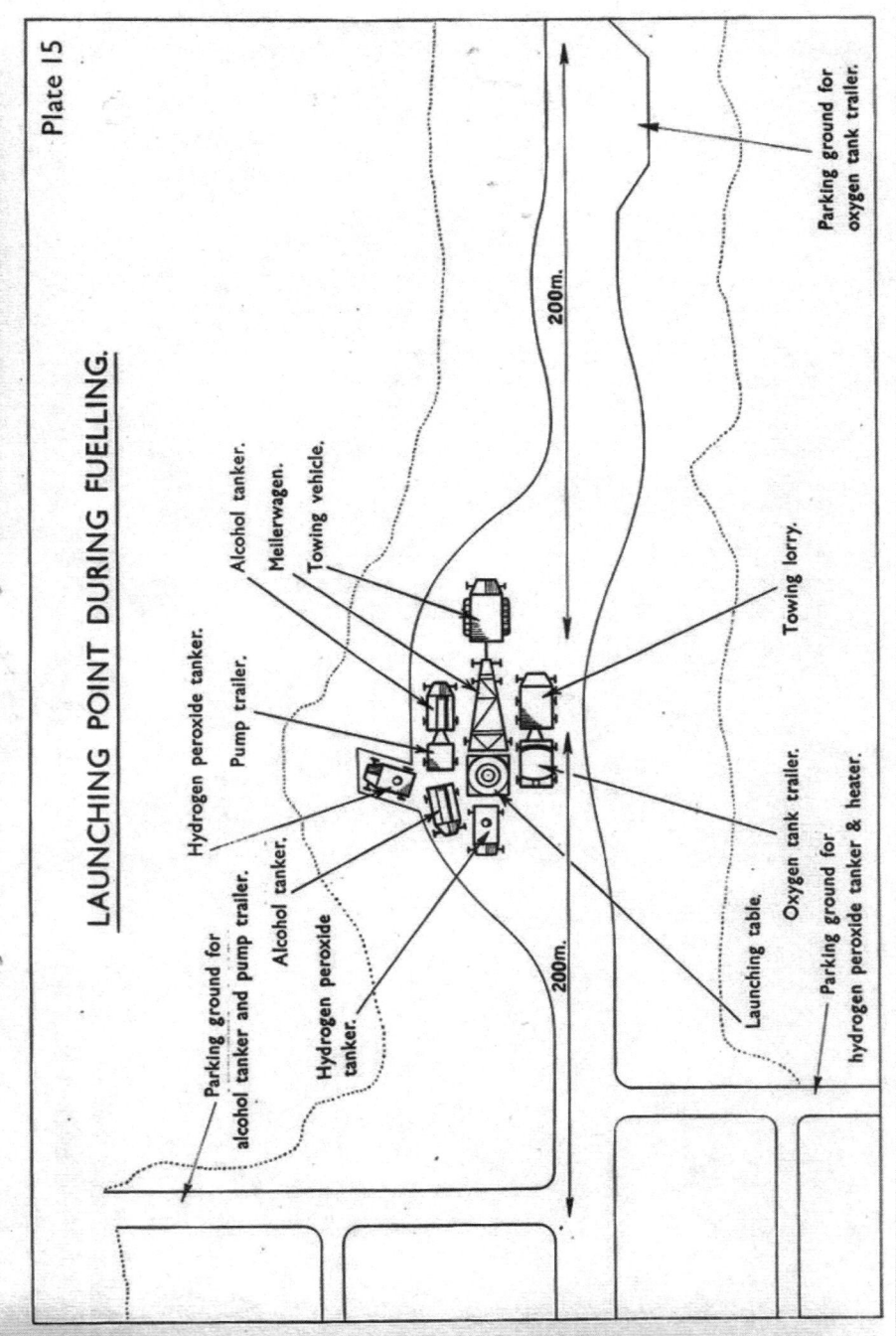

Plate 15

LAUNCHING POINT DURING FUELLING.

Alcohol tanker.
Meilerwagen.
Towing vehicle.

Hydrogen peroxide tanker.
Pump trailer.

Alcohol tanker.

Hydrogen peroxide tanker.

Parking ground for alcohol tanker and pump trailer.

Launching table.

Oxygen tank trailer.

Towing lorry.

Parking ground for hydrogen peroxide tanker & heater.

Parking ground for oxygen tank trailer.

200 m.

200 m.

Typical layout of service vehicles distributed around the V2 during the fuelling process. Operation Backfire, October 1945.

APPENDIX 11

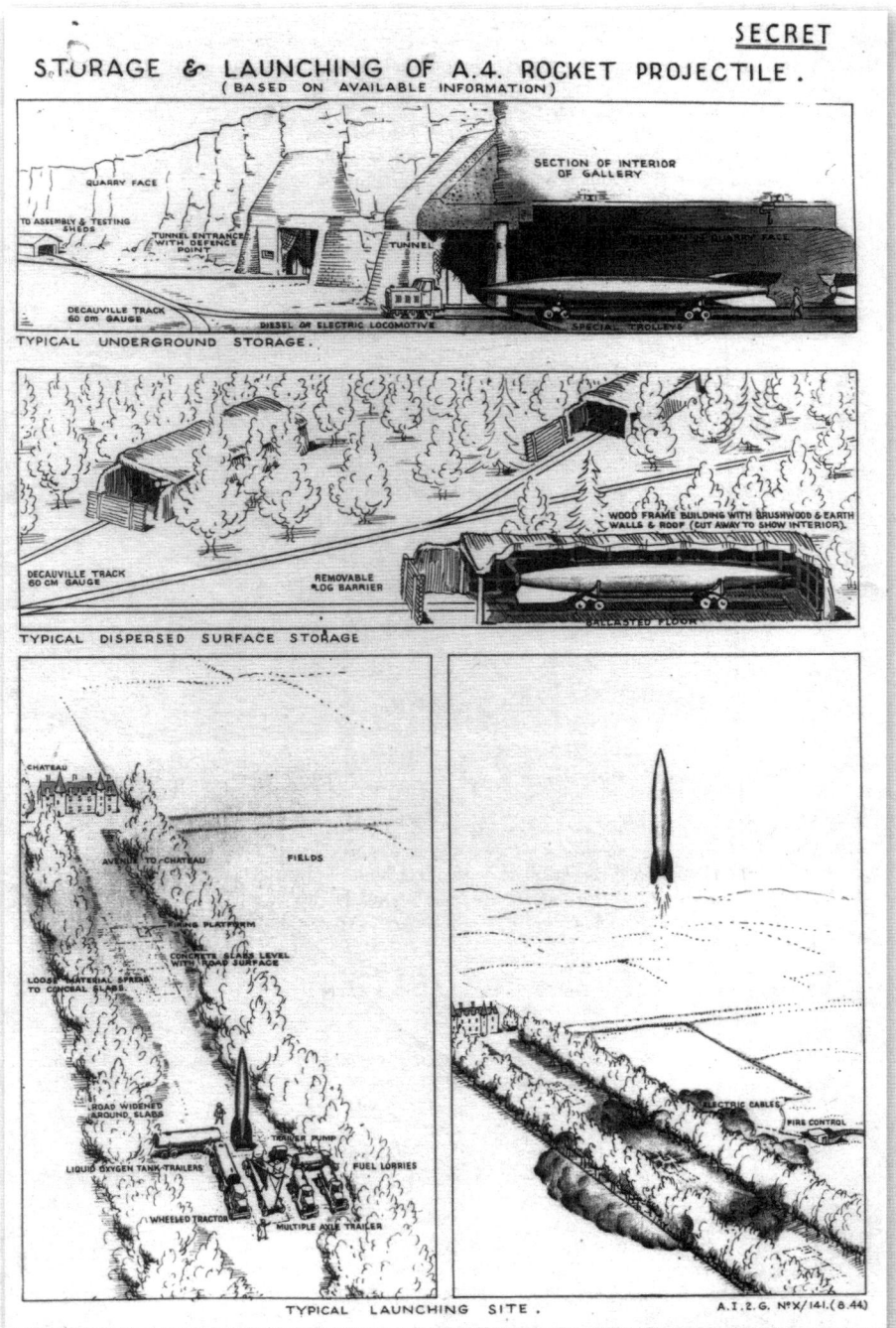

A pictorial representation of the storage and firing of a V2 Rocket drafted by British Air Intelligence prior to the start of Operation Pinguin and based upon information then available. August, 1944.

CHAPTER NOTES

CHAPTER ONE

1. '*Recollections of Childhood – Early Experiences in Rocketry as told by Wernher Von Braun 1963* [sic]', NASA Marshall Space Flight Center History Office, Hunstville, Alabama, USA
2. Ibid.
3. Konrad Dannenberg, correspondence.
4. Conquest of Space – 1959 interview, Wernher von Braun and Willy Ley.
5. *V2*, Major-General Walter Dornberger, Scientific Book Club, 1952.
6. Conquest of Space – 1959 interview, Wernher von Braun and Willy Ley.
7. Ibid.
8. Ibid.
9. Konrad Dannenberg (with permission) from *Aviation Week & Space Technology*, March 24, 2003.

CHAPTER TWO

1. UKNA/AVIA 13/1149: *Examination of Big Ben (V2 Rocket) Equipment.*
2. UKNA/AIR 37/1167: SHAEF (Main and Rear): *German "emergency development" programme, 1944-1945.*
3. UKNA/AIR 37/1253, SHAEF (Main and Rear): *H.Q. 2nd T.A.F.: Air Technical Intelligence Reports.*
4. UKNA/AVIA 13/1149.
5. via Dr. Frenk.
6. UKNA/AVIA 13/1149.
7. *Gerätebeschreibung A4, Baureihe B.* Reisig, Gerhard, Deutsches Museum.
8. UKNA/AIR 37/1167.
9. Cor Lulof, IV2RG, correspondence.
10. *Gerätebeschreibung A4, Baureihe B.* Reisig, Gerhard, Deutsches Museum.
11. UKNA/AIR 20/4137: *German A.4 Rocket Organisation: Operational Aspects, July-August 1945.*
12. UKNA/WO 231/22 and 23: *Backfire* Report.
13. UKNA/AIR 37/1167.
14. UKNA/AIR 37/1253.
15. UKNA/AIR 20/4137.
16. UKNA/WO 231/22 and 23.
17. Ibid.
18. UKNA/AIR 20/4137.

CHAPTER THREE

1. UKNA/DEFE 40/22, *The German Long Range Rocket. War Office MI4-14,* 30 October 1945.
2. IWM, AL 1552, *The Employment of V-Weapons by the Germans in World War II*, Lieut. M.C. Helfers, Office of the Chief of Military History, Department of the Army, 1954.
3. *V2*, Major-General Walter Dornberger, Scientific Book Club, 1952.
4. V-*Missiles of the Third Reich*, Dieter Hölsken, Monogram Aviation Publications. 1994.
5. UKNA/DEFE 40/22.
6. John Pridige, IV2RG, correspondence.
7. *V2*, Major-General Walter Dornberger, Scientific Book Club, 1952.
8. Ibid.
9. Ibid.
10. *The Business of Genocide (The SS, Slave Labor, and the Concentration Camps)*, Michael Thad Allen, The University of North Carolina Press, 2002.
11. *The Case for Auschwitz*, Robert Jan Pelt, Indiana University Press, 2002.
12. *V2*, Major-General Walter Dornberger, Scientific Book Club, 1952.
13. *Der Schuss in Weltall*, Walter Dornberger, Esslingen, 1952, page 258.
14. *V2: A Combat History of the First Ballistic Missile,* Tracy D. Dungan. Westholme Publishing, 2005.
15. Ibid.
16. UKNA/DEFE 40/22.
17. IWM, F.1 AL 1552, *The Employment of V-Weapons by the Germans in World War II*, Lieut. M.C. Helfers, Office of the Chief of Military History, Department of the Army, 1954.
18. WO 208/3155, *V2 Organisation, War Establishment and Supplies: Information Obtained from German POWs.* September 1945.
19. UKNA/DEFE 40/22.

20. Ibid.
21. Ibid.
22. Ibid.
23. Ibid.

CHAPTER FOUR

1. *German Railroad Guns in Action*, Joachim Engelmann, Squadron/Signal Publications, Armor Number 15, 1976.
2. *The JG 26 War Diary*, Volume One 1939-1942, Donald Caldwell, Grub Street, 1996.
3. Jiří (Jirzy) Komprda, IV2RG, (www.jirzy.webzdarma.cz).
4. *Ultimate Sound Pressure Level Decibel Table*, William Hamby, 2004.
5. *V2*, Major-General Walter Dornberger, Scientific Book Club, 1952.
6. Wernher von Braun interview recollection, NOVA PBS television program '*Hitler's Secret Weapon*' first broadcast, 5 January 1977.
7. *The Peenemünde Raid*, Martin Middlebrook, Allen Lane, Penguin Books Ltd., 1982.
8. *Das nationalsozialistische Lagersystem,* Anne Kaiser and Ursula Krause-Schmitt, VKA-Buchladen und Versand, 2000.
9. *Conquest of Space* – 1959 interview, Wernher von Braun and Willy Ley.
10. *Peenemünde to Canaveral*, Dieter K. Huzel, Prentice-Hall Inc., 1962.
11. UKNA/WO33/2554: *Report on Operation Backfire: Vol 1 Scope and Organisation of Operation*. 1946.
12. *The Rocket Team* Frederick I Ordway III, Mitchell R. Sharpe, Thomas Y. Crowell, 1979.

CHAPTER FIVE

1. *V-Missiles of the Third Reich*, Dieter Hölsken, Monogram Aviation Publications, 1994.
2. *The Peenemünde Raid*, Martin Middlebrook, Allen Lane, Penguin Books Ltd., 1982.
3. *V2, A Combat History of the First Ballistic Missile,* Tracy D. Dungan. Westholme Publishing, 2005.
4. The Fondation pour la Mémoire de la Déportation, Paris. Cyrille Le Quellec. This organization also holds correspondence written by Maurice Moreau, February 1967 to 'Le Chef du Bureau des Indemnisations et de la Documentation.'
5. Vernichtung, Auftrag und Vollendung. *Heimatverein Rehmsdorf e. V. Lothar Czoßek.*

CHAPTER SIX

1. MCI is German rail nomenclature for indicating weight and length and that the passenger coach is based upon a freight van design. M: Behelfswagen, Mannschaftswagen (substitute carriages) C: Wagen 3. Klasse (carriages 3rd class) I: Durchgang und offene Übergänge (open connections between the carriages).
2. *Obersturmführer* = SS Senior Assault [or Storm] Leader (British/US = First Lieutenant).
3. BA–MA Freiburg: RH 8 / 1278. *Abteilung für Sondergerät und Heeresversuchsanstalt Peenemünde.*
4. BA–MA Freiburg: RH 26-1022-3, *Kriegstagebuch (Nr. 1 und 2) Division z. V. Tätigkeitsberichte der Abteilungen Ia tech., Ia Meß, Ic/III , IIa/b, III, IVa, IVb, V. Sept. 1944 - April 1945.*
5. It is possible that this event took place at an earlier date at Peenemünde.
6. UKNA/FO1031/128. *Brief Interrogation Report on Prof. Dr. Wernher von Braun*, July 1947.
7. V2 Firing Time Line, Tracy Dungan et al.
8. Ibid.
9. Arthur O. Bauer, Foundation Centre for German Communication and Related Technology, The Netherlands.
10. Zena Stein, *Famine and Human Development: Dutch Hunger Winter of 1944-45*, 1975.
11. Jos Borsboom and Paul Waayers correspondence.
12. V2 Firing Time Line, Tracy Dungan et al.
13. Jos Borsboom and Mart Keuning.
14. Ibid.
15. Henk Koopman, IV2RG, correspondence. *Police Report Municipality of Wassenaar*, dated September 28, 1945 Nr. 817.
16. Foot, M.R.D., *SOE in the Low Countries*, 2001.
17. BA–MA Freiburg: RH26 1022/6. *Verschußmeldungen, Verschußnachweise Division z. V. Sept.* 1944-Jan. 1945. In spite of the poor condition of this document, the following information is known of the V2s fired on New Year's Eve just prior to midnight 1944 by *Batterie* 444: Rocket 20881, Firing site number 77 and Rocket 20880, Firing site number 74. Both entries recorded as *Früh Zerleger* ('air-bursters').

18. V2 Firing Time Line, Tracy Dungan et al.
19. BA–MA Freiburg: RH 26–1022-3, *Kriegstagebuch (Nr. 1 und 2) Division z. V. Tätigkeitsberichte der Abteilungen Ia tech., Ia Meß, Ic/III , IIa/b, III, IVa, IVb, V.* Sept. 1944 – April 1945.
20. Ibid.
21. Walter Naasner, *SS-wirtschaft und SS-verwaltung,* Droste. 1998.

CHAPTER SEVEN

1. *V2,* Major–General Walter Dornberger, 1954.
2. Via Henk Koopman, IV2RG and Mart Keuning, correspondence.
3. V2 Firing Time Line, Tracy Dungan et al.

CHAPTER EIGHT

1. Confusingly, due to the style of German handwriting popular during the first half of the last century and the similarity of capital characters, the 'I-*Gerät*' was sometimes referred to as the 'J-*Gerät*'.
2. UKNA AIR 40/2517, *Blizna (Poland) Experimental Station. 1944.*
3. Ibid.
4. UKNA DEFE 40/18, *German rocket development: report on test firings in Poland. 1944.*
5. Bundesarchiv- Militärarchiv, Freiburg: RH 26–1022-3, *Kriegstagebuch (Nr. 1 und 2) Division z. V. Tätigkeitsberichte der Abteilungen Ia tech., Ia Meß, Ic/III , IIa/b, III, IVa, IVb, V.* Sept. 1944 – April 1945.
6. Vincent Milano, *Wehrmacht Brothels* at *Der Erste Zug. A Heer Living History Organization* see www.dererstezug.com
7. Harvard University Library, Open Collection Program, Contagion, Historical Views of Diseases and Epidemics, Syphilis
8. *V2, A Combat History of the First Ballistic Missile,* Tracy D. Dungan. Westholme Publishing, 2005.
9. BA–MA/RH 26–1022-3
10. Cornelie Jochems, Duindigt, Wassenaar.
11. Tracy D. Dungan, IV2RG, correspondence.

CHAPTER NINE

1. *Feld-Hell* system, Murray Greenman: internet resource.http://www.qsl.net/zl1bpu/HELL/Feld.htm
2. *The Rise and Fall of the Luftwaffe – The Life of Field Marshall Erhard Milch,* David Irving, Futura Publications, 1976.
3. *The Rocket and the Reich: Peenemunde and the Coming of the Ballistic Missile Era,* Michael Neufeld), Simon and Schuster, 1994.

CHAPTER TEN

1. UKNA/WO208/4292: CSDIC – German rocket operations: information obtained from interrogation of enemy POWs.
2. IWM: F.1 MI 14/864V, *Art. Abteilung 836. (mot.) (Art. Regt. (mot.) z. V. 901) War Diary,* 5.9.44 – 7.4.45.
3. UKNA/WO208/4292.
4. Michel Baert and Gilles Bouillon, National Museum of Military History (Belgium) and Association (Belgo-Luxembourgeoise) des Musées de la Bataille des Ardennes.
5. V2 Firing Time Line, Tracy Dungan et al.
6. Ibid.
7. *V2 gefrorene Blitze. Einsatzgeschichte der V2 aus Eifel, Hunsrück und Westerwald 1944/45,* Wolfgang Gückelhorn, Detlev Paul. Helios Verlag, 2007.
8. Frau Priebe: Interview, summer 2007.
9. Ibid.
10. Ibid.
11. Ibid.

CHAPTER ELEVEN

1. *The Fire: The Bombing of Germany, 1940-1945,* Jörg Friedrich, Columbia University Press, 2006.
2. *V2 Firing Time Line,* Tracy Dungan et al.
3. John Pridige, IV2RG, correspondence.
4. UKNA/AIR 37/1253 *SHAEF (MAIN AND REAR): H.Q. 2nd T.A.F.: Air Technical Intelligence Reports.*
5. John Pridige, IV2RG, correspondence.
6. BA-MA Freiburg: RH 41-1195, *Anlagen zum Kriegstagebuch Band 2:* 1945.

CHAPTER TWELVE

1. Dr. David Lee, Holsworthy Medical Centre, Devon.
2. Bundesarchiv-Militärarchiv, Freiburg, RH 41/1192: *Kriegstagebuch Art.Abt. (mot.) 836 / Art.Rgt. z.V. 901. 6.9.43 - 8.4.1945.* via correspondence with John Pridige.
3. RAF History Bomber Command. http://www.raf.mod.uk/bombercommand/apr45.html
4. Rudolph J. Rummel, Center for National Security Law, University of Virginia. Published work, '*Statistics of Democide*', 1997.
5. *Personelle Verluste der deutschen Bevölkerung durcht Flucht und Vertreibung,* Rüdiger Overmans, 1995 and *The Expulsion of 'German' Communities from Eastern Europe at the end of the Second World War,* Steffen Prauser and Arfon Rees, European University Institute, Florence.

CHAPTER THIRTEEN

1. *Raketenforschung in Deutschland: Wie die Menschen das All eroberten* Gerhard H. R. Reisig.
2. UKNA/DEFE 40/22. *The German Long Range Rocket.* War Office MI4-14, 30 October 1945. Unknown author. This document refers extensively to the history and activities of *Art.Ers.Abt.* 271.
3. Bundesarchiv-Militärarchiv, Freiburg. RH 26-1022-3, *Kriegstagebuch (Nr. 1 und 2) Division z.V. Tätigkeitsberichte der Abteilungen Ia tech., Ia Meß, Ic/III , IIa/b, III, IVa, IVb, V. Sept. 1944 - April 1945.*
4. Michel van Best, IV2RG, correspondence.
5. Patrick Clancey and David Newton of the HyperWar Foundation.
6. Reverend Douglas McRoberts, transcript and Love's early flying career.
7. Source, Dr. Helmuth Frenk.
8. Via Sergeant Graham Galloway (RAF), serving Bomb Disposal Expert and Instructor.
9. UKNA WO205/41 War Office: 21 Army Group: Military Headquarters, *Operation Crossbow: radar counter-measures, civil defence in the United Kingdom against V2 rockets and lessons learnt.*
10. Reverend Douglas McRoberts, correspondence.
11. Jack Love, correspondence.
12. Reverend Douglas McRoberts, correspondence.
13. Ibid.
14. Jack Love, correspondence.

CHAPTER FOURTEEN

1. Bert Koopman. IV2RG, correspondence.
2. UKNA/WO208/3155: *V2 Organisation, War Establishment and Supplies: Information Obtained from German POWs.* Hauptmann G. Salomon, *Art. Abt.* 2./485 (*mot.*), September 1945.
3. *En Nooit Was Het Stil...,* Kroniek Van Een Luchtoorlog. Gerrit J. Zwanenburg. Koninklijke Luchtmacht, 1990.
4. Henk Koopman. IV2RG, correspondence.
5. Ibid.
6. Arthur O. Bauer, Foundation Centre for German Communication and Related Technology, The Netherlands, correspondence.
7. UKNA/AIR 27/1893: Operations Record Book, 453 Squadron, R.A.A.F.
8. V2 Firing Time Line, Tracy Dungan *et al.*
9. *V2, A Combat History of the First Ballistic Missile,* Tracy D. Dungan. Westholme Publishing, 2005.

SOURCES AND BIBLIOGRAPHY

Various author interviews and correspondence with:
Raymond Baxter, OBE
Stefan Blomberg
Konrad Dannenberg
Helmut Fredenhagen
Helmuth Frenk
Eduard Jericha
Heinz Junker
Walter Klein
Fritz Meibert
Wilhelm Priebe
Oswald Schneider
Franz Stolle
Heinz Wunderlich

Bundesarchiv – Militärarchiv, Freiburg (BA–MA)
RH 8 / 1278: *Abteilung für Sondergerät und Heeresversuchsanstalt Peenemünde*
RH 26-1022-3: *Kriegstagebuch (Nr. 1 und 2) Division z.V. Tätigkeitsberichte der Abteilungen Ia tech., Ia Meß,*
     Ic/III , IIa/b, III, IVa, IVb, V. Sept. 1944 - April 1945
RH26 1022/6: *Verschußmeldungen, Verschußnachweise Division z.V. Sept. 1944 - Jan. 1945*
RH 41/1192: *Kriegstagebuch Art.Abt.(mot.) 836 / Art.Rgt. z.V. 901. 6.9.43 - 8.4.1945*
RH 41-1195: *Anlagen zum Kriegstagebuch Band 2: 1945*

UK National Archives (UKNA), Kew, London
AIR16/925: *German flying bomb and rocket offensives: air operations by ADGB and Fighter Command,*
     1944 - 1945
AIR 20/4137: *German A.4 Rocket Organisation: Operational Aspects, July-August 1945*
AIR20/9200: *V Weapons: Rockets (Code 97/1): Production and disposition of German A4 (V2) rockets: study*
     by USAF
AIR27/1893: Operations Record Book, 453 Squadron, R.A.A.F. July 1941–May 1945
AIR37/657: *2nd Tactical Air Force: Anti-'Big Ben' organisation*
AIR37/1167: SHAEF (MAIN AND REAR): *German 'emergency development' programme, 1944 - 1945*
AIR37/1253: SHAEF (Main and rear): *H.Q. 2nd T.A.F.: Air Technical Intelligence Reports*
AIR40/1676: *Work of the G.A.F. experimental station at Peenemunde - Karlshagen in the field of guided*
     projectiles: organisation and history, II technical A.I.D.(K) reports 413 & 415/1945
AIR40/1692: *German long range rocket: programme of investigation*
AIR40/2114: *German activity including long range rocket and flying bomb sites and attacks: Crossbow weekly*
     and special reports by A.I.1(h), January – May 1945
AIR40/2517: *Blizna (Poland) Experimental Station. Includes 48 photographs depicting: 'Crossbow' sites,*
     interpretation reports: Blizne, Poland (aerial mosaics). 1944
AIR40/2541: *V2 rocket, transporter and associated equipment, 1945*
AVIA13/1149: *Examination of Big Ben (V2 Rocket) Equipment*
DEFE40/22: *The German Long Range Rocket. War Office MI4-14, 30 October 1945.* [Unknown author].
HS7/161: *Clandestine activity in Netherlands; Dutch investigation report; evaluation of SOE activities*
     in Netherlands
HS 8/302: *CROSSBOW: use of resistance groups, 1944 - 1945*
WO33/2554: *Report on Operation Backfire: Vol 1 Scope and Organisation of Operation. 1946*
WO205/41: War Office: *21 Army Group: Military Headquarters, Operation Crossbow: radar counter-measures,*
     civil defence in the United Kingdom against V2 rockets and lessons learnt. June-October 1944
WO208/3155: *V2 Organisation, War Establishment and Supplies: Information Obtained from German POWs.*
     September 1945

WO208/4292: CSDIC *German rocket operations: information obtained from interrogation of enemy POWs. 1943-1946*

WO291/871: *Location of rocket launching sites: army ground equipment, 1945*

WO219/1975: *Movements of German divisions into the battle area, with maps, July - September 1944*

WO219/4929: *Operation Crossbow: outline of the organisation of German long range rocket forces, intelligence and operational reports, November 1944 – April 1945*

Imperial War Museum, London (IWM)

F.1 MI 14/832V: File of V2 Procedure

F.1 MI 14/864V: Art. Abteilung 836. (mot.) (Art.Regt. (mot.) z.V. 901) *War Diary*, 5.9.44 – 7.4.45

F.1 MI 14/870V: I. Abt./ Art.Regt. 902 (mot.) *War Diary*, 19.9.44 – 1.4.45

F.1 MI 14/873V: III. Abt./ Art.Regt. 902 (mot.) *War Diary*, 12.10.44 – 15.4.45

F.1 MI 14/874V: II. Abt./ Art.Regt. 902 (mot.) *War Diary*, 2 – 15.2.45

F.1 AL 1552, *The Employment of V-Weapons by the Germans in World War II*, Lieut. M.C. Helfers, Office of the Chief of Military History, Department of the Army, 1954

Magazines and Journals

The V-Weapons, After the Battle, Number 6, 1974

The Peenemünde Rocket Centre, After the Battle, Number 74, 1991

Nordhausen, After the Battle, Number 101, 1998

Dannenberg, Konrad, *Present at the Creation, Aviation Week & Space Technology*, March 24, 2003

Engelmann Joachim, *German Railroad Guns in Action*, Squadron/Signal Publications, Armor Number 15, 1976

Books

Allen, Michael Thad, *The Business of Genocide (The SS, Slave Labor, and the Concentration Camps)*, The University of North Carolina Press, 2002

Baxter, Raymond, (Collaboration, Dron, Tony), *Tales of My Time*, Grub Street. 2005

Cabell, Craig and Thomas, Graham A. *Operation Big Ben, The Anti-V2 Spitfire Missions 1944-45*, Spellmount, 2004

Caiden, Martin, *Rockets Beyond Earth*, Arco Publishers Ltd., 1955

Caldwell, David, *The JG 26 War Diary*, Volume One 1939-1942, Grub Street, 1996

Collier, Basil, *The Battle of the V-Weapons 1944 - 45*, The Elmfield Press, 1976

Czossek, Lothar, Vernichtung, Auftrag und Vollendung. *Nachtrag zur Ausgabe Dezember 1997: Documentation über das Aussenlager Rehmsdorf des KZ Buchenwald*, Heimatverein Rehmsdorf, 2005

Davis, Brian L. *Flags of the Third Reich*, Osprey History, 2000

Davis, Brian L. *German Army Uniforms and Insignia 1933 - 1945*, Military Book Society, 1971

Dornberger, Walter (Major-General), *V2*, The Scientific Book Club, 1954

Dungan, Tracy D., *V2, A Combat History of the First Ballistic Missile*, Westholme Publishing, 2005

Engelmann, Joachim, *V2, Dawn of the Rocket Age*, Schiffer Military History, 1990

Foot, M.R.D., *SOE in the Low Countries*, St Ermin's Press, 2001

Friedrich, Jörg, *The Fire: The Bombing of Germany, 1940-1945*, Columbia University Press, 2006

Gückelhorn, Wolfgang and Paul, Detlev. *V2 gefrorene Blitze: Einsatzgeschichte der V2 aus Eifel, Hunsrück und Westerwald 1944/45*, Helios Verlag, 2007

Hölsken, Dieter, *V-Missiles of the Third Reich*, Monogram Aviation Publications, 1994

Huzel, Dieter K., *Peenemünde to Canaveral*, Prentice-Hall Inc., 1962

Irving, David, *The Rise and Fall of the Luftwaffe – The Life of Field Marshall Erhard Milch*, Futura Publications, 1976

Jones, R.V, *Most Secret War, British Scientific Intelligence, 1939 - 1945*, Hamish Hamilton, 1978

Kaiser, Anne and Krause-Schmitt, Ursula, *Das nationalsozialistische Lagersystem* VKA–Buchladen und Versand, 2000

King, Benjamin and Kutta, Timothy, *IMPACT, The History of Germany's V-Weapons in World War II*, Sarpedon, 1998

Middlebrook, Martin, *The Peenemünde Raid*, Allen Lane, Penguin Books Ltd., 1982
Naasner, Walter, *SS-wirtschaft und SS-verwaltung*, Droste. 1998
Neufeld, Michael, *The Rocket and the Reich: Peenemunde and the Coming of the Ballistic Missile Era*, Simon and Schuster, 1994
Ogley, Bob, *Doodlebugs and Rockets – The Battle of the Flying Bombs*, Froglets Publications, 1992
Ordway III, Frederick I. and Sharpe, Mitchell R. *The Rocket Team*, Thomas Y. Crowell, 1979
Overmans, Rüdiger, *Personelle Verluste der deutschen Bevolkerung durcht Flucht und Vertreibung* (with Polish translation), Dzieje Najnowsze. 1994
Payne, L.G.S. (Air Commodore), *Air Dates*, Heinnemann, 1957
Pelt, Robert Jan, *The Case for Auschwitz*, Indiana University Press, 2002
Porezag, Karsten, *Geheime Kommandosache*, Verlag Wetzlardruck GmbH, 1997
Prauser, Steffen and Rees, Arfon, *The Expulsion of 'German' Communities from Eastern Europe at the End of the Second World War*, European University Institute, Florense, 2004
Reisig, Gerhard, *Raketenforschung in Deutschland: Wie die Menschen das All eroberten*, Wissenschaft & Technik Verlag. 1997
Rummel, Rudolph J. *'Statistics of Democide'*, Lit Verlag; annotated edition, 1998
Stein, Zena, *Famine and Human Development: Dutch Hunger Winter of 1944-45*, Oxford Medicine Publications, 1975
Whiting, Charles, *'45, The Final Drive from the Rhine to the Baltic*, Guild Publishing, 1985
Wood, Tony and Gunston, Bill, *Hitler's Luftwaffe, A Pictorial History and Technical Encyclopedia of Hitler's Air Power in World War II*, Crescent Books, 1978
Zwanenburg, Gerrit J., *En Nooit Was Het Stil... Kroniek Van Een Luchtoorlog. Deel 2: Luchtaanvallen Op Doelen in En om Nederlan*, Koninklijke Luchtmacht, 1990

Websites and other Sources
Von Braun, Wernher and Ley, Willy, *Conquest of Space* [1959 interview]
www Dungan, Tracy T. D., The A4 / V2 Resource Site (www.v2rocket.com)
www.v2rocket.com/start/others/part_1_society_for_space_travel.mp3
www.v2rocket.com/start/others/part_2_peenemunde.mp3
www.v2rocket.com/start/others/part_3_future.mp3
Timeline for V-2 attacks, 1944-45: Extracts from *Hitler's Geheimwaffen im Westerwald* by Dr. U. Jungbluth: Complied by Charles Ostyn, Henk Koopman, John Pridige, Detlev Paul, Wolfgang Gückelhorn, Robert Collis, Mike Grube, Laurent Bailleul, Ed Straten and Rudi Velthuis: www.v2rocket.com/start/deployment/timeline.html
Von Braun, Wernher, *Recollections of Childhood – Early Experiences in Rocketry. 1963* [sic], NASA Marshall Space Flight Center History Office: (history.msfc.nasa.gov/vonbraun/index.html)
Komprda Jiří (Jirzy): Information related to A4 test footage filmed at Peenemünde and other locations (www.jirzy.webzdarma.cz)
Oehler, Pat and Bocek, Jon, Der Erste Zug. *A Heer Living History Organization* (www.dererstezug.com)
Greenman, Murray, *Feld-Hell* system. (www.qsl.net/zl1bpu/HELL/Feld.htm)
Clancey, Patrick & Newton, David. HyperWar Foundation. (www.ibiblio.org/hyperwar)
Hamby, William, *Ultimate Sound Pressure Level Decibel Table*, 2004 (www.makeitlouder.com/Decibel Level Chart.txt)
Czoßek, Lothar, *Vernichtung, Auftrag und Vollendung*, Heimatverein Rehmsdorf e.V. (www.amberroom.org/books-armament.htm)
Harvard University Library, Open Collection Program, Contagion, Historical Views of Diseases and Epidemics, Syphilis. (ocp.hul.harvard.edu/contagion/syphilis.html)

INDEX